Continuing the Revolution

——— *John Bryan Starr* ———

CONTINUING THE REVOLUTION

THE

POLITICAL THOUGHT

OF MAO

PRINCETON UNIVERSITY PRESS

For Marilyn

CONTENTS

PREFACE

> The Hunanese often say, "Straw sandals have no pattern—they shape themselves in the making."[1]

The long and controversial political career of Mao Zedong having ended, and time having passed since his death, it is now possible to gain a new perspective on that career and on the political ideas that derived from and guided it. Like the straw sandals to which he alluded in the passage cited above, the shape or pattern of Mao's career and his ideas are perhaps best discerned in retrospect. This book is an attempt to discern retrospectively the pattern of one important aspect of his political thought—that of what came to be called his "theory of continuing the revolution under the dictatorship of the proletariat"—by means of a study of the corpus of his works as they are presently available to us.

Mao's career as a revolutionary actor spanned nearly sixty years of modern and contemporary Chinese history. He was not only a man of action, but also a man of ideas; he both wrote and spoke prolifically during the course of these years. This study rests on the assumption of the historical importance of Mao's political career and, without raising new claims for the truth, originality, or applicability of the political ideas that grew out of, and in turn shaped that career, proceeds on the further assumption of the intrinsic historical importance of those political ideas.

The purpose of this study is therefore not to mount a defense of Mao's ideas against those of his critics; indeed, although I have alluded from time to time to the important secondary literature that treats Mao's ideas, I have not attempted in any systematic way to juxtapose my own interpretations of his ideas against those found in the substantial and growing body of interpretive literature that deals with those ideas. To have done so would have resulted in a far longer and unnecessarily complex work. Nor is it my purpose here to explicate thoroughly the intellectual origins of Mao's political ideas. Although I admit to a fascination with that difficult question, my own training lies in

[1] 1958d:94. References to Mao's writings appear here in this form. Complete information for each entry is found in the bibliography.

ix

the realm of Chinese politics and political theory, not in the field
of intellectual history, and my speculations concerning the historical roots of Mao's thought must be taken as those of an
interested amateur. With regard to the related and much-debated
question of Mao's relationship—whether legitimate or illegitimate
—to his forebears in the Marxist-Leninist tradition, I defer to
those for whom this question assumes a greater importance than
it does for me. There is no question, I think, that Mao saw himself as starting from and working within an intellectual framework drawn from his interpretation of the ideas of Marx and
Lenin. I have attempted to set forth here the positions taken by
Mao's predecessors in the Marxist-Leninist tradition alongside of
his own, so that comparisons between these positions can be made.
As I believe this study succeeds in showing, however, Mao was
acutely and increasingly aware, as his career unfolded, of the
unique characteristics of the revolution he helped to make, of
the society within which that revolution was made, and of the
historical period in which he was living and working. The question of what constitutes a legitimate or an illegitimate revision of
the ideas of Marx and Lenin is one that must ultimately be resolved on political grounds. To be sure, Mao himself was deeply
concerned with that political question, particularly in the latter
years of his career, and I have attempted to explicate his position
with regard to this political question. Beyond that, however, it
is not my purpose here to offer yet another external judgment on
the question of the legitimacy or illegitimacy, originality or
derivativeness of his thought in relation to that of his forebears
in the Marxist tradition.

Finally, this study is not conceived of as biographical in any
complete sense. While it is impossible to speak of the evolution
of Mao's ideas during the course of his career without alluding
from time to time to certain events in that career, and while I
have attempted to relate major shifts in his ideas to the events
that I believe influenced those shifts, I have not set out to relate
his political ideas to his political biography in a systematic fashion.
Rather, it is my purpose here to explicate one important aspect
of Mao's political thought by means of an investigation of its internal logic and evolution. The aspect chosen—that of his theory
of continuing the revolution—is important first, because it has
been treated both by Mao himself and by his successors as the
culmination of his theoretical activity; and second, because it is

an aspect the explication of which involves a broad investigation of the political themes, concepts, and ideas on which it is based and from which it proceeds, and thus offers a view of a wide range of Mao's political ideas. I have chosen to study this aspect of Mao's thought by investigating nine interrelated themes. The choice of a thematic, rather than a historical, presentation of Mao's political ideas was a carefully considered one, though it involves certain attendant costs that should be pointed out here. As we shall see in the chapters to follow, a fundamental concept in Mao's theory of knowledge is that there is a necessary, dialectical relationship between revolutionary theory and revolutionary practice. Theory divorced from practice is, as he made clear on numerous occasions, both illegitimate and useless. Because of this fundamental principle, there is a certain illegitimacy in treating his theoretical conclusions in isolation from their practical context. A historical presentation of his political ideas—that is, one that took as its basic outline the various phases of his political career—might approximate more closely his own sense of the necessary relationship between theory and practice. On the other hand, the disadvantage in such a format is that of an inevitable redundancy. Because each of the themes that I think important to treat in order to understand Mao's theory of continuing the revolution was relevant to, and was altered by, the events of each of the periods of his career, a historical treatment would necessitate picking up each of a number of strands in each period, carrying it forward a short distance in time, and then dropping it once again. What is gained in epistemological fidelity does not compensate for the attendant loss in clarity.

There were, it is true, specific issues or conflicts that Mao regarded as being salient in each period of his political career—"principal contradictions," as he referred to them—and it is crucial to understand what these issues were, and the effect they had on his thought. Rather than treating those issues or conflicts chronologically, I have treated them in relationship to the broad themes I have chosen, discussing each theme in terms of the way its treatment by Mao evolved during the course of his career. The resultant study is thus by no means disembodied from historical contexts, but it does proceed on the assumption that certain of the ideas that emerged from Mao's political practice transcend the limited relevance of the moment of their conception, form an integrated whole, and thus can usefully be studied as such. Because of the framework adopted here, the reader who is unfamiliar with the history of the period may find a biography of Mao or a history of the period of his career a helpful companion to this study. Even more important as a complement to this work is a chronological reading of Mao's works themselves. Indeed, even for the reader who is well versed in the history of the period, this book is intended as an introduction and a companion to a reading of those works, and not in any sense as a substitute for that first-hand encounter.

The starting point for a reading of Mao's works is the official edition of his *Xuanji* (Selected Works), which covers the period 1926 through 1957.[2] Two other collections have been published in Beijing, the one covering Mao's military writings,[3] the other a selection of pre- and post-Liberation writings in a single volume of "readings."[4] The officially published *Xuanji*, however, contains only a portion of Mao's writings during the period it covers. A more complete and highly reliable edition of his pre-Liberation works has been published in Tokyo in a Chinese-language edition as *Mao Zedong ji* (Collected Works of Mao Zedong).[5] We have, moreover, been promised a complete edition of Mao's works, editorial work on which has been begun under the supervision of Mao's successor as chairman of the Chinese Communist party, Hua Guofeng.

[2] *Mao Zedong xuanji*, single volume edition (Peking: Renmin chubanshe, 1969), translated as *Selected Works of Mao Tse-tung* 4 vol. (Peking: Foreign Languages Press, 1965). These two works cover selections from his writings from 1926 to 1949. The fifth volume, covering the period 1949-1957, was published under the same title and auspices in 1977.

The *pinyin* system of Romanization is used in this book in place of the more familiar Wade-Giles system. This choice was made because *pinyin* is the system that has been devised and adopted for use by the Chinese themselves as a part of their ongoing program to reform and simplify their language. In the summer of 1975 the Chinese announced that the use of this system would be extended to replace Wade-Giles Romanization of Chinese proper nouns in material published in the People's Republic. This announcement was rescinded in the fall, before it had been implemented, but was restated three years later and implemented in January 1979. For this reason and for the sake of consistency, both proper nouns and terms appear here in *pinyin*.

[3] *Selected Military Writings of Mao Tse-tung* (Peking: Foreign Languages Press, 1966).

[4] *Selected Readings from the Works of Mao Tse-tung* (Peking: Foreign Languages Press, 1966).

[5] *Mao Zedong ji* (Tokyo: Mō Takutō Bunken Shiryō Kenyūkai, 1970).

Translations of excerpts from a number of pre-Liberation works not included in the official *Selected Works* are included in Stuart R. Schram's useful volume, *The Political Thought of Mao Tse-tung*,[6] which contains nearly three hundred pages of extracts from Mao's writings dating from the beginning of his career through the Cultural Revolution. Of particular help are Schram's notes indicating alterations in the texts of various pre-Liberation works that have been edited and emended prior to publication in their current, authorized editions. In collaboration with Nancy Anne Dyer, I compiled a reasonably complete bibliography and index of Mao's post-Liberation writings, which contains references both to Chinese sources and to English-language translations for nearly eight hundred documents dating from the period 1949-1975.[7] Finally, a project is currently underway at Brown University under the editorship of Ying-mao Kau, the object of which is to produce a complete edition of Mao's writings in Chinese and English.

This study began, over a decade ago, with my fascination with the idea of "permanent revolution"—the notion that a revolution could and should be prolonged after the successful seizure of state power—since such an idea seemed to contradict many of the fundamental theories on revolution current among Western social scientists. As a student of post-Liberation Chinese politics, I was intrigued by the fact that, whereas Mao and his colleagues appeared to be attempting to implement such a theory in their own practice and, indeed, spoke of the necessity of doing so at the time of the Great Leap Forward, they nonetheless maintained that, both in theory and in practice, their concept of permanent or uninterrupted revolution bore no relationship to that of Leon Trotsky, who had written on the subject nearly a half century earlier. During the period of my research for a dissertation on the Chinese concept of permanent revolution, the Chinese press began once again to speak explicitly of the concept, referring to it at that point as "Chairman Mao's theory of continuing the revolution under the dictatorship of the proletariat." At the same time, thanks to the voluminous publications of Red Guard organiza-

[6] Stuart R. Schram, *The Political Thought of Mao Tse-tung*, 2nd, rev. ed. (New York: Praeger, 1969).

[7] John Bryan Starr and Nancy Anne Dyer, compilers, *Post-Liberation Works of Mao Zedong: A Bibliography and Index* (Berkeley: University of California, Center for Chinese Studies, 1976).

tions in China during the Cultural Revolution, a vast new corpus of Mao's previously unpublished speeches and writings became available in, and subsequently outside of, China.[8] As a result of the availability of this new material, the dissertation focused on the more recent period, relating this theory of continuing the revolution to its implementation during the course of the Cultural Revolution.[9] A summary of the argument there appeared in article form in 1971.[10]

During the course of the last six years I have developed my interpretation of Mao's political thought through offering a course on the subject at Berkeley and at Yale. This experience has put me in regular contact with those for whom Mao's political ideas are novel, and has thus helped me with the problem of how best to approach these ideas in a pedagogical sense. Moreover, through the dialectic of the classroom I have been able to develop my own command and interpretation of those ideas: my students have been, in a genuine and much-appreciated sense, my teachers. I am particularly grateful for the detailed comments on an earlier version of this manuscript that I have received from Edward Friedman, Hanna Pitkin, Stuart Schram, John Service, and Frederic Wakeman. I appreciate as well the invaluable editorial and research assistance of Nancy Levenberg during the final stages of preparing the manuscript. For her patient instruction and helpful advice with regard to translations from the Chinese, and particularly for her calligraphy, which graces the jacket and glossary of this book, I owe my sincerest thanks to Mei-hsia Tseng. I want to express my appreciation to the American Council of Learned Societies-Social Science Research Council Joint Committee on Contemporary China for a grant in 1970-71, which made possible

[8] Among the most important of these Red Guard collections are *Mao Zedong dui Peng-Huang-Zhang-Zhou fandang jituan de pipan* (Mao Zedong's Criticism of the Peng-Huang-Zhang-Zhou Anti-Party clique) (1967); four collections that appeared under the title, *Mao Zedong sixiang wansui!* (Long Live the Thought of Mao Zedong!), the first three of which appeared in 1967, the fourth, and by far the largest, in 1969; *Mao zhuxi wenxuan* (Selected Texts from Chairman Mao) (n.d.); and *Mao zhuxi jiaoyu yulu* (Quotations from Chairman Mao on Education) (July 1967).

[9] John Bryan Starr, "Mao Tse-tung's Theory of Continuing the Revolution under the Dictatorship of the Proletariat: Its Origins, Development and Practical Implications," Ph.D. Dissertation, University of California, Berkeley, 1971.

[10] John Bryan Starr, "Conceptual Foundations of Mao Tse-tung's Theory of Continuous Revolution," *Asian Survey* 11:6 (1971), 610-628.

a year of research and reflection in Hong Kong—a year without which this study could not have been undertaken. Finally, I owe special thanks to my wife, Marilyn, whose unwavering support in hard times has made all the difference. It is to her that this book is dedicated.

Mao assumed many roles during the course of his long revolutionary career: student activist, peasant organizer, military strategist, poet, political founder, statesman, political theorist. In addition, a number of roles have been ascribed to him by his admirers and detractors. He was, for them, a Great Helmsman or a ruthless dictator; a creative innovator in the Marxist-Leninist tradition, or an ill-informed charlatan falsely using Marxism-Leninism as a means to his own personal or nationalistic ends; a dedicated revolutionary leader, or an unpredictable autocrat bent on manipulating his colleagues and his subjects in the interest of acting out his own changing whims. Mao's image of himself as his career drew to a close is an interesting one. He did not want to be remembered, he told his biographer and friend, Edgar Snow, as the "Great Leader, Great Supreme Commander, Great Teacher, or Great Helmsman"—Cultural Revolutionary epithets that he dismissed as a "nuisance." Rather, he said, "only the word, 'teacher' would be retained—that is, simply schoolteacher."[11] He was, he told Snow in concluding their visit, "not a complicated man, but really very simple."[12] It is toward the end of enriching our understanding of the political ideas of this man, and of providing the basis for making our own respective evaluations of his accomplishments and shortcomings, that the pages which follow are devoted.

Domaine Bonfils
Puyricard, France

[11] 1970b:169.   [12] Ibid., p. 175.

Continuing the Revolution

Chapter One

ON CONFLICT

> Contradiction exists in the process of the devel-
> opment of all things, and . . . in the process
> of the development of each thing a movement
> of opposites exists from beginning to end.[1]

The central idea around which the political thought of Mao
Zedong was constructed was that of conflict or contradiction and
the change to which it gives rise. Each of the important political
themes with which he dealt in his political writings was grounded
in his view of conflict and change as aspects of the natural or
given state of the political realm, as they are in the realm of nature. Because his theory of knowledge was based on this central
idea, he regarded his political ideas not only as an explication of,
but also as an example of this view of conflict and change, and
thus as subject to the same laws of development that govern
natural and political phenomena. In order, therefore, to understand the logic of Mao's theory of "continuing the revolution
under the dictatorship of the proletariat," we must begin by ex-
ploring this fundamental concept of conflict.

Mao's view of contradiction, conflict, and change can usefully
be considered in terms of four aspects: first, as I have suggested,
he took conflict to be a given, natural condition in society and
nature alike; second, he regarded it as a ubiquitous condition;
third, he viewed conflict as a beneficial characteristic of the
world, in that the change it promotes is positive and progressive;
and finally, he believed that conflict is a permanent condition of
nature and society. It is the purpose of this chapter to use these
four aspects as a means for organizing our exploration of the
origin, nature, and implications of the idea of conflict and change
that lay at the heart of Mao's political thought.

[1] 1937g:280/1, 316. The first number after the colon refers to the page
number in the Chinese edition, the second number to the page number in
the English-language translation.

CONFLICT AS GIVEN

Although it contravenes certain very fundamental principles underlying contemporary Western social and political thought, a view of the interaction of opposing forces as the natural state of society and nature is nevertheless very old and very widespread. It is found in the historical antecedents of modern Chinese thought, as well as in the historical antecedents of modern thought in Europe and America. Its pervasiveness may be explained by the fact that it is a view that can occur quite spontaneously to anyone who observes the natural world closely, and who entertains a sense that men and women are a part of that world, subject to its laws of change. This view of nature and of the relationship of men and women to nature—a view that we might think of as "pre-Promethean"—was common to preclassical Greek thought in the European intellectual tradition, and to pre-Confucian thought in the Chinese tradition.

In order to explore these early views of the interaction of opposing forces and their relationship to Mao's use of the concept of conflict, we must first make some rather basic linguistic distinctions. At a very general level, we might think of opposition as one of several possible relationships between two items. In turn, it is useful to think of conflict as one of two possible types of relationships between opposites, the other being complementarity. Whether one regards conflict or complementarity as the appropriate way to conceive of the relationship between opposites affects, and is in turn affected by, one's concept of and attitude toward change. The idea of opposition and that of change are, of course, conceptually distinguishable, but they appear closely linked in both early Greek and early Chinese thought. In both cases, a view of opposition as involving, most importantly, the interrelationship of complementary elements lent itself naturally to a view of change as repetitive, preordained, and cyclical. By contrast, a view of opposition as involving most importantly the relations of conflicting elements can give rise to a view of change as linear and progressive.

In the writings of Heraclitus of Ephesus one finds evidence of a view of the natural world as characterized by the interaction of opposed forces: "Living and dead, waking and sleeping, youth and age are one in the same; for they undergo change into one

4

another."[2] The primary emphasis in Heraclitus' treatment of opposition appears to be on the complementarity of, rather than on the conflict between opposites.[3] Despite this emphasis, he does not ignore the occurrence of conflict: "Things taken together . . . and especially extremes or 'opposites' . . . are in one sense wholes or continua, in another sense not wholes, but separate and opposed. In one sense they tend together, to unity, while in another sense they tend apart, to plurality."[4] To the extent that he treats opposed elements as complementary, he sees change as cyclical in nature. To the extent that opposed elements are treated as being in conflict with one another, change of a different sort is implied: "One must know that conflict is common and right and that all things are necessarily brought about through conflict."[5]

This view of nature as involving the often complementary and occasionally conflictual relationship of opposing forces was largely abandoned, or at least thoroughly transformed, as Greek thought developed into its maturity. By contrast, the association of opposition with nature in ancient Chinese thought was both

---

[2] Heraclitus, Fragment 88. The paraphrase is that found in J. Katz and R. W. Weingartner, *Philosophy in the West* (New York: Harcourt, Brace and World, 1965), p. 12. A good deal more literal translation is found in G. S. Kirk, *Heraclitus: The Cosmic Fragments* (Cambridge: Cambridge University Press, 1954), p. 135: "And as the same thing there exists in us living and dead, and the waking and sleeping and young and old: for these things having changed round are those, and those things having changed round *again* are these ones."

[3] Kirk sees his attempt at showing the unity of opposites as involving first the argument that "opposites are 'the same' relative to different observers, or to different aspects of the same subject," and second the argument exemplified by the fragment just quoted—that "opposites are 'the same' because they inevitably succeed one another" (Kirk, *Heraclitus*, p. 72). Charles H. Kahn, in his article, "A New Look at Heraclitus," differs from previous interpreters of Heraclitus, Kirk among them, in seeing a continuity behind the fragments that places Heraclitus in proximity to the poets and philosophers of his age rather than to the natural scientists. "His real subject," Kahn writes, "is not the physical world but the human condition, which for the Greeks means the condition of mortality. His aim is to conceive the relationship of life and death within a universal doctrine of opposition, transformation and hidden unity." *American Philosophical Quarterly* 1:3 (1964), 194.

[4] Kirk, paraphrasing Fragment 10, in *Heraclitus*, p. 176.

[5] My own modification of Kirk's translation of Fragment 80, ibid., p. 238.

more pervasive and more influential in shaping succeeding modes of thought in the Chinese tradition than it was in the Greek case.

The earliest manifestation of the widespread interest in the relationship of opposing forces in Chinese thought is found in the *Yi Jing*—the Book of Changes. The dates of the various parts of this classic are the subject of considerable scholarly debate, but the system of divination on which the commentary is based is traditionally held to date from the eleventh century B.C.[6] This system of trigrams and hexagrams is based on combinations of solid and broken lines, the solid representing the dominant or strong principle, the broken representing the recessive or weak principle. All possible combinations of three solid or broken lines form the eight trigrams. Two trigrams combined into a single six-line figure form a hexagram, of which there are sixty-four possible combinations.[7]

In the commentaries that accompany the hexagrams, the treatment of opposing forces is one that emphasizes their complementarity and, consequently, holds to a cyclical view of change: "The way of the Creative works through change and transformation, so that each thing receives its true nature and destiny and comes into permanent accord with the Great Harmony; this is what furthers and what perseveres."[8] Indeed, the hexagrams themselves are often shown arranged in a circle, suggesting that each gives rise to another in a cyclical sequence.

The complementary relationship between dominant and recessive forces symbolized by the broken and solid lines was further

[6] Wing-tsit Chan describes the problem of dating as follows: "Tradition has ascribed the Eight Trigrams to legendary Fu-hsi, the sixty-four hexagrams to King Wen (r. 1171-1122 B.C.), the two texts (1 and 2) to him or Duke Chou (d. 1094 B.C.), and the 'ten wings' to Confucius. Most modern scholars have rejected this attribution, but they are not agreed on when and by whom the book was produced. Most probably it is a product of many hands over a long period of time, from the fifth or sixth century B.C. to the third or fourth century B.C." *A Source Book in Chinese Philosophy* (Princeton: Princeton University Press, 1963), p. 262n. Cf. Joseph Needham, *Science and Civilization in China* (Cambridge: Cambridge University Press, 1962), II, 306f., who agrees with those who carry the process up through the first century A.D.

[7] Helmut Wilhelm's translation of the *Yi Jing* into German has been rendered into English by Cary F. Baynes, *The I Ching or Book of Changes* (Princeton: Princeton University Press, Bollingen Series XIX, 1967).

[8] Commentary on the judgment on the first hexagram, *Ch'ien (Qian)*/The Creative, ibid., p. 371.

developed and formalized through the use of the terms, *yin* and *yang*. Among the earliest antecedents of the school of thought devoted to the study of these terms and the concepts for which they stood is the comment in the fifth chapter of the *Xi Ci* or "Great Appendix" of commentary on the *Yi Jing*: "One *yin* and one *yang*: that is the *Dao*."[9] The character *yin*, standing for the recessive principle, coldness, darkness, femaleness, that which is inside or hidden, depicts the shadows of hills and clouds, and originally referred to the shady side of a mountain or valley. The character *yang*, standing for the dominant principle, warmth, light, maleness, that which is outside or manifest, depicts either a flag fluttering in the sunshine, or a figure (possibly a male ritual dancer) holding up a perforated jade disk, symbol of heaven and thus of light, and referred originally to the sunny side of a mountain or valley.[10] The relationship of the two forces was symbolically represented by the *tai ji tu*—a circle divided into light and dark segments, each of which in turn contains a spot of the other.[11]

Although conflict of opposing forces is not ignored in the *I Jing*, the principle emphasis there is on their complementarity. Deriving from this emphasis, as Wilhelm has pointed out, are three types of change that are distinguished from one another in the classic: "nonchange, cyclic change, and sequent change. Nonchange is the background, as it were, against which change is made possible." Harmony and order are seen in the *I Jing* as transitory conditions, giving way in each instance to change.[12]

Daoist thought[13] emphasizes particularly clearly the interrela-

---

[9] *Yi yin yi yang zhi wei dao.* Wilhelm and Baynes translate the phrase, "That which lets now the dark, now the light appear is *tao*" (p. 297), thereby emphasizing the dynamic and cyclical implications of the passage. Needham's comment on the sentence is that "the general sense must be that there are only these two fundamental forces or operations in the universe, now one dominating, now the other, in wavelike succession." *Science and Civilization*, II, 273.

[10] Ibid., II, 273f.

[11] As Wilhelm points out, the emphasis in this diagram is on the *ji*—a character with the original meaning of ridgepole or line. "With this line, which in itself represents oneness, duality comes into the world, for the line posits an above and a below, a right and a left, front and back—in a word, the world of the opposites." Wilhelm and Baynes, *I Ching*, lv.

[12] Ibid., pp. 280ff.

[13] There is considerable disagreement with regard to the period in which Daoism originated. Some argue that Lao Zi, generally regarded as the author of the *Dao De Jing*, was Confucius' senior by a half century and

tionships of opposites in nature as found in *yin-yang* thought. Daoist writings are filled with references to opposites in nature and to the cyclical change that results from the complementarity of these opposing forces, as is suggested in this passage from the *Zhuang Zi*: "Light came from darkness, order from the formless. . . . Life springs into existence without a visible force and disappears into infinity. . . . Such is the operation of the *Dao*. . . . Awe-inspiring, beginning again in cycles ever new."[14] In the *Dao De Jing* the implications of this emphasis on the complementary relationship of opposing forces and the resultant cyclical nature of change are spelled out yet more clearly: "Prosperity tilts over to misfortune and good fortune comes out of bad. Who can understand this extreme turning point? For it recognizes no such thing as normality. Normality changes into abnormality."[15]

As Needham convincingly argues,[16] the result of this concern over opposition is a focus on the *relationship* of the opposite forces rather than on their separate qualities. Another passage from the *Dao De Jing* illustrates this point:

> Being and non-being produce each other;
> Difficult and easy complete each other;
> Long and short contrast each other;
> High and low distinguish each other;
> Sound and voice harmonize with each other;
> Front and back follow each other.[17]

The dominance of the idea of the complementarity of opposing

---

that his work is thus the product of the fifth and sixth centuries B.C. Others see the *Dao De Jing* as the product of the third or fourth centuries B.C. Chan summarizes the argument and sides with the earlier date. *Source Book*, p. 138.

[14] *Zhuang Zi*, chapter 22, translated by Legge, cited in Needham, *Science and Civilization*, pp. 38f.

[15] *Dao De Jing*, chapter 58, cited in Needham, *Science and Civilization*, p. 75.

[16] Ibid., pp. 199f.

[17] *Dao De Jing*, chapter 2, translated in Chan, *Source Book*, p. 140. Zhang Dongsun refers to the Daoist tendency toward "correlative logic" in the article: Chang Tung-sun, "A Chinese Philosopher's Theory of Knowledge," *Yenching Journal of the Social Sciences* 1:2 (1939), 155, reprinted in *Etc: A Review of General Semantics* 9 (1952), 203. Zhang bases his argument on the linguistic grounds that Chinese lacks a clear-cut equivalent to the verb "to be."

forces is suggested by the fact that none of the relationships described here can, strictly speaking, be conceived of as conflictual.

Of the various schools of thought that emerged in the sixth
and fifth centuries B.C., however, it was Confucianism which,
through its many transmogrifications, became the dominant philosophical school in the public realm in China. As compared with
Daoist thinkers, Confucius was less inclined to view man as a part
of nature, subject to its forces. Taken as a whole, his teachings
were less concerned with natural relations than with human relations, and less concerned with conflict than with harmony. Such
an interpretation is called into question by those who hold to the
traditional view that Confucius not only studied the *I Jing*
closely, but also wrote the *Tuan Zhuan* or "Commentary on the
Decisions"—the first two of the ten "wings" or sets of commentary that subsequently became a part of the classic.[18]

Whichever position one takes, however, one must acknowledge
that Confucianists attempted to integrate the ideas on opposition
contained in the *Yi Jing* with Confucius' own teachings. Among
others, the philosopher most responsible for the elevating of
Confucianism to the position of state ideology that it subsequently held, Dong Zhongshu, undertook this integration. Associated with what has subsequently come to be called the
"*Yin-yang* School" of Confucianism, Dong interpreted the inter-
relational logic of the *Yi Jing* through the framework of a
Confucian emphasis on harmony and stability. Opposition there
was in the natural world, Dong argued, but the opposite forces
represented in the hexagrams were complementary, not contradictory, and together they comprised unity, wholeness. Since the
achievement of harmony and balance was the desired goal of the
Confucian, the opposite forces of *yin* and *yang* were to be har-
nessed by men and women to achieve that harmony and balance.[19]

[18] There is a passage in the *Lun Yu* (Analects) in which Confucius is
reported as having said, "Give me a few more years so that I can devote
fifty years to the study of the *I Jing*. I may be free from great mistakes"
(*Lun Yu* 7:16, in Chan, *Source Book*, 32). Those who do not accept so
early a date for the *I Jing* regard this passage as a later addition to the
Lun Yu aimed at confirming the Confucian legitimacy of the philosophy
of change. See Needham, *Science and Civilization*, II, 307.

[19] Dong Zhongshu, for example, incorporates the following passage in his
Qun Qiu Fanlu (Luxuriant Gems of the Spring and Autumn Annals):
"Heaven possesses *yin* and *yang* and man also possesses *yin* and *yang*. When
the universe's material force of *yin* arises, man's material force of *yin* arises

Dong's explicit incorporation of *yin-yang* theory into the corpus of Confucianism resulted in a subtle but important modification both of the Confucian concept of harmony and of the *yin-yang* concept of opposition: harmony was now regarded as a goal to be striven for by human endeavor rather than simply a natural characteristic of the world. By treating harmony as the result of the actions of moral men and women, Dong and his followers left open the implication that, left to itself, the world would be naturally conflictful and, according to the values assigned by the Confucianist, evil. Thus, while Confucianism came to the point of conceding the givenness of conflict, it did not go so far as to accept an assessment of that natural conflict as being productive of social growth and development, nor the idea that, in the very process of resolving conflict, new conflicts are produced.[20]

Thus we see that both of the major schools of philosophy in traditional China took cognizance of the problem of opposition and its relationship to change.[21] Confucianism, which became in Han times the dominant philosophy in the public and political

---

in response. Conversely, when man's material force of *yin* arises, that of the universe should also rise in response. He who understands when he wishes to bring forth rain, will activate the *yang* in man in order to arouse the *yang* of the universe."

[20] Needham carries his discussion of the relationship between science and the dominant modes of thought in traditional China through Zhu Xi and Song Neo-Confucianism. He says, "I shall suggest that Chu Hsi's philosophy was fundamentally a philosophy of organism, and that Sung Neo-Confucians thus attained, primarily by insight, a position analogous to that of Whitehead, without having passed through the stages corresponding to Newton and Galileo. They thus present a parallel with Mohist and Taoist thinkers of the Warring States period, who may be said to have attained gleams of dialectical logic thereby anticipating Hegel, without ever having passed through the logic of Aristotle and the scholastics"; *Science and Civilization*, II, 458.

[21] Derk Bodde explores views of conflict and change in his article, "Harmony and Conflict in Chinese Philosophy," in Arthur F. Wright, ed., *Studies in Chinese Thought* (Chicago: University of Chicago Press, 1953), pp. 19-80. There he concludes, "prominent in all these schools [of Daoist, *yin-yang*, and Confucian thought] is the belief that the universe is in a constant state of flux but that this flux follows a fixed and therefore predictable pattern consisting either of eternal oscillation between two poles or of cyclical movement within a closed circuit; in either case the change involved is relative rather than absolute, since all movement serves in the end only to bring the process back to its starting point" (p. 21).

realm, resolved whatever ambiguity existed in *yin-yang* thought between the conflict or complementarity of opposites in favor of what we might term an enforced complementarity. This tendency was enhanced as Confucianism became transformed into a kind of state doctrine or ideology that served both to explain and to justify the existing political order. The elevation of Confucianism to a position of dominance in the political realm did not result in the weakening of Daoist thought, however. Indeed, the latter, with its relatively more ambiguous response to the question of whether relationships between opposed forces in the natural world were to be conceived of as primarily conflictual or primarily complementary, and with its advocacy of the position of *wu-wei*, or nonaction, for human beings confronted with this natural opposition, continued to thrive. Just as Confucianism became associated with the function of statecraft, so Daoism became associated with the functions of other, generally more private realms of life. Popular religious practices, moreover, many of which antedated the formal elaboration of these philosophical schools, came to be associated with both of them, resulting in the popularization (and often the bastardization) of the philosophical position on which each rested.

Consequently Confucianism and Daoism, and the ideas of opposition and change incorporated in each, survived well into the nineteenth century and beyond, as much-modified but nonetheless still viable modes of philosophical inquiry. In a similar fashion, these ideas also survived in the popular culture as much-modified but still viable sources of moral and ethical principles and of religious practices. Western thought, by contrast, lacked this continuity of concern with a view of opposition as a given condition of the natural world.

Two ideas basic to the development of Western thought after Heraclitus and his contemporaries contravene the assumptions underlying a view of nature as characterized by the interaction of opposite forces. The first is the Aristotelian concept of identity, on which logic is based. The second is the Newtonian concept of motion, on which foundation not only the physical sciences but also much contemporary social thought rests. The idea of identity, developed by Aristotle as a fundamental element of his theory of logic, postulates that an object cannot at the same time possess or manifest opposite qualities or characteristics. In these terms, it is logical to say that the object is either x or non-x. It cannot be both at once.[22] This exactly contravenes a view such as that of Heraclitus who, looking for internal conflicts within every aspect of the natural and social worlds, argued that every item must at the same time be both x and non-x. It is the Aristotelian and not the Heraclitan view that prevailed in the development of Western logic.

The second idea that became ascendent in opposition to the view of natural opposition was formalized in Newton's laws of motion, but had long been in currency before Newton's time: bodies are naturally at rest; motion is the result of the impetus imparted from without by another moving body.[23] Translated from the physical to the social realm, this postulate forms the basis of a view prevalent in European and American thought, one that sees society as existing naturally in a state of equilibrium and stasis rather than one of opposition, movement, and change. The existence of social conflict and change necessarily must, following this view, be induced and explained, since they constitute deviations from the normal or natural.[24] For Heraclitus and his ancient Chinese counterparts, opposition and change are the given states of the natural and social worlds, and it is the existence of equilibrium and stasis that requires inducement and explanation.

[22] See, for example, his statement in the *Ethics* in response to the question, "what is science?": "We all see that scientific knowledge is of things that are never other than they are . . ."; Book VI, chapter 3, translated by J.A.K. Thomson (Hammondsworth, England: Penguin, 1955), p. 174.

[23] Newton's first law of motion reads as follows: "Every body continues in its state of rest, or of uniform motion in a right [i.e., straight] line, unless it is compelled to change that state by forces impressed on it"; *Philosophae naturalis principia mathematica* (1687) translated by A. Motte, in Paul Edwards, ed., *Encyclopedia of Philosophy* (New York: Macmillan Company and Free Press, 1967), v, 49. See also Michael J. Buckley, *Motion and Motion's God* (Princeton: Princeton University Press, 1971). It is a view that was also held by Mao in his pre-Marxist phase. In his 1917 article on physical education he commented, "in general, that which is at rest cannot set itself in motion; there must be something to move it" (1917:159). Earlier in the same article, however, in an attempt to distinguish his views from the Daoist idea of nonaction, he commented, "in my opinion, however, there is only movement in heaven and earth" (ibid., p. 157).

[24] Barbara Russett, *The Concept of Equilibrium in American Thought* (New York: Harcourt, Brace and World, 1966) attributes the ascendency of the concept of equilibrium in social thought to the work of Comte and Spencer in the late nineteenth century, and traces its origins to Archimedes and Hippocrates in the Greek tradition.

Mao consistently treats the interaction of opposing forces as a natural, given state of things. "Imbalance," he wrote in 1958, "is a universal, objective law. Things forever proceed from imbalance to equilibrium and again, from equilibrium to imbalance in a cycle, but each cycle brings about a higher plane. Imbalance is constant and absolute, while equilibrium is temporary and relative."[25] The opposite point of view, one that sees equilibrium as natural or given, Mao (citing Engels and Lenin) labeled "metaphysical."[26]

Mao was exposed to and assimilated, through his experience of and education in Chinese culture, the view that the natural and social realms are inherently fraught with the interaction of opposing forces—a view we have found articulated in both the Daoist and the Confucianist traditions. Nonetheless, he came to reject the emphasis placed in these schools of thought on the complementarity of these opposing forces. He rejected, as well, the corollary that followed from this idea of complementarity, namely, that the change in which that opposition eventuates must be cyclical or sequential in nature. In their place he substituted the idea, gleaned from his study of Marx, that it was conflict, not complementarity, that characterizes the inherent opposition in nature and society, and that change must, as a result, be progressive and not cyclical.

Conflict as Ubiquitous

There is a distinction to be drawn between those who have seen the world as naturally fraught with the interaction of opposing forces and those who go on to argue that one's mode of analysis— the logic of one's inquiry—should reflect this interaction. The link that we find in Hegel and his successors between opposition as subject matter and opposition as method—a link that we associate with the term, "dialectic"—is a recent development in Western thought. In Greek thought the origins of what is called the dialectical method do not coincide with the origins of a view of the world as governed by the dynamic of internal conflict. In the history of Chinese philosophy it is at least possible to consider the two strains of thought as having had a common origin. And in the exploration of this common origin, we will find

[25] 1958e:7; see also 1955f:28; 1958v:112; and 1959c:201.
[26] 1937g:275/I, 312.

suggestions of the idea that even within the Chinese tradition itself there was a place for the concept of opposition as conflictual and of change as progressive.

The word "dialectic" has a common root with the word "dialogue," both of which can be traced to the Greek word, *dialegesthai*, to converse. The origin of the dialectical method is ordinarily ascribed to Zeno of Alea, who based his method on the principle of unitary identity—the idea that a thing cannot possess opposite qualities at the same moment.[27] Zeno thus refuted his opponents in argumentation by leading them to the point of affirming two contradictory positions. The argument was won when Zeno pointed out the contradiction. This dialectical method became the basis of the Sophists' approach to argumentation.[28]

Socrates and Plato used the term "dialectic" in a somewhat different sense to describe the method of arriving at truth through a dialogue—through a series of questions and answers.[29] Aristotle regarded the dialectic in a narrower sense as an inferior form of argumentation based, as he saw it, on secondary premises rather than on the primary premises of direct observation, characteristic of what he called the "demonstrative method."[30]

As it emerged from its origins in Greek thought, then, the dialectical method was firmly grounded not on the idea that conflict or contradiction was a natural characteristic of the world, and thus that any method of analysis should reflect those contradictions, but rather on one of two different views: either that associated with Aristotle, which contended that, since internal contradiction was *not* a characteristic of the world, logical proofs could be based on the demonstration and refutation of such contradictions; or that associated with Socrates and Plato, which divorced the dialectic from any necessary association with the

[27] See, for example, Zeno's defense of his concept of monism in H.D.P. Lee, *Zeno of Elea: A Text with Translation and Notes* (Cambridge: Cambridge University Press, 1936), pp. 18f.

[28] See, for example, Socrates' dialogue with Thrasymachus concerning the conventional conception of morality in *Republic*, Book I, 11.336-357, translated by H.D.P. Lee (Hammondsworth, England: Penguin, 1955), pp. 62ff.

[29] Ibid., Book VII, 11.532-538, pp. 300-304. Plato also uses the term more narrowly in the *Republic* to refer to the hierarchical arrangement of the forms from specific to general.

[30] Aristotle, *Ethics* VI, 3, pp. 174f.

natural order, and which employed it as a means for seeking the truth through the interaction of conflicting ideas.

While these views of the dialectic were influential in shaping medieval thought, it was in the hands of German philosophers, beginning with Kant and leading through Fichte, Schelling, and Schleiermacher to Hegel that the dialectic was both transformed and given renewed importance. What Hegel and his predecessors attempted was, in effect, an integration of the Aristotelian and Platonic constructions of the dialectic: contradictory ideas do in fact negate one another, they argued, but that negation results not in the invalidation of the original idea, but in its supercession through the emergence of a new idea. A thesis, as Fichte described the process, interacted with its opposite idea, the antithesis, to produce a new synthesis. An idea, to use Hegel's terms, naturally gives rise to its negation and out of the conflict between these two there emerges as the result of an *Aufhebung* or supercession a new idea, the negation of the negation. Hegel viewed each instance of this process as a part of the gradual realization of the Absolute Idea through history.[31] Because this historical process is fraught with the conflict of opposed elements, the dialectic— our method for comprehending that process—likewise must incorporate the interaction of conflicting opposites.

When Marx set about "standing Hegel on his feet" by translating his idealist dialectic into materialist terms, he took the Hegelian transformation of the dialectic a step farther by integrating with it a Heraclitan view of the natural world as characterized by natural opposition. Whereas Heraclitus had emphasized the complementarity of that inherent opposition, however, Marx emphasized its conflictual character.

In the Chinese tradition, the split between conflict as phenomenon and conflict as analytical method was by no means so pronounced. The *Yi Jing* was at the same time a description of the world as multifarious combinations of conflicting elements, and a mode of analysis, however primitive, for understanding these natural phenomena by reflecting their conflict. As we have seen,

---

[31] Gustav Mueller, in a spirited defense of Hegel against the over-simplifying "thesis-antithesis-synthesis" formula, attributes its association with Hegel's thought to Marx, for whom, in Professor Mueller's view, "brutal simplifications" are his "specialties." "The Hegel Legend of 'Thesis-Antithesis-Synthesis,' " *Journal of the History of Ideas* 19 (1958), 414.

these primitive methods were refined in Daoism into a kind of prototypical dialectic. This is most clearly suggested in the second chapter of the *Zhuang Zi*: "The sages harmonize the affirmations 'it is' and 'it is not,' and rest in the natural equalizations of Heaven. This is called 'following two courses at once.' "[32] In Needham's view, this dialectical bent in Daoism made it considerably better able to deal with change as observed in nature, and it was thus in its inception a type of thought considerably more conducive to the development of natural science than was what he calls the "rigid Aristotelian formalism" of Western thought.[33]

These views in Daoism are made even more explicit in the philosophical writings of Mo Zi.[34] "That which 'must be so' is not a terminus. Every affirmation is accompanied by a negative, every natural phenomenon meets another one behaving opposite to it. Wherever there is a must-be-so there will also be a must-not-be-so. Wherever there is an 'is' there will also be an 'isn't.' And this is what really 'must be so.' "[35] He continues: "Some affirm that certain things are so, and are convinced that their affirmation is right. Others deny it and raise questions about it. But [ultimate truth] is like the sage; it contains all the negations but has no [more] contradictions."[36]

[32] Several writers have noted the affinity between this chapter of the *Zhuang Zi* and the much later use of the dialectic by Hegel and others. The argument is most complete in Tang Qunyi's article, "*Heigeer de bienhua xingershangxue yu Zhuang Zi de bienhua xingershangxue bijiao*" (A Comparison of the Metaphysical Transformation in Hegel and Zhuang Zi), *Quarterly Review of the Sun Yat-sen Institute for the Advancement of Culture and Education* 3:4 (1936), 1301-1315. The article is abstracted in *China Institute Bulletin* (New York) 1:4 (1937), 27. See also Needham, *Science and Civilization* II, 74-77; and Chan, *Source Book*, p. 183.

[33] Needham, *Science and Civilization*, II, 76f. He attributes the failure to realize this potential for scientific development in China to what he calls "unfavorable environmental conditions," ibid., p. 194.

[34] Mo Zi (fl. 479-438 B.C.) developed his philosophy based on the idea of universal love between the time of Confucius and that of Confucius' disciple, Mencius. Chan argues that Moism is a relatively unimportant school of Chinese thought, and that "modern interest in Moism arose in China because of its utilitarian spirit and in the West because of its superficial resemblance to the Christian teachings of the will of God and universal love"; Chan, *Source Book*, p. 212.

[35] *Jing shang* proposition 51, as numbered by Tan Jiefu, *Mo Jing I Jie* (Shanghai: Commercial Press, 1935), cited in Needham, *Science and Civilization* II, 180.

[36] *Jing xia* proposition 1, cited ibid., II, 181.

A second strand of proto-dialectical thought exists within the Chinese tradition, this one traceable to Indian dialectical logic, introduced into China with Buddhism. The Indian school in question is that of Nāgārjuna,[37] whose texts elaborating his theory of Mādhyamika ("the doctrine of the middle") were translated into Chinese as the *Zhong Lun* in the fifth century A.D.[38] A central principle of this school of thought has been paraphrased as follows: "Everything is in perpetual change, not for one moment the same, and therefore not real."[39] The two Chinese philosophers most closely associated with Buddhist dialectic are Seng-zhao (A.D. 384-414) and Ji-zang (A.D. 549-623). Whereas Seng-zhao emphasized the natural affinities between this mode of thought and similar strains in Daoism, Ji-zang elaborated the dialectical method of refutation and negation by means of which the highest level of Truth—the "True Middle"—is to be reached.[40]

As is evident in these passages, the dominance of a view of the relationship between opposed elements as complementary, which we found in the treatment of the natural world in ancient Chinese thought, gives way to some extent in these methodological discussions to the suggestion that conflict as well as complementarity may occur. It is also evident that the combination that Marx effected between a concept of the world as characterized by the interaction of opposed forces and the concept of an investigative method as characterized by the interaction of opposed forces had been effected in at least a primitive way centuries earlier in the Chinese tradition.

The observation that there are parallels to be drawn between the development of the dialectic in China and the West has been made by Mao and his colleagues. Speaking with the French politician and writer, Alain Peyrefitte, in 1972, the Chinese writer Guo Moro observed that both ancient Greek and ancient Chinese thought had had a dialectical strain. Western thought had lost its dialectic, Guo argued, through the ascendence of the ideas of Aristotle and Descartes, whereas the ancient dialectic had re-

---

[37] See S.C.A. Vidyabhusana, "History of the Mādhyamika Philosophy of Nāgārjuna," *Journal of the Buddhist Text Society* 5 (1897), 3.

[38] The translation was made by Kumārajīva (A.D. 344-413). See Chan, *Source Book*, p. 343.

[39] The paraphrase is that of Needham, *Science and Civilization* II, 405.

[40] Excerpts from Seng-zhao's *Zhao Lun* and Ji-zang's *Er Di Zhang* (Treatise on the Two Levels of Truth) in which their dialectical views are expressed are found in Chan, *Source Book*, pp. 344-356 and 360-369.

mained a viable mode of thought in China. Indeed, he suggested—
perhaps not without a note of irony—Fichte, Schelling, Hegel,
and Marx may have borrowed their concept of the dialectic from
China.[41] When Mao himself spoke of the relationship between
ancient and modern uses of the dialectic in China and the West,
he did so in a somewhat different way from Guo. Each relationship, he argued, was itself dialectical: in the West, Greek dialectics were negated by medieval metaphysics, and both were superceded by the dialectic of Hegel and Marx. In China, similarly,
ancient dialectics were negated by the metaphysics of the feudal
classics, and both were superceded by the introduction of Marxism into China.[42]

This idea of the continuity of a tradition of protodialectical
thought in the Chinese setting is critical to an understanding of
the way in which Mao assimilated and developed the dialectical
ideas he found in Marxism. Where Hegel and Marx were able to
argue with considerable reason that their ideas were a novel rejection and supercession of the Western philosophical tradition,
Mao's development of these ideas of Marx in the Chinese setting
took place in the context of the vital resonances with the Chinese
philosophical and cultural traditions that these ideas struck. We
can say of Mao that he was, by virtue of his familiarity with the
protodialectical aspect of the Chinese philosophical and cultural
traditions, a "natural dialectician," in the same sense that Stuart
Schram described him as a "natural Leninist" because of his innate receptivity to Lenin's emphasis upon political struggle and
to his principles of revolutionary organization.[43] At the same time,
it is important to realize that this same point can be made about
the audience to whom Mao addressed himself in writing and speaking about the dialectic. That he was aware of this fact may be
seen from the examples that he typically used to illustrate his dis-

[41] Alain Peyrefitte, *Quand la Chine s'eveillera, le monde tremblera* (Paris:
Fayard, 1973), pp. 47f.

[42] 1958s:98. He explained the reason for the necessity of this supercession
in both cases in an earlier formulation of the same argument: "Ancient
dialectics . . . had a somewhat spontaneous and naive character; in the
social and historical conditions then prevailing, it was not yet able to form
a theoretical system, hence it could not fully explain the world and was
supplanted by metaphysics"; 1937g:273/1, 315. Cf. similar arguments in
1958l:109f., and 1959c:205.

[43] Stuart R. Schram, *Political Thought of Mao Tse-tung* (New York:
Praeger, 1963), p. 33.

cussions of the dialectic—examples that give the dialectic in Mao's hands a uniquely Chinese character.[44] This unique character is particularly evident in his treatment of the concept of the ubiquity of conflict, a concept by means of which nature, society, and method are linked by the common trait of conflict.

As I have suggested, Marx effectively combined the view of conflict as method, which he drew from Hegel and his immediate predecessors, with his reinterpretation of a much earlier strain of thought, which saw the material world as naturally fraught with opposition—a reinterpretation that emphasized the conflictual rather than the complementary nature of that opposition. This reinterpretation is suggested by the use in the work of Marx's successors of the term "contradiction" to describe dialectical relationships. The use of this term, however, obscured what had been a fairly clear distinction between the more general concept of conflict and the specific type of conflict described with that term, contradiction. In common parlance we ordinarily distinguish between objects, forces, or ideas that are in conflict with one another, and objects, forces, or ideas that are in opposition or contradiction with one another. Conflict and contradiction have in common the implication of a common framework within which the objects, forces, or ideas interact. However, where the concept of conflict allows for some possible common ground of agreement within that framework, the idea of contradiction, suggesting as it does diametric or antipodean opposition, does not.

It is in the material realm that the idea of contradiction or antipodean opposition makes most sense. Marx, however, was concerned with the natural world only as it related to the human process of production. As a result, he concerned himself principally with economic, social, and political conflict, rather than the antipodean opposition as observed in nature. It was Engels, and later Lenin, who sought for and found examples in the material realm of forces in diametric opposition to one another. They used these examples to illustrate by analogy their conception of the dialectic in human affairs. They went on to argue that, because it was equally applicable both to the natural and to the human world, dialectical materialism was thus the more scientific.

---

[44] This is particularly evident in a collection of his comments on dialectics drawn from speeches in 1958, especially in his treatment of birth and death as examples of dialectical interaction (1959c:216, 219).

Explaining his interest in mathematics and in the natural sciences, Engels wrote,

> my recapitulation of mathematics and the natural sciences was undertaken in order to convince myself in detail—of which in general I was not in doubt—that amid the welter of innumerable changes taking place in nature, the same dialectical laws of motion are in operation as those which in history govern the apparent fortuitousness of events; the same laws as those which similarly form the thread running through the history of the development of human thought and gradually give rise to consciousness in the mind of man.[45]

About a decade earlier he set down three "general laws" abstracted "from the history of nature and human society." These laws were:

> The law of the transformation of quantity into quality and vice versa.
>
> The law of the interpenetration of opposites.
>
> The law of the negation of the negation.[46]

Neither in the *Anti-Dühring* nor in the *Dialectics of Nature*, from which these passages are drawn, does one find a particularly systematic application of these laws to the natural world, despite what was obviously a considerable effort on Engels' part to become conversant with contemporary scientific developments. The *Anti-Dühring* was written as a critique of the loosely structured and wide-ranging work of Eugen Dühring. *Dialectics of Nature* was never completed by Engels, but remains a collection of disorganized notes. In these notes his approach was to draw examples for his three laws from different fields of scientific inquiry rather than to apply all three in a systematic explanation of a single science.[47] He draws examples of his first law of dia-

[45] Frederich Engels, Preface to the second edition of *Herr Eugen Dühring's Revolution in Science* (known as *Anti-Dühring*) (1885), translated by *Emile Burns* (New York: International Publishers, 1939), pp. 15f.

[46] Engels, *Dialectics of Nature*, translated by Clemens Dutt (New York: International Publishers, 1940), p. 26.

[47] He indeed argues that he is not engaged in "writing a handbook of dialectics but only with showing that the dialectical laws are really laws of development of nature and therefore are valid for theoretical natural sciences. Hence," he continues, "we cannot go into the inner interconnection of those laws with one another"; ibid., p. 27.

lectical development—the transformation of quantity into quality —from the field of chemistry. The interpenetration of opposites, his second law, he illustrates by referring to the realm of physics. The law of the negation of the negation is demonstrated in his discussion of biology and particularly of botany. The reader is thus left with the task of conceptualizing the way in which the other two laws might apply in the scientific fields Engels has chosen to illustrate the third. For instance, he suggests that it is useful to conceive of the development of the barley plant from the grain as a "negation" of the grain and of the development in turn of the grain from the plant as a "negation of the negation,"[48] but fails to treat the question of how useful it is to think of plant and seed as "opposites" that interpenetrate, or how the law of the transformation of quantity into quality applies in this botanical example.

Lenin was considerably more direct in his discussion of the applicability of dialectical laws to natural phenomena. He devoted considerable attention to the problem in his *Materialism and Empirio-criticism*, and returned to the question several years later in a briefer essay, "On Dialectics." In this latter essay he set forth a list of examples of what he regarded as "contradictory, mutually exclusive, opposite tendencies":

In mathematics: + and −. Differential and integral.

In mechanics: action and reaction.

In physics: positive and negative electricity.

In chemistry: the combination and dissociation of atoms.

In social science: the class struggle.[49]

In both cases, Engels and Lenin made reference to the natural sciences in order to establish the material, physical bases of the dialectical pattern of development. Both wanted to show not only an *analogy* between dialectical development in the natural, social, and philosophical spheres, but an *identity*. In asserting this identity, however, they not only took a very different view of nature and its relationship to men and women from that of Marx, but, as their critics aver, they rigidified and oversimplified beyond recognition what had been, in the hands of Marx, a subtle and

[48] Engels, *Anti-Dühring*, p. 149.
[49] V. I. Lenin, "On Dialectics," in *Selected Works* (New York: International Publishers, n.d.) XI, 81.

flexible mode of understanding the world, and of changing it.[50] In so doing, moreover, they intentionally blurred whatever distinction it is possible to make between the general category, conflict, and the particular type of conflict, contradiction. As a result, the usefulness of the dialectic for understanding nonantipodean opposition—which is far more common in social, political, and economic life than is antipodean opposition—is vitiated by the use of the term contradiction, and the consequent failure to attend as well to the complementarity of opposites that earlier, proto-dialectical observers of change in nature had stressed.

Although Mao makes frequent use of the term "contradiction," he uses it to include both antipodean and nonantipodean conflict. In his use of the dialectic we find a dual emphasis on complementarity and contradiction. He effected this dual emphasis through his use of the principle of the unity of opposites. Here, as we shall see, however, the idea of complementarity, rather than being a permanent characteristic of conflict, becomes a "moment" in the dialectical process. Citing Engels and Lenin, Mao did refer frequently in his discussion of the dialectic to the identity of the process of the interaction of contradictory elements in natural, social, and philosophical settings. He began by citing Engels' grounding of the theory of contradiction in the laws of motion ("motion itself is a contradiction")[51] and went on to point out, "contradiction exists universally and in all processes, whether in the simple or the complex forms of motion, whether in objective phenomena or ideological phenomena."[52] Indeed, he went on to suggest in his discussion of the "particularity" of contradiction that individual natural sciences are defined on the basis of a specific contradiction that constitutes the focus of the study.[53] At

---

[50] This is the argument found in the editorial comments of Frederic L. Bender in his anthology entitled *The Betrayal of Marx* (New York: Harper and Row, 1975), particularly 56-59, 66f., and 82f. In making the case for Marx, the humanist, betrayed by Engels, Plekhanov, and Lenin, the rigid and scientific materialists, however, Bender fails fully to acknowledge the degree to which Marx's own writings are suffused with the scientism of his age and thus themselves provide an impetus in the direction in which some of his successors moved. See Paul Thomas, "Marx and Science," *Political Studies* 24:1 (1976), 1-23.

[51] 1937g:280/1, 316.   [52] 1937g:281/1, 317.

[53] 1937g:284/1, 320. The passage is reminiscent of Thomas Kuhn's description of the creation of new branches of science on the basis of the breaking off of new paradigms from a previously established science in *The Structure of Scientific Revolutions* (Chicago: University of Chicago Press, 1962).

the same time that he sided with Engels and Lenin on the links between the applicability of the dialectic to the natural and social sciences, he nonetheless advanced a characteristically practical explanation for the emergence of the dialectic as a method of analysis—an explanation that reunited nature with the activity of men and women in a way more in consonance with the pattern of Marx's own approach: "In human practice—in the struggle against nature, in class struggle, and in scientific experimentation, year after year and month after month, for the necessity of living and struggle—men and women considered the laws of material reality and proved the correctness of the philosophy of materialism."[54]

Elsewhere, in a particularly interesting passage, Mao suggested that the wave-like motion of dialectical development (which we will discuss in greater detail below) is a law that is manifested not only in human affairs but also in the movement of electromagnetic and sound waves. The implication of the passage is clearly that more than mere analogy links the two types of movement, though the dialectics of electromagnetism and sonics is not spelled out (1959k:175). His enthusiasm for linking the natural and social sciences through the dialectic is manifested as well in his approbation of the dialectical nuclear physics of Sakata Soichi (1964g:319 and 1964r).

[54] 1937a:5. Considerable controversy has surrounded the authenticity of this article. Arthur Cohen argued that the crudeness of the article (which, on the basis of information then available to him, he dated 1940) as contrasted with the polish of the 1937 article, "On Contradiction," proved that the latter was either a much later product that had been predated and added to Mao's *Selected Works*, or a very substantial revision of an earlier work; *The Communism of Mao Tse-tung* (Chicago: University of Chicago Press, 1964), pp. 25ff. Dennis Doolin and Peter Golas published a translation of the first section of this article and substantially agreed with Cohen's assessment of the disparity between this and his other works purporting to date from the same period; " 'On Contradiction' in the Light of Mao Tse-tung's Essay, 'On Dialectical Materialism,' " *China Quarterly* 19 (1964), 38ff. Karl Wittfogel and C. R. Chao found the article to be largely a plagiarism of an article in the *Bol'shaya sovetskaya entsiklopedia*; "Some Remarks on Mao's Handling of Concepts and Problems of Dialectics," *Studies in Soviet Thought* 3:4 (1963), 251-277. John Rue, on the other hand, argued that the article was actually published by Party elements hostile to Mao and allied with Moscow, in an attempt to discredit him; "Is Mao Tse-tung's 'Dialectical Materialism' a Forgery?" *Journal of Asian Studies* 26:3 (1967), 464-468. Mao added his own comment to the controversy when, early in 1965, Edgar Snow reported to him the argument among Western scholars with regard to the article. Mao's reply to Snow's query was that, although he recalled clearly the date of writing "On Practice" and "On Contradiction" because they were delivered as lectures at Kangda in Yan'an, he had never written an essay entitled "Dialectical Materialism." "He thought that he

He alluded to his Chinese antecedents as a means of introducing what he took to be the central tenet of the dialectic, the law of the unity of opposites. "We Chinese often say," he pointed out, " 'Things that oppose each other also complement each other.' That is, things opposed to each other have identity."[55] Explaining the unity of opposites Mao said, "the fact is that no contradictory aspect can exist in isolation. Without its opposite aspect, each loses the conditions for its existence."[56] He then went on to illustrate his point with a passage that is virtually a paraphrase of the *Dao De Jing*, and that strongly reasserts the sense of the complementarity of opposites lost in Engels' and Lenin's formulations: "Without life there would be no death; without death there would be no life. Without 'above' there would be no 'below'; without 'below' there would be no 'above.' . . . Without facility there would be no difficulty; without difficulty there would be no facility."[57] Elsewhere he contends that Engels' three laws of the dialectic are reduceable to one, namely the law of the unity of opposites. "The unity of opposites is the most basic law," he explained in 1964. "Transmutation between quality and quantity is the unity of opposites between quality and quantity, but there is basically no negation of negation."[58] Although the law of the

would remember it if he had," he added (1965b:206f.). Stuart Schram appears to have resolved the question, Mao's memory to the contrary notwithstanding, with his discovery of a set of serialized lecture notes from talks delivered by Mao at Kangda in 1936-1937. The notes were published in the magazine, *Kangzhan Daxue* in 1938, and include the text of both the article "On Dialectical Materialism" and the article "On Practice." Moreover, the notes indicate that the lecture "On Contradiction" was to follow. All of these pieces thus appear to date from late 1936 and early 1937 and, although crude and uneven in quality, apparently reflect the quality of Mao's thought at the time; Schram, *Political Thought*, pp. 85-88.

A somewhat similar treatment of the relationship between human and natural conflict—one that uses natural conflict as evidence, in a sense, of the necessity of human conflict—is found in a brief comment dating from 1964 in which he says, "ideas of stagnation, pessimism, inertia and complacency are all wrong. They are wrong because they agree neither with the historical facts of social development over the past millions of years, nor with the historical facts of nature so far known to us (i.e., nature as revealed in the history of celestial bodies, the earth, life and other natural phenomena)" (1964x).

[55] 1937e:305/I, 343.   [56] Ibid., 302/I, 338.

[57] Ibid. See p. 8 above, where the relevant passage of the *Dao De Jing* is cited.

[58] 1964g:393. The following year he reiterated his point, suggesting that

unity of opposites was to be emphasized, that emphasis should not, in Mao's view, be an exclusive one. This was made clear when a serious dispute broke out in philosophical circles in the early 1960s over the question of the emphasis to be given to the unity of opposites and to their conflict. Yang Xianzhen advanced the argument that it was important to focus on the phase of two combining into one—the creation of a new stage of unity resulting from an antecedent conflict of contradictory forces.[59] Mao attacked Yang's position, both because of the political ramifications of his argument (which emphasized conciliation over struggle at a time—just prior to the Cultural Revolution—when Mao was attempting to make the opposite point), but more importantly because of its broader methodological implications. He suggested that overemphasizing the unity of opposites rather than their potential contradiction was a Hegelian error that gave rise to satisfaction with the status quo. The correct position, he insisted, was one that emphasized the moment of one splitting into two, thereby pointing up the continuity of conflict and the temporary character of unity and equilibrium.[60]

As Mao's argument in opposition to that of Yang makes clear, the dialectical resolution of the apparent paradox of opposition in unity and unity in opposition is to regard the two conditions as moments that alternate over time in an ongoing process. There

---

where Stalin had expanded Engels' three laws to four, the three could profitably be reduced to one, namely, "the law of contradiction: the remainder, quantity and quality, affirmation and negation, phenomenon and essence, content and form, necessity and freedom, possibility and reality, are all unity of opposites" (1965j:54).

[59] Yang Xianzhen's ideas as conveyed in lectures to his students are summarized in the article "One Divides into Two, Two Combines into One," by Ai Hengwu and Lin Qingshan, *Guangming Ribao* (29 May 1964). It was refuted in the article, "A Discussion with Comrade Yang on Problems of Two Combining into One," by Wang Qing and Guo Peiheng, *Renmin Ribao* (hereafter *RMRB*) (17 July 1964). See also Merle Goldman, "The Role of History in Party Struggle, 1962-1964," *China Quarterly* 51 (1972), 500-519.

[60] 1964g:387, 392. It was not a new position for Mao, who pointed out in 1959 that the unity of opposites is to be seen as "conditional, temporary, transitional and relative" (1959c:201). Similarly, commenting on the use in a Soviet text on political economy of the phrase "complete consolidation" of the socialist system, he pointed out that in dialectical terms the phrase is erroneous, since nothing can be completely consolidated when it is in a state of constant development (1961a:262f.).

are points in the process of development at which struggle, disunity, and qualitative change are its characteristics; similarly, there are points at which complementarity, unity, and quantitative change are its characteristics. Although both stages are necessary to the process of change, it is the former that he identifies as "absolute" or given. The latter—complementarity and unity—are thus to be conceived of as relative or temporary.

Deriving from Mao's conception of this dialectical resolution are two of the most pervasive metaphors in his writings: that of the wave and that of the spiral as illustrative of the movement of progress and development. "Any development," he wrote in 1961, "is not a straight line, but in the shape of a wave or a spiral."[61] The spiral illustrates the fact that, as "things proceed from imbalance and back to balance," "each cycle brings about a higher plane."[62] The wave suggests the shift between high and low speed,[63] between tension and relaxation.[64] "A wave-like form of progress is the unity of opposites, deliberation and haste," he wrote in 1958, "the unity of [the] opposites, toil and dreams."[65]

Finally (and in a certain sense paradoxically, as we shall see when we move on to speak of Mao's view of the human role in the dialectical process), he spoke often of the wave as symbolic of nature as a whole, in that it is something against which men and women must struggle in the process of pushing forward. He cited a Confucian interpretation of the symbolism of waves in his poem, "Swimming," with the lines, "Standing at a ford, the Master once said:/ Thus life flows into the past." But the symbolism is strikingly altered by the preceding lines:

> A swim cuts across the Long River.
> A glance gauges the sky's width.
> Let the wind blow and the waves strike,
> This surpasses an aimless stroll in the court.[66]

Waves thus served Mao as a symbol for the dialectical movement of nature in a way very reminiscent of that in which they served his Chinese forebears, but in his treatment of the posture of men

[61] Ibid., p. 279.   [62] 1958e:7; 1958c:80.
[63] 1959c:202.
[64] 1958t:105; 1959c:206. Cf. 1961a:284, where he suggests that "shock tactics" are sometimes appropriate as a variation in pace to sustain the alternation between the two.
[65] 1958l:106.   [66] 1956f.

and women in the face of this movement, he diverges sharply from them: "Swimming is a sport," he commented in 1964, "in which the swimmers battle against nature."[67] They also served him in the same way as a symbol in his political life: in July 1966 he plunged into the Yangtze once again as a signal of his reemergence as a vigorous, "first line" leader prepared to take an active role in the nascent Cultural Revolution.[68]

It is significant that Mao suggested abandoning Engels' third law of the dialectic—the law of the negation of the negation. Richard Bernstein suggests by means of a helpful analogy what Hegel had in mind in using this term to describe the process of achieving an innovation: "One 'moment' of a dialectical process, when it is fully developed or understood, gives rise to its own negation; it is not mechanically confronted by an antithesis. The process here is more like that of a tragedy where the 'fall' of the tragic hero emerges from the dynamics of the development of his own character."[69] By contrast, Mao's conception of the process of reaching a synthesis is more mechanistic than organic, perhaps because he found Hegel only by way of Engels. He describes the period of relative balance as one in which change is quantitative in nature, and may be brought about by external, as well as internal causes.[70] Conflicts during this period, he states elsewhere, "develop," "sharpen," and "deepen."[71] A ruling class in decline in the face of a rising advanced class is one of his favorite examples of quantitative change.[72] During this period of relative balance and quantitative change, the dialectic becomes, as Mao described it, a "comparative method" by means of which two aspects of a contradiction are brought together and their relative strength measured.[73] Qualitative change of a situation, by contrast, presupposes an *Aufhebung*—a supercession of what has come before: a "leap" in Mao's terms—to a qualitatively new situation that must be brought about by forces internal to the contradiction itself.[74]

In setting forth his alternative to the Hegelian term for the dialectical supercession of the old by the new—the stage that

[67] 1964g.
[68] 1966h.
[69] Richard Bernstein, *Praxis and Action* (Philadelphia: University of Pennsylvania Press, 1971), p. 20.
[70] 1937g:277, 297/I, 314, 333.
[71] 1930a:97f./I, 120f.
[72] 1958xx:73.
[73] 1958j:200; 1959c:201.
[74] 1958v:112; 1961a:263.

others have referred to as that of the achievement of a synthesis—
Mao is at his most vague and ambiguous. "What is synthesis?"
he asked rhetorically in 1937. "It is eating something up. . . .
Synthesis is the big fish eating the small fish."[75] He clarified this
unusual explanation some thirty years later and in so doing made
the process seem more eclectic than synthetic:

> Synthesis means swallowing up the enemy. How did we syn-
> thesize the Guomindang? We did it by taking enemy material
> and remoulding it. . . . Those we did not use we have *"Auf-
> gehoben"* to use a philosophical term. . . . The process of eating
> is also one of analysis and synthesis. For example, when eating
> crabs you eat the meat but not the shell. The stomach will
> absorb the nutritious part and get rid of the useless part. You
> are all foreign-style philosophers. I am a native-style philoso-
> pher.[76]

What is crucial here is not only the degree to which he returns
self-consciously to his own "native" sources rather than to the
Western origins of the dialectic in his explanation of its most
critical stage, but also the expansiveness with which he applies the
concept of qualitative change, a concept that he equates with the
term, "revolution." "All kinds of mutations and leaps," he pointed
out in 1958, "are a kind of revolution and must go through struggle. The 'theory of no struggle' is metaphysical."[77]

In order to complete this brief explication of Mao's use of the
dialectic, we must turn to the question of the role of human
actors in the dialectical process. For the moment it is important
to emphasize that the dialectic—the use of contradictions as a
method of investigation and analysis—is not treated by Mao as
merely one of many possible methods or paradigms that can be
imposed on a disorderly world to create an orderly explanation.
Although any scientist, as Thomas Kuhn describes scientific activity,[78] uses the dominant paradigm of the moment in the belief

[75] 1937a:28.

[76] 1965k:238f. He goes on to suggest that this definition derives from his
study of Marx, who "removed the shell of Hegel's philosophy and absorbed
the useful inner part, transforming it into dialectical materialism. He absorbed Feuerbach's materialism and criticized his metaphysics." His miscon-
strual of Hegel's and Marx's use of the term *Aufgehoben* here is instructive
of his departure from their conception of synthesis.

[77] 1958e:6; 1961a:273.

[78] Kuhn, *Structure of Scientific Revolutions.*

that it corresponds, in some sense, with the natural phenomena under observation, Mao the dialectician takes this correspondence much more literally.[79] Dialectical materialism is, in his view, the one satisfactory mode of analysis because its basis in contradiction is the same basis on which rest both the natural and the social worlds. Because contradiction is ubiquitous—"absolute" to use Mao's term—the dialectic, too, takes on an absolute character. To understand how the contradictory nature of the world and the contradictory nature of the dialectic relate to human nature and to the process of human action, we must explore the third characteristic of conflict as Mao saw it: its beneficiality.

CONFLICT AS BENEFICIAL

In his speech at Marx's graveside, Engels spoke of him as having made the contribution to the social sciences that Darwin, his contemporary, had made to the natural sciences.[80] The link between the work of the two men amounts to more than contemporaneity and significance, however. Both were, in addition, contributing importantly to the profound faith in the positive character of forward movement so characteristic of nineteenth-century European and American thought.[81]

For Darwin, the naturalist, the concept of progress was defined

[79] To be sure, most scientists engaged in what Kuhn calls "normal science," or "puzzle solving" within the framework of an accepted paradigm believe that there is a correspondence between their models and the phenomena under observation. The normal scientist's idea of correspondence, however, is, I would argue, much less self-conscious than that of the dialectician. Moreover, there is a considerably greater belief of open-endedness in the scientist's view of his own operations than in the self-image of the dialectician. The scientist's self-image of his openness includes, importantly, a professed willingness to abandon the old methods and hypotheses if they fail to account for apparent anomalies. That this self-image is often misfounded is one of Kuhn's principal points. The dialectician, on the other hand, seldom poses questions in such a way as to make them effectively verifiable, and thus "anomalies" in Kuhn's sense of that term have little possibility of calling into question the paradigm as a whole.

[80] Engels, "Speech at the Graveside of Karl Marx," in Robert C. Tucker, ed. *The Marx-Engels Reader* (New York: W. W. Norton, 1972), p. 603.

[81] A fascinating attempt to depict the intellectual climate prior to the general acceptance of the ideas of Marx and Darwin, and thereby to illuminate the degree to which we are now affected by those ideas is found in John Fowles' novel, *The French Lieutenant's Woman* (Boston: Little, Brown, 1969).

in terms of "fitness," where that word is close to that of an earlier form: "fittedness"—correspondence, in other words, to a given set of environmental conditions that are themselves in a process of change. When these ideas were carried into the social realm, the concept of fitness took on a more abstract set of positive connotations. Whereas for Darwin himself the process of evolution was a relatively open-ended one, those who came to be called "social Darwinists" almost invariably treated social evolution as directed toward some predetermined set of goals.[82]

Marx was sufficiently impressed with the work of Darwin to have considered dedicating *Das Kapital* to him. It was perhaps on the basis of the fact that Darwin's work, interpreted in light of the dialectic (for it is clearly not inherently dialectical) gave material and scientific substance to the rather more vague concept of inevitably forward movement that Marx had found in his study of Hegel and the work of Hegel's students.[83] The dialectic in the hands of its earliest exponents in Greece and China had a triadic structure. The two complementary elements of an opposition were contained within a third element, an unaltering framework within which the conflict took place. This unaltering framework was in some instances the natural cycle of the seasons, in others the life cycle. In China it was symbolized by the *tai ji tu*: a circle within which the conflict of *yin* and *yang* is bound. In the hands of the modern dialecticians, however, the circle is broken. Conflict replaces complementarity as the dominant form of opposition; the metaphor of the circle is replaced, as we have seen, by that of the spiral, which conveys the sense of simultaneous circular and forward or upward movement. For Marx and Mao, as for their idealist predecessors, each resolution of conflict, each synthesis, marked a forward step in development, incorporating as it did only the positive elements of the conflicting forces that had given rise to it. "When one contradiction has been conquered, another emerges. The same process of competition repeats itself. In this way society forges ahead continuously," Mao wrote in 1955.[84]

[82] See Richard Hofstadter, *Social Darwinism in American Thought* (Boston: Beacon, 1944).

[83] Bender discusses the relationship of Marx to Darwin in conjunction with Plekhanov's attempts to emphasize and build on that relationship his own ideas of the scientific nature of dialectical materialism; Bender, ed., *Betrayal*, pp. 110-113.

[84] 1955b:52.

This marriage of the dialectic to a Darwinesque concept of progress results in altered roles for the human actor. Within the ancient, naturalistic dialectic there are posited two roles for men and women: that of victim or passive experiencer of the forces of natural conflict, and that of observer of those forces. To these two roles Hegel and his successors added two additional ones, the one implicit and the other explicit in their schema. The implicit role is that of the defining authority—the individual who moves beyond mere observance of the conflict to a position of setting or descrying the goals toward which social conflict is to move and, in so doing, defining what are the positive and what the negative forces in that conflict. The explicit role is that of the human agent of change—the Marxist revolutionary actor who, by means of experience and intellection, moves beyond the philosopher's attempt to understand the world and seeks actively to change it.

Mao has relatively little to say on the act of setting the broad and long-range goals of social development. Indeed, as we shall see, his view of the dependence of thought upon empirical observation and praxis precludes for him, as a similar view precluded for Marx, in an important way, the possibility of fleshing out distant goals. In terms of more immediate goals, however, the role of the definer or arbitrator of conflict is more obvious. We will explore this question at greater length when Mao's epistemological views have been described, and the concept of authority that they contain explicated. Suffice it to say at this point that the implicit role of arbitrator or definer arises because of the potential conflict between the givenness and ubiquity of contradiction, on the one hand, and the beneficiality of contradiction, on the other. What is it that insures that all conflict will naturally resolve itself in a manner that fosters positive, progressive development? The deterministic side of Hegelian and Marxist thought (as is the case with the determinism implicit in the ideas of the social Darwinists) presupposes that the motor which pushes history forward is internal to the contradiction itself, and independent of the action of human agents. If historical development *inevitably* moves forward, then the conflicts that give rise to that progressive development must resolve themselves naturally, and in such a way as to contribute to progress. Just as conflict itself is given, so must the naturally correct resolution of conflict also be given. Incorrect or retrogressive resolutions are possible only over the short run, and constitute exceptions to the rule. A position such as this one

31

gives no weight to the effect of human judgment. What constitutes progress and development is determined by the conflict itself, and not by the men and women who observe and participate in that historical process.

Marx, however, was a humanist, by which he meant, in Feuerbachian terms, that men and women must be made the subject of philosophy in place of the abstractions that men and women have created. Subsequently moving beyond Feuerbach's position, he argued that the focus should be upon men and women as active subjects—as political, social, and economic actors transforming their world.[85] This humanism prevented Marx from taking a rigid, determinist position which he and certain of his successors were inclined to reject with the label, "mechanical materialism." A dialectic thus placed, as Marx placed it, in the service of humanism presupposes, I would argue, a human arbiter capable of defining the problem of human alienation, and of at least suggesting what the unalienated state of species being will be, toward the realization of which the historical process is moving. Progress can then be understood in terms of the movement toward that realization. Although, as we shall see, Mao redefined Marx's central problem—that of alienation—the need of a defining authority in his human-centered dialectic is nonetheless immanent.

To turn to the second role for the human actor added to the dialectic by its modern proponents, that of the agent of change, it is important to take note of the debate that has occurred regarding the relative importance of voluntarism and determinism in the Marxist tradition. A close reading of Marx's own writings on the subject reveals an ambiguity on the question: he speaks both of "iron laws" and of the necessity of human action to effect social progress.[86] Engels endeavored to resolve this ambiguity following

[85] Marx discussed what he then took to be Feuerbach's positive contributions to German philosophy in the opening pages of the "Economic and Philosophical Manuscripts" of 1844; Tucker, ed., *Marx-Engels Reader*, pp. 54ff. His statement of the ways in which he saw his own work as a supercession of that of Feuerbach is found in the "Theses on Feuerbach" and in the first part of *The German Ideology* (ibid., pp. 107ff., 111-164). A useful analysis of the evolution of this relationship is found in Shlomo Avineri, *The Social and Political Thought of Karl Marx* (Cambridge: Cambridge University Press, 1968), pp. 8-12 and 66-74.

[86] While it is possible to find in Marx statements with a particularly "deterministic" ring, I nonetheless subscribe to the position persuasively argued by Andrew Walder, "Marxism, Maoism and Social Change," *Modern*

Marx's death in favor of a greater determinism. Within the frame-work of Marxist thought, then, there are a number of positions that may be taken regarding the role of the actor in bringing about historical development. At one end of a continuum, the human actor is seen as wholly at the mercy of forces beyond his or her control. Midway along the continuum the actor is treated as unable to alter the course of events, but at least as able to affect the pace at which they move. At the opposite end, the actor can, by actions positive or negative, affect not only the pace of history, but its direction of movement, as well.

It is possible to find Mao, like Marx, taking positions all along this continuum at various points in his writings. In "On Contra-diction" (1937), for example, Mao says, "The development of things should be seen as their internal and necessary self-move-ment. . . . The fundamental cause of the development of a thing is not external but internal; it lies in the contradictoriness within a thing."[87] Several pages later in the same essay, however, he takes this position: "Qualitatively different contradictions can only be resolved by qualitatively different methods. . . . Processes change, old processes and old contradictions disappear, new processes and new contradictions emerge, and the methods of resolving con-tradictions differ accordingly."[88] The first statement presupposes a strongly determinist position. The latter, on the other hand, conveys both the idea that the "methods for resolution," even though derived from particular contradictions, are conceptually separable from the contradiction, and the implication of the need for an agent who will "apply" the apposite method. As a result, the latter statement must be taken as representative of a position far along the continuum toward voluntarism.[89] He attempts to

---

China 3:1 and 2 (January and April 1977), 101-118, 125-160, which sees voluntarism and determinism in Marx's work as dialectically related to one another, and thus as inappropriately conceived of as isolated, dichotomous positions, only one of which adequately characterizes Marx's (or Mao's) thought.

[87] 1937g:276f./I, 313.   [88] Ibid., 286/I, 321f.

[89] A similarly "voluntaristic" point of view is reflected in Mao's 1955 definition: "To break through and then seek balance is dialectics" (1955f:28). Martin Glaberman, in his provocative article, "Mao as a Dialectician" (*In-ternational Philosophical Quarterly* 8 [1968], 102-107), takes particular issue with the 1937 passage, arguing that Mao's position regarding the resolution of contradictions is "external and manipulative," and separates him from the Hegelian dialectical tradition. Glaberman's argument is correct as far as he

resolve the apparent contradiction in his position by arguing that "external causes are the condition of change and internal causes are the basis of change, and that external causes become operative through internal causes." He goes on to illustrate his point with a homely, if somewhat too clear-cut example: "In a suitable temperature an egg changes into a chicken, but no temperature can change a stone into a chicken because it has a different basis."[90]

Applied to the social and political realms, the relationship of internal and external causation delimits the range of effective human action:"When the economic basis reaches a certain stage of development, the old superstructure will no longer correspond to it. At that time changes of a fundamental nature must inevitably occur. Whoever tries to resist such change is discarded by history."[91] Thus, "the socialist system will replace the capitalist system. This is an objective law independent of human will. No matter how hard the reactionaries may try to prevent the advance of the wheel of history, revolution will take place sooner or later and will surely triumph."[92] The limits are thus defined as follows: "Whatever is not needed by history is bound to collapse; it is impossible to maintain it artificially. Whatever is in keeping with the demands of history will never collapse and it will be futile to disband it artificially. This is the great truth of historical materialism."[93]

Looking at it from the opposite side—that of the freedom to act—he summarized his view thus in 1962: "Freedom means the recognition of necessity and it means transforming the objective world. Only on the basis of recognizing necessity can man enjoy freedom of activity. What we call necessity is an objectively existing law."[94] On balance, then, Mao followed Marx in his tendency to regard historical development as the product of the interaction of human praxis and the conflict of natural forces.

---

takes it, but he fails to take account of the degree to which "externality" and "manipulation" are implicit in Marx's recasting of the Hegelian mode of thought. Without a degree of externality and manipulation, there is, after all, no role for the revolutionary actor who, while not central to Marx's theory as he or she is to Lenin's, is nonetheless not absent from that theory, either.

[90] 1937g:277f./1, 314.

[91] 1956n:34. See also his comment on the treatment of "unavoidability" in that article in 1957b:370.

[92] 1960e:34; cf. 1963e:22f.   [93] 1959t.

[94] 1962a:180.

Where he parted company with Marx in the direction of assigning a greater weight to the effect of human action is at the point in the development of his thought at which, as we shall see, he came to believe that by their errors men and women can reverse the course of historical development.

In spelling out the role of human praxis in resolving contradiction and thereby in fostering development, Mao was precise, detailed, and considerably more formularistic than might be wished by those who criticize his thought from the point of view of its departures from a humanistic Marxism. He used two terms when discussing human action with regard to social conflict—"to resolve" (*jiejue*) and "to handle" (*chuli*). While his use of the term "to resolve" tends more frequently to be in the passive than in the active voice—conflicts "are resolved," with the agent accomplishing the resolution unspecified—his use of the idea of the handling—"managing" we might say—of conflict is clearly an active one. In the context of his discussion of the handling of contradictions Mao elaborated the four crucial distinctions that he contended must be drawn in dealing with a particular set of contradictions. First is the determination of what elements in a given social situation are actually in contradiction with one another. Second is the distinction between what he referred to as "principal" (or dominant) and "nonprincipal" (or secondary) contradictions. Third is the calculation as to which aspect of the contradiction is dominant. Finally, a distinction must be made between what he refers to as an antagonistic and a nonantagonistic contradiction.

What are the relevant social conflicts at a particular time and place? Whereas the contradictions in the realm of nature that Mao and others use to exemplify their argument are compelling ones, which it would be difficult for the observer to overlook, social contradictions might appear to us to be somewhat less self-evident. Not so, Mao argued: "No matter what realm [we consider and this is] particularly [true of] a class society of course, it is always full of contradictions. Some people say that it is possible to 'find' contradictions in a socialist society. To me this seems to be an incorrect interpretation. One cannot say 'find' contradictions when the world is full of them. Nowhere do contradictions not exist."[95] Given this plethora of contradictions, it is the function of the experienced observer in direct contact with the em-

95 1959c:212; translation modified.

pirical situation—as we shall see explicated in greater detail in
the next chapter—to search out the relevant contradictions in a
particular objective situation. This process might usefully be
thought of as one of drawing up a list of contradictions among
which will ultimately be found the principal contradiction that
provides the key to the development of the situation. Mao alluded
to this process in 1958 as one of the "setting up of opposites":
"When we say setting up the opposite, it does not mean setting
up something not in objective existence. The so-called opposite
can only be set up when it is in objective existence."[96] "What is
absent in nature," he added when returning to this subject later,
"can be manufactured by man, but there must be a material foundation."[97] An example of his own implementation of this process
is found in a speech in 1956, in which he set forth the "ten major
relationships" relevant to Chinese development—those between
industry and agriculture, between coastal and inland regions, between economic development and national defence and so on.[98]

Once the relevant conflicts within a social situation have been
determined, the second distinction that must be drawn is that
between the principal and secondary contradictions. Based on the
goals toward which the conflict is progressing, the principal contradiction is the one that "plays a leading and decisive role,"
"whose existence and development determine or influence the
existence and development of the other contradictions,"[99] and
whose resolution will advance society toward the next stage in
its development.

The third distinction that must be made in the handling or
managing of contradictions is a crucial one. Within the principal
contradiction, which is its principal and which its "nonprincipal"
or secondary aspect? Mao's discussion of this latter distinction[100]
is pervaded by an ambiguity between a differentiation based on
the relative strength of the two aspects, and one based on a more
abstract qualitative judgment—an ambiguity that illustrates, in-
cidentally, Mao's adherence to Hegel's and Marx's implicit denial

---

[96] 1958s:98.   [97] 1958v:114.

[98] 1956e. We shall return to this document subsequently in this study,
since it is one that Mao viewed as his own first attempt to present an indigenous alternative to the Soviet developmental model which China had
adopted at Liberation; see, for instance, 1958j:101.

[99] 1937g:295f./I, 331f.   [100] Ibid., 297-300/I, 333-337.

of the validity of a separation of fact from value.[101] Mao spoke, for example, of the principal aspect of a contradiction as being "the aspect which has gained the dominant position" resulting from its having experienced an "increase in force" through its struggle with the other aspect of the contradiction.[102] At the same time, however, he introduced a quite different distinction—that between "old" and "new"—suggesting that in any given contradiction "the new aspect changes from being minor to being major and rises to predominance, while the old aspect changes from being major to being minor and gradually dies out."[103] If one takes seriously the idea of the passage of time as inevitably bringing about positive change, as Mao did at this stage in his career, then what he has put forward here in the guise of what one might at first assume to be a potentially verifiable quality—that of novelty—is a distinction that in practice involves nonverifiable judgments of value, for clearly there is a pejorative sense to "oldness" which derives from this context. This implicit distinction between the "good" and the "bad" aspects of a contradiction is a crucial one, since any action that is to be taken to further the course of development must be taken by putting one's weight on the side of (and thereby enhancing the force of) the "new" or positive aspect of the contradiction.[104]

Finally, a fourth distinction that must be made in handling a

[101] Bernstein's discussion of Marx's position is a helpful one; *Praxis and Action*, pp. 75ff.

[102] 1937g:297/I, 333.

[103] Ibid. See also, for example, 1940a:646f./II, 361f., where the young, vital communist movement is contrasted with the old and moribund capitalist system.

[104] The distinction being made here is reminiscent of that found in Mao's discussion in 1938 of just and unjust wars: "History shows that wars are divided into two kinds, just and unjust. All wars that are progressive are just and all wars that impede progress are unjust. We Communists oppose all unjust wars that impede progress, but we do not oppose progressive, just wars" (1938d:443/II, 150). The Cultural Revolution provides interesting examples of situations in which, in any particular contradiction, the novel, the good, and the powerful were not always associated with the same aspect of a contradiction, as seems to be implied in this discussion of the problem of distinguishing principal from nonprincipal aspects of a contradiction. Indeed, as we shall see in our subsequent discussion, once having seized power, a revolutionary may well find that the novel is often out of phase with what is powerful and, in turn, with what he or she regards as positive.

contradiction is that between nonantagonistic and antagonistic contradictions—contradictions among the people and those between the people and their enemies. This latter distinction depends in turn on the second distinction—that between principal and secondary contradictions—in that the line which separates the people from their enemies is one that is drawn on the basis of attitudes toward the principal contradiction at a given time in a given society.[105] This distinction determines, in turn, what kind of action will be taken to resolve the contradiction—whether struggle, as in the case of an antagonistic contradiction, or what Mao calls the "democratic" methods of persuasion and criticism that are appropriate to the case of a nonantagonistic contradiction.

Under the broad rubric of the "handling" of contradictions, then, one finds a range of action which, as Mao presented it, must be taken in order for the contradiction to be correctly resolved, and for forward development to take place as a result of that resolution.

In summarizing his brief explication of Mao's views on the positive contribution of conflict toward social development, and of the role of the human actor in fostering this positive contribution, it is perhaps useful to recall a teleological distinction made by Kant when he noted that, whereas man desires harmony, nature seeks struggle and pushes man from what would otherwise be an indolent life.[106] This differentiation between the proclivity for

---

[105] 1957d:80. This distinction between antagonistic and nonantagonistic contradictions is found originally in his 1937 article, "On Contradiction" (1937g:308ff./I, 343ff.). It was elaborated upon in an article written in December 1956 (1956n). He suggested in his 1957 speech that the association of the distinction between antagonistic and nonantagonistic contradictions, and that between the people and their enemies, could be traced to his argument concerning the treatment of allies and enemies in his article, "On the People's Democratic Dictatorship" (1949d:1357-1371/IV, 411-424) of 1949 and in a June 1950 speech (1950c:93). Arthur Cohen has traced the origin of the idea from its roots in a comment of Lenin's that Mao cited in 1937 ("Antagonism and contradiction are by no means the same. Under socialism the first will vanish, the second will remain."), through its development by Soviet and Chinese theorists prior to its enunciation by Mao in 1957 (*The Communism of Mao Tse-tung*, pp. 140-149). The comment of Lenin is found in his notes on Bukharin's *Economics of the Transitional Period, Selected Works*, Russian ed. (Moscow: Foreign Languages Publishing House, 1931) XI, 357. Mao's schema is reiterated in 1958p:89.

[106] Cited in Paul Foulquié, *La dialectique* (Paris: Presses Universitaires, 1949), p. 97. Kant's distinction is found in his *Idea of Universal History*

conflict in nature and the lack of a proclivity for conflict in humans is generally unacceptable to Mao and his predecessors in the development of the modern dialectic, as it would have been unacceptable or even incomprehensible to ancient practitioners of protodialectical thought. Indeed, there is an apparently intentional effort on Mao's part to blur the distinction between human and natural conflict. Conflict among humans is ultimately reduceable for him to the conflict of natural forces, since human purposes are ultimately determined by their relationship to material forces. Thus, not only would he have disagreed with the distinction drawn by Kant, he would have been likely to have had certain problems with Kant's view of the human psyche. The possibility that men and women may "by nature" prefer stability and harmony to conflict is a problem for social-psychological investigation. It is not an hypothesis that finds explicit expression in Mao's writings. However, as we shall see, there is implicit in a number of the tenets of the "theory of continuing the revolution under the dictatorship of the proletariat" the suggestion that, left to their own devices, men and women may prefer to stagnate rather than to exist in an inherently unstable environment of perpetual conflict. The Kantian idea, then, that conflict in the physical world is natural or given, and that conflict among humans is an unnatural, aberrant condition is rejected on principle by Mao, but implicitly acknowledged both in theory and in practice. On the other hand, Mao is consistent in his rejection of the possible implication in Kant's comment that, while nature's conflicts are beneficial, conflict among humans is baneful except when instigated by natural forces.

THE PERMANENCE OF CONFLICT

In his early philosophical writing, as we have seen, Mao emphasized what he referred to as the "absoluteness" of conflict: "Contradiction exists in and runs through all processes from beginning

---

from a Cosmopolitan Viewpoint, and is also discussed by Kurt Singer, when he differentiates between what he refers to as a "somatic" and a "noëtic" conflict. Somatic conflict is that which results from the physical fact that no two objects can occupy the same space simultaneously; noëtic conflict is that which arises from the interaction of opposed purposes among human actors; *The Idea of Conflict* (Melbourne: Melbourne University Press, 1949), pp. 14ff.

to end; motion, things, processes, thinking—all are contradictions. To deny contradictions is to deny everything. This is a universal truth for all times and all countries, which admits of no exception."[107] As we shall see when we investigate Mao's theory of knowledge in the next chapter, any concept that is taken to be universally and eternally true violates in a fundamental way that theory. Despite this important inconsistency, Mao makes his point forcefully: contradiction, he contends, is a permanent feature of the natural and the social worlds alike. The nature of the conflict—particularly that of social conflict—may change under the conditions of a socialist society, but conflict itself is a constant.

On this particular point Mao's position became, if anything, more positive over the course of his career. As a result, he modified in recent years Marx's, Lenin's, Stalin's, and even his own earlier treatment of this question. This modification is a conceptual cornerstone, as we shall see, of his theory of continuing the revolution. Marx viewed the socialist revolution as conducted by the proletariat as a unique historical turning point. The social modifications that would be brought about by a dictatorship of the proletariat following this revolution would bring an end to classes, and with them, an end to the most fundamental of social and political contradictions, the class struggle.[108] He alluded only infrequently to the specific nature of this classless society, but these allusions convey the impression of an essentially static situation. Marx does not *deny* the continued existence of conflict in a classless society, but then neither does he affirm it.[109]

[107] 1937g:294/I, 330.

[108] Marx, "Letter to Joseph Weydemeyer" (5 March 1852) in Lewis S. Feuer, ed. *Marx and Engels: Basic Writings on Politics and Philosophy* (New York: Doubleday, 1959), p. 457.

[109] In the *Communist Manifesto*, Marx and Engels rejected the "castles in the air" of the utopian socialists and spoke of the new society merely as being one in which "in place of the old bourgeois society, with its classes and class antagonisms, we shall have an association, in which free development of each is condition for the free development of all"; Tucker, ed., *Marx-Engels Reader*, pp. 353, 361. Earlier, in the 1844 Manuscripts, Marx expanded on his idea of the communist society: "This communism, as fully developed naturalism equals humanism, and as fully developed humanism equals naturalism; it is the *genuine* resolution of the conflict between man and nature and between man and man—the true resolution of the strife between existence and essence, between objectification and self-confirmation, between freedom and necessity, between the individual and the species. Communism is the riddle of history solved, and it knows itself to be this solution" (ibid., p. 70). I have discussed the utopian strain in the

Lenin had little time to devote to the study of a socialist society, much less to speculate about the communist stage beyond, prior to the Bolshevik Revolution, because his primary task was the anterior one of bringing about a socialist revolution; and after the revolution his active career was cut short by his illness and his death during the initial stages of the process of the socialist transformation of Russian society. Stalin, when he turned to the question of the existence of contradictions in a socialist society, reached an opposite conclusion to that of Mao: in 1936 he declared that Soviet society, as a result of the gradual evolution of socialism in that society, was essentially free of contradiction. Mao took particular issue with this position of Stalin's,[110] despite the fact that he acknowledged that, shortly before his death, Stalin had modified his earlier position and had asserted that contradictions did exist between the forces and relations of production in Soviet society—contradictions that could, if mishandled, become antagonistic.[111]

Prior to 1956, by Mao's own reckoning, China was still in the stage of the transition to socialism, and thus Stalin's earlier ideas concerning contradiction in a socialist society were, temporarily at least, irrelevant to China. Not only did these earlier ideas of Stalin's go against Mao's previously articulated and strongly phrased belief in the perpetuity of conflict, however, but subsequent events within the Soviet bloc—specifically the uprisings in Hungary in 1956—appeared to Mao to belie their validity. In their place Mao elaborated, as we have seen, the ideas of the continued existence and the change of character of contradictions during the socialist stage. He emphasized anew the distinction between antagonistic and nonantagonistic contradictions, and argued that, if correctly handled, antagonistic contradictions would gradually give way to nonantagonistic contradictions in a socialist society. Applied to the question of social classes, as we shall see, the implication of this position was clearly that over the course of the socialist stage, class struggle would gradually diminish in intensity.

A decade later, however, Mao came to denounce this same

---

thought of Marx and his successors in "Maoism and Marxist Utopianism," *Problems of Communism* 26:4 (1977), 56-62.

[110] 1958l:108; 1958p:89; 1961a:266, 272, 294. Stuart Schram cites and discusses the relevant Soviet texts in *La "Révolution permanente" en Chine* (Paris: Mouton, 1963), xxxiii-xxxvi.

[111] 1958t:106.

position, which he referred to as a "theory of the dying out of the class struggle," associating it with Liu Shaoqi. Implicit in this rejection was a reassessment of the characteristics of a socialist society with the conclusion that, far from dying out over the course of the socialist stage, antagonistic contradictions may well increase in number and intensity. The theory of continuing the revolution under the dictatorship of the proletariat predicates what is referred to as a "fairly long" socialist stage fraught with "classes, class contradictions, class struggle . . . [and] the struggle between the road of socialism and the road of capitalism."[112] In his later years Mao took to speaking with visitors in terms of very long historical epochs, emphasizing anew that the one element of continuity in these epochs will be the continued existence of conflict.[113]

This permanence of conflict extends even beyond what Marx

[112] 1962c.

[113] Klaus Mehnert has described Mao's visit with a German delegation shortly before his death, during which he indicated that his thought had been strongly influenced by "four Germans: Hegel, Marx, Engels, and Haeckel." The latter, Ernst Haeckel, was a late nineteenth-century evolutionist whose views on the long-term development of the universe were read by Mao in translation, and are mirrored in a number of his comments beginning in the late 1950s. Compare, for example, Mao's comment in 1959: "There is nothing in this world that does not go through emergence, development and extinction. Ape changed into man and man emerged. The ultimate outcome of mankind as a whole is extinction. Man will possibly change into another kind of thing. By then the earth will no longer exist. The sun will have cooled. . . . There are only two infinites: time and space. Infinites are composed of finites. All kinds of things develop and change gradually" (1959c:205), with Haeckel's comments: "The fate of those branches of the human family, those nations and races which have struggled for existence and progress for thousands of years, is determined by the same 'eternal laws of iron' as the history of the whole organic world which has peopled the earth for millions of years. . . . While many of the stars are probably in a similar stage of biogenetic development to that of our earth, . . . others have advanced far beyond this stage, and, in their planetary old age, are hastening towards their end—the same end that inevitably awaits our own globe. The radiation of heat into space gradually lowers the temperature until all the water is turned into ice; that is the end of all organic life. . . . Yet in this 'perpetual motion' the infinite substance of the universe, the sum total of its matter and energy, remains eternally unchanged, and we have an eternal repetition in infinite time of the periodic dance of the worlds, the metamorphosis of the cosmos that ever returns to its starting point. Over all rules the law of substance"; Ernst Haeckel, *The Riddle of the Universe at the Close of the Nineteenth Century*, translated by Joseph McCabe (New York: Harper and Bros., 1900), pp. 270, 372.

called the end of prehistory—the end of the class struggle. Mao explained his view in 1964 as follows: "I don't believe that there won't be qualitative change in communism and that it won't pass through stages of qualitative change. . . . I cannot believe that a specific characteristic can go on for millions of years without undergoing some change. According to dialectics this is inconceivable."[114] The nature of the conflict and development in the communist stage may not be wholly clear, but Mao suggested that it will take the form of continued struggle between old and new, true and false,[115] subjective and objective, the forces and relations of production, materialism and idealism, and the individual and the collective.[116] To deny the permanence of change, he suggested in 1956, is to deny the very fundamentals of Marxism.[117] A decade later he suggested that even Marxism itself was subject to the transcience implicit in a view of permanent conflict: "Marxism also has its birth, its development, and its death. . . . To say that it won't die is metaphysics. Naturally, the death of Marxism means that something higher than Marxism will come to replace it."[118]

CONFLICT IN MAO'S POLITICAL PHILOSOPHY

Having considered aspects of Mao's view of conflict as a central idea around which his political philosophy is constructed, it may prove useful to put this view into perspective by contrasting it with that prevalent in our own approach to social questions. Here I am less concerned with philosophical schools and social science models than with our common perceptions of conflict and harmony. As I have suggested above, in these common perceptions we have moved away from a naturalistic tendency to view the world in terms of conflicting forces—a tendency which, with the exception of the nineteenth-century dialecticians, was not reinforced by the major philosophical schools in the West, as it was in China. Our tendency is to regard conflict as aberrant—as a problem that requires a solution.

Our evaluation of conflict thus tends to be negative rather than positive. Conflict is regarded as a hindrance rather than as a help to development. Conflicts are obstacles that must be surmounted

---

[114] 1964q:394f. Cf. 1959c:221; 1961a:264; and 1971:41.

[115] 1964x.   [116] 1956d:10.   [117] 1956a:96.

[118] 1964r:399. Cf. his comments to Edgar Snow on the subject the following year (1965b:222).

before progress can be made; they are certainly not regarded as the motor of progress. Our conception of the "management" of conflict, unlike Mao's "correct handling" of contradictions, seeks to prevent conflict from hindering forward development, rather than to use conflict to promote that development.

As we have seen, Mao tended to conflate the terms conflict and contradiction. By contrast, our common language seeks to distinguish the two terms. Where we treat the concept of conflict or opposition as permitting of a range of degrees of difference, we reserve the concept of contradiction—of antithetical or antipodean difference—for complete negation, sharp, unmistakable contrast or antagonism. Because of its use in logic, we tend to view contradiction as impossible—as making nonsense of any proposition in which it appears. Far from being a creative force in the realm of nature and of ideas, we regard it instead as confined to the realm of ideas, and as constituting a criterion of invalidity. Thus, whereas we see conflict as occurring in both human affairs and in the natural world, we treat contradiction, which we consider to be an impossible condition in the natural world, as referring by extension to an equally impossible condition in the realm of ideas. Far from regarding conflict as ubiquitous—as equally characteristic of natural, social, and conceptual processes—our tendency instead is to confine the concept within much narrower limits.

Mao's position on these questions was not, as we have seen, wholly free from ambiguity. Although he took conflict as a given, natural state, he was too much concerned with the effect of human activity to argue that this natural conflict among things and among people will work itself out through time in foreordained, positive ways. Taken as a whole, in Mao's treatment of the question he held that it is a good thing, not a bad thing that conflict pervades our experience, but at the same time he argued that men and women have an active part to play in bringing about that progressive development through the correct handling and resolution of social and natural conflict. The presence of conflict in the world requires, in his view, the use of a mode of thought that reflects this conflict. As will become increasingly evident, the dialectic, or Mao's variant form of that mode of thought, pervaded and permeated his approach to virtually every question.

For Marx, the central problem with which he initiated his work and toward the solution of which that work is directed, is very clearly that of the alienation of men and women in the productive process as it is conducted in a capitalist system. Conflict and contradiction in the human and natural realm—the dialectical method—Marx treated as the tool appropriate to the conceptualization and resolution of this central problem. Alienation is a problem that interested Mao not at all.[119] Because economic, social, and political development is the problem with which he did, in fact, concern himself, contradiction, conflict, and the dialectic to which they give rise came to constitute the central idea and fixed pole around which all other ideas in his political thought revolved.

As I have noted, there is, however, an apparent and crucial contradiction between Mao's contention that conflict is absolute or permanent, and a tenet in the theory of knowledge which he based on his conception of conflict—the tenet that would invalidate any statement purporting to affirm the permanency of any aspect of human experience. We will explore this contradiction further as we turn now to an investigation of his theory of knowledge.

[119] Donald J. Munro, "The Chinese View of Alienation," *China Quarterly* 59 (1974), 580-583. Cf. Starr, "Mao's Self-Image as a Marxist Thinker," *Modern China* 3:4 (1977); and "Marxism and the Political Legacy of Mao Tse-tung," *International Journal* (Winter 1976-1977), pp. 128-155.

Chapter Two

ON KNOWING AND DOING

> Where do correct ideas come from? Do they
> drop from the skies? No. Are they innate in
> the mind? No. They come from social prac-
> tice, and from it alone; they come from three
> kinds of social practice—the struggle for pro-
> duction, the class struggle and scientific experi-
> ment. It is man's social being that determines
> his thinking.[1]

In the same set of lectures at Kangda in which he addressed himself to the problem of contradiction, Mao devoted another lecture
to the problem of the theory of knowledge—a lecture which he
entitled, "On Practice: On the Relations between Knowledge and
Practice, between Knowing and Doing."[2] In this lecture he put
forward an explicitly dialectical theory of knowledge, which he
modified but slightly in the intervening years. In this chapter I
will begin by investigating Mao's description of the origin and
development of ideas—the process of cognition—looking particularly at the dialectical characteristics he ascribed to this process.
In the latter section of the chapter I will take up his treatment of
the verification of ideas and, in conjunction with that treatment,
the various criteria on the basis of which he differentiated between and evaluated ideas. Having done so, it will be possible to
reexplore the paradox with which the last chapter closed: that
of how, in an epistemological system in which all ideas derive
from practice, certain ideas—notably that of the ubiquity and
permanence of contradiction—can have a validity not bound by
time.

THE PROCESS OF COGNITION

In the previous chapter I cited a passage in which Mao spoke of
freedom as cognizance of the constraints of the inevitable.[3] He

[1] 1963d:58.   [2] 1937e:259-273/I, 295-309.
[3] 1962a:180.

returned to this idea two years later, and in clarifying his interpretation gave a sense of the interrelatedness he saw between understanding and action: "Engels spoke of moving from the realm of necessity to the realm of freedom, and said that freedom is the understanding of necessity. This sentence is not complete, it only says one half and leaves the rest unsaid. Freedom is the understanding of necessity *and* the transformation of necessity— one has some work to do too. . . . It won't do just to understand necessity, we must also transform things."[4] Mao turned to the explication of the dialectical link between understanding and transformation in his discussion of his theory of knowledge.

There are at least two grounds on which to base the interpretation that Mao's theory of knowledge was dialectical in nature. First, as we have seen in the previous chapter, when speaking of the universality of contradiction, he argued that thought processes, like society and nature, are fraught with contradiction.[5] Second, in his description of the process of cognition itself, he uses the language of the dialectic in describing the movement from stage to stage in the process. This movement he characterized as a "sudden change" (*tubian*) or "leap" (*feiyue*), which brings about a qualitative transformation, suggesting thereby that the stage which follows is synthetic in nature, and that the movement to that stage has resulted from the conflict of opposites in the preceding stage. He describes the process of cognition in this 1937 article as involving three such stages—perception, conception, and revolutionary practice—the third giving rise once again to the first, so that the process, like Mao's concept of the dialectic itself, becomes spiral in form.

It would be incorrect to suggest that any one of the three interrelated stages of the process of cognition is more important than the others. It is true, however, that Mao devoted more attention to the stage of perception than to the other two—more in an exhortatory than an explanatory mode, to be sure—presumably because it was the stage he most frequently saw being given short shrift by his comrades. He put it bluntly in 1930: "No investigation, no right to speak."[6] Perceptions, the product of this first

---

[4] 1964q:228.

[5] Enumerating examples of fundamentally important contradictions, Mao included that between the forces of production and relations of production, that between economic base and superstructure, and that between theory and practice (1937g:300/I, 335).

[6] The statement was originally made in 1930 in his article, "Oppose Book

stage of the process, are the result of the interaction of the observer and the phenomenon. Again and again in his discussion of the perceptual stage, Mao emphasized the need for direct, even physical contact between the observer and the phenomenon observed.[7] In one of his earliest articles he made the point as follows: "Knowledge consists in knowing the things in the world, and in observing their laws. In this matter we must rely on our body, because direct observation depends on the ears and eyes, and reflection depends on the brain. . . . When the body is perfect, then knowledge is also perfect."[8] Later in the same article he cited an analogy that conveys his sense that observations must be made directly to be reliable: "If we look at flowers from a galloping horse, even though we may look at them daily, it is as though we have not seen them at all."[9] Stopping to look at the flowers is more effective, he said, but if one really wants to see the flowers, the only way to succeed in doing so is to dismount and observe them directly.[10] This insistence that it is only through "going down" to the basic level, observing conditions, and speaking to people to ascertain their opinions that one can form perceptions of a situation, is one to which Mao returned frequently,[11] basing his injunctions on his own extensive investigatory experience.[12]

Worship" (1930b:40). He reiterated it in 1941 in his preface to *Rural Surveys*, pointing out that many had accused him of "narrow empiricism" on the basis of that slogan, but that he would stand by it, since those who spoke without having made their own investigations could offer nothing but "ignorant twaddle" (1941a:749/III, 13). He repeated the comment once again in 1965 (1965c:122).

[7] For example, see 1937e:261f./I, 297, where Mao illustrates his description of the process with the experience of a hypothetical inspection party touring the Yan'an base area. "In the first day or two, they see its topography, streets and houses; they meet many people, attend banquets, evening parties and mass meetings, hear talk of various kinds and read various documents. . . . These particular things in Yan'an *act on the sense organs* of the observation group [and] evoke sense perceptions" (emphasis added). Cf. 1930b:233f.

[8] 1917:156f.   [9] Ibid., p. 160.

[10] He returned to the image again in 1958 in encouraging bureaucrats to visit local areas and "dismount to look at the flowers" (1958e:8).

[11] See, for instance, 1958a; 1961b:237, 241f.; 1963d:69; and 1965a:437. Idealists, by contrast, have it easy, he suggested, since they have no need for grounding their ideas in objective reality (1955b:53).

[12] Although he said relatively little about himself in the articles and speeches available to us, Mao did emphasize his investigatory experience during his early years in the party. We have already referred to two early

Philosophy, he pointed out in 1963, is not the product of university specialists; "philosophy comes out of the mountains and valleys."[13]

Phenomenon and observer are not, as Mao describes them, in opposition or contradiction during the process of observation, although the phenomenon itself is seen as internally contradictory or conflictful. Indeed, as we have seen in the previous chapter, the process of observation at the perceptual stage is one of looking for the conflicts or contradictions in the phenomenon under consideration.

Although he acknowledged that each individual observer is incapable of experiencing directly all of the phenomenal world about which he or she needs to know, Mao did argue that the indirect knowledge upon which we need to rely at times must be traceable back to direct observation: "What is indirect experience for me is direct experience for other people. Consequently, considered as a whole, knowledge of any kind is inseparable from direct experience. All knowledge originates in perception of the objective, external world through human physical sense organs."[14]

---

articles that allude to this experience (see note 6 above). He referred to it subsequently in 1956e:25, 1964c:341, and 1964q:389. He spoke in 1955 of the extensive reading he had accomplished in material dealing with local conditions (1955e:21); the publication at the end of that year of a collection of this material with his editorial comments appended gives evidence of the accuracy of his claim (1955g). During the Great Leap Forward—a period during which he has been accused by some of being particularly out of touch with the realities of rural life in China—the Chinese press carried more than two dozen reports of his visits to cooperatives, communes, schools, mines, factories, and ships, giving validity to his comment to his party colleagues in 1965 that "I myself have met people of all kinds and government officials big and small" (1965j:54). Reports of his 1958 visits are found in 1958f; 1958g; 1958h; 1958k; 1958n; 1958r; 1958y; 1958z; 1958aa; 1958bb; 1958cc; 1958dd; 1958ee; 1958ff; 1958gg; 1958hh; 1958ii; 1958jj; 1958kk; 1958nn; 1958oo; 1958pp; 1958qq; 1958rr, and 1959l.

[13] 1963b:320.

[14] 1937e:264/I, 300. Elsewhere he reiterated the importance of indirect knowledge: "It is also necessary to learn with an open mind from other people's experience, and it is sheer 'narrow empiricism' to insist on one's own personal experience in all matters and, in its absence, to adhere stubbornly to one's own opinions and reject other people's experience" (1936:197/I, 223). On the other hand, he also advocated, where possible, the verification of second-hand knowledge, which "consists of theories set down by [our] predecessors in summarizing experience of the struggle for production and of the class struggle" (1942a:774/III, 39).

Phrasing his comment in this way, Mao glosses over substantial problems of intersubjectivity and communication between observers—problems that will reemerge when we consider the criteria he provided for testing the validity of one idea against that of another. Nonetheless, his basic point is clear: the closer one is as an observer to direct experience of the phenomena under observation, and the broader that direct experience, the more reliable will be that observer's perceptions. "If you want to know the taste of a pear, you must change the pear by eating it yourself."[15]

His description of the process of perception makes Mao a thoroughgoing empiricist, at least at the outset of the process of cognition. But empiricism of the perceptual stage alone results only in the "cataloguing of great piles of superficial phenomena," as he described it at one point.[16] Perception must serve, he said elsewhere, as an "usher at the threshold of grasping the essence of the phenomenon."[17] To fail to cross this threshold is to be guilty of the fault he calls "narrow empiricism."

The second stage in the process of cognition is that of conception, and the movement from perception to conception is, as Mao describes it, a dialectical one: "As social practice continues, things that give rise to human sense perceptions and impressions in the course of practice are repeated many times; then a sudden change (leap) takes place in the brain in the process of cognition and concepts are formed."[18] Conceptions differ from perceptions in that they "grasp the essence, the totality and the internal relations of things," whereas perceptions are phenomenal, isolated and external.[19] By way of illustration, he referred to a frog in a well who says, "the sky is no bigger than the mouth of the well." By contrast, "a Marxist should see the whole as well as the parts."[20] "In studying a problem," he said in 1961, "we must start from appearance that people see and feel in order to explore the essence behind appearance and thereupon expose the essence and contradictions of objective things."[21] A peasant, for instance, can only conceptualize oppression on the basis of the experience of oppression at the hands of a particular landlord.[22]

Using concepts, he continued, it is possible to form judgments, inferences, and logical conclusions. A part of the process is merely

[15] 1937e:264/I, 200.
[16] 1965c:126.
[17] 1930a:96/I, 119.
[18] 1939e:262/I, 298.
[19] Ibid.
[20] 1935:135/I, 159.
[21] 1961a:303.
[22] 1963b:319.

cumulative: conceptions are the result of multiple perceptions.[23] The accumulation of multiple perceptions, however, accounts for only the quantitative change involved—the change he posits between perception and conception is synthetic in nature, and must, therefore, be qualitative as well. Addressing the problem in the context of setting forth prescriptions for the improvement of analytical writing, Mao argued that the process of conceptualization is one in which the problem, or contradiction observed in the process of perception, is submitted to a "systematic and thorough investigation and study" to reveal the "internal relations of things." This having been done, it is then possible to "make a synthesis," and thereby to provide the method to solve the problem.[24] Left unspecified, however, are the opposing forces, the conflict of which is resolved by the leap to a new, synthetic stage of conception. The process is described merely as one of "synthesiz[ing]" (*zhonghe*) the data by arranging and reconstructing them."[25]

As I interpret it, the contradiction here—the resolution of which constitutes the formation of concepts—is that between the sense perceptions and what might usefully be conceived of as the "preconceptions" that the observer brings to the process of conceptualization. I choose this term not because it appears in Mao's own description of the process, but because the logic of his description of the process of cognition as a whole suggests the appropriateness of such a term. Because the process of cognition as he sees it is necessarily cumulative, then there must be a point at which "old" conceptual knowledge about the phenomenal world comes into interaction with new perceptions of the world. The movement from perception to conception—the process of arrangement and reconstruction about which Mao speaks—appears to me to be the point at which this contradictory interaction must occur. This interaction between perceptions and preconceptions is contradictory because, as we shall see in a moment, the product of any completed process of cognition is twofold: new

[23] "It is only when the data are very rich (not fragmentary) (*shifen fengfu* [*bushi lingsui buquan*]) and correspond to reality (are not illusory) that they can be the basis for forming correct concepts and theories" (1937e:267/1, 302). "A thing has both an appearance and an essence," he commented in 1963. "We must penetrate the superficial to see the essence." This is accomplished, he went on to argue, by intensive investigation— "squatting on a spot," as the slogan of the time described it (1963b:320).

[24] 1942b:795f./III, 61f.   [25] 1937e:262/1, 298.

ideas *and* a changed world are its results. The changed world, however, is the product of another dialectical transformation beyond the formation of concepts, and thus the concept and the world do not coincide directly with one another. Rather, when it is perceived once again after the change has been effected, the world is found to be in contradiction with concepts that have been formed on the basis of perceptions prior to the change, and which are brought to bear as preconceptions in the new process of cognition.

It is within this stage of the process of cognition that the groundwork is laid for qualitative rankings of ideas and observers. The process of perception seemed to Mao to be one of such compelling contact with the "real" material world that there is little possibility for error, though, as we shall see, some observers are regarded as better suited, more thorough, and more reliable than others. There is a greater possibility for error in the stage of conception, where not only the competence and experience of the observer—his or her ability to "arrange and reconstruct" perceptual data—but also the legitimacy or validity of the preconceptions that the observer brings to bear on the perceptual data may affect the successful outcome of the process. If the observer is inept, or if his or her preconceptions are faulty because of an insufficient empirical base or an incorrect process of conceptualization, then the product of the new cognitive process will inevitably be incorrect, as well. Since some observers are seen as more effective than others, and some preconceptions are seen as more accurate than others, there is an implicit need for the qualitative ranking of observers and ideas, and for a set of criteria by means of which these rankings can be achieved. We will turn to a discussion of these criteria in the latter half of this chapter.

The interrelationship and inseparability of the stages of perception and conception in the process of cognition were emphasized and reemphasized by Mao,[26] who made this point by suggesting the deviations from correct practice that occur when perception and conception are divorced from one another. As he described it during the party's rectification campaign in the early 1940s, he saw this correct process of cognition as standing in contradistinction, on the one hand, to that of party members who, primarily because of their ties to Moscow, overstressed Marxist-Leninist principles; and, on the other hand, to that of party members who,

[26] See, for example, ibid.; 267/1, 302f.; and 1942a:774/III, 39.

because of their lack of theoretical training in Marxism-Leninism, overstressed the concrete details of their own immediate revolutionary experience. The former he referred to as dogmatists, the latter as empiricists, and he regarded both groups as guilty of a form of subjectivism. Empiricists, as we have seen, concentrate on the perceptual stage of the cognitive process and ignore the stage of conception. As a result, like the frog in the well, they "mistake fragmentary experience for universal truth."[27]

Dogmatists, by contrast, are those who focus upon the stage of conceptualization and neglect the stage of perception. They concentrate their attention on their own theories or those of others, and ignore the requisite empirical base for that theory, as a result of being "divorced from social practice."[28] Citing the example of the relationship between Marxist-Leninist theory and the social practice of the Chinese revolution, Mao made use of an analogy to describe dogmatists in a 1942 speech: "How is Marxist-Leninist theory to be linked with the practice of the Chinese revolution? To use a common expression, it is by 'shooting the arrow at the target.' As the arrow is to the target, so is Marxism-Leninism to the Chinese revolution. Some comrades . . . merely stroke the arrow fondly, saying, 'What a fine arrow! What a fine arrow!' but never want to shoot it."[29] They "regard Marxism-Leninism as dogma," he said in a portion of the same speech that has been omitted from the reedited version, and they thus must be told, " 'Your dogma is of no use,' or, to use an impolite formulation, 'Your dogma is less useful than shit.' We see that dog shit can fertilize the fields and man's can feed the dog. And dogmas? They can't fertilize the fields, nor can they feed a dog. Of what use are they?"[30] The tendency of the dogmatist is to ignore the fact that, because the world is continually developing, and because different areas of the world are at different stages in that developmental process, no one set of ideas can be mechanically applied to all areas in all periods.[31] The correct use of these ideas is not as a set formula mechanically applied to every case, but rather as a set of preconceptions brought to bear on one's own perceptions in order to create conceptual sense out of one's experience, which will, in turn, guide revolutionary praxis.[32] The

[27] 1945a:995/III, 314.
[28] Ibid.
[29] 1942a:777f./III, 42.
[30] 1942a:179 (Schram version).
[31] 1956d:15.
[32] Mao made this point on a number of occasions. See, for instance, 1938c:499f./II, 209, where he is speaking of the need for the "Sinification of

same principle applies not only to the "classics" of Marxism, but to Mao's own ideas as well. In 1964 he spoke of the need to revise the articles "On Practice" and "On Contradiction" in the light of subsequent experience in the Chinese revolution,[33] and the following year he cautioned visitors from the Palestine Liberation Organization against the mechanical application of the Chinese revolutionary theory to their own movement: "Do not tell me that you have read this or that opinion in my books. You have your war and we have ours. You must create the principles and ideology on which your war stands. Books obstruct the view if piled up before the eyes."[34]

The danger of dogmatism does not, however, obviate the role of the theorist who is correctly able to conceptualize on the basis of perceptual knowledge. Theory is "crystallized in the subjective world in the mind of the theorist," he wrote in 1958.[35] "When the subjective reflects the objective, it becomes subjective activity, not subjectivism," he said the following year, and, in the same speech, concluded, "in the union of theory and practice, theory is the spirit and spirit reflects substance."[36]

Although new ideas have emerged as a result of the conceptual stage in the process of cognition, "the movement of knowledge does not end here," Mao insisted. Equating perception here with practice, he continued: "Knowledge begins with practice and theoretical knowledge is acquired through practice and must then return to practice. The active function of knowledge manifests itself not only in the active leap from perceptual to rational knowledge, but—and this is more important—it must manifest itself in the leap from rational knowledge to revolutionary practice."[37]

Again, despite his sense of the interdependence of the three stages, Mao placed great emphasis on the importance of the stage of revolutionary praxis. Were the process to stop with conceptualization, he said, "only half the problem would be dealt with. And, as far as Marxist philosophy is concerned, only the less important half at that."[38] "In the contradiction between theory and practice, practice is the principal aspect."[39] Practice is crucial

---

Marxism" by means of this process. See also 1942a:772/III, 38; 1956h; and 1956i:9.

[33] 1964e:341.   [34] 1965f; cf. 1960e:34.   [35] 1958w:117.

[36] 1959e:156.   [37] 1937e:269/I, 304.   [38] Ibid.

[39] 1937g:300/I, 335.

because understanding is incomplete without it. Just as in learning the rules of grammar and logic, Mao pointed out, so all understanding is incomplete until the student has had experience in applying the rules.[40] But the more important function of practice is to carry out Marx's injunction[41] to supersede mere understanding, and actively to change the world through revolution.

Once again, the movement between the conceptual and the practical stages is described as a leap, and thus once again we should expect that movement to be predicated upon a conflict of opposing forces. As before, Mao does not stipulate the contradiction, the resolution of which constitutes the dialectical leap in this third stage. It seems clear, however, that the opposition involved is that between the new idea that emerges from the stage of concept formation, and the unaltered world—the world as it was initially perceived. Because the new idea is, in effect, a prescription for change, the world does not yet conform to that idea. The notion that the two are in contradiction with one another is one that bears further thought. Our ordinary sense of the relationship between a problem and its solution is that the former ought to conform, in a rough way, to the latter. In Mao's schema, by contrast, the solution to a problem is regarded as being in a relationship of contradiction with that problem, rather than in one of correspondence to it. It is the introduction of contradiction at this particular point in the cognitive process that underscores the revolutionary, rather than ameliorative, bent to Mao's view of the cognitive process.

A schematic presentation of the foregoing explication of Mao's description of the cognitive process may help to clarify the argument:

```
                          (Stage 1)        (Stage 2)        (Stage 3)
Phenomenon¹ + Observer——>Perception
(itself                      ↑
contradic-                   |————————>Concept
tory)                    Preconceptions   ↑————— ——>Phenomenon² + Observer . . .
                                      Phenomenon¹   (itself tem-   (the process
                                      (itself       porarily       repeats it-
                                      contradic-    noncontradic-  self)
                                      tory)         tory, but
                                                    becoming so)
```

[40] 1964s:23.

[41] Contained in the eleventh "thesis on Feuerbach," in Robert C. Tucker, ed., *Marx-Engels Reader* (New York: W. W. Norton, 1972), p. 109.

One or two comments are called for by this schematization of Mao's description of the cognitive process in his 1937 lecture. The first relates to the mechanical or manipulative character of his use of the dialectic. There is no question that the contradictions described here bear little resemblance to the organic and natural dialectic extolled by some of Mao's critics.[42] At least to a degree, I do not believe that such a characterization of his understanding and use of the dialectic is inaccurate, however, since that understanding and use owes more, as I have already suggested, to Engels and Plekhanov than to Hegel and Marx. To the extent that there are distortions, however, the context of the explanation must be taken into account. The lecture in which the explanation is given was delivered to a class at Kangda consisting primarily of Red Army cadres who were rich in revolutionary experience, but almost wholly unfamiliar with the subtleties of Marxist analysis. Mao's pedagogically wise attempt to present in a simple and straightforward way a complex and ambiguous process is likely to have rendered his description of the process of cognition more mechanical than he himself understood it to be. My own attempt here to elaborate and make more explicit his already schematic description renders that description even more unrepresentatively mechanistic and inflexible.[43]

Second, the three-stage process set forward here obscures the interrelationship between praxis and perception in a way I find incompatible with Mao's treatment of that interrelationship elsewhere. A clue to the error is found in the way in which the observer-theorist role appears divorced from that of a revolutionary actor. That this is not what Mao intended is suggested by his denunciation as "idealist" (and thus as illegitimate) that division of labor by which some individuals engage in mental labor divorced from contact with the world.[44] It is further suggested

[42] As, for example, Martin Glaberman, "Mao as a Dialectician," *International Philosophical Quarterly* 8 (1968), 94-112. See also Arthur Cohen, *The Communism of Mao Tse-tung* (Chicago: University of Chicago Press, 1964), pp. 7-28.

[43] I am reminded of Professor Mueller's scorn for those who "impose a Procrustean methodological regularity of 'thesis-antithesis-synthesis' on the subtleties of Hegel's logic"; "The Hegel Legend of 'Thesis-Antithesis-Synthesis,'" *Journal of the History of Ideas* 19 (1958), 411. On the other hand, as indicated here and earlier, I believe that Mao was more comfortable in this bed of regularity than Hegel would have been.

[44] 1937a:1-3. Cf. 1937g:275/1, 311f.

by his equating, in a passage cited above, perception and practice: "knowledge begins with practice." While such a formulation suggests Mao's idea of the interrelatedness of the two activities, it confuses his explanation by equating what we are accustomed to think of as two quite different activities—that of understanding the world, and that of acting upon it. Whether it was Mao's intention to argue that the act of perception is a form of practice, or that one perceives in the process of practice, is not made clear here.

The evolution of Mao's theory of knowledge in his speeches and writings after 1937 was gradual.[45] A discussion of the problems of theorizing in 1942 contains essentially the same three-stage formulation that he had employed in 1937. He did, however, explicitly address himself to the problem of the bifurcation between observer and actor when he took up the case of intellectuals who had recently joined the revolution, and whose perceptual and conceptual knowledge was derived primarily from reading and study. He contended that their knowledge was incomplete until they had taken part in practical work and had studied practical problems. This bifurcation is seen here, however, as a remediable, and thus temporary problem, exemplified by the case of Marx himself, who began as an intellectual without practical experience, but subsequently corrected that shortcoming. Ultimately he "became a most completely developed intellectual . . . [who] undertook detailed investigations and studies in the course of practical struggles, formed generalizations and then verified his conclusions by testing them in practical struggles."[46]

He reiterated his argument concerning the need for the integration of theorist and actor at the Second Session of the Eighth Party Congress in 1958, when he noted that "our thinking can only be formed through the stimulation of our senses by the objective world. It is formed from objective practice."[47] That the achievement of such an integration is by no means unproblematic, however, is suggested in his statement two months earlier

[45] An interesting parallel description, which antedates "On Practice" by six months, is found in the article "Strategy in China's Revolutionary War," where Mao described the process of forming a strategy as involving first, thorough reconnaissance; second, correct judgments based on that reconnaissance; and finally, correct strategic decisions based in turn on those judgments (1936:163f./I, 188).

[46] 1942a:773f./III, 39f.   [47] 1958t:104.

in the "Sixty Work Methods." There he spoke of the brain as a "processing plant" which, in forming concepts, draws information from the masses and, once having formed these concepts, transmits the viewpoints and ideas so that they may be "tested by the masses of people" to ascertain whether or not they are "fit for use or correct."[48] The implication here is clearly that the party leaders' brains are the conceptualizing "plants," and that the masses provide the perceptual raw material for and evaluate the products of these plants.

The most complete discussion of the theory of knowledge from the post-Liberation period is found in a section of a Central Committee resolution on the Socialist Education Campaign.[49] Extracted under the title, "Where Do Correct Ideas Come From?" it appears as the fourth of the *Four Essays on Philosophy* published as a collection in the mid-1960s. There Mao recast his theoretical schema, this time describing the process of cognition as involving two, rather than three stages. Perception and conception have been combined into a single process: "At first knowledge is perceptual. The leap to conceptual knowledge, i.e., to ideas, occurs when sufficient perceptual knowledge is accumulated. This is *one process* in cognition."[50] The dialectical nature of the process as described here is considerably less clear-cut than in the earlier formulation. Although the move from perception to conception is referred to here as a "leap," in the same sentence it is also spoken of as the result of the accumulation of perceptions.[51] Yet, as we have seen earlier, simple quantitative change in Mao's view does not involve a dialectical movement.[52]

---

[48] 1958e:11.   [49] 1963d:58f.

[50] Ibid., p. 58. Emphasis added.

[51] "The leap to conceptual knowledge, i.e., to ideas, occurs when sufficient perceptual knowledge is accumulated" (ibid.). Essentially the same argument is found in 1958e:11 and in 1958t:104.

[52] An exception to this rule is suggested in the following example, in which quantitative change appears to take on a qualitative character: "If a three-year-old child is asked whether his mother is a human being or a dog, he will be able to reply that she is a human being, not a dog. This is a judgment of the child. Mother is an individual, while human being is general, yet there is a unity between the two. It is the unity of opposites between the individual and the general" (1958t:104). The suggestion here is that the concept is the result of the contradiction between the specific and the general, but the "general" and the concept seem to be one and the same.

The second step in this process is essentially the same as the third stage in the earlier discussion:

> Then comes the second stage in the process of cognition, the stage leading from consciousness back to matter, from ideas back to existence, in which the knowledge gained in the first stage is applied in social practice to ascertain whether the theories, policies, plans or measures meet with the anticipated success. . . . Man's knowledge makes another leap through the test of practice. This leap is more important than the previous one, for it is this leap alone that can prove the correctness or incorrectness of the first leap.[53]

Once again, in this stage, although the terminology is dialectical, the process itself seems to have little that is overtly dialectical about it. That his conception of the process remained, in fact, a dialectical one, however, is suggested by his summary of the process of cognition here as being one whereby "matter is transformed into consciousness and consciousness into matter; . . . such leaps are phenomena of everyday life."[54]

By simplifying the process from three stages to two, the basic contradiction in the process as a whole—that between theory and practice—is accentuated, and the unity of observer and actor clarified. At the same time, his earlier conflation of the process of perception and that of practice—of understanding and change— is reiterated here in even more direct terms. Indeed, the summary statement in Mao's 1937 lecture seems more appropriately associated with the more recent formulation: "Discover the truth through practice, and again through practice verify and develop the truth. . . . This form repeats itself in endless cycles, and with each cycle the content of practice and knowledge rises to a higher level."[55]

What is most often regarded as salient in his 1963 discussion of his theory of knowledge is the emphasis Mao placed there on the power of ideas—an emphasis which has sometimes been taken to constitute a move toward the very idealism that he has consistently criticized so vigorously. "Once the correct ideas characteristic of the advanced class are grasped by the masses," he said, "these ideas turn into a material force which changes society and

[53] 1963d:58f. [54] Ibid., p. 59.
[55] 1937e:273/I, 308.

changes the world."[56] There are several grounds for rejecting an interpretation of this passage as indicative of the emergence of a new idealism in Mao's work during his latter years. First, the formulation is not a novel one. In almost identical words he described the ideas of Stalin a decade earlier as "gripping the hearts of the masses," and thereby "becoming an invincible force."[57] Second, a careful reading of the language itself suggests that the "idealism" here has been hedged about with important materialist qualifications. It is only "correct" ideas that become a material force, and, as the passage as a whole makes clear, correct ideas come from contact with the material world through perception-conception and revolutionary praxis. The means by which correct ideas become a material force is their implementation by the revolutionary masses. Finally, it is also important to recognize that it is far from a rejection of Marxism and an espousal of a kind of neo-Hegelian idealism to put forward the idea of a reciprocity between the realm of ideas and the material world. Although Marx did indeed argue that his revision of Feuerbachian materialism was the means whereby Hegel could be stood on his feet, he saw himself as doing so, as Richard Bernstein has insightfully observed, in a dialectical way. That is, rather than denying the force of ideas, Marx moved dialectically beyond a position of ascribing primary causal force to ideas: "Marx's materialism can best be understood as an *Aufhebung*—in precisely the sense in which Hegel used this concept—of previous materialistic and idealistic doctrines; he at once negates, affirms, and goes beyond these polar 'moments.' "[58] Thus to see an *interaction* between

[56] 1963d:59. He made much the same point earlier the same month by noting the effect of "a single word": "a single word may rejuvenate a country [as was the case with Marx's explication of the proletarian revolution] or a single word may bring disaster to a country [as in the case of Khrushchev's denial of revolution and class struggle]" (1963b:319). In 1966 he was quoted as saying, "we also—and indeed must—recognize the reaction of mental on material things, of social consciousness on social being and of the superstructure on the economic base" (1966r).

[57] 1953c:112. Mao's formulation of the relationship between consciousness and the material realm is reminiscent of a discussion of the relationship between superstructure and base in Stalin's 1950 article, "Marxism and Linguistics": "No sooner does the superstructure arise than it becomes an exceedingly active force, actively assisting its base to take shape and consolidate itself"; Bruce Franklin, ed., *The Essential Stalin* (New York: Doubleday, 1972), p. 408.

[58] Richard Bernstein, *Praxis and Action* (Philadelphia: University of Pennsylvania Press, 1971), p. 43.

ideas and material things, as the passage suggests that Mao saw, is by no means to abandon in favor of idealism a materialist dialectic as interpreted by Marx and his successors.

CRITERIA FOR EVALUATING OBSERVERS AND THEIR OBSERVATIONS

There are, in Mao's epistemological writings, at least three ways in which ideas are compared and evaluated. The first is on the basis of the correctness or incorrectness of an idea, its truth or falsity. The second, closely related, criterion we might call that of "relevance." For what length of time does a correct idea remain correct—what is the duration of its relevance—given the fact that the world to which it refers is an ever-changing one? The third criterion by which ideas are evaluated is an *ad hominem* one: who it is that perceives, conceives, and acts upon an idea can, under certain circumstances, make a difference in the relative validity of the idea.

Correct or true ideas, Mao begins by arguing in a straightforward way, are those that work in social practice.[59] In its simplest form this argument sees the process of verification as one in which the ideas developed in the conceptual stage of the process of cognition "correspond (*fuhe*) to objective reality" in the subsequent stage of social practice.[60] He acknowledges that the question cannot be quite so simply resolved as that, as the passage continues: if the purpose of conceptualization is not to understand but to change the world, then, as we have seen, correct concepts cannot merely correspond to the world, but must be in contradiction with the world. The more complicated test of validity based on this premise is described as follows: "The only way to solve this problem [of verification] completely is to redirect rational knowledge to social practice, apply theory to practice and see whether it can achieve the objectives one has in mind."[61] The complication, of course, is the means by which

[59] "There is but one truth and the question of whether or not one has arrived at it depends not on subjective boasting but on objective practice" (1940a:623/II, 339).

[60] 1937e:269/I, 304. Cf. 1938d:445/II, 151: "All ideas based upon and corresponding to objective facts are correct ideas, and all deeds or actions based upon correct ideas are correct actions." Looking at it from the opposite point of view, he argued in 1961 that there cannot be correct ideas which have not met the test of praxis. As a result, "there never were men of foresight and vision" (1961a:274).

[61] 1937e:269/I, 304. Cf. 1963d:53.

one acquires these "objectives one has in mind." Clearly they are a part of the preconceptions employed in the process of cognition, but the complication of how they are acquired and evaluated is perhaps best set aside for a moment, and treated as an aspect of the question of relevance, our second criterion for evaluating ideas.

There are other problems that arise in the process of verifying ideas, which do merit our attention here, however. It is not always the case, Mao pointed out, that a correct line achieves the desired objectives immediately. Time is sometimes needed for the correctness of a particular policy to manifest itself.[62] In some instances this is the case because of circumstances extraneous to the idea itself, and here a third complication is added to the process of verification: that of the power of the observer-actor to implement his idea. It is alluded to in Mao's 1963 article: "Generally speaking, those [ideas] which succeed are correct and those that fail are incorrect and this is especially true of the human struggle with nature. In social struggle, the forces representing the advanced class sometimes suffer defeat not because their ideas are incorrect but because, in the balance of forces engaged in the struggle, they are not as powerful for the time being as the forces of reaction."[63] Powerful opposition to a correct idea may arise either as the result of conscious malfeasance, or simply through ignorance. Indeed, elsewhere he suggests that opposition is requisite to the discovery of truth: a correct line can only be formed in a struggle with an incorrect line, the two constituting a unity of opposites. "Truths are developed from struggles with fallacies."[64] Moreover, he suggested that in this inevitable struggle between truth and falsehood, the forces of truth will initially be less powerful than those of falsehood: "In the beginning, truth is not in the hands of the majority of people, but in the hands of a minority," he commented in 1962.[65] As a consequence, minority views are to be protected, since they may well prove to be correct.[66]

Who constitutes that minority, however, is of crucial significance, since ultimately the test of the validity of an idea may rest outside the realm of practice: as we have seen, if a concept does

---

[62] 1957d:115; 1959q:45.   [63] 1963d:58f.   [64] 1959c:205, 207.

[65] 1962a:183. Cf. 1964e:339, where the views of Copernicus are cited as an example.

[66] 1966m:121.

not correspond with the material world it may be untrue, or it may yet be true because it corresponds instead with the world as it should be according to a set of goals previously posed. If it does not correspond to the world as it should be, again it may be untrue, or else the passage of time may reveal its validity. If the concept is unverified even after the passage of a period of time, once again it may be untrue, or it may be that its exponents are insufficiently powerful to implement it successfully. Finally, even this test may prove insufficient to verify an idea, in which case it becomes a question of who expounds the idea: the ideas of the "advanced class," as Mao put it in his 1963 argument, "are bound to triumph sooner or later."[67] Ultimately, then, the idea is true in an instance such as this not because it has been proven in practice, but because it is held by members of the advanced class. It is the observer-actor and not the idea that is being evaluated.

To turn back from the most complicated to the simplest case, if the "anticipated results" are not achieved in the process of cognition, where does the observer-actor look for possible errors? Mao speaks of the necessity for reviewing and repeating the process in the case of initial failure.[68] What is involved in this review? It would appear that there are three aspects to the process of cognition to which error may be attributable. First, a correct idea may be incorrectly put into practice. Any number of the errors in work style that we will discuss in subsequent chapters may creep into the actor's praxis, thus nullifying the validity of the idea he or she is attempting to implement. Second, the concept or idea may be incorrect, and this, in turn, can be attributed to two possible causes: either the "raw material" of conception—the observer's perception of the problem—is flawed, or the preconceptions that he or she has brought to bear in the stage of conception are incorrect and thus inappropriate to the process. Finally, the desired results may not be achieved in the process of cognition because of the illegitimacy, in some respect, of the observer-actor. It is to the latter two potential errors—incorrect preconceptions and illegitimate observer-actors—that we turn in our discussion of the criteria by which the relevance of ideas is measured and the criteria by which observers are compared.

[67] 1963d:59.

[68] Ibid.: "Often a correct idea can be arrived at only after many repetitions of the process leading from matter to consciousness and then back to matter, that is, leading from practice to knowledge and then back to practice."

Franz Schurmann advanced an explication of the Chinese system for the evaluation of ideas on the basis of the duration of their relevancy in his seminal book, *Ideology and Organization in Communist China*. There Schurmann distinguishes between what he calls "pure ideology" and "practical ideology"—terms he uses as synonyms for the Chinese words *lilun* (theory) and *sixiang* (thought).[69] He finds this distinction to be one which, particularly during the period between Liberation and the Cultural Revolution, the Chinese themselves made with some degree of consistency. He sees pure ideology as an essentially static, unchanging set of ideas.[70] Practical ideology is the product of the attempt to relate these static ideas to specific and changing circumstances. He summarizes his view in the following passage: "Ideology arises, not by applying truths to real problems but by uniting universal theory (which may or may not have relevance for real problems) and correct practice (which may or may not be determined by the truths). Thus, according to Mao's epistemology, ideology (or knowledge) is the product of action, and not the reverse."[71] He sees Marxism-Leninism as having served the function of pure ideology,[72] and the "thought of Mao Zedong" as having operated as practical ideology. Although Schurmann's formulation reflects the tendency in Mao's own epistemological works to argue that some concepts remain valid and useful longer than others, there are, nonetheless, several interrelated problems with it.

The first problem arises from the fact that, since the mid-1960s, specifically since the publication of Lin Biao's article on people's war in 1965,[73] the distinction between Marxism-Leninism as pure

[69] H. Franz Schurmann, *Ideology and Organization in Communist China*, revised edition (Berkeley and Los Angeles: University of California Press, 1968).

[70] Ibid., p. 33.   [71] Ibid., p. 29.

[72] Here Schurmann departs somewhat from the Chinese treatment of the problem. He sees all ideology as necessarily associated with particular organizations: ideology is an *organizational* ethos. Since there is no supranational organization that encompasses all Marxist-Leninists at the present time, there can be no universal Marxism-Leninism. The Chinese, by contrast, because they do not share Schurmann's view of the relationship between ideology and organization, believe that at least certain principles of Marxism-Leninism are universally valid (cf. ibid., pp. 22, 24).

[73] Lin Biao, "Long Live the Victory of People's War," RMRB (3 September 1965); translated in A. Doak Barnett, *China After Mao* (New York: Praeger, 1969).

ideology and Mao's thought as practical ideology no longer holds, since Mao is seen more recently as having himself contributed to the creation of theory.[74] This shift in Chinese usage—assuming, as Schurmann does, that the earlier usage was intentional—calls into question more completely than he is prepared to acknowledge his distinction between pure and practical ideology. Indeed, the distinction was fundamentally problematic from the outset, since it provides no explanation for the origin of pure ideology or theory. More importantly, it cannot account for the change and development of theory over time, and treats pure ideology in a fundamentally un-Maoist way as static and unchanging. Lenin's ideas are regarded as a part of present-day pure ideology, but during Lenin's lifetime they must have constituted practical ideology for the Russian revolution. Schurmann's formulation provides no suggestion as to what brought about the "promotion" of these ideas from the realm of practical to that of pure ideology. Another problem with Schurmann's explication is raised by Frederic Wakeman, who criticized Schurmann for the implication that revolutionary ideas (pure ideology) had their origin in a process wholly exogenous to the Chinese revolution, and thus that the Chinese were capable of producing for themselves only a lower order of truth, that is, practical ideology. Theory is foreign and must be imported; only thought is a domestic product.[75] Explicitly, Schurmann takes a different stance, arguing that although the CCP *thinks* of Marxism-Leninism as universal, it is in fact *Chinese* Marxism-Leninism (the product of the Chinese party organization) that constitutes pure ideology for the Chinese. Implicitly, however, it is clear from his discussion that he regards these ideas as rooted in experience external to China.[76]

Despite the fact that there are problems with the categories that Schurmann devised, the problem of finding criteria by which to measure the longevity of a valid idea remains one that is posed by Mao's epistemological arguments themselves. It seems clear that there is a distinction to be made between ideas on the basis

[74] Schurmann himself acknowledges this shift in the "Supplement" to his volume, but fails to explore its ramifications for his earlier explication.

[75] Frederic Wakeman, "The Use and Abuse of Ideology in the Study of Contemporary China," *China Quarterly* 61 (1975), 127-151.

[76] Indeed, as Wakeman correctly argues, "Strictly speaking, only the 'practical' kind [of ideology] fits Schurmann's systematic definition [of its being 'a manner of thinking characteristic of an organization'] at all" (ibid., p. 147).

of their relevance over time, but that this distinction cannot be taken to constitute fixed categories into which particular ideas must permanently be assigned. It would appear that the distinction should be a tripartite one among ideas of permanent relevance, ideas of relatively long-term relevance, and ideas of only short-term validity.[77]

There are two and only two concepts that fall into the first category—that of ideas with permanent validity and relevance. The first is a fact, the second a method. The fact, as we saw in the first chapter, is the existence—naturally, ubiquitously, beneficially, and permanently—of contradiction. Contradiction is absolute, that is, it is a *permanently* true condition. The second concept that Mao treated as permanently valid is the dialectical method of analysis set forward in his epistemological writings. Although, as we have seen, the ideas to which this method gives rise are ever-changing, the method itself remains constant. It is, as Mao noted in 1936, citing Lenin, "the most essential thing in Marxism, the living soul of Marxism."[78]

The importance that Mao accords to method is not to be underestimated.[79] "One must respect materialist dialectics," he commented in 1958. "Why?" he asked rhetorically. "Because *Weltanschauung*, epistemology, and methodology are one and the same thing."[80] Earlier he spoke of the Marxist method as a telescope and microscope, permitting not only the long view but also the detailed view of social conditions.[81] What is enduring in Marxism

[77] James Chieh Hsiung also sets out a tripartite distinction between elements of Maoist ideology in his book, *Ideology and Practice* (New York: Praeger, 1970), pp. 126-133. He sees ideology as made up of three components: a conceptual framework or epistemological component (*guannian xingtai*), a theoretical component (*lilun*), and thought (*sixiang*), which acts as the "link between theory and practice." Hsiung's distinction is unsatisfactory in two respects. First, like Schurmann's, it is static and fails to provide for movement between categories and change over time. Second, it obscures the fact that *sixiang*, as Mao uses that term and as others use it to refer to Mao's work, refers not only to a process, but also to the product of that process.

[78] 1936:175/I, 195f.

[79] He used a metaphor in 1934 to suggest the primacy of method: "If our task is to cross a river, we cannot cross it without a bridge or a boat. Unless the bridge or boat problem is solved, talk about the task is useless" (1934b: 125/I, 150. Cf. 1936:162/I, 187; 1957f:20; 1961a:275; and 1963k:86f.).

[80] 1958t:104. Six years later he said, "What is philosophy? Philosophy is the theory of cognition, nothing else" (1964r:397).

[81] 1936:196/I, 222. Three months later, in a speech marking the first anni-

—and, by extension, in Maoism—is not so much the substance, but rather the method that is found therein.

The most intriguing aspect of this category of permanently valid ideas is the fact that no provision is found in Mao's theory of knowledge for the existence of such ideas. Within that system ideas depend for their origin on an ever-changing world, and for their validity on the effort to foster and promote that change; therefore, no idea is seen as having permanent validity. "Marxists are not fortune-tellers," Mao commented in 1930. "They should, and indeed can only indicate the general direction of future developments."[82] The givenness of contradiction and the dialectical theory of knowledge based on that givenness are exceptions to this process of the development of ideas because, as Mao saw it, they constitute that process in a fundamental sense. They are ideas that originated in practice, and they are continually validated in practice, but change over time will not invalidate them. It is their permanence in a changing world that gives them their authoritativeness.

The second category—that of ideas of relatively long-term relevance—is a considerably larger category. Herein are the "abstract principles" which, as Mao described it, are to be applied to "concrete circumstances." They are neither fixed nor exclusively derived from non-Chinese experience. Moreover, ideas in this category do not constitute a closed set, but may be added to or subtracted from on the basis of a changing world and changing projects in that world. Ideas in this category constitute the preconceptions that interact with perceptions of the world in the stage of conceptualization. These preconceptions must themselves be rooted in experience to be legitimate, and they are continually modified, however slightly, by every interaction with the material world, because that world is itself in a state of perpetual development. This interaction may result in the continued affirmation of the validity of these ideas, or it may result at some point in their invalidation. No idea in this category (unlike those in the first category described above) is immune from such invalidation. New ideas are continually raised as potential candidates for in-

---

versary of the death of Lu Xun, he used the phrase once again: "Lu Xun's first characteristic was his political vision. He examined society with both a microscope and a telescope." The phrase reappeared in the Cultural Revolution, this time used to describe Mao's thought.

[82] 1930a:103/I, 127.

clusion in this category, but they are included there only if their validity is proven over the course of many tests in practice. Mao uses the term "law" and "science" to describe ideas in this second category. He speaks of laws in the context of the Chinese revolution generally,[83] and in the more specific context of military strategy,[84] but always insists on the evolution of laws and the dangers inherent in their mechanical application out of context. Although they are to be applied in the present to change the future, because of their dialectical origin, laws must inevitably be retrospective: "The transformation of ideology into a system invariably occurs at the end of the movement of things in general. . . . Things have to appear again and again before they become laws and can be recognized as such by the people."[85] Similarly, he defined science as "correct and systematic knowledge":[86] correct and systematic knowledge of the struggle for production is natural science, correct and systematic knowledge of the class struggle is social science.[87] Finally, as we have seen, correct and systematic knowledge, when applied to change the material world, is the source of freedom. Social science thus contributes to freedom in society, just as natural science contributes to freedom in nature.[88]

The emphasis in Mao's treatment of the ideas that make up this second category of concepts with a relatively long-term validity is on their ultimate transitoriness. The mutability of conditions make fixed criteria, fixed labels, and fixed laws ultimately incorrect and irrelevant.[89] This rule applies as aptly to the criteria, labels, and laws of Marxism-Leninism—ideas that constitute the bulk of those in this category—as they do to any other ideas. Marx was concerned with the economic, social, and political relationships unique to a capitalist system. As a result, there are limits,

[83] 1962a:175. [84] 1936:157/I, 181f.
[85] 1961a:303. [86] 1954b.
[87] 1942a:773f./III, 39. Cf. 1942b:792f./III, 59: "For the proletariat, the sharpest and most effective weapon is a serious and militant scientific attitude. The Communist Party lives by the truth of Marxism-Leninism, by seeking truth from facts, by science, and not by intimidating people."
[88] 1940b:204f.
[89] 1942c:826/III, 89; 1955e:24f. In 1940 he cited Stalin's criticism of an opponent for having "quot[ed] outside of space and time, without reference to the living historical situation and thereby violat[ed] the most elementary requirements of the dialectic, and ignor[ed] the fact that what is right for one historical situation may prove to be wrong in another historical situation" (1940a:631/II, 346).

Mao argued, to the applicability of some aspects of Marxism to the conditions of an industrially relatively backward socialist economy such as that of contemporary China.[90] He noted in his speech at the Eighth Party Congress in 1956 that Chinese practice, like that of Lenin, had surpassed that of Marx.[91] "A thousand years from now," he told Edgar Snow in 1965, "all of us . . . even Marx, Engels, and Lenin, [will] probably appear rather ridiculous."[92] As a result, preconceptions in the process of cognition should not be limited to the Marxist-Leninist canon alone, but must be augmented with concepts derived from Chinese praxis.[93]

A critical concept for Mao in determining the limits of the validity of certain of the ideas in this second category is that of the historical epoch. "Leninism," he pointed out in 1960, "is Marxism in the epoch of imperialism and proletarian revolution, Marxism in the epoch of the victory of socialism and communism."[94] Similarly, Mao's own political ideas have more recently been described as "the Marxism-Leninism of the era in which imperialism is headed for a total collapse and socialism is advancing to worldwide victory."[95] We will consider in greater detail this concept of historical epoch when we turn to Mao's views of political history. The idea of the historical epoch as a period during which a given set of preconceptions are likely to be valid appears, however, to form a critical part of his theory of knowledge.

The third category—that of ideas of relatively short-term validity—is quickly covered, since we have discussed at length the problems involved in verifying the ideas it contains. Included

[90] 1961a:301. Cf. 1959a:195, 199.

[91] 1958s:91. "Recently I met a friend from West Germany," he commented the following year. "I said to him, 'Your Marx is busy with matters in our country and has completely neglected matters in his own home. But having worked a good bit in our country, he will return home'" (1959g:6).

[92] 1965b:222.

[93] 1961a:305. A list of those Marxist-Leninist texts which Mao commended to the attention of cadres in 1960 is contained in 1960b. Mao's earlier ideas on the Sinification of Marxism are found, as we have seen, in 1938e:498-500/II, 208ff. Cf. 1956a:98.

[94] 1960e:9. During his lifetime Stalin was praised by Mao for having "developed Marxism-Leninism" and "advanced Marxism to a new [but unspecified] stage" (1949f; 1953c:112). After Stalin's death, Mao described him, perhaps more honestly, as an inferior theoretician because of his imperfect command of the dialectic and because of his being "divorced from reality" (1958p:87).

[95] 1968l:170.

within this third category are those ideas that are the product of a specific process of cognition. Until they are further tested, these ideas are valid only in the instance in which they were produced. Nonetheless, they do form a part of the preconceptions that the observer-actor brings to his or her subsequent attempt to conceptualize the changed world he or she has observed. Those ideas in this category that prove to be reliable as preconceptions in a number of such processes are, as we have seen in Mao's discussion of the way in which laws are derived, taken to be concepts or theories of the second category—which includes ideas of relatively long-range validity.

In addition to the tests of validity and relevance as a means of ranking ideas there is, as we have seen, a third test that emerges from the implications of Mao's argument: that is, there is a ranking of ideas based on characteristics of the observer-actors who perceive, conceptualize, and put them into practice. All observers, in Mao's epistemological system, are not necessarily equal, and thus the products of all processes of cognition are not equally valid. Because, as we have seen, the role of observer is linked to that of actor, and because all praxis, as Mao saw it, has a political content, the criteria for legitimacy of observers in his epistemological system are the same criteria by which legitimacy is measured in the political sphere. It is to this subject and these criteria that we will turn in the next chapter.

PRAGMATISM AND REVOLUTIONARY ROMANTICISM

The theory of knowledge described here is one which, as I have argued at length elsewhere,[96] bears striking resemblance to that of the American pragmatist, John Dewey, whose thought exerted considerable influence on the Chinese intellectuals with whom Mao had contact during the May Fourth period. Like Dewey, Mao sees ideas growing out of practical experience and, in turn, shaping that experience. For both, the world is regarded as a series of problems, which are the occasion for both theory and action.[97] Indeed, the resemblance was clear to Mao, since he

[96] Starr, "On the Possibility of a Pragmatic Ideology: Epistemological Principles of Mao Zedong and John Dewey," unpublished paper for the Seminar on the Comparative Study of Communist Societies, University of California, Berkeley, 1975.

[97] "What is a problem?" Mao asked rhetorically in 1942. "A problem is a

on more than one occasion described himself as a pragmatist. Even on the eve of the Great Leap Forward, a time when he is ordinarily taken to have acted least pragmatically, he insisted that the contrary was the case: "When we ask the river to yield the way, it must yield! Is such a hypothesis groundless? No, we are not insane, we are pragmatists; we are Marxists, seeking truth from facts."[98]

In Mao's view, however, pragmatism alone is not enough. What is needed, he said later in the same year, is to "walk on both legs, with Russia's revolutionary fervor and America's practical spirit."[99] It is the revolutionary fervor—"revolutionary romanticism" as he referred to it on other occasions during that year[100]—which informs the objectives toward which praxis is directed. As we have seen, however, these objectives are neither created from whole cloth, nor are they fixedly held. "We are revolutionary utilitarians aiming for the broadest and most long-range objectives," he commented in the Yan'an Forum Talks in 1942, "not narrow utilitarians concerned only with the partial and the immediate."[101] As I hope to have shown here, and as I shall attempt to illustrate in greater detail in the concluding chapter, which deals with Mao's concept of political development, his political thought challenges the validity of a dichotomous classification of pragmatists and visionaries by attempting to achieve a new synthesis of the respective approaches of the two.

---

contradiction in a thing," he responded, and went on to describe the process of solving problems using the same stages he had used five years earlier to describe the process of cognition (1942b: 796/III, 61). Elsewhere he employed a metaphor to make the point: "Catch a sparrow [that is, a problem while it is still a small one] and dissect it. Although the sparrow is small, the gall and the liver are all complete. Chinese and foreign sparrows are alike. You don't have to dissect them all" (1955e:21).

[98] 1958s:96. Cf. 1958d:94.   [99] 1958zz:138. Cf. 1959e:16.

[100] 1958l:106; 1958m:124.   [101] 1942c:821/III, 85.

ON AUTHORITY

> Whoever has the truth will be obeyed, be he
> a manure carrier, coal miner, street sweeper,
> or a poor peasant. No matter how high the
> official position, if truth is not in his hands,
> there is no reason to obey him.[1]

The opening sentences in Mao's *Selected Works*, drawn from a
1926 analysis of the classes in Chinese society, read as follows:
"Who are our enemies? Who are our friends? This is a question
of the first importance for the revolution."[2]

A first reaction might be to take this as the dichotomous view
of the world we would expect to find in the work of a political
thinker concerned, as Mao is, with contradiction. In fact, he
alludes to three parties here: enemies, friends, and "ourselves."
The revolutionary "we" implicit in Mao's question is an individual
or group that has succeeded in becoming an authoritative par-
ticipant in and arbiter of the conflict between friends and enemies
in a revolutionary situation. It is the basis on which Mao evalu-
ates the legitimacy of such a participant-arbiter that is the subject
of our explorations in this chapter.

An analogous need for an authoritative arbiter in a conflictful
world is found in the epistemological introduction to Thomas
Hobbes' *Leviathan*.[3] Like Engels and Mao, Hobbes rooted his
system of cognition in what he understood to be the nature of the
physical world. Beginning with a discussion of movement, he then
took up sensation and next perception. Perception led him, however, to one of the same problems which, as we have seen, Mao
faced in his epistemological arguments: how does a conceptual

---

[1] 1958v:110.   [2] 1926:3/I, 13.

[3] Thomas Hobbes, *Leviathan*, edited by Michael Oakeshoot (New York:
Collier Books, 1962). Steven Andors interprets the relationship between
Mao's ideas and those of Hobbes in a quite different way from that which
follows here, emphasizing their dissimilarities; "Hobbes and Weber vs.
Marx and Mao: The Political Economy of Decentralization in China,"
Bulletin of Concerned Asian Scholars 6:3 (September-October 1974), 19-34.

system that begins with the individual perceiver deal with the problem of intersubjectivity among many diverse observers? Hobbes sees the situation first in epistemological terms, then in social and political terms, as a "war of each against all" in which life could only be, in his famous phrase, "solitary, poor, nasty, brutish and short."[4] His solution for this intolerable situation was the creation of a sovereign Leviathan whose definitional decisions —epistemological, social, and political—would be accepted as binding by common agreement of his subjects, who "created" him by this agreement.

In a political cartoon drawn by Gerald Scarfe during the Cultural Revolution, the illustration from the cover of an early edition of Hobbes' *Leviathan*, depicting a sovereign whose body is composed entirely of the figures of his subjects, who thus "constitute" him in a double sense, has been redrawn to depict Mao.[5] The satirist's image suggests a number of questions that can profitably be raised in our discussion of Mao's concept of authority: in what sense do Mao's questions, "Who are our friends? Who are our enemies?" presuppose the creation of a defining Leviathan? On what basis is this Leviathan to be imbued with legitimacy? What concrete institutions or individuals in the Chinese political system should, in Mao's view, function as such a Leviathan?

Power as an Element of Authority

In his discussion of Hobbes' epistemology, Sheldon Wolin points out the interrelatedness of two apparently disparate definitions of authority in common usage. In an intellectual sense, we think of authorities as those who know; in a political sense we think of authorities as those who legitimately wield power. For Hobbes, Wolin points out, it is the sovereign's function to enforce with his political authority the definitions he reaches with his intellectual authority.[6] Like Weber, who subsequently discussed the question in greater detail, Hobbes saw authority as combining elements of power and legitimacy. It was the supreme power of the sovereign that enabled him to create order from the chaos of

[4] Hobbes, *Leviathan*, Part I, Chapter XIII, p. 100.
[5] *Atlas Magazine* 14:6 (1967).
[6] Sheldon Wolin, *Politics and Vision* (Boston: Little, Brown, 1960), pp. 265-272.

the state of nature. This power was legitimate because it derived from the agreement of his subjects.

In Mao's political scheme of things, there is an implicit need for authoritative definitions at critical points. Although, as we have seen, contradictions are evident to all who observe the world directly, distinguishing between contradictions in order to handle or resolve them in a way conducive to bringing about the broader goals of the betterment of society (as well as the very act of setting these goals) presupposes the presence of an observer or a set of observers who are authoritative, and whose distinctions and priorities are thus trustworthy. The determination of the principal contradiction in a particular period of historical development is a crucial first step, not only in resolving that contradiction,[7] but also in distinguishing friend from enemy within the social system during that period.[8] The principal contradiction may in some instances be so compelling as to be obvious to any observer (as was true, to cite an example to which Mao alluded frequently, in the period of the anti-Japanese war of resistance). It is more frequently the case, however, that social and political systems are confronted with a number of equally pressing projects, an assessment of priorities among which may well vary from observer to observer. The resolution of a conflict such as this should, of course, come through praxis, but under conditions of limited time, resources, and manpower, implementation of a number of lines for purposes of comparing and verification is not always possible.

Mao was well aware of the need for power to make one's definitions, distinctions, and priorities stick. At the same time, he was aware of the limitations of power alone. As we saw, when he discussed the verification of ideas in practice he noted that the verification of a correct idea is sometimes thwarted by its exponents' lack of the power to implement it.[9] Nevertheless, it is clear from the passage cited that it is not power alone that determines the correctness of the idea. The idea was *potentially* correct, needing proof through practice. Its opponents were not seen as "correct" or valid merely because theirs was the power temporarily to thwart its implementation. Legitimacy, then, is clearly separable from power in Mao's view, so that all that is powerful

[7] 1937g:295-301/I, 331-337.   [8] 1957d:80f.
[9] 1963d:59.

74

is not necessarily legitimate, and all that is legitimate is not necessarily powerful.

It is, however, difficult to overestimate the position of power in Mao's equation for authority, the balance having been permanently tipped in that direction by his oft-cited reference in 1938 to the "truth" that "political power grows out of the barrel of a gun."[10] The subsequent sentence is sometimes quoted together with this maxim to suggest a mitigation or even a reversal of the idea expressed in the maxim itself: "Our principle is that the Party commands the gun and the gun must never be allowed to command the Party." Whatever mitigating effect this sentence may have, however, is in turn attenuated by the passage that follows:

> Yet, having guns, we can create Party organizations, as witness the powerful Party organizations which the Eighth Route Army has created in northern China. We can also create cadres, create schools, create culture, create mass movements. Everything in Yan'an has been created by having guns. All things grow out of the barrel of a gun. According to the Marxist theory of the state, the army is the chief component of state power. Whoever wants to seize and retain state power must have a strong army.[11]

The effect of the passage as a whole is to render unmistakable Mao's view of the intimate relationship between political power and physical coercion, and the dominance of the latter within that relationship.

It is possible to observe a gradual evolution of Mao's views on power over the course of the first decade or so of his writings. In his 1919 article, "The Great Union of the Popular Masses," he argued that the sheer numbers of the masses, if united, would insure revolutionary victory against the "aristocracy, the capitalists, and the other powerful people . . . [who] . . . rely . . . firstly

[10] 1938h:512/II, 224f.

[11] Ibid. Hannah Arendt takes issue with Mao's attempt to equate his view with that of Marx. For Marx, she contends, the old, prerevolutionary society died as a result of its internal contradictions. Violence certainly accompanies, but is not the cause of the overthrow of the bourgeoisie for Marx ("Reflections on Violence," *New York Review of Books* 12:4 [1969], 19). Her view is reminiscent of that of Glaberman, cited in Chapter One above.

on knowledge, secondly on money, and thirdly on military force."[12] Although there is some indication of an increased sophistication regarding power and its uses in the intervening years,[13] even the Hunan Report, written eight years later,[14] is pervaded by a certain naiveté that made it possible for Mao to underestimate the power of counterrevolution in China at the time, and consequently to think of the peasants as possessing a force as irresistible as that of a hurricane.

The events of 1927-1928 were crucial in changing Mao's views on power. The defeat of the communist forces at the hands of their erstwhile allies in the Northern Expedition taught them the lesson of the indispensability of an independent military force directly controlled by the Communist party. The maturation of his thought on this subject as a result of this experience is evident as early as 1928, when he explained how "Red political power" could survive in China's hinterlands. He attributed this possibility to complementary splits among the enemies of the revolution— warlords and imperialists—and to the experience of revolution in the area in which the bases were located. Even more important, however, was the independent Red Army, created only months before, and a strong party organization as its complement.[15] Reviewing the progress of the revolution a decade later, he pointed up the error of those who "underestimate[d] the strength of the enemies of the revolutionary Chinese people."[16] The use of force—the setting up of "positions of strength"—is ultimately a characteristic of class society, and as a consequence

[12] 1919a:77. Despite the naiveté evident in this passage regarding the possession and use of political power, when recounting his autobiography to Edgar Snow in 1936, Mao spoke of his realization of the need for political power to bring about revolutionary transformation as having dated from 1919; Edgar Snow, *Red Star over China* (New York: Grove Press, 1968), pp. 154f.

[13] See, for example, his letters to Cai Hosen in the winter of 1920-1921 (1920-21:297), where he noted that "no despot, imperialist or militarist throughout history has ever been known to leave the stage of history of his own free will without being overthrown by the people."

[14] 1927:12-44/I, 23-59.

[15] 1928a:50/I, 66f. Cf. 1929:87/I, 106, where he speaks of the complementary nature of political and military power.

[16] 1939j:597/II, 316. He echoed this view in criticizing the Soviet view of peaceful coexistence, arguing that this view overlooked the crucial fact of the control of the armed forces by the bourgeoisie (1964f:7).

can be expected to continue to figure as an element of authority so long as classes exist.[17]

Power as an element of authority, then, presupposes the possession of superior means of coercion. The expectation of obedience that derives from that superiority provides the power holder with a freedom to act that those who lack power do not possess. This freedom of action is another aspect of the concept of authority, which is suggested by its derivation from the Latin word *auctor*, meaning "originator," "doer," or "author." In one of his earliest essays, Mao addressed himself to the question of the freedom to act granted the powerful: "In reality, for thousands of years the Chinese people of several hundred millions all led a life of slaves. Only one person, the 'Emperor,' was not a slave (or rather one could say that even he was a slave of 'heaven'). When the emperor was in control of everything, we were not allowed to exercise our capacities. Whether in politics, study, society, etc., we were not allowed to exercise our capacities."[18] His discussion here is reflected in a subsequent treatment of the problem, in a much more specialized context in which freedom of action is not exclusively the prerogative of the more powerful. Speaking of guerrilla strategy, Mao warned of the danger of a guerrilla force losing the initiative (*zhudongxing*), being "forced into a passive position and ceasing to have freedom of action." Maintaining the initiative is crucial to a guerrilla force because of its relative weakness *vis-à-vis* its enemies. Occasionally it is this very weakness that helps it regain the initiative, since the small number in a guerrilla unit can "mysteriously appear and disappear . . . and thus enjoy a freedom of action such as massive regular armies never can."[19] In this context, it is not so much power that guarantees the freedom to act as it is the reverse: seizing that freedom can enhance one's power.

There are therefore circumstances under which authority is not reduceable simply to a question of power. The less powerful

[17] 1961a:265.　　　　[18] 1919a:87.

[19] 1938c:379/II, 85ff. Recovering the initiative once lost, he contended, is not "an innate attribute of genius, but is something an intelligent leader attains through open-minded study and correct appraisal of the objective conditions and through correct military and political dispositions" (ibid., p. 87). Cf. 1937l:98. Translating this term into the political context, Mao spoke of the necessity for the CCP to maintain its initiative (*duli zizhu*) *vis-à-vis* the Guomindang in the wartime united front (1938g:505/II, 216).

may, under certain circumstances, be the possessors of truth, and thus the locus of authority. If it is not their strength of numbers that is the defining characteristic of their authority, then there are obviously other elements in the concept of authority besides power alone. It is to an exploration of Mao's treatment of those elements that we turn now.

THE BASES OF LEGITIMACY

In her article, "Reflections on Violence," Hannah Arendt complained of what she saw as a failure in contemporary political science to differentiate between "such key terms as power, strength, force, might, authority and, finally, violence."[20] The attempt to redress this failure in the study of the Chinese polity is made the more complicated by the fact that, in linguistic terms, the Chinese tend to draw different lines of distinction in this conceptual area from those drawn in Western languages.[21] The problem is epitomized in the translation of a recurring phrase in the Chinese press during the Cultural Revolution: revolutionaries were encouraged to "seize *power* from those in *authority* taking the capitalist road." At first glance, the phrase appears to have a familiar, Weberian ring to it. Closer examination, however, reveals that ring to be a spurious one. The phrase officially translated as "seize *power*" (*naquan*), could equally well be translated "seize *authority*," since the character *quan* is the same as that which appears in the phrase officially translated, "those in authority," *dangquanpai*.

Two characters are associated with the concept of authority in modern Chinese. The first, *quan*, derives from the name of a weight used to balance a steelyard; its relevant contemporary meanings are "power," "influence," "authority," and "service as an official."[22] The second, *wei*, means "dignity," "solemnity," and "awe-inspiring power." Together, in the compound *quanwei*,

20 Arendt, "Reflections on Violence," p. 21.
21 D. S. Carne-Ross has spoken of "the difference, for the translator, between the 'close distance' separating English and French and the far greater, but thinner, culturally inactive space through which the translator of Chinese must work"; "Cracking the Code," reviewing George Steiner, *After Babel: Aspects of Language and Translation* (Oxford: Oxford University Press, 1975), in *New York Review of Books* 22:17 (1975), 39.
22 *Hanyu cidian* (A Dictionary of the Chinese Language) (Hong Kong: Commercial Press, 1967), p. 603.

the characters are often translated with the word "authority," with reference either to political or to intellectual authority. The compound, *quanli*, formed with the character *li*, meaning physical strength, is frequently translated "power" to distinguish it from *quanwei*. On the other hand, official translators with equal frequency translate *quanli* with the word "authority," and a recently published dictionary holds the two compounds to be potentially interchangeable.[23] Finally, as we shall see, the compound *weifeng* (in which *feng* could be rendered "style") is usually translated "air of importance," or "prestige."[24]

One of the few times when the term "authority" (here the official translation of the Chinese compound *quanli*) appears in Mao's writings occurs in his 1927 "Hunan Report," where he described the populace of rural China as controlled by four "systems of authority" (*you xitong de quanli*): the state system, the clan system, the supernatural system, and the marital system. To each of these systems, a form of authority is appropriate: the authority of the husband over the wife in the marital system, religious authority in the supernatural system, the authority of the clan leaders in the clan system, and the many levels of "political authority" (*zhengquan*) in the state system.[25]

Earlier in the same article he described the process of overthrowing the landlords in such a way as to suggest what he regarded as the components of the concept of authority. The official English translation speaks of the process of "pulling down

[23] *Hanyu da cidian* (A Large Phrase Dictionary of the Chinese Language) (Hong Kong: Shanghai Book Co., 1970), p. 567.

[24] The problems of conceptualization and translation are exemplified by a *Hongqi* article early in 1967 in which Engel's essay, "On Authority" was cited. The passage cited reads as follows: "A revolution is certainly the most authoritarian thing there is; it is the act whereby one part of the population imposes its will upon the other part by means of rifles, bayonets and cannons—authoritarian means if such there be at all; and if the victorious party does not want to have fought in vain, it must maintain this rule by means of the terror which its arms inspire in the reactionaries"; "On Revolutionary Discipline and Revolutionary Authority of the Proletariat," *HQ* 3 (3 February 1967), 19-21; translated in *PR* 10:7 (10 February 1967), 17-19. The title of Engel's essay is rendered in Chinese with the compound *quanwei* which, as I have suggested, carries with it connotations of awesomeness and prestigiousness. Similarly, "authoritarian" in the Chinese text is *you quanwei de*. Elsewhere in the article there is a careful distinction made by official translators between *quanwei*, or "authority," and *quanli*, which they translate as "power."

[25] 1927:31/I, 44.

landlord authority" (*quanli*) as being one of "smashing the political prestige (*weifeng*) and power of the landlord class." A rendering of the sentence which remains more faithful to the construction of the Chinese shows him speaking of two processes:
the "tearing down of the landlord class's *prestige* in the political
realm," and the "tearing down of the landlords' *power*, which is
based on their social position within the village." These two
processes are seen as the necessary prerequisites to the emergence
and growth of peasant power.[26] There seems, then, to be two
component parts to Mao's concept of political authority: power
and prestige.

Because of the weight he placed on power as an element of
authority, there is a concomitant deemphasis, in Mao's treatment
of the concept, of the other element of authority, prestige.
"Prestige," in fact, seems to be a particularly felicitous choice of
words to translate the compounds containing the Chinese character, *wei*, as Mao used them in the passage just cited, since that
English word derives from the Latin *praestigiae*, meaning "decep-
tions," or "juggler's tricks." According to its derivation, there is
something phony about prestige and, similarly, the landlords'
weifeng in the passage just cited—their "prestige" or "awesomeness"—was effective only because it deluded the peasantry; but
it was something quite separate and easily distinguishable from
their actual power.

This distinction between power and prestige is a continuing
theme in Mao's thought, though prestige is sometimes treated
in a more positive way than it was in 1927. Such a positive treatment is found in his comments concerning those who had been
the targets of the movement to "seize power" early in 1967: "All
those who have made mistakes should correct them resolutely.
If they fail to correct their mistakes, they will sink deeper and
deeper into the mire and in the end they will still have to correct
them, but by then they will have suffered considerable loss in
prestige. If they correct their mistakes early, their prestige can
only be higher than before."[27] Here the concept of prestige and
the more personal concept of face are less closely associated. In
the case of the landlords as depicted in the 1927 article, once face
was lost there was little possibility of its restoration (perhaps a

[26] 1927:23/1, 35; emphasis added. He made it clear subsequently in the
same article that his notion of prestige (*weifeng*) is closely associated with
the idea of losing (or saving) "face" (*diulian*) (1927:25/1, 37).

[27] 1967d.

fallacious assumption, as subsequent emphasis by the Chinese on the lingering influence of members of the former landlord class in China's countryside would seem to suggest). In the case of the deposed power holders, prestige appears to derive either from performing their tasks correctly from the outset, or, equally, from admitting to and correcting a mistaken performance. Unlike that of the landlords, the prestige of the power holders can thus be recaptured if lost.

Prestige has also been treated in a negative way in recent years. For example, Cultural Revolutionary discussions of the lingering prestige of those who had been dismissed from office, but who resisted reform, speak disparagingly of that prestige. One article spoke of individuals such as this who continued to possess "great political capacity" (*zhengzhi nengliang*).[28] As a result of this capacity, the effect of their resistance to reform was proportionally much greater than their small numbers would indicate. The following explanation was given for this situation:

> Their dismissal from office (*chezhi*) does not mean complete seizure of power (*quan*) from them. Since position (*zhi*) and power (*quan*) are interrelated, those who hold positions have power, but those who no longer hold positions may also still have power.
>
> Power (*quan*) not only means authority (*quan*) to issue organizational and administrative commands, but also authority to issue political and ideological commands. When one has political influence (*zhengzhi shili*) among the masses, his commands will be heeded by some people and at the opportune moment this influence will turn into organizational and administrative authority to give commands. . . . Their political-ideological power . . . can only be seized by unfolding from below a mass campaign to expose, criticize and repudiate them.[29]

The prestige of the dismissed office holders is treated here as a form of illegitimate "political-ideological power."

[28] "Politically and Ideologically Overthrow Completely the Handful of Capitalist Roaders within the Party," New China News Agency, 21 July 1967, *HQ* 12 (1 August 1967); translated in *PR* 10:34 (18 August 1967), 27f. Although the term "political capacity" more accurately represents the sense of the Chinese *zhengzhi nengliang*, the official translators employed the term "political influence."

[29] Ibid.

Mao's explicit comments on political authority as composed of power and prestige are thus quite different from definitions of authority with which we, as Western social scientists, are more familiar. One of those familiar definitions is that of Max Weber, who treats power and *legitimacy* as the constituent elements of political authority.[30] Mao's concept of prestige is by no means identical to the concept of legitimacy as Weber used it. In fact, as the examples cited above make clear, the term prestige, as it was used by Mao and other Chinese writers, very often carried overtones of *illegitimacy*.

On the other hand, the idea of legitimacy is, as we have already begun to see, by no means absent from Mao's political thought. We have, for example, found an implicit notion of legitimacy in his discussion of the theory of knowledge, which is much closer to Weber's use of that term. When he discussed the verification of ideas through practice, Mao spoke of the situation in which the correctness of an idea held by members of the advanced class is not immediately validated, "because in the balance of forces engaged in struggle they are not as powerful for the time being as the forces of reaction."[31] There is implied here an idea of the separability of the power to implement one's ideas and the correctness or legitimacy of those ideas, which is not unlike that found (in a very different context) in Weber's political sociology.

Given this use of the idea of legitimacy in Mao's treatment of intellectual authority, we must next consider the criteria by which this legitimacy is to be measured. His criteria of intellectual legitimacy are summarized in a statement in the 1942 article, "Rectify the Party's Style of Work," where he defines correct theorists as those who "can, in accordance with the Marxist-Leninist stand, viewpoint and method, correctly interpret the practical problems arising in the course of history and revolution and give scientific explanations and theoretical elucidations of

[30] This oversimplified and abbreviated statement of Weber's conceptually rich and multifaceted argument, and the subsequent discussion of the relationship between Mao's and Weber's ideas, is based on Weber's discussion of authority in *The Theory of Social and Economic Organization*, edited by Talcott Parsons (New York: Free Press, 1964), pp. 152ff. A stimulating discussion of Weber's concept of authority and its applicability to the Chinese context is found in the initial chapters of Anne Fretter Thurston, "Authority and Legitimacy in Post-Revolutionary Rural Kwangtung: The Case of the People's Communes," Ph.D. dissertation, University of California, Berkeley, 1975.

[31] 1963d:59.

China's problems."[32] What is meant here by "stand, viewpoint, and method" as criteria of intellectual legitimacy is the question to which we turn next. The political relevance of these criteria is evident when we recall that, as Mao insisted, the legitimate observer is, at one and the same time, the legitimate political actor and, by extension, the legitimate political leader.

It is most feasible to take up first the third of Mao's three criteria—that of method—since we have already discussed that method with some thoroughness. As we saw, Mao's descriptions of correct method emphasize the importance of direct, even physical, contact between observer and phenomenon. Translated into political terms, the method becomes the mass line, a leadership principle based on the necessity of direct contact between leader and led. Just as in his description of the effective observer in the process of perception, so the legitimate political actor is one who *knows* those whom he leads through direct contact and observation.[33] Indeed, as we shall see, one of the basic problems of organizations, in his view, is that they tend to break down—through both their structure and their scale—this fundamental prerequisite for legitimate leadership. Perception, correct conceptualization, and verification through practice constitute the legitimate method for the formation of ideas. Similarly, contact with one's constituency, formation of policies based on that contact, and proof of the policies through their dissemination to and implementation by the masses constitute the legitimate method for the exercise of political leadership. Just as phenomena under observation are found by the observer to be conflictful by nature, so the leader finds that those he leads are divided by conflicts. It is these conflicts that result in the triune division between leaders, friends, and enemies alluded to earlier. In sum, just as those observers who correctly implement the method as outlined in "On Practice" are regarded by Mao as legitimate observers, so he regards as legitimate those political actors who practice the

---

[32] 1942a:772/III, 38. At two other points Mao offered comments that can be taken as statements of his criteria of legitimacy, neither of which is incompatible with the argument here: in 1943 he cited with approval the four criteria for a leading group advanced by Georgi Dmitrov: "absolute devotion to the cause, contact with the masses, ability independently to find one's bearings, and observance of discipline" (1943b:854/III, 119). In 1961 he noted that "in our work three things are required: understanding of circumstances, great determination and correct orientation" (1961b:242).

[33] 1943b.

mass line method, and as illegitimate those who misconstrue or misapply it.

As a corollary of this criticism, Mao treated those whose experience is extensive as more legitimate than those with limited experience. Whereas all experience on the part of an observer or actor is not to be construed as inherently legitimizing, and Mao is not merely cloaking a traditional respect for authority in new revolutionary trappings, nonetheless he did regard the revolutionary actor with correct and successful experience behind him or her as more reliable and more legitimate than one who has little experience.[34] As we shall see in our discussion of socialization, technical, scientific, and managerial expertise is as important an aspect of experience as the experience of political praxis. "We cannot transform what we do not know about," he said in 1961.[35]

The second of Mao's criteria of legitimacy is that of viewpoint, by which I take him to mean the acceptance and employment of correct preconceptions both in the process of conceptualization and in the process of political action. As we have seen, Mao distinguishes not only between correct and incorrect ideas, but also between ideas of short and long-term relevancy. The legitimate political actor, like the legitimate observer, is the one who uses as preconceptions ideas that are both correct and relevant to the current historical epoch.

The last of the three elements of Mao's concept of legitimacy is that of stand. As Mao uses the term, stand is associated with class. Although we have treated the problem of authority heretofore as one involving individuals, in most instances in which the problem is discussed, Mao spoke in terms of the authority of groups—classes—rather than that of individuals. It is his view

[34] In 1960 he spoke of the CCP as having "experience, guiding principles, policies and methods" in political and military affairs and in class struggle (1960f). During the Cultural Revolution the problem of legitimization based on experience loomed especially large. In 1967 Mao commented on more than one occasion on the necessity to take experience into account when criticizing cadres (for example, 1967g:467), and lamented the lack of experience of the student rebels who were conducting that criticism (for example, 1967c:4).

[35] 1961b:240. As early as 1943 Mao was writing on the necessity for cadres to become leaders in production in order to be taken seriously as political leaders by the masses (1943d:866/III, 133). After Liberation, when the tasks of development became more complex, Mao's emphasis on the need for technical expertise as a legitimating factor in political leadership increased, as the cited passage indicates.

that members of a particular class during a particular historical epoch are more likely to possess (or to be capable of possessing) correct, and hence legitimate, ideas than are members of the other classes in that society at that time. As we have seen, he refers to this class as the "advanced class" of that epoch. At least in the initial stages of his treatment of class (and in an attenuated form in the subsequent discussions of the subject), he argues that the class standing of an individual is very likely to have a dominant effect on that individual's ideas and actions, and thus those who take the stand of the advanced class in the present epoch—that is, the proletariat—are legitimate, and those who take the stand of the bourgeoisie are illegitimate as actors as well as observers.

Also included in this criterion of correct stand is the idea that action and conception are only legitimate if they are practiced unselfishly in the interests of the masses. Indeed, as I shall show in the next chapter, authority misused to further one's own personal interests is, in Mao's view, the principal cause of the creation of new class enemies—of the process of embourgeoise-ment—in a socialist society. Power gives an individual the capac-ity to act, but if the action taken is a self-interested one, rather than one that will further the interests of the masses, that power is illegitimate and the power holder pursuing selfish ends mani-fests thereby the defining characteristic of the bourgeoisie. It is the goal of organizational reform and cultural revolution to mini-mize this corrupting misuse of authority.

Stand, as an aspect or criterion of legitimacy can, under certain circumstances, be in contradiction with experience used as a criterion of legitimacy. Mao spoke on more than one occasion of the Chinese peasantry as "poor and blank." By endorsing this condition as a good one, he implied that legitimacy based on the criterion of stand was more important than that based on correct experience.[36] It is this legitimacy of uncorruptedness that con-stituted a part of the basis for his argument on the need for super-vision of the party by the masses or, more recently, seizure of power by student rebels.[37]

[36] The phrase "poor and blank" first appeared in Mao's talk on the ques-tion of intellectuals in January 1956 (1956a:99). Although he used it fre-quently in the ensuing years, it is most often associated with the article "Introducing a Cooperative," which he wrote for the inaugural issue of *Hongqi* in 1958 (1958q).

[37] See, for example, 1941c:768/III, 34, and 1958m:123. In 1965c:125 he

Mao's treatment of authority, then, greatly emphasizes power. In addition, he speaks explicitly of prestige; prestige and power are the complementary elements of authority. What we refer to as legitimacy is related to elements of what Mao treats under the concepts of power and prestige, but is more commonly treated by him as a separate problem, often in the context of discussions of his theory of knowledge. Reassembling these views of legitimacy, we find that there are three criteria by which legitimacy is measured: stand, viewpoint, and method. These criteria are applicable to the epistemological as well as to the political realms. It now remains to explore the difficult problem of his idea of the locus of authority—whether he saw it as correctly resting in an institution, an individual, or a set of ideas.

THE LOCUS OF AUTHORITY

Mao's view of the concept of authority as composed of power and prestige locates him precisely in the interstice between two Weberian stools. At the same time it suggests, even perhaps more strongly than at other points in his treatment of organizational life, his reaction against traditional Chinese modes of bureaucratic behavior. Weber distinguished between two types of legitimate authority: rational-legal (with which bureaucracy is associated), in which legitimacy rests in an office; and charismatic, in which legitimacy resides in a person. Weber's distinction between individual and office as the locus of legitimacy is blurred in Mao's concept of prestige. As we have seen in the case of the landlord class as described in the "Hunan Report," and in the much more recent comments concerning "party persons in authority," cited above, prestige may derive from office, but it may well adhere to the individual, even when it happens that he or she is dismissed from office. I would contend that this concept of prestige and its relationship to authority is predicated upon traditional Chinese concepts of authority that exceeded the bounds of the political organization. Political, economic, cultural, and social authority in the traditional system were all vested in a single group of individuals for whom officeholding was an important source of legitimacy, but by no means the only such source.

---

spoke of the need for supervision of cadres "from above and from below. The most important supervision is that which comes from the masses."

It derives, as well, from a view of legitimacy vested in a particular class. In the waning stages of the capitalist society it is the proletariat that is the chosen or elect class, and thus any member of the proletariat during that period possesses a particular authority *vis-à-vis* members of other classes. As we shall find when we take up the idea of social class in the next chapter, Mao changed in fundamental ways the bases on which class is determined and this, in turn, has made more ambiguous the role of social class in determining political legitimacy. Despite the changes in the basis on which membership in the class is determined, however, the authority of the proletariat in the socialist stage of historical development is never called into question; indeed, it has been reaffirmed the more strongly in the last decade or so.

Closely related to the idea that the proletariat is the locus of legitimacy in a socialist system is the idea that the Communist party and its system of dictatorship should constitute that locus. There is a crucial distinction to be drawn between those who are members of a social class merely because of their economic position, and those whose affiliation with a class is a self-conscious identification determining, at least to a degree, their thought and action. Although any proletarian is authoritative, by virtue of his or her class standing, those proletarians who are imbued with class consciousness, take a class stand, and are thus prepared to act on their class sentiments, are viewed as more authoritative. Building on this point, Lenin developed the concept of the vanguard party as embodying proletarian consciousness and readiness to act.[38] Possessing these characteristics, the party comes to serve as the locus of legitimacy in both the revolutionary and the post-revolutionary political systems.

The power that renders that legitimacy authoritative is that of the dictatorship of the proletariat—the state structure which is, in Lenin's view, an instrument of oppression of one class over another. When the proletariat has smashed the state machinery of the bourgeoisie it creates its own state machinery—its own dictatorship. Although this new state machinery is legitimate, it

[38] Lenin's discussion of the "professional revolutionary" and the appropriate form for an organization of professional revolutionaries in "What Is To Be Done?" (1902) is instructive in this connection; see James E. Connor, ed., *Lenin on Politics and Revolution: Selected Writings* (New York: Pegasus, 1968), pp. 67ff.

is its supervision by the proletarian party, and not simply its characteristics as a state structure, that invests it with this legitimacy. Indeed, its oppressive function is seen as an undesirable necessity until the class struggle is over, at which time the state structure will simply wither away, its nondictatorial functions subsumed by the essentially conflict-free society itself.[39]

Mao accepted Lenin's view of the legitimacy and authoritativeness of the revolutionary party. Indeed, as we have seen, in his opening comments in the article with which the *Selected Works* begins, he sees the revolutionary party as serving the function of mediating between the revolution's friends and its enemies.[40] The function of the party, he said citing Lenin in 1960, is to organize the proletariat for the class struggle.[41] The bases of the legitimacy of the revolutionary party are those I have discussed above: the party is only legitimate if the stand, viewpoint, and method of its members and its leaders are correct: "No political party can possibly lead a great revolutionary movement to victory unless it possesses revolutionary theory and a knowledge of history and has a profound grasp of the practical movement."[42] The stand of the party is crucial. It is only because it takes the stand of the proletariat that it is capable of speaking for "the whole people," a capacity that derives from the universal character of the proletariat.[43] Mao has been accused, particularly by Soviet writers, of having permitted the Chinese party to lose its proletarian quality by the oversubscription of petty-bourgeois peasant members,[44] but, as we shall see, while Mao acknowledges the imbalance in party composition,[45] he has also redefined in critical ways the term "proletariat," thereby changing the frame of reference of the question.[46] Thus, whereas the 1969 party constitution spoke of

[39] See, for example, his discussion of the dictatorship of the proletariat in "State and Revolution," *ibid.*, pp. 184-230.

[40] 1926:3/I, 13.   [41] 1960e:5.

[42] 1938e:498/II, 208.   [43] 1963e:42.

[44] See, for example, Boris Leibson, *Petty-bourgeois Revolutionism*, translated by Don Danemanis (Moscow: Progress Publishers, 1970).

[45] For example, 1950b:110.

[46] The question of Mao's view of the role of the peasant in the socialist revolution has been taken by many writers to be the central one in the discussion of the legitimacy or illegitimacy of Mao's Marxism-Leninism. The most important sources in this debate are Benjamin Schwartz, *Chinese Communism and the Rise of Mao* (Cambridge: Harvard University Press, 1951), and the debate between Schwartz and Karl Wittfogel over the

the party as the "vanguard organization of advanced elements of the proletariat capable of leading the masses in the struggle against the class enemy,"[47] the meaning of the terms used there is very different from that found in Lenin's very similar description of the function of a revolutionary party.

Mao took seriously the criteria of stand, viewpoint, and method in evaluating the legitimacy of the party. That is, if the revolutionary party violates these criteria it can, to the extent of the violation, lose its legitimacy thereby. This conditional acceptance of the authority of the party may perhaps result from the substantial periods in Mao's career when he found himself in opposition to the duly constituted Chinese Communist party, as well as those periods in which circumstances caused him to question the correctness of the Soviet party. In 1936, for example, shortly after the point in the revolution at which Mao assumed a leading position in the Chinese party, he noted that it was only by avoiding errors of policy that the CCP could continue to lead the revolution. For the party to err would be for it to lose its position of revolutionary legitimacy.[48] Beginning in 1958, he began to suggest that the legitimacy of the party did not extend to all its members. It was necessary to prepare for splits within the party, he argued. Indeed, "partial splits" were to be conceived of as a normal phenomenon.[49] As the Cultural Revolution drew near, he spoke more and more explicitly of the illegitimacy of the "representatives of the landlord class and the bourgeoisie" who had infiltrated the party.[50] By late 1965, he was suggesting that this illegitimacy had penetrated even to the level of the Central Committee,[51] and it was at this point that he found himself, on the

---

"legend of Maoism" in the pages of *China Quarterly* 1 and 2 (1960). See also Arthur Cohen, *The Communism of Mao Tse-tung* (Chicago: University of Chicago Press, 1964), and James Chieh Hsiung, *Ideology and Practice* (New York: Praeger, 1970), pp. 53-84.

[47] The phrase first appeared in 1968a. Its use in the context of the constitution is found in 1968l:169. Essentially the same wording is found in the party's 1977 constitution, *PR* 20:36 (2 September 1977), 16.

[48] 1936:177/I, 192.

[49] 1958t:108f.; 1958yy:146. A year later he reminded his listeners that he had spoken of splits the previous year: "There were no salient signs yet, but they have appeared now" (1959v:61; cf. 1959q:45).

[50] 1961b:238f., 244; 1962a:181; 1964w; and 1964y:427.

[51] 1965i.

one hand, once again in a position of opposition and, on the other hand, powerless to act on that position because of his retreat, six years earlier, to the "second line" of party decision making.[52]

Although the explicit attack of the Cultural Revolution was on the malfeasance of individual party members and the overgrown and rigidified party structure, there seemed to be in the initial stages of the movement an implicit attack on the party as an institution, in the call for new organizational forms to take the place of the party.[53] Whether in pursuit of his original goals, or as a compromise of those goals, however, Mao began late in 1968 to call for the rebuilding of the party structure, arguing with a biological metaphor the necessity for "getting rid of the stale and taking in the fresh."[54] That it was pursuit and not compromise of his goals is suggested in his comment early in 1967 that the party continued to be a necessary institution in the Chinese system: "I think we will need it because we must have a hard core, whether it is called the Communist party or a social democratic party. In short, we still need a party."[55] With this approach in the ascendance, the Cultural Revolution came to appear more like

[52] Speaking of the creation of two "lines" of leadership—the first for day-to-day decision making, the second for broad policy guidance—Mao attributed its implementation to his desire to provide potential successors with experience, but contended that the first line became an "independent kingdom" wherein he had no power. He dated his realization of the gravity of this state of affairs to the issuing of the "Twenty-three Articles" (1965c) in January 1965 (1966o:71; 1966q:75).

[53] The subject of organizational reform in the Cultural Revolution is treated at greater length in Chapter Five below. There has been considerable debate concerning Mao's goals in this organizational reform. Whether the new, Paris Commune-like forms spoken of in the Sixteen-Point Decision of the Central Committee (1966m) were to be complementary to a reformed party, or a replacement for an irreformable party, is the question at issue. *Cf.* Stuart R. Schram, "The Party in Chinese Communist Ideology," in John W. Lewis, ed., *Party, Leadership and Political Power in China* (Cambridge: Cambridge University Press, 1970), pp. 170-202; Starr, "Revolution in Retrospect: The Paris Commune through Chinese Eyes," *China Quarterly* 49 (1972), 106-125; and Harry Harding Jr., "Mobilization, Bureaucracy and Professionalism: The Organizational Issue in Chinese Politics," Ph.D. dissertation, Stanford University, 1974).

[54] 1968k.

[55] 1967c:17. Schram agrees that Mao's aim was always the reform of and never the destruction of the party. See his article, "The Cultural Revolution in Historical Perspective," in Schram, ed. *Authority, Participation and Cultural Change in China* (Cambridge: Cambridge University Press, 1973), pp. 1-108.

the most recent of a series of party rectification movements, and less like an unprecedented attack on the very legitimacy of the party as an institution.

As in Lenin's case, Mao's treatment of the legitimacy of the party is closely related to his view of the necessity of a state structure in the form of a dictatorship of the proletariat to enforce the legitimacy of party and class through the entire period of transition to a communist society. The function of the dictatorship of the proletariat, he wrote in 1960, is to conduct a "persistent struggle, both sanguinary and bloodless, violent and peaceful, military and economic, educational and administrative against the resistance of the exploiting classes, against foreign aggression, and against the forces and traditions of the old society."[56] A "state of the whole people" as a substitute for the dictatorship of the proletariat when the transition period was well advanced—as was advocated by Khrushchev in the Soviet Union—Mao denounced as erroneous and contrary to the spirit as well as to the letter of Marxism-Leninism.[57] During the year before his death, in a series of remarks launching a campaign to study the theory of the dictatorship of the proletariat, Mao reiterated his belief in the necessity of that state form, particularly because he saw it as a necessary means for controlling newly emergent bourgeois elements in a socialist society.[58]

At any of the several points in its history when Mao has called into question the legitimacy of the party or certain of its members, he has done so by referring, implicitly or explicitly, to his own greater legitimacy or to the greater legitimacy of his political solution to the problem at hand. In so doing he has entered the rock-strewn channel of his own profoundly ambivalent views on the vesting of authority in an individual—the fourth of the loci of legitimacy to be discussed here.

Mao first dealt in detail with the question of the authoritative leader in response to Khrushchev's attack on Stalin at the Twentieth Party Congress of the CPSU. His initial response to this attack (of which he apparently had no advance warning) came

---

[56] 1960e:4. In 1958 he pointed out that the division of labor as between party and the state structure should be on a functional basis rather than simply split equally between the two. His point was made at a time characterized by an increasing integration of party and state during the Great Leap Forward (1958b:79).

[57] 1963e:38f.   [58] 1975a.

in two articles, one written in April, the other in December 1956. There, contrary to what one might expect of a man whose revolutionary career was hardly abetted by Stalin's actions, Mao was quite restrained in his criticism. Stalin was treated as a legitimate leader with regard to his experience and his command of theory; it was his divorcement from the masses, brought about by the "cult of personality," that was the principal source of his illegitimacy, Mao argued. Stalin became "conceited and imprudent," "counterposed his individual authority to the collective leadership," and "isolated himself . . . from the masses of the people and from real life." But—and here Mao parted company with his Soviet colleagues—Stalin's merits and accomplishments outweighed his errors, and Khrushchev was wrong to have one-sidedly attacked his predecessor.[59]

At the same time that Mao criticized Stalin's errors, he elaborated upon what he indicated was a correct position regarding the authority of individual leaders. Citing Lenin, Mao noted that a society is divided into classes, that classes are led by political parties, and that parties, in their turn, are led by "stable groups of authoritative, influential, and experienced members."[60] "Collective leadership and personal responsibility are not antagonistic, but are integrated with each other," he noted in 1955. "Personal responsibility and personal dictatorship which violates the principle of collective dictatorship are two entirely different things."[61] The cult of the individual, which violates the principle of collective leadership, he denounced as a "foul carryover from the old society . . . in contradiction with the economic forces as well as the political and cultural forces of the new society."[62]

Individual leadership is thus appropriate and legitimate, in Mao's view. "If we did not have Stalin," he put it succinctly in 1939, "who would give the orders?"[63] It is blind obedience to individual

[59] 1956d:7f., 11. A later version of the list of Stalin's errors added two additional failings: a theoretical lapse in his belief that contradiction ended during the socialist stage of development, and a tendency to misadvise foreign parties in the conduct of their revolutions (1963g:5f.).

[60] 1956d:8, 11. Much the same argument is reiterated in 1963e:43, 1963g: 13, and 1965g:102.

[61] 1955a. A return to this point occurs in 1962a:43f., where emphasis is placed on collective, rather than one-man leadership of party committees.

[62] 1956d:8f.

[63] 1939k:47. Cf. 1958zz:137, where he comments on the necessity for an "idol": "a class must have a class leader," he concludes there.

leaders that is illegitimate.[64] Nonetheless, in a widely cited remark
to Edgar Snow in 1965, he took what appeared to be a different
position regarding the cult of the individual. He noted that
Khrushchev had probably been overthrown because he lacked a
cult of personality.[65] Moreover, immediately after this conversation, there began the encouragement of a cult of personality
around Mao that culminated during the Cultural Revolution, and
that appeared to rival Stalin's excesses in this regard. Are we to
take this as an abandonment of Mao's earlier position in opposition
to the vesting of legitimacy in a single individual or, if not, how
is it to be reconciled with that opposition?

Clearly the relationship between leader and led characteristic
of Weber's description of a charismatic system of authority[66] is
one that violates one of the fundamental criteria of legitimacy for
Mao. While it is true that mass support is an important aspect of
the power of a leader, and the lack of organized mass support
made it considerably easier for Khrushchev's colleagues to strip
him of office, the follower of a charismatic leader contributes
nothing but his adulatory support to that leader. The charismatic
leader's legitimacy is based on his or her "gift of grace." It does
not depend on the flow of information and interests upward,
which permits a leader to maintain that contact with the concrete
experience of those whom he or she leads that is requisite to his
legitimacy, in Mao's terms. In considering the use of charismatic
authority in the Cultural Revolution, there are important counter-
vailing elements that one must balance against the more obvious
of its excesses. First, there is Mao's own denunciation of the excesses of this aspect of the movement.[67] Five years after his comment to Snow on Khrushchev's lack of a cult of personality, he
took up the question with Snow once again. He noted then that
adulation of himself had been carried to extremes and that the
"Mao cult" was in process of being dismantled.[68] Subsequently,
during the course of the campaign to discredit Lin Biao in 1974,
Mao placed the responsibility for these excesses on the shoulders

[64] 1958j:99. [65] 1965b:205.

[66] Max Weber, *Economy and Society: An Outline of Interpretive Sociology*, edited by Guenther Roth and Claus Wittich (New York: Bedminster, 1968), I, 215f.

[67] In July 1966 he spoke of the cult as follows: "The higher a thing is
blown up the more seriously it is hurt in the fall. I am now prepared to be
broken to pieces" (1966g:96).

[68] 1970b:169f.

of his former comrade-in-arms, and a letter was released purportedly written by Mao to his wife in 1966 denouncing Lin's tendency toward encouraging public adulation of Mao for purposes of enhancing his own position.[69]

It is also important to realize, I think, that even at the height of its excesses there was a subtle but significant difference between the Mao cult and the cult of personality surrounding Stalin. Whereas Stalin's cult was focused directly on his person, Mao's was, to a great extent, focused on his thought. With some important exceptions, it was ordinarily Mao's ideas, rather than his personal characteristics, that were invoked in the creation of his cult—a situation that was symbolized by the almost ubiquitous appearance of the red plastic-covered book of quotations from his writings that served as a sort of talisman during the Cultural Revolution.

Mao may have abandoned his earlier opposition to a Stalin-like cult; encouraged the development of a cult of his own, despite the violation of his own definitions of authority which that constituted; and only subsequently found, perhaps because of the opposition of his colleagues, that this cult was untenable because counterproductive to the maintenance of his own power. More likely, I think, is the interpretation that Mao realized the need for a new, temporary locus of legitimacy in the Chinese system if the legitimacy of the party (or at least of certain of its leaders) were to be called into question and its errors rectified. He saw the creation of a cult of personality as a less than desirable but necessary consequence of launching an attack from the basis of his own personal legitimacy as a leader of the Chinese revolution. He attempted to mitigate its ill effect by emphasizing the legitimacy of his ideas more strongly that that of his personality. Although the development of the cult far exceeded his stated expectations, it was nevertheless further mitigated for him as a result of the fact that his personal authority and that of his thought alone were insufficient to achieve his evolving goals in the Cultural Revolution. Ultimately the weight of the power, and particularly the legitimacy, of the People's Liberation Army were required to insure the eventual success of the movement, even a success more modest in scope than Mao had initially hoped for.

Mao's own self-image as a leader is an interesting one to follow in his writings. While there is no evidence there that he attempted

[69] 1966g. Cf. 1971:36f.

to minimize his contribution to the Chinese revolution, by the same token it appears that he had an image of himself as having held to his own standards of legitimate leadership.[70] As he insisted should be the case in his discussion of the relationship between individual responsibility and the responsibility of the collective, he argued that when credit is due it should accrue to the collectivity and not to the individual, but that it was appropriate that he take individual responsibility for mistakes made by the party. "I don't think it is right to say that one cannot refute the Chairman," he said.[71] Similarly, he saw it as appropriate that he engage in self-criticism, and argued that his self-criticism should be widely distributed.[72]

A recurrent analogy to the Chairman in the eyes of his critics, and in his own eyes as well, is the emperor Qin Shi. Although credited with the successful unification of China, Qin Shi Huang Di is frequently remembered in China for his repressive policies. Despite the fact that his critics alluded to this repressiveness in associating Mao with Qin Shi Huang Di,[73] Mao himself took a different view, praising the emperor for his innovativeness and for the effectiveness of his repressive measures.[74] While the Chin

[70] Early in 1958, at a work conference in Nanning, Mao spoke at some length of his own position as a leader. He acknowledged that his position on cooperativization—that it should be pressed rapidly toward completion—had alienated some of his fellow leaders, and had cost him popularity. He held, however, to the correctness of his stand, and indicated that he would be satisfied even if he retained the support of only one in ten (1958c:82). Later in the same year he commented that he did not believe in "following without discrimination," and that he should only be followed when he was correct (1958t:107).

[71] 1959r:39; 1962a:167. The most virulent response to this suggestion came at the time of the Lushan Plenum in 1959, at which point, he contended, his critics accused him of having begun to resemble the aging Stalin, of becoming "despotic and dictatorial," of refusing to permit democracy and mass participation, and, finally, of being vain and boastful.

[72] 1961c. Cf. 1959r:39.

[73] 1959r:28. Lin Biao's plan for an attempted coup contained a similar derogatory reference associating the two; Michael Y. M. Kau, ed., *The Lin Piao Affair: Power Politics and Military Coup* (White Plains, N.Y.: International Arts and Sciences Press, 1975), p. 83. Some attributed the subsequent effort in the anti-Confucius campaign to build up the image of Qin Shi Huang as a response to this derogatory association.

[74] 1958s:98. In 1964 Mao commented, "we must issue strict orders. There must be a Qin Shi Huang Di. Who is Qin Shi Huang Di? It is [name omitted in text]. I am his aide" (1964w:422).

Shi Huang comparison may account for one side of his self-image, the other side is characterized, particularly in later years, with considerable self-effacement. A document in which this view is particularly evident is the letter allegedly written by Mao to his wife in the summer of 1966, in which he denounced the "supernatural power" attributed to his writings, and described his position as follows: "When tigers are absent from the mountain the monkey then becomes king. I have become such a king."[75] More recently, he remarked to Edgar Snow that, among the various titles which had been bestowed on him, only that of teacher was wholly appropriate, and that it was by this one which he hoped to be remembered.[76]

There is, Mao remarked in 1967, "no single absolute authority. All authorities are relative."[77] In his writings on his theory of knowledge and in the application of that theory to the political realm, the final authority—that of the idea of contradiction and the method for comprehending the world which derives from it —is an authority which is at the same time mutable and fixed, impersonal and dependent on human action. Mao's system of authority is one that attempts to provide the basis for a position from which a political leader can legitimately define, channel, and direct conflict and change. But because the legitimacy of that position depends at least in part on involvement in the conflict itself; because there are limits to what praxis can accomplish in defining, channeling, and redirecting the course of history; and, finally, because of the mortality of any single set of political actors, that position of leadership is relative and temporary, not absolute and permanent. If there is a Leviathan in Mao's system— one that has taken, at various times, the form of a party, of a small handful of powerful leaders, or of Mao himself—this "sovereign definer" ultimately takes the form of an idea, the idea of the permanence and ubiquity of contradiction and change.

[75] 1966g:95. A year later he complained of the exaggerated adulation in the Chinese press of himself and his thought, though his complaint was addressed specifically to the release of articles to the foreign media (1967f.).

[76] 1970b:175. A particularly useful collection of "images" of Mao is contained in the volume, *Mao Tse-tung in the Scales of History*, edited by Dick Wilson (Cambridge: Cambridge University Press, 1977).

[77] 1967l.

Chapter Four

ON CLASS AND CLASS CONFLICT

> In a class society everyone lives as a member
> of a particular class, and every kind of think-
> ing, without exception, is stamped with the
> brand of a class.[1]

A theory of continuing the revolution under the dictatorship of
the proletariat, in which revolution is defined, in part, as a class
struggle, must of necessity contain within it an explanation for
the continued presence of class enemies. The simple explanation
for the continued presence of class enemies after the revolutionary seizure of power treats that presence as deriving from the
imperfect results of individual transformation or resocialization.
Such an explanation may be satisfactory over the short run, but
imperfections in the process of resocialization are potentially
correctable, and thus cannot serve to explain the long-term presence of class enemies. Rather, extending significantly the period
of the existence of such enemies implies that the new order established by the revolutionaries is itself responsible for the creation
of new enemies. An explanation for embourgeoisement, then, is a
logical prerequisite to a theory that envisions a protracted struggle
between proletariat and bourgeoisie.

Seeking an orthodox foundation for the development of a
theory of embourgeoisement, Mao paraphrased Lenin's thoughts
on the subject—without citing the specific sources—as follows:

After the October Revolution, Lenin pointed out a number of
times that:

(a) The overthrown exploiters always try in a thousand and
one ways to recover the "paradise" they have been deprived of.

(b) New elements of capitalism are constantly and spontaneously generated in the petty-bourgeois atmosphere.

---

[1] 1937e:260/I, 296.

(c) Political degenerates and new bourgeois elements may emerge in the ranks of the working class and among government functionaries as a result of bourgeois influence and the pervasive, corrupting atmosphere of the petty bourgeoisie.

(d) The external conditions for the continuance of class struggle within a socialist country are encirclement by international capitalism, the imperialists' threat of armed intervention, and their subversive activities to accomplish peaceful disintegration.[2]

"Life has confirmed these conclusions of Lenin's," is Mao's succinct comment on this passage.[3]

It is significant that in Lenin's view, as it is presented here, the only source of systematically generated new bourgeois elements is what Lenin referred to as "spontaneous capitalism." The other bourgeois elements in the postrevolutionary society are either "remnants" of the old system, or newly degenerated individuals who had been adversely influenced, either by these remnants or by surrounding capitalist countries. As a consequence, if a truly *new* class is to be depicted as arising in a socialist society, a rigorously Leninist explanation for that phenomenon should concentrate on the economic question of spontaneous capitalism.

As we shall see, however, Mao came to regard politics and ideology as having an effect equally important as that of economics in altering the nature and composition of classes in a socialist society. This is particularly evident in his discussion of a change in class status stemming from the remolding of an individual's economic, political, and ideological orientations through revolutionary education and "socialist transformation." The same idea of multicausality is also evident in his treatment of the reverse of this process—the change of class status that he sees as stemming from the deterioration of an individual's economic, political, and ideological orientations.

To lay the foundation for this argument, I want to begin by reviewing the evolution of Mao's ideas on class and class struggle —ideas which are surely Marxist in origin but which, in Mao's treatment of them, have come to diverge significantly from their origins. In the second section of the chapter it will then be possible to analyze Mao's description of the cause and manifestations of embourgeoisement in a socialist society.

[2] 1963e:36.   [3] Ibid.

ORIGIN AND DEVELOPMENT OF THE CONCEPT OF CLASS IN MAO'S THOUGHT

In *The German Ideology*, Marx set out a twofold process for the formation of a social class. On the one hand, property relationships are the most significant determinant of class. "Industry and commerce, production and the exchange of the necessities of life, themselves determine distribution, the structure of the different social classes and are, in turn, determined by it as to the mode in which they are carried on."[4] Holding material property relations to be the causal basis of the social process, Marx saw the property relations of a particular class as giving rise to the political power and intellectual outlook of that class.

In addition to property relations and their attendant political and intellectual superstructures, there is a second element which, in Marx's view, is a prerequisite to the formation of a class: a second class, to which the first is opposed. "The separate individuals form a class only insofar as they have to carry on a common battle against another class."[5]

Marx's concept of class thus combines both a materialist and what we might call an existential element. If property relations are a contributory cause for the formation of classes, then struggle with another class is the immediate cause for the coalescence of the class and the formation of class consciousness. Like Marx, Mao, too, speaks of class in terms of both its economic basis and the development of class consciousness—of the "class-in-itself" as well as the "class-for-itself."[6] Unlike Marx, however, Mao

[4] Marx and Engels, *The German Ideology*, in Robert C. Tucker, ed., *The Marx-Engels Reader* (New York: W. W. Norton, 1972), p. 134. "The property question," he said elsewhere, "relative to the different stages of development of industry, has always been the life question of any given class"; "Die moralisierende Kritik und die critische Moral," in Franz Mehring, ed., *Aus dem literarischen Nachlass von Karl Marx und Frederich Engels*, 3rd ed. (Stuttgart, 1920), cited in Ralf Dahrendorf, *Class and Class Conflict in Industrial Society* (Stanford: Stanford University Press, 1959), p. 11.

[5] Marx and Engels, *The German Ideology*, p. 143.

[6] He speaks of the transformation of the proletariat from a class-in-itself to a class-for-itself as the result of "conscious and organized economic and political struggles" (1937e:295/1, 301; cf. 1964r:399). The Chinese terms Mao uses are interesting: class-in-itself is *zizai de jieji*, a relatively literal translation; the term for class-for-itself, however, *ziwei de jieji*, conveys,

places considerably more emphasis on what I have called the existential side of the determination of class than he does on the materialist side.

In a revolutionary society, the concept of class must serve both as what Marion Levy has called an "analytical structure," and as what he terms a "concrete structure."[7] As evolved by Marx, a social class is primarily an analytic structure. His purpose was to describe society not as a static entity, but rather as a dynamic process. As a consequence, he was less concerned with the identification and the composition of specific classes (possibly because the distinction between the proletariat and the bourgeoisie seemed to him to be a very obvious one in English industrial society during the late nineteenth century), and more concerned with discovering the effect on society of major alterations in the class structure. But if static description did not satisfy Marx, neither did the mere explanation of a process, for his aim was to transform the world. Such transformation through revolution requires the "application" of his theory in specific, concrete, historical circumstances. The result in retrospect is an ambiguity in Marx's concept of class: he treats it now as an analytical structure, now as a concrete one, and makes no attempt to distinguish rigorously between the two.

"Application" of this concept in any revolutionary situation necessitates an act of reification, since application involves the process of "classification"—the assigning of a class status to each member of the society. This process presupposes the formulation of a specific and detailed definition of each class to serve as a set of criteria against which each individual can be measured and classified. The creation of these definitions—which must consti-

---

with its use of the active *wei* (to act, to do), much more of the sense of action implicit in the term than do its equivalents in Western languages.

[7] See Marion Levy, "Some Aspects of 'Structural-Functional Analysis' and Political Science," in Roland Young, ed., *Approaches to the Study of Politics* (Evanston: Northwestern University Press, 1958), pp. 52-65, where he makes the distinction as follows: concrete structures are "those patterns that define the character of units that are at least in theory capable of physical separation (in time and/or space) from other units of the same sort"; analytical structures "are not even theoretically capable of concrete separation" from one another. The concrete structure of a table consists of its top and legs; the analytical structure of a table consists of its height, width, weight, and so on. Analytic structures "do not refer to different things, but rather to different ways of looking at the same things."

tute at least temporarily static descriptions of concrete structures —inevitably involves a significant exegesis on the work of Marx, whose dynamic description of analytic structures offers little to guide the revolutionary actor in this work.

In his "Analysis of the Classes in Chinese Society," with which his *Selected Works* begins, Mao sets out to draw what is an essentially static description of the structure of Chinese society. Writing in March 1926, when his acquaintance with Marxism was still relatively rudimentary, he listed six classes as comprising this structure: the landlord class, the "comprador" class (consisting of those whose interests were closely allied with those of the imperialists in China), the middle bourgeoisie, the petty bourgeoisie, the semiproletariat, and the proletariat. He further dissects certain of these classes, and in the process he divides them, as we have seen, into the three important categories of "ourselves," "our friends," and "our enemies."[8] This he bases on the argument that class analysis requires not only an investigation of the economic status, but also, equally importantly, an investigation of the attitude of each class toward the revolution.[9]

When completed, these superordinate categories and the classes they contain are as follows: (1) "ourselves" is composed of the industrial proletariat;[10] (2) "our friends" consists of the petty bourgeoisie, the left wing of the middle bourgeoisie, and the semiproletariat, which he described as being made up of semiowner peasants, poor peasants, small handicraftsmen, shop assistants, and peddlers. (3) "our enemies" includes warlords, landlords, bureaucrats, compradors, reactionary intellectuals, and the right wing of the middle bourgeoisie. It is important to note the criteria by which the categories and the classes are distinguished from one another. The criteria that separate the classes from one another are clearly economic ones.[11] The composition of the three super-

[8] 1926. This text is a heavily edited version of the original article, which appeared in *Zhongguo Nongmin* (Chinese peasantry) in February 1926. Another article, published the previous month, dealt exclusively with the peasantry as a grouping of classes, and the attitudes of members of those respective classes toward the revolution. Excerpts from the two are found in Stuart R. Schram, *Political Thought of Mao Tse-tung* (New York: Praeger, 1969), pp. 210-214, 241-247.

[9] 1926:3/I, 13.

[10] Which, elsewhere, he described as having emerged pursuant to the May Fourth Movement (1940a:633/II, 348).

[11] As Stuart Schram has pointed out, the classes are differentiated both

ordinate categories, however, is determined on the basis of political or attitudinal criteria. Describing the basis for this analysis, Mao said, "to distinguish real friends from real enemies, we must make a general analysis of the economic status of the various classes in Chinese society and of their respective attitudes toward the revolution."[12]

It was in turning his attention to the borderline classes—those on either side of the line separating friends from enemies—that he began to look beyond purely economic definitions for classes. In his description of the "Struggle in the Jinggang Mountains" in 1929 Mao spoke of what he called an "intermediate class" (*zhongjian jieji*) consisting of small landlords and rich peasants. Here, though the two groups were distinguishable from one another on economic grounds, it was their political tendencies—namely, the likelihood of their becoming counterrevolutionary either under the pressure of the "white terror" or under what he referred to as the "pressure of daily life"—that linked them together as an "intermediate class."[13]

As the revolution progressed, and as Mao came more and more to treat the Chinese class structure as a simplified dichotomy of bourgeoisie and proletariat, he came to apply the same sort of analysis to the bourgeoisie that he had to the "intermediate class" in Jiangxi—a mode of analysis in which both economic and political considerations separated one *class* from another. Class was thus coming to be seen by Mao as determined not only by economic factors, but by political ones as well.

In general, the political tendency of the bourgeoisie as a whole was seen to be one of vacillation, a propensity to compromise.[14] This tendency, however, was unequally manifested in the various segments of the bourgeoisie. In general, the petty bourgeoisie was seen as a reliable ally,[15] but within this class certain elements were more reliable than others. The difference, he argued in 1926, was

---

on the basis of ownership or nonownership of the means of production, and on the basis of relative wealth and status; "Mao Ze-dong and the Role of the Various Classes in the Chinese Revolution, 1923-27," in *The Polity and Economy of China: The Late Professor Yuji Muramatsu Commemoration Volume* (Tokyo: Toyo Keizai Sinposha, 1975) pp. 227-239.

[12] 1926:3/I, 13.

[13] 1928b:71ff./I, 87ff. Earlier he treated the "middle peasant" in much the same way, emphasizing the quality of vacillation (1927:20/I, 31f.).

[14] 1937d:266/I, 290, and 1937k:382/II, 65.

[15] 1939g:597f./II, 289.

based on income: those within the petty bourgeoisie having a surplus income generally feared the revolution; those who were just able to make ends meet—the majority, in fact, of the petty bourgeoisie—would not oppose the revolution, but were unlikely to contribute significantly; finally, those who had a deficit at the year's end were most likely to be genuinely revolutionary.[16] The middle bourgeoisie or national bourgeoisie he saw as having "inconsistent" or "contradictory" (*you maodun de*) attitudes toward the revolution. On the one hand, they feared the revolution; on the other, they were concerned about the effects of imperialism in China.[17] The big bourgeoisie, finally, could be counted upon to oppose the revolution except when there developed contradictions between themselves and their "imperialist masters."[18] It was on the basis of his view of the bourgeoisie as characterized by their vacillation, finally, that he was able to conclude that the effect of the Japanese invasion in 1937 would be one of "altering class relations in China."[19]

Students and intellectuals were a group that posed problems for Mao's attempt at classification. Following Stalin, he defined the category of intellectuals as including all those with at least a middle-school education or the equivalent.[20] He argued that the members of this category did not comprise a separate class or stratum. Rather, they were for the most part members of the petty bourgeoisie.[21] They were to be separated into "revolutionary" and "counterrevolutionary" categories, he said, on the basis of their willingness to "integrate themselves with the workers and peasants," and the degree to which they actually did so.[22]

[16] 1926:5f./I, 16. It is interesting that, whereas in 1926 "owner peasants" were included as a part of the petty bourgeoisie, in a note to the 1928 article, "Why Is It That Red Political Power Can Exist in China?" they are excluded from the category: "By the term, 'petty bourgeoisie' Comrade Mao Tse-tung means those elements other than the peasants . . ." (1926:5/I, 15, and 1928a:55/I, 72).

[17] 1926:3f./I, 14; 1935:139/I, 155f.   [18] 1939g:597f./II, 289.

[19] 1937h:339/II, 41.   [20] 1939i:613/II, 302.

[21] 1939j:636/II, 322.

[22] 1939c:554/II, 246. More recently, Mao argued that even those intellectuals who come from working-class backgrounds are bourgeois as a result of the education they receive (1957f:11). In 1962, however, he appears to have returned to his earlier view: "Intellectuals such as scientists, engineers, technicians, professors, writers, actors, artists, medical workers and journalists do not always constitute a class. They belong either to the bourgeoisie or to the proletariat" (1962a:169).

As a consequence of his treatment of the vacillation of these "intermediate" classes, Mao came increasingly to emphasize the importance of political and ideological criteria over purely material ones. Aside from his early treatment of the petty bourgeoisie as having sentiments governed by their annual incomes, he subsequently argued that what vacillates among the bourgeoisie is their political attitude, even when their economic position remains essentially unchanged. While, as we have seen, he was willing in the Jiangxi period to describe an "intermediate class," constituted on the basis of its attitude toward the revolution, in the subsequent periods of the Second United Front and of the New Democracy, political and ideological criteria were used with increasing frequency to determine which members of an economically constituted class should be considered as falling into the broader categories of friends and enemies.[23]

Whereas the problem of vacillation focussed Mao's attention on questions of class *status*, the vast project of the classification of the Chinese population focussed attention on class *origin*. The standard initially used for rural classification was Mao's October 1933 document entitled, "How to Differentiate the Classes in Rural Areas."[24] In this document Mao differentiated between five classes: landlords (including warlords, officials, local tyrants, and evil gentry as well as rent collectors and property managers), rich peasants, middle peasants, poor peasants, and workers (including farm laborers). The classes were differentiated on the basis of the amount of land and number of farm implements owned, and on the basis of the disposition of labor—whether an individual employed the labor of others, worked for himself, or was forced to sell his own labor. Here the categories are clearly economic

[23] Mao's position on the relative determinative power of economic position and of political action is never resolved wholly in favor of the latter, but the emphasis is clearly on the latter and not on the former. One finds him stating in late 1939 that class attitude and class stand are "entirely determined by [one's] economic status in society" (1939j:601/II, 319). Seven months earlier, and on many occasions later, however, he took a different position: in May 1939 he spoke of the effect of "hard struggle" in bringing about a correct political attitude (1939b:147), and in 1955, when discussing the attitudes of various sectors of the rural population toward the project of cooperativization he noted that, while "these sections are fairly similar in their economic position," nonetheless their "enthusiasm" for cooperativization "varies—some are very keen, some are not so keen for the time being, and others prefer to wait and see" (1955d:15).

[24] 1933b.

in origin and relatively explicit, despite the fact that no precise figures are used, presumably in order to allow for local variations. The categories are inevitably static and inflexible, as well.

In distinguishing between emphasis on class origin and class status, it is well to reflect upon the distinction between what I have called the material and the existential notion of class. With regard to the material basis for class, class origin was of paramount importance, because of the effect of inheritance on an individual's relationship to the means of production. With regard to the existential basis for the creation of classes—their formation in the course of struggle with opposing classes—class status is obviously crucial, since the effect derives from an individual's personal experience of the struggle, and this experience can be only imperfectly transmitted by inheritance.

If we find, in Mao's treatment of the subject of class, a greater emphasis on the existential side of the concept—on the class as formed in struggle, and thus on class status rather than class origin—this emphasis can be attributed both to his theory of knowledge and concept of contradiction, on the one hand, and on the other, to ideas on class inherited from the Chinese tradition. Change and praxis are two interrelated central concerns in Mao's thought, and both of these concerns led him to an emphasis on the mutability of class standing rather than to its fixed "givenness." Traditional Chinese views are significant, too, however. Whereas many of the overtones of fixedness and inheritability of class status in our own use of the concept may be attributed to the experience of a feudal past—an attribution particularly evident in Marx's own derivation of the concept—the Chinese historical experience contained different lessons. In China there was, with few exceptions, no system of primogeniture or "strong property," to use Karl Wittfogel's term,[25] as there was at the base of the Western (and Japanese) feudal systems. Rather, a system of "weak" property prevailed, in which sons shared equally in the paternal inheritance. The result of this system was to bring about changes in the fortunes of a family from generation to generation. The question of the magnitude of the effect of these generational changes, and of the related effect of the sys-

[25] Karl Wittfogel, *Oriental Despotism* (New Haven: Yale University Press, 1957), pp. 116ff. There were examples of the system of primogeniture. See, for example, Fei Xiaotong's description of the role of "second sons" in his *Peasant Life in China* (London: Kegan Paul, 1939).

tem of "open" entry into officialdom upon the social mobility of the society as a whole, has been debated in the literature.[26] Nonetheless, one can argue with considerable confidence that the system was sufficiently open to have provided no firm basis for a view that the class status of one generation would inevitably pass unaltered to the next. On the contrary, the prevailing myth appears to have been one in which the road from peasantry to officialdom and back to peasantry again was described as taking five generations or so to traverse.[27]

As we have seen, attention to political attitude led Mao at an early point to superimpose the supraclass categories of friends and enemies upon his delineation of the classes themselves. In a similar way, one can observe an evolution in his treatment of the class content of one third of these supraclass categories—that of "ourselves." As it was described in 1927, this category was limited to members of the urban working class. A significant aspect of the Chinese Communists' experience after 1927, however, was the absence of a proletarian element in China sufficiently numerous and powerful to assume the vanguard role in the party. As Benjamin Schwartz has pointed out, the plenitude of peasants and the paucity of proletarians in the movement resulted in a series of tactics designed to conceal the severance of the Chinese Communist party from its proletarian base. Schwartz contends that, in effect, these tactics resulted in the substitution of the party for

[26] Ho Ping-ti, for example, argues in his *Ladder of Success in Imperial China* (New York: Columbia University Press, 1962) that "in the Ming-Ch'ing period as a whole, the status system was fluid and flexible and there were no effective legal and social barriers which prevented the movement of individuals and families from one status to another" (p. 257).

[27] It would be wrong, of course, to dichotomize in too stark a way the Chinese and European cases, since the decline of the feudal system in the West and its replacement with capitalism was marked by a substantial increase in social mobility, perhaps best typified by what Rostow has called, referring to Thomas Mann's novel, the "Buddenbrooks dynamic." Rostow explains the meaning of his term in a note as follows: "In Thomas Mann's novel of three generations the first sought money; the second, born to money, sought social and civic position; the third, born to comfort and family prestige, looked to the life of music. The phrase is designed to suggest, then, the changing aspirations of generations, as they place a low value on what they take for granted and seek new forms of satisfaction"; Walt Rostow, *Stages of Economic Growth: A Non-Communist Manifesto* (Cambridge: Cambridge University Press, 1961), p. 11. Mann's novel is *Buddenbrooks*, translated by H. T. Lowe-Porter (New York: Random House, 1952).

the class as the locus of "proletarian nature."[28] Mao contributed evidence in support of Schwartz's hypothesis when, in 1964, he wrote as follows: "The party of the proletariat has members of other class origins. But the latter do not join the party as representatives of other classes. From the very day they join the party they must abandon their former class stand and take the stand of the proletariat."[29] Put in these terms, the argument reveals the conclusions that follow logically from Mao's emphasis on the possibility of a change of class status, and from his assumption that there are experiential determinants of class which are equally, if not more, important than the material, and which have to do with the political and ideological realms as well as the economic realm. Once an individual has joined the party and has acquired the experience of participating in the political life of the party, he or she is, for all practical purposes, Mao contended, a member of the proletariat. Thus, while the nominal class content of the category, "ourselves," remained fixed and limited to the proletariat, the number and nature of those regarded as members of the proletariat was significantly altered.

Turning next to the question of the duration of the class struggle, it should be noted that stress on the economic or material basis of class gives rise to a view of that struggle as inevitable, but also finite. Stress on the existential aspect of class—that is, that the class is finally constituted only through class struggle—gives rise to a view of that struggle as more contingent upon human choice and action but also, as we shall see, as of potentially longer dura-

[28] Benjamin I. Schwartz, *Chinese Communism and the Rise of Mao* (Cambridge: Harvard University Press, 1951), pp. 192ff.

[29] 1964n:19. He made much the same point many years earlier, but it was the army and not the party that he saw as effecting a change of class. Speaking of the class origins of the recruits into the Red Army during the Jiangxi Soviet period, he noted that, despite their varied background, "their character changes once they are in the Red Army, which thus serves as a furnace, transmuting its recruits" (Mao 1928b:62/1, 81). The following year he reaffirmed his belief that, despite the fact that most soldiers are of peasant or petty-bourgeois origin, the incorrect ideas that derive from that background could be corrected by education conducted by the party (1929: 83/1, 105). An undated excerpt in the *Wansui* (1969) collection puts the problem like this: "It is . . . important to distinguish between class background and one's own performance, with emphasis on the latter. . . . The question is whether you take the stand of your original class or take a changed class stand, that is, taking the side of the workers and poor and lower-middle peasants" (n.d.:433).

tion. Emphasis on the contingency of struggle on human choice, however, is very much out of character with Mao's idea that contradiction, and class struggle as a form of contradiction, exist independently of such choice and are more than merely a tool, the use of which is subject to "adjustment." More in character with this view is his statement contained in the June 1963 "Proposal Concerning the General Line of the International Communist Movement": "For a very long historical period after the proletariat takes power, class struggle continues as an objective law *independent of an individual's will*, differing only in form from what it was before the taking of power."[30]

This explicit linking of the concept of class struggle to the concept of contradictions that are ubiquitous and permanent came only in Mao's later work, however. Earlier, when writing in June 1949 on the subject of the "People's Democratic Dictatorship," he had argued that the extinguishing of classes would bring about an end of parties and state power, and he contended that their eventual extinction was "inevitable."[31] The question left unresolved here is at what point classes can be considered to have been extinguished, and the class struggle thus ended. Two references to the question in 1955 make it clear that Mao did not believe that the class struggle had been completed at that point. Yet to be overcome were the "attempts of the counterrevolutionary classes, cliques, and individuals, to oppose the revolution and restore their own power."[32] On the other hand, Mao's initial reactions to the Soviet Twentieth Party Congress in 1956, formulated in a pair of articles "On the Historical Experience of the Dictatorship of the Proletariat," contain a suggestion that he believed that the process of extinguishing of classes was a relatively short one. Stalin was chided, in fact, for taking the opposite view: "After the elimination of the exploiting classes and the wiping out in the main of the counterrevolutionary forces, it was still necessary for the dictatorship of the proletariat to deal with counterrevolutionary remnants—these could not be wiped out completely so long as imperialism existed—but by then its edge should have been mainly directed against the aggressive forces of foreign imperialism."[33]

[30] 1963e:36. Emphasis added. [31] 1949d:1357/IV, 411.
[32] 1955b:51. Later in the same year he predicted that the class struggle during the first five-year plan (1953-1957) would be "very acute" (1955e: 16).
[33] 1956n:48f.

While the "edge" of the dictatorship of the proletariat was being directed outward, the criticism continues, "democratic procedures" should have been developed to deal with internal administration. "After the elimination of classes, the class struggle should not continue to be stressed as though it were being intensified, as was done by Stalin, with the result that the healthy development of socialist democracy was hampered."[34] The implication here is clearly that the process of the elimination of classes had already taken place in the Soviet Union under Stalin, and the CPSU is praised as being "completely right" in having "corrected Stalin's mistakes" in this connection.

Mao's speech "On the Correct Handling of Contradictions among the People" before a Supreme State Conference in February 1957, published the following June in what we must assume was a considerably altered form,[35] constitutes a kind of watershed document with regard to Mao's formulation of his conception of class and class conflict in a socialist society. He does speak there of the continued existence of class struggle, but the emphasis is on what has been accomplished since Liberation and the effect of those accomplishments on the gradual diminution of class struggle: "Today, matters stand as follows: the large-scale and turbulent class struggles of the masses characteristic of the previous revolutionary periods have, in the main, ended, but class struggle is by no means entirely over."[36]

The speech is, moreover, the *locus classicus* for the definition of the supraclass categories of "people" and "enemies of the people," which had come more and more to replace class labels in the discussion of social problems and their solutions. As was implied in his early use of these supraclass categories two decades earlier, they were to be defined on the basis of political attitude toward the principal contradiction facing the society at any

[34] Ibid., p. 49.

[35] We have no published version of the February speech except for a second-hand report from a Polish visitor who heard the speech delivered and reported it abroad (1957e). The official published version (1957d) postdated the Hundred Flowers period and contains within it strictures against criticism of the party that cannot have been contained in the spoken version.

[36] Ibid., p. 95. Eight months later he spoke of the class struggle as "fundamentally ended," but noted that conflicts remained in the superstructure over "ideology and political power" (1957j:73). In the spring of the following year he described the former exploiting classes as having been "reduced to mere drops in the ocean of the working people" (1958g).

particular moment: "At the present stage, the period of building socialism, the classes, strata, and social groups which favor, support, and work for the cause of socialist construction all come within the category of the people, while the social forces and groups which resist the socialist revolution and are hostile to or sabotage socialist construction are enemies of the people."[37] As he had indicated in 1949, the distinction was crucial because of the difference in methods appropriate to the two groups: among the people, democratic methods were to be employed to resolve contradictions, whereas contradictions with the enemy were said to be antagonistic and were to be resolved by dictatorial methods.[38]

A somewhat clearer indication of the relationship between class struggle and struggle between the people and their enemies is found in the "Sixty Work Methods" published the following year. There Mao reiterates the idea that "as far as China is concerned, classes have not been finally wiped out and there is still class struggle." On the other hand, the implication is clear that this situation is only a temporary one, since he goes on as follows:

> After the complete abolition of classes at the end of the transition period, as far as the domestic situation is concerned, politics

[37] 1957d:80f. Mao first referred to the distinction between antagonistic and nonantagonistic contradictions in his 1937 article, "On Contradiction," and attributed it to Lenin (1937g). The relationship drawn in his 1957 speech between the people and their enemies, and between antagonistic and nonantagonistic contradictions appeared in nearly the same form in the article, "More on the Historical Experience of the Dictatorship of the Proletariat," which was published the preceding December (Mao 1956n:24f.). Cohen has traced at some length the Soviet roots of Mao's treatment of this relationship, and points out that the argument owes much to a symposium of Chinese theorists held in the fall of 1956, at which several points of view were set forward concerning the nature of contradictions in a socialist society. The position taken by Mao in these articles of December and February was one of those points of view; Arthur Cohen, *The Communism of Mao Tse-tung* (Chicago: University of Chicago Press, 1964), pp. 139-148. Martin Glaberman, commenting on Mao's 1957 speech, regards it as wholly political and not at all philosophical—an abandonment of the dialectic in favor of "categories . . . made so rigid and meaningless that they are juggled any way which pleases Mao"; "Mao as a Dialectician," *International Philosophical Quarterly* 8 (1968), 111.

[38] 1957d:82f. Cf. 1949d:1363/IV, 417f., where the category "people" is defined and distinguished from "reactionaries," and where democracy and dictatorship are indicated as the appropriate means for dealing with problems arising within each category.

is entirely a relationship among the people. By that time there will still be ideological struggle, political struggle, and revolution among men, and it is not possible to do away with them. But the nature of the struggle and revolution is different from the past; it is not a class struggle, but a struggle between the advanced and backward among the people, a struggle between advanced and backward science and technology.[39]

Much of the optimism underlying his view of the gradual elimination of class conflict in China and its replacement by peaceful conflicts "among the people" can be traced, I believe, to the speed with which cooperativization had been accomplished in the Chinese countryside and the relative lack of resistance encountered by the CCP in carrying out this major transformation. This latter achievement was the culmination of a long series of accomplishments for Mao: indeed, each project to which he had turned his attention during the two decades since the beginning of the Yan'an period had, from his point of view, succeeded. His optimism is mirrored in his editorial comments to the collection of articles on cooperativization published in December 1955 under the title, *The Socialist Upsurge in China's Countryside*.[40] By mid-1958, however, despite the atmosphere surrounding the Great Leap Forward, he was beginning to take a somewhat more cautious view: "The annotations to *The Socialist Upsurge in China's Countryside* should be printed. . . . It was a little too optimistic to predict that the socialist revolution had gained a basic victory. I did not expect such a big revolution. As for China's bourgeoisie, I predict that there will still be struggles, long-term struggles to eliminate the deep-rooted influence of the bourgeoisie and its intellectuals."[41]

The problems encountered in the wake of the Great Leap Forward and the formation of communes, and his colleagues' reactions to these problems as expressed at the "Lushan Plenum" in the summer of 1959, replaced whatever optimism Mao may have felt with a considerably darker, if more realistic, picture of

[39] 1958e:6.

[40] 1955g, particularly p. 139, where he sees 1955 as a turning point in the balance of power between class forces. Cf. 1955e:15, where he speaks of the fact that the ranks of the proletariat will soon be substantially augmented with "several million members of the bourgeoisie" who will have been effectively transformed.

[41] 1958u:121. Cf. 1958t:107.

the situation in China. Deeply affected by his colleagues' criticisms of his policies, he attempted to comprehend what had transpired at the meeting. His conclusion was that what he had witnessed during the course of the Central Committee's meetings was, despite the obvious expectations to the contrary, a class struggle.[42]

In the years that followed—years during which Mao was devoting himself to theorizing, having resigned his position as head of state—he developed a new hypothesis concerning class struggle in a socialist system. Rather than a gradual elimination of the salience of classes and class struggle, and their consequent replacement as analytical and practical constructs by broader, supraclass categories such as people and enemies, he came to see a sharpening of class struggle during this period, and thus a renewed relevance of class categories. During the Cultural Revolution, Liu Shaoqi was accused, among other faults, of having favored a "theory of the dying out of class struggle." Texts were cited showing that he had believed that the transition period was marked by a gradual diminution of the class struggle.[43] Careful analysis of these texts,

[42] He seemed to be unsure of the situation in July: noting that a segment of the party leadership disagreed with the general line, he said, "What kind of class shall we call it, bourgeoisie or petty bourgeoisie?" (1959r:34). By the following month he was unequivocal: "The struggle that has arisen at Lushan is a class struggle. It is the continuation of the life and death struggle between the two great antagonists of the bourgeoisie and the proletariat in the process of the socialist revolution during the past decade." "I consider these words to be extremely important," he concluded the document (1959z:73, 76). At the same time, it is important to note both the fact that the bourgeois elements involved in this struggle were not newly created ones, but rather were individuals who were influenced by the remnants of bourgeois and petty bourgeois ideology, and who had "sneaked" into the party (1959z:74, 80f. Cf. 1959aa:77 and 1959bb:80). Moreover, he was not prepared to abandon his ideas of people and enemies, describing the conflict not only as a class struggle but also (somewhat inconsistently) as a contradiction among the people, different from previous "renegades" such as, *inter alia*, Chen Duxiu and Gao Gang, who were enemies of the people (1959z:75).

[43] See excerpts from a speech made by Liu in March 1957 before the Shanghai Municipal Party Committee cited in "A Theoretical Weapon for Making Revolution under the Dictatorship of the Proletariat," *HQ* 10 (1967) (21 July 1967), translated in *PR* 10:26 (23 June 1967), 27-32; excerpts from a speech given to the graduates of Beijing Geological Institute in May 1957, in *Dongfanghong Bao* (The East is Red News) 28 (28 April 1967), translated in *JPRS* 41858 (17 July 1967), 1ff. Additional elaborations of these charges are found in "*Chedi pipan 'jieji douzheng xiaomie lun' de*

however, and comparison of them with texts from Mao dating from the same period, suggests not only that both Liu and Mao had seen class struggle as "dying out" during the socialist period, but also that both men had moved away from this position between 1957 and 1962. The act of making the accusation against Liu in Mao's name, however, served to underscore the conviction with which Mao had himself abandoned the "theory of the dying out of class struggle."

Mao did not reach his new position on class and class conflict immediately. Although in 1960 he accused Tito of "completely writ[ing] off the question of class contradictions and class struggle in the world," the class contradictions that he enumerates to substantiate this charge do not include those within a socialist system.[44] The following year, annotating a Soviet textbook on political economics, he agreed with the statement he found there that there is "no class in a socialist system which is making every effort to maintain outdated economic relations." He did note, however, that there are conflicting strata and interest groups, contradictions between manual and mental labor, between urban and rural areas, between workers and peasants, between the advanced and the backward in a socialist society. There are also, he noted, individuals (not a class) who strive to maintain these outdated relations.[45] Elsewhere in the same set of notes he observed that "to say that class struggle in China is not acute is out of keeping with reality," but the examples which follow that statement are all drawn from the period prior to and immediately following Liberation.[46] Finally, he points out that there is still a class struggle underway in the Soviet Union, but it is one in opposition to the remnants of capitalism.[47]

Although the speech that Mao gave at the Central Committee's Tenth Plenum in late September 1962 is usually cited as the source for his new view on class struggle in socialist society,[48] he

---

fandun miulun" (Thoroughly Repudiate the Reactionary Fallacy of the 'Theory of the Dying out of the Class Struggle'), *RMRB* (20 August 1967). Lowell Dittmer, in his illuminating study of Liu, puts this theoretical accusation into the context of the range of criticism against Liu in the Cultural Revolution; *Liu Shao-ch'i and the Chinese Cultural Revolution: The Politics of Mass Criticism* (Berkeley and Los Angeles: University of California Press, 1974), pp. 222f.

[44] 1960e:10, 14, 31.   [45] 1961a:273.
[46] Ibid., p. 268.   [47] Ibid., p. 299.
[48] 1962e:86f. Cf. 1962b; 1962c.

had made much the same point nine months earlier at an enlarged Central Work Conference. There he observed that, while the system of exploitation had been eliminated and the economic foundation of the bourgeoisie and landlord classes had been removed, nevertheless, "We must . . . continue to wage a struggle against them. The overthrown reactionary classes may attempt a comeback. In a socialist society, meanwhile, new elements of the bourgeoisie may emerge. Classes and class struggle remain during the entire period of socialism. The class struggle is protracted, complex, and sometimes violent."[49] Pursuant to this new view, Mao offered a reinterpretation of the four-class model of Chinese society prevalent in his writings in 1958 and 1959. That model depicted the society as composed of remnants of the exploiting classes, the national bourgeoisie, workers, and peasants.[50] The reinterpretation integrated these classes with the earlier supraclass categories of people and enemies in a new way. The category of "the people" now included workers, peasants, urban petty bourgeois elements, and patriotic intellectuals (though the latter group was not to be conceived of as a class). This category included, he estimated, approximately 95 percent of the population. Enemies— the remaining 5 percent—consisted of landlords, rich peasants, counterrevolutionaries, bad elements, and anticommunist rightists.[51]

Given his revived concern over the problem of the continued existence of classes in a socialist society, it is interesting to see that he takes a relatively restrained position here on the question of the role of class struggle in political life as a whole. He alludes to the "truism" that "our work must not be affected by the class struggle. . . . Work and class struggle should be taken side by

[49] 1962a:168. Referring to his comment in the editorial notes to *The Socialist Upsurge in China's Countryside* to the effect that after the elimination of the bourgeoisie, only the remnants of the bourgeois ideology would remain, he said, "I misspoke and I am going to correct it" (1962d:22).

[50] 1958p:87; 1958l:112. The four classes listed were the exploiting class, the national bourgeoisie, workers, and peasants. Compare his characterization in 1941 of Chinese society as "small at both ends and large in the middle"—few exploiters, few workers, many peasants and petty bourgeois (1941c:766/III, 32).

[51] 1962a:169. In an earlier attempt at integrating these categories, Mao suggested that nonantagonistic contradictions were those between strata within a single class, and that antagonistic contradictions were those between the two supraclass categories, "exploiters" and "nonexploiters" (1958p:90).

side. Though class struggle is imperative, we need special persons to do this work."[52] Subsequently he evolved a formula calling for a link between "class struggle, production struggle, and scientific experimentation," apparently putting the three on a par with one another, and separating class from production in such a way as to emphasize the noneconomic content of class as he had come to conceive of it.[53] It was only after more than a decade had passed that Deng Xiaoping, operating on the assumption that the three were, in fact, to be taken as being on a par, elicited from Mao the clarifying point that class struggle was intended to be taken as the "key link" among the three.[54]

Thus the evolution was completed whereby a broad-based alliance of classes friendly to the purposes of the Chinese Communist revolution, initially referred to as "new democratic forces," became known instead as "the people," and finally were reconceptualized into a class-based category that prepared the way for their being referred to during the Cultural Revolution as the "proletariat." Those who resisted this united front, initially referred to as "reactionaries," became "enemies of the people," and, finally, in the more recent shorthand, members of the "bourgeoisie." Supraclass categories gave way to the reintroduction of class categories, and the transition period was seen as one of intensified, rather than diminishing, class struggle. Socialist transformation was now viewed as a process that carries within itself the potential for its own reversal. We now turn to consider Mao's perception of the process of embourgeoisement or negative trans-

---

[52] 1962e:92. The point made here is reminiscent of that made prior to Liberation when he explained that when class struggle had to give way to anti-Japanese resistance, it was not a question of "denying the class struggle," but of "adjusting (*tiaojie*) it" (1938e:513/II, 200). He maintained this position until mid-1963, when he called for mass mobilization to carry out the class struggle, since it was ineffectual to leave that task to the public security organs (1963a:317).

[53] See, for example, 1963d:70 and 1964e:342. Glaberman takes particular issue with this formulation, arguing that, for Marx, the class struggle is inseparable from the process of production and scientific experimentation, and derives from them ("Mao as a Dialectician," p. 99).

[54] 1976. Given the questions that have been raised regarding Mao's position *vis-à-vis* Deng Xiaoping and the "Gang of Four" during the year immediately preceding his death, one needs to read the comments Mao is said to have made during this period with considerable care. The emphasis Mao placed on class struggle during his latter years, however, lends credence to this particular comment.

formation in a socialist society, for it is this process that, he argues, necessitates the continuation of the revolution under the dictatorship of the proletariat.

Mao's initial efforts to understand the process of embourgeoisement hewed closely to Lenin's view as cited at the beginning of this chapter, and explored only the effects of bourgeois influence on otherwise upright cadres. Addressing the Central Committee in March 1949 he observed that,

> with victory, the people will be grateful to us and the bourgeoisie will come forward to flatter us. It has been proven that the enemy cannot conquer us by force of arms. However, the flattery of the bourgeoisie may conquer the weak-willed in our ranks. There may be some communists, who were not conquered by enemies with guns and were worthy of the name of heroes for standing up to these enemies, but who cannot withstand sugar-coated bullets; they will be defeated by sugar-coated bullets.[55]

So great was the threat from these "sugar-coated bullets," that Mao went on to describe the nearly three decades of the Chinese Communist revolution theretofore as "only the first step in a long march of ten thousand *li*," and a "comparatively tiny" one at that.[56]

His subsequent efforts at explaining the process took as their subject not post-Liberation China, but rather Yugoslavia and, by indirection, the Soviet Union, which two systems he had, by the early 1960s, increasingly come to see as negative examples for China. It is useful to contrast Mao's view with the views of Milovan Djilas on the formation of a "new class" in a socialist system. Such a comparison benefits from the fact that both Djilas and Mao use Yugoslavia as their exemplary case. The comparison is important, as well, because, apart from Mao, Djilas is one of the very few writers to have advanced a systematic explanation for the process.

Djilas ascribes responsibility for the emergence of the new

[55] 1949b:1439f./IV, 374.   [56] Ibid.

class in Yugoslav society to a "stratum of professional revolutionaries who made up its core even before it attained power."[57]
Unlike most classes, however, which have "attained power *after*
new economic patterns had taken shape in the old society," the
new class "did not come to power to *complete* a new economic
order but to establish its own and, in so doing, to establish its
power over society."[58] Although this formulation seems to suggest
a series of purposeful acts by a social grouping conscious of
itself as such, and aiming at establishing its position as a group,
Djilas' subsequent argument suggests that this was not the case.
The new class, he later argues, is "the most deluded and least
conscious of itself." "A Communist member of the new class . . .
thinks that he belongs to a group with prescribed ideas, aims,
attitudes and roles. That is all he sees. He cannot see that at the
same time he belongs to a special social category: the ownership
class."[59] Its emergence as an *economic* class, in other words, must
thus have been an unintended consequence of the actions of a
group of individuals united on the basis of a shared perception of
the desirability of a course of *political* action.

Initiated by a "stratum of professional revolutionaries," the new
class is intimately connected with the Communist party in a
socialist system. Djilas draws an important distinction—one to
which we shall return in a moment—between political bureaucracies (the party) and administrative bureaucracies (the government and, presumably, the economic structure in the socialist
system). The power base of the new class is in the political
bureaucracy, but this class constitutes, in effect, a parasitic growth
on the party; for, as the class grows in power, the party lan-
guishes as a result.[60] He contends that Marx foresaw the problems
arising from the parasitic nature of an administrative bureaucracy,
but failed to foresee that a political bureaucracy might itself become an exploitative force in a socialist system, as has been the
case in the Soviet Union.

But if the origins of the new class lie in the realm of political
action, the definition of the class as it has now evolved is an economic one. The class is composed, in Djilas' words, of "those
who have special privileges and economic preference because of

[57] Milovan Djilas, *The New Class: An Analysis of the Communist System*
(New York: Praeger, 1957), p. 39.
[58] Ibid., p. 38.   [59] Ibid., p. 59.
[60] Ibid., pp. 39f.

117

the administrative monopoly they hold."[61] He sees this "administrative monopoly" as amounting to the "ownership" of nationalized property. Thus membership in the class is defined by a large income in goods and privileges.[62] Its base of power thus grounded in the ownership of the means of production, the new class is plagued with what Djilas calls a "profound internal contradiction." On the one hand, it is unable to renounce the ownership that provides its power. On the other hand, that ownership is fundamentally illegitimate within the socialist legal framework, and cannot be made legitimate except at the cost of revealing the nature of the new class to the rest of the society. As a result of this contradiction, the greatest threat to the new class comes from the expansion of freedom within the system, for freedom, in Djilas' eyes, would bring with it a popular awareness of the illegitimacy of the rule of the new class. In a passage that bears an interesting resemblance to Mao's thoughts on the subject, Djilas concludes, "circumstances may drive the new class, no matter how monopolistic and totalitarian it may be, to retreat before the masses."[63]

Although positing economic criteria for defining membership in the new class, Djilas is disappointingly vague in describing the boundaries that separate the new class from the rest of society. "Although it is sociologically possible to prescribe who belongs to the new class," he says, "it is difficult to do so; for the new class melts into and spills over into the people, into other lower classes, and is constantly changing."[64]

Despite this analytical fuzziness, however, he does see the possibility of describing certain common characteristics shared by members of the class. They are voracious and insatiable, exclusive and isolated from the masses. Though eschewing an individualistic ethos, they nonetheless selfishly pursue individual ends. Finally, as a class, they possess a monopoly of power that far exceeds that of any other class in the society.[65]

It is perhaps misleading to discuss Djilas' argument under the rubric of "embourgeoisement," since, unlike Mao, he does not refer to this class as being bourgeois. When he refers to it as being a "new" class, he means not only that it is a new phenomenon in a socialist system, but also that it manifests unprecedented quali-

[61] Ibid.
[63] Ibid., p. 68.
[65] Ibid., pp. 6of., 69.

[62] Ibid., p. 44.
[64] Ibid., p. 61.

ties that distinguish it from similar classes in other systems. Its most important distinguishing feature, in his view, is the process by which it originates—a process that is unlike Marx's conception of how new classes emerge. In comparing the new class specifically with the bourgeoisie in other systems, Djilas notes that the two classes share their worst qualities, but that the new class lacks what appears to him as a redeeming feature of the bourgeoisie, namely, its frugality and economy.[66]

Taken as a whole, then, Djilas' account of the new class and its origins offers us interesting insights, but by no means provides us with a thorough analytical explanation. In large measure this is the result of the polemical framework in which his argument is embedded. His primary object is to show that the actions of certain individuals—the "stratum of professional revolutionaries" whom he holds responsible for the formation of the new class— were at best misguided, and at worst malevolent. Thus individual actions loom larger in his explanation than do structural defects as the cause for the rise of the new class.

In this respect, his argument more closely resembles the criticisms that Leon Trotsky leveled against Stalinist Russia than they do Mao's perception of Khrushchev's failings. Siegfried Bahne, in his inclusive review of Trotsky's condemnations of Stalin's errors, pointed out that "as early as his first open attack after Lenin had been incapacitated, [Trotsky] had emphatically warned of the increasing 'bureaucratization' of the party apparatus, which Lenin had already observed with anxiety and which was 'linked with a development of conservative traditionalism and all its side effects.' "[67] By 1936, Trotsky was speaking in terms strikingly close to those of Djilas: "The Party now ruling in the Soviet Union is nothing but the political machine of the privileged class."[68] The Stalinist purges of 1936 to 1938 led Trotsky to the view that "the 'new aristocracy' of the Soviet Union, whose rule was based on deception of the masses, feared both criticism and the people, not least because it was the embodiment of a monstrous inequality and had to hide the truth."[69]

Thus for Djilas, as for Trotsky two decades earlier, the problem of the formation of a new class is less one of the retrogression of individuals previously embued with a correct perception of a

[66] Ibid., p. 60.
[67] Bahne, "Trotsky on Stalin's Russia," *Survey* 41 (1962), 29.
[68] Ibid., p. 41.   [69] Ibid.

course of revolutionary action, than it is one of naive or calculating individuals who, in large measure, still remain ignorant of the disastrous results of what they profess to perceive as having been a correct course of action. In this connection, both accounts differ importantly from the view advanced by Mao.

In 1963 Mao wrote, or contributed to the writing of, an article entitled, "Is Yugoslavia a Socialist Country?" Written as one of nine "comments" on the "Open Letter" sent by the Communist Party of the Soviet Union in July 1963, the article advanced a political, rather than an economic fact as being causal and defining of the process of the "restoration of capitalism": "In the final analysis, the fact that capitalism has swamped Yugoslavia in both town and country, the degeneration of an economy owned by the whole people into a state capitalist economy and the decline of Yugoslavia into a dependency of U.S. imperialism are all due to the degeneration of the party and state power in Yugoslavia."[70] The process is described in greater detail in the passage that follows this one, and six steps or stages are listed. The first of these steps suggests that the political causation of the process had an antecedent cause of its own, which was ideological in nature. This first step was taken when "the leading group of the Yugoslav Communist party betrayed Marxism-Leninism and embarked on the path of revisionism, bringing about the gradual degeneration of the party and state power in Yugoslavia." As a result of opposition to this first step in the Communist party, the "Tito clique," as the villains in the piece are called, made important changes in the party. The clique first "used its power to expel and purge from the party a great number of Communists loyal to Marxism-Leninism," and then replaced them with "counterrevolutionaries, bourgeois elements, all kinds of antisocialist elements and careerists seeking position and wealth through their membership cards." At this point the party was renamed "The League of Communists of Yugoslavia," a symbolic act that reflected the transformation of the party into a "virtual instrument for maintaining [the clique's] dictatorial rule." This restructuring of the party constitutes the second stage in the process of degeneration.

The relationship between steps two and three hinges on the idea that the nature of state power is unavoidably dependent upon the class structure of the society and the class composition of the political parties therein. Thus "with the degeneration of a com-

[70] 1963h:23.

munist into a bourgeois political party, state power inevitably degenerates from the dictatorship of the proletariat into the dictatorship of the bourgeoisie." There follows an elaboration on the explanation of this important step: "The degeneration of the state power in Yugoslavia did not occur through the overthrow of the original state power by violence and the establishment of a new state power, but through 'peaceful evolution.' In appearance, the same people remain in power, but in essence these people no longer represent the interests of the workers, peasants, and the working people, but those of imperialism and the old and new bourgeoisie of Yugoslavia."[71]

The fourth step, too, is an important one. During the course of this stage, the Tito clique, "utilizing state power and controlling the economic lifeline of the country . . . exploited the Yugoslav working people to the utmost extent and *brought into being* a bureaucrat-capitalist class."[72] It is only at this point, the fifth step in the process, that the effects are finally felt in economic terms. The socialist economy is now "destroyed," and a capitalist economic system restored. The sixth and last stage in the process suggests a reciprocal relationship between the political and the economic realms typical, as we have seen, of Mao's later thought on the subject. Once a capitalist economic restoration has taken place, the bourgeoisie then "demands the intensification of the bourgeois dictatorship and the development of a political system suited to the capitalist economic system so as to consolidate its ruling position."[73]

The process of embourgeoisement in Yugoslavia thus began, in Mao's view, with the acceptance of revisionist ideas by certain influential leaders. Imbued with these ideas, the "clique" set about repopulating the party with sympathetic elements. This transformation of the character of the party was reflected in the subsequent transformation of the character of state power, and this new power was used to "create" a new class. The "bureaucrat-capitalists" who constitute the membership of this class then brought about the transformation of the economy into a capitalist system, which in turn necessitated the creation of a more thoroughly bourgeois political system. The process as a whole Mao sardonically refers to as "peaceful evolution," thereby reversing the meaning ascribed to that term by those whom he regarded as

[71] Ibid., p. 24.   [72] Ibid. Emphasis added.
[73] Ibid.

121

revisionists. "The whole history of the dictatorship of the proletariat," he explained, "tells us that peaceful transition from capitalism to socialism is impossible. However, there is already the Yugoslav precedent for the 'peaceful evolution' of socialism back into capitalism."[74] No effort is made to elucidate the interesting and significant theoretical question raised by this treatment. Implicit here is the idea that development in a "forward" or "progressive" direction must involve a dialectical-revolutionary process, whereas movement in the opposite, retrogressive direction can proceed in a nondialectical, evolutionary process.

Mao's interest in Yugoslavia was only an indirect one. The problems he saw as having reached a mature state there he believed were equally seriously affecting the Soviet Union. Most important, the degeneration of Yugoslavia and the Soviet Union provided an admonitory example of a potential course that China itself might follow unless corrective measures were taken. What distinguishes Mao's explanation for the process of embourgeoisement from that of Djilas is that he emphasizes to a much greater degree than does Djilas a multiplicity of factors—political, economic, and ideological—that contribute to degeneration.[75]

At about the same time that he was devoting his attention to the problems of Yugoslavia, Mao also wrote about the problems of embourgeoisement in his own society. In a "Draft Resolution on Some Problems in the Current Rural Work," more commonly known as the "First Ten Points," he set forth nine manifestations of the continuing class struggle in China. Of the nine problems noted, five involve activities of the overthrown reactionary classes using various illegitimate means in an attempt to recover their lost position. Of the other four, three touch on economic activities such as speculation, profiteering, exploitation of labor, and usury. The last manifestation includes, among other groups, "degenerates" within political and economic organization who, by their actions, have become "a part of the new bourgeoisie or their ally."[76] In his most complete analysis of the situation in the Soviet Union, written the following year, he made his multicausal argument even clearer:

[74] 1964f:20.
[75] As early as 1959 he spoke of these three "fronts"—ideological, political, and economic—as those on which revisionism was to be combated (1959x: 72).
[76] 1963d:60f.

The activities of the bourgeoisie . . . , its corrupting effects in the political, economic, ideological, and cultural and educational fields, the existence of spontaneous capitalist tendencies among urban and rural small producers, and the influence of the remaining bourgeois rights and the force of habit of the old society all constantly breed political degenerates in the ranks of the working class and party and government organizations, new bourgeois elements and embezzlers and grafters in state enterprises owned by the whole people, and bourgeois intellectuals in the cultural and educational institutions and intellectual circles.[77]

It is by no means the case that Mao ignored the economic factor in his discussions of embourgeoisement. Indeed, in later years, that factor came to be emphasized even above political and ideological considerations. The creation through economic causes of a new bourgeois class in the countryside is a problem that Mao long pondered. Land reform left class inequities in the countryside, he noted in 1955,[78] and the relatively well-off shared in the spontaneous tendency toward capitalism of which Lenin warned.[79] The problem was exacerbated by the fact that, after the end of cooperativization, no further attention was devoted to the problem of the class struggle in the countryside; and, left to itself, such a situation could only deteriorate, not ameliorate.[80] Furthermore, and even more interestingly, Mao suggested that the polarization of city and countryside, particularly as that is manifested in the system of ownership and the distribution of resources, can put the urban proletariat in the position of exploiting the rural peasantry—a position analogous to that of the bourgeoisie *vis-à-vis* the proletariat in a capitalist society. So long as the industrial sector is dominated by state ownership—"ownership of the whole people"—and the rural sector is dominated by collective ownership, and so long as capital derived from agriculture is used to finance industrialization, this potential for polarization remains, he argued.[81]

Shortly before his death, discussing the economic causes of embourgeoisement, Mao once again took up the question of "bourgeois right." The term is Marx's, drawn from his *Critique*

[77] 1964n:9.
[78] 1955g:137.
[79] 1955d:20f., 25f.
[80] 1963b:318f.
[81] 1961b:245; 1963e:41.

of the Gotha Program, in which he describes the inequalities that arise from the fact that, although individual laborers vary with regard to their productivity, they are nonetheless paid equal amounts on the basis of the time they have spent.[82] Lenin summarized the concept in *State and Revolution* as follows: "Bourgeois right . . . gives to unequal individuals in return for unequal (really unequal) amounts of labor, equal amounts of products."[83]

The problem, as Mao identified it in late 1958, is that an economy in transition to socialism, by engaging in the production of commodities and establishing a multilevel wage system, incorporates within itself a system of inequality that is likely to lead, in turn, to a polarization and to the creation of a new exploitative class.[84] Although he was optimistic in 1958 that the communes might be able to institute a system of distribution according to need, rather than one based on labor contributed,[85] the failure of the communes to achieve such a system rendered him increasingly concerned with this problem, which he ultimately came to view as one that can only be controlled, not eliminated, over the short run, and that by means of the continued reliance on the dictatorship of the proletariat.[86]

The problem of embourgeoisement is more than merely economic in origin, however. It has, as well, its ideological side. Here Mao focussed on two aspects: the fact that socialist systems are surrounded by powerful functioning bourgeois societies with ideological systems in conflict with socialism is an important cause of the corruption of those within the socialist system. There is, moreover, what Mao referred to frequently as the "force of habit

[82] Tucker, ed., *Marx-Engels Reader*, p. 387.

[83] James E. Connor, ed., *Lenin on Politics and Revolution: Selected Writings* (New York: Pegasus, 1968), p. 223.

[84] At Zhengzhou at the height of the Great Leap Forward, he observed that bourgeois right "must be destroyed, destroyed every day, such as the emphasis on qualification, the emphasis on grade levels, the failure to see the benefit of the supply system. . . . The grade level system is the father-son relationship, the cat-mouse relationship. It must be destroyed all the time" (1958uu:131). The following year, commenting on a text of Stalin's, he made the same point: "The concept of bourgeois rights must definitely be eliminated. Wages, [preferential] treatment and grades are all wrong" (1959b:189f.).

[85] 1958pp:5.

[86] "Our country is at present practicing a commodity system, and the wage system is unequal too, there being the eight-grade wage system, etc. These can only be restricted under the dictatorship of the proletariat" (1975a).

of the old society." This problem is compounded by the fact that the socialization of young people in the socialist society is inevitably placed in the hands of intellectuals, that group in the society most likely to be adversely affected by external and historical sources of bourgeois ideas. "At this crucial moment of class struggle," he said in 1967, "it is necessary to stress the transformation of one's own world outlook. . . . Otherwise, if bourgeois ideology is not liquidated, one is bound to head in the wrong direction."[87] The nature of this ideology is suggested in a pair of comments dating from the early 1960s. In the first, arguing the necessity of eliminating bourgeois ideology, he offered the following examples of what he had in mind in using that term: "contesting for position, contesting for rank, wanting to increase wages and giving higher wages to the intellectual worker and lower wages to the physical laborer are all remnants of bourgeois ideology. To each according to his worth is prescribed by law, and it is also a bourgeois thing."[88] Three years later he turned to yet another aspect of bourgeois ideology, citing a work style of arrogance and complacency as a manifestation of a small-producer mentality linked with an idealist position, with individualism, and thus with the bourgeoisie.[89] In an especially interesting passage, he suggested how the force of these ideas resulted in a change of class. As we have seen, class is defined in the recent period as much on the basis of political attitude as on the basis of economic position. In 1959 he suggested that rightist views in the political sphere were to be linked with the bourgeoisie and that, in turn, those who espoused these views, despite their class origins, should thus be linked with the bourgeois class.[90] Those who espouse "rightist" ideological principles are likely to undergo a process of embourgeoisement. Once that process is complete, members of the new class construct their own ideological justification of what they have experienced, attempting to defend it in Marxist-Leninist terms. This ideological justification Mao identified with the term "revisionism."[91]

[87] 1967j:10.   [88] 1960a.

[89] 1963k:88. In 1959 he posed the problem thus: "I say that anyone who is malicious is bound to go to his opposite side. As regards the class of the world, the party of the world, class enterprises as well as people's enterprises, anyone who is malicious is bound to go to his opposite side" (1959bb: 79).

[90] 1959s:50.

[91] In 1956 Mao listed five points which, he argued, encompass the "funda-

The third aspect of the process of embourgeoisement—the political—is in many respects the most important element of Mao's explanation of the process. This aspect of the question was paramount in the Cultural Revolution when he called for the defeat of the "handful of persons in authority taking the capitalist road," "not only organizationally, but also politically, ideologically, and theoretically."[92] It is not merely a question of individuals of dubious class background wielding power in organizations that troubled Mao, but rather a belief that the wielding of power in an organization may bring about the embourgeoisement of an individual of good class background. Individuals in authority divorce themselves from those whom they are there to serve, assume "bureaucratic airs," and come to be totally absorbed in the maintenance and preservation of their own positions and the perquisites associated with them.[93] All of these are characteristics,

---

mental experience of the Soviet Union in revolution and construction," which "we commonly refer to as the path of the October Revolution," and which constitute "universally applicable truths of Marxism-Leninism." The points are as follows: (1) The formation of a Communist party by the proletariat using Marxism-Leninism as its guide, and based on the principles of democratic centralism. The party establishes "close links with the masses, strives to become the core of the laboring masses and educates its party members and the masses of people in Marxism-Leninism." (2) Led by the party, the proletariat seizes state power from the bourgeoisie by means of violent revolution. (3) The proletariat, led by the party, establishes a dictatorship of the proletariat under which counterrevolution is crushed, and nationalization of industry and collectivization of agriculture are undertaken, "thereby eliminating the system of exploitation, private ownership of the means of production and classes." (4) "The state, led by the proletariat and the Communist party, leads the people in the planned development of the socialist economy and culture . . . and works for the transition to communist society." (5) The foreign policy of this state involves opposition to imperialist aggression, support of the equality of all nations, defense of world peace, and adherence to the principles of proletarian internationalism (1956n:29f.). These five points, then, are the core concepts, in Mao's eyes, of Marxism-Leninism, and, although they should be adapted to local and historical circumstances, deviations from them are to be regarded as revisionism. Cf. 1964f.

[92] 1967j:7.

[93] In 1958 he spoke of the error of cadres who "seek honor and position" and thereby adopt bourgeois patterns of thought. In 1965 he spoke of bureaucrats who follow the capitalist road as "new bourgeois elements" "in a state of class conflict with the workers," and poor and lower-middle peasants (1965c:99, 120). He has on many occasions denounced the practice

as we have seen, of the bourgeoisie, as Mao described that class.

The causes of embourgeoisement are, in Mao's view, intricately interrelated, and the fact of embourgeoisement necessitates his theory of the continuation of the revolution under the dictatorship of the proletariat. As we have seen, he argues that the causes of retrogressive transformation in a socialist society are threefold: there are economic, ideological, and political causes of embourgeoisement. Economic causation works on leaders and led alike. Wherever there are wage differences or potentials for one individual or group to exploit another economically, the possibility of embourgeoisement exists. The solution here is a continuation of the revolution in the form of an unceasing imposition of the dictatorship of the proletariat to avoid the ill effects of a temporarily necessary unequal system.

Similarly, the ideological causes of embourgeoisement are as likely to affect those who are led as those who lead. The solution for this problem is one of correct socialization and resocialization. A continuation of the revolution is necessary here, to insure that both personnel and methods of socialization are legitimate and correct.

Political and organizational causes of embourgeoisement, on the other hand, affect the levels of society differentially. Those in positions of authority are those who are most likely to suffer the ill effects that those positions have the potential of inflicting. For this reason, the political-organizational problem becomes the most acute, for if the very leaders in whose hands is vested the responsibility for conducting a *révolution en permanence* are subject to corruption as a result of that responsibility, then special measures are required, and this becomes the central problem in dealing with the question as a whole.

In the mid-1960s the extreme solution that Mao proposed for the problem of embourgeoisement was a Cultural Revolution, which he described in advance as the "final test which will eliminate class distinction and reduce the 'three great differences.' "[94] Two years later the solution seemed less than final: he described the movement as a "great victory," but acknowledged that the

---

of according special privileges to cadres as a group, a practice particularly subject to attack during the Cultural Revolution (see, for example, 1961a: 306f.; 1964b; 1964p).

[94] 1966i:25.

"defeated class" would continue to struggle for decades.[95] It is to a closer investigation of the problem of authority within organizations and its potential for corruption that we turn in the next chapter.

[95] 1968i.

Chapter Five

ON ORGANIZATION

> Forms of revolutionary organization must be
> adapted to the necessities of revolutionary
> struggle. If a form of organization is no longer
> adapted to the necessities of the struggle, then
> this form of organization must be abolished.[1]

Mao had, on balance, a profoundly ambivalent attitude toward organizations. On the one hand, he saw organization as the indispensable means that makes revolution possible; on the other hand, he came to believe that the revolutionary organization itself can become both locus and cause for the corruption of revolutionary goals and their abandonment in favor of goals that move society in the opposite, counterrevolutionary direction. As an illustration of this ambivalence, we find him at one point extolling the fact that the Chinese Communist party succeeded in organizing the Chinese population—a population that Sun Zhongshan had referred to as analogous to a sheet of sand in its lack of cohesion.[2] At another point, he spoke of the advantages of the fact that, when the party and army were engaged in guerrilla warfare, organization was of necessity very loose and cadres were, as a consequence, all "travelers." The post-Liberation organization is a much different, and, he implied, less satisfactory one because of its fixity. Speaking of its members he said, "we should think of ways and means to chase them out the door and turn them into travelers."[3]

This ambivalent attitude of Mao's with regard to organizations is reminiscent of the later work of Jean-Paul Sartre. The two theorists start, it is true, from very different problems and premises. Although there are existential elements in Mao's treatment of the concept of class, he is far from taking the radically individualist point of view typical of the early Sartre. Despite their differences, however, the conclusions the two men reached con-

[1] 1943a:422. [2] 1955b:53.
[3] 1958p:88.

cerning the relationship between the organization and individual praxis are strikingly similar. Moreover, it is instructive to refer to Sartre's argument, since nowhere in Mao's writing did he make fully explicit his own line of reasoning that led him to conclude, as did Sartre, that the organization, which begins by making concerted effort possible, ends by preventing any action from taking place. It will thus be possible for us to understand how such an argument might be made, and we can then match this argument against what we know of Mao's position on the question.

In his early philosophic work, *L'Etre et le néant*, Sartre considered man's freedom to be absolute. "There is only one limit to freedom, and that is freedom itself; we can, so to speak, be nothing else but free."[4] The condition of scarcity, which he later came to regard as a tragic flaw in our age, impinges on this freedom. In his *Critique de la raison dialectique* Sartre considered the problem of social relations in the context of scarcity. He saw individuals as obliged to enter relationships of cooperation and conflict with others for the scarce objects that are necessary to sustain life, and as thereby jeopardizing the absolute nature of their individual freedom.

The existential person is defined by his or her action, and the nature of that action for Sartre is the "project." In response to a perceived need, individuals "pro-ject" themselves into a future state where this need is fulfilled.[5] There are four stages or types of relationships through which this process of group formation proceeds: the series, the *groupe en fusion*, the group, and the institution. The first relationship between the individual and his fellow humans that results from the condition of scarcity, the "series," is a group of individuals united only by their interest in a common object. Sartre uses the example of a group waiting for a bus to describe this concept: "these separate men form a group *insofar as* they are all standing on the same sidewalk protecting them from the cars crossing the square, *insofar as* they have grouped around the same bus stop, etc. And especially, these individuals form a group in that they have a *common interest*."[6]

[4] Wilfrid Desan, *The Tragic Finale* (New York: Harper and Row, 1960), p. 97.

[5] Jean-Paul Sartre, *L'Etre et le néant* (Paris: Gallimard, 1953), p. 173.

[6] Robert Denoon Cumming, ed., *The Philosophy of Jean-Paul Sartre* (New York: Modern Library, 1965), p. 459.

The series is characterized by a succession (the individuals at the bus stop have formed a line), but lacks a structure or hierarchy, and is incapable of common action.[7]

Structure and hierarchy come as a response to pressure from outside the nascent group. Such pressure transforms the series into what Sartre terms a *groupe en fusion*. Here his analogy is taken from the formation of a revolutionary force from isolated individuals as a result of a perception of being encircled, and the subsequent act of storming the Bastille in 1789. His concept here is related to that of Marx, who, as we have noted, saw class consciousness arising as a response to oppression by another class; it is related as well to the same theme as developed by Georg Simmel and the "conflict theorists" for whom his thought was seminal.[8]

Looking at the *groupe en fusion* from the point of view of the individual, Sartre argues that, when confronted by an organized opponent, the individual concludes that his or her project will best be served by an alliance with those individuals who have roughly similar projects. For purposes of the moment, those projects that the group do not have in common are overlooked. The action taken on the basis of this temporary alliance constitutes an objective, if shortlived, bond that unites the *groupe en fusion*.

The temporary nature of the *groupe en fusion* means that, if left to itself, it will naturally disband again into new "series" in which men and women are once again acting on the basis of individual projects. If preservation of the group becomes the object, additional bonds are necessary. "When freedom becomes a common *praxis* in order to establish the group's permanence, producing its own inertia by itself and in mediated reciprocity, this new status is called *the oath*."[9] While the oath brings about the third stage in this process—the group—it is by itself insufficient to prevent individuals from leaving the group, and the counteracting of this insufficiency gives rise to a state of *terreur*. "The fear is now that of seeing the group itself dissolve into seriality. In order to avoid that danger, the group itself exerts pressure on its members, and they themselves are thus in danger *within* the group.

[7] Wilfrid Desan, *The Marxism of Jean-Paul Sartre* (New York: Doubleday, 1965), p. 110.

[8] Georg Simmel, *Conflict* (New York: The Free Press, 1964).

[9] Cumming, ed., *The Philosophy of Jean-Paul Sartre*, p. 474.

Violence threatens them not from the outside, but from the inside, that is, from the group itself. . . . This results in what Sartre calls a state of *terreur*."[10]

The final stage in the progression away from individual action is the formation of the institution. Whereas each of the preceding structures has been analytical, the institution, on the other hand, Sartre refers to as being "both *praxis* and thing."[11] On the one hand, the institution is "ossified *praxis*," which "receives its ossification from our powerlessness."[12] On the other hand, it is a structure that "posits itself, by and in its inert-being, as essentiality, *defining men as the inessential means* of its perpetuation."[13]

In Desan's words, "when individual freedom is alienated, or entrusted to the group, and only the 'function' is left, we are on our way to what we call an institution. This implies two main transformations: the introduction of a certain desired inertia, and the appearance of authority."[14]

If Sartrian philosophical prose tends occasionally to obscure the thrust of his argument, the language of his plays is considerably clearer. In *The Condemned of Altona*, Father von Gerlach, magnate of a large shipbuilding firm, is preparing to turn over his position at the head of that institution to his reluctant son:

Father: The largest shipbuilding firm is handed to you and that breaks your heart. Why?

. . .

Werner: To decide! To decide! To be responsible for everything. Alone. On behalf of a hundred thousand men. And you have managed to live.

Father: It's a long time since I have decided anything. I sign the correspondence. Next year you will sign it. . . . For repairs, Gelber will be there. A remarkable man, you know, who has been with us for twenty-five years. . . . He is your employee. You pay him to let you know what orders to give.[15]

In short, then, it is Sartre's view that the institution reduces inno-

---

[10] Desan, *The Marxism of Jean-Paul Sartre*, p. 140.
[11] Cumming, ed., *The Philosophy of Jean-Paul Sartre*, p. 477.
[12] Ibid., p. 479.   [13] Ibid., p. 477. Emphasis added.
[14] Desan, *The Marxism of Jean-Paul Sartre*, p. 175.
[15] Jean-Paul Sartre, *The Condemned of Altona* (New York: Vintage, 1961), pp. 10f.

vative human action to a mere response to stimulus; strategic decisions give place to tactical ones. Action, as Hannah Arendt has defined that term—public, creative, and heroic[16]—is precluded within the confines of the institution.

Despite the fact that Mao believed strongly in the need for authority, it is the Sartrian categories of *groupe en fusion* and group that are most characteristic of the organization of the revolutionary party as he saw it. The anarchic freedom of the individual in seriality, and the rigidification implied in the institution must both be avoided, particularly if the revolution is to be maintained *en permanence*. The project of revolutionary change requires sufficient cohesion so that individual members of the group may be transformed, but at the same time, sufficient freedom so that innovative and novel action is still possible.

Sartre's view of the tendency toward institutionalization, however, is in some sense a fatalistic one.[17] For the revolutionary, the Sartrian group is only a compromise solution. The truly malleable individual is the individual in the institution who has sacrificed his or her essentiality to that of the structure; and the truly effective authority is that which accrues to the sovereign power in the institution in proportion as it is abdicated by the individual. This expanding power over the increasingly malleable individual is essentially directionless power: "It is a long time since I have decided anything. I sign the correspondence." The power to act at will is gained at the cost of the capacity to act creatively.

Thus it is that at least a part of the strong mistrust which Mao manifested toward organizations was based on his perception, which he shared with Sartre—though he reached it by a very different route—that the structure and operation of organizations can sap away the very freedom to initiate, which power should permit. It was clearly this problem that he had in mind when he complained that, on the eve of the Cultural Revolution in 1965, he found himself "unable to insert even a pin" into the tight structure of the Party Committee in Beijing,[18] despite the fact that its leaders were his nominal subordinates in his capacity as chairman of the party. He felt himself, he said to André Malraux, who visited him in the summer of that year, wholly alienated

[16] Hannah Arendt, *The Human Condition* (New York: Harcourt, Brace and World, 1963), pp. 326ff.
[17] Desan, *The Marxism of Jean-Paul Sartre*, p. 181.
[18] 1966q:75.

from the institutions he had helped to create. "I am," he said, "alone with the masses, waiting."[19]

Mao's experience and observations of organizations and organizational behavior were by no means confined to that type of organization we most commonly associate with the term "bureaucracy." Although the Chinese Communist party has created modern bureaucratic structures in the economic, political, and social realms, and although many such structures existed in China prior to Liberation, the term "bureaucracy" in the Chinese context must also encompass the very long history of "bureaucratic" rule in China by a scholar-gentry class whose behavior in office is not manifestly illuminated by a Weberian analysis of organizational performance. Mao's critique of organizational behavior as a contribution and at the same time as a threat to the achievement of the goals of the revolution must be read in the context both of our own experience of bureaucratic organization, and of the very different experience of bureaucratic behavior in "traditional" China.

I have thus organized the discussion that follows around five elements of the Weberian ideal type of a rational-legal bureaucratic organization: the division of labor, the hierarchical structure of organizations, the tendency toward routinization, the formalistic impersonality of officials, and the goal of efficient operation toward which the bureaucracy strives.[20] Alongside each of these elements I have set the equivalent elements of an ideal typification of the traditional Chinese bureaucracy. Since any such effort at constructing an ideal type involves a distortion or exaggeration of actual practice, I have included, as well, indications of the way in which Chinese and Western bureaucracies have been observed to function so as to deviate from the ideal typification. Finally, with each of these elements of the Weberian ideal type I have included Mao's comments on the relevant aspect of organizations.

Mao's emphasis in these comments on organizational life is

[19] 1965h:377.

[20] These categories are derived from those used by Peter M. Blau in his discussion of the Weberian ideal type in *Bureaucracy in Modern Society* (New York: Random House, 1956), pp. 28ff. They are in turn derived from Weber's own description. Cf. H. H. Gerth and C. Wright Mills, eds., *From Max Weber: Essays in Sociology* (New York: Oxford University Press, 1958), pp. 196-198.

consistently upon performance rather than on structure—on the actions of individuals within the organization rather than on the nature of the setting in which they operate. Because of this, his comments generally refer to modes of behavior—both descriptive and prescriptive—of men and women in organizations. It is nonetheless perfectly possible to extrapolate from these modes of behavior a reasonably clear sense of Mao's perception of the structure of organizations and the relationship of that structure to the behavior of the members of those organizations.[21]

THE DIVISION OF LABOR

"The regular activities required for purposes of the organization," Weber wrote, "are distributed in a fixed way as official duties."[22] Peter Blau, commenting on this element of Weber's concept, noted that "the clear-cut division of labor makes it possible to employ only specialized experts in each particular position and to make every one of them responsible for the effective performance of his duties."[23]

Western observers of contemporary bureaucracies have noted that the escalation of technical specialization in the purposes of specific bureaucracies has brought about a bifurcation within those bureaucratic organizations as between the function of operation and that of management—a bifurcation that is not encompassed in Weber's conception. Thus it has come to be the case that the manager is placed in his position not because he possesses the specialized expertise appropriate to the execution of the "official duties" associated with that office, but rather because he possesses managerial skills seen as requisite to the control of those who do possess specialized expertise. Under such circumstances there may well arise a conflict of loyalties based on this bifurcation of functions, where managers tend to become "locals," loyal

[21] Alternative discussions of Mao's organizational principles as they are related to Western concepts of organization are found in Stephen Andors, *China's Industrial Revolution: Policy Planning and Management, 1949 to the Present* (New York: Pantheon, 1977); Harry Harding, Jr., "Mobilization, Bureaucracy and Professionalism: The Organizational Issue in Chinese Politics," Ph.D. dissertation, Stanford University, 1974; and Martin King Whyte, "Bureaucracy and Mobilization in China: The Maoist Critique," *American Sociological Review* 38:2 (1973), 149-163.

[22] Gerth and Mills, eds., *From Max Weber*, p. 196.

[23] Blau, *Bureaucracy*, pp. 28f.

to the organization, and where technical personnel tend to become "cosmopolitans," loyal to their technical profession.[24]

In contrast to Weber's formulation, the duties formally associated with office in the traditional Chinese bureaucracy required the qualities of a generalist, rather than those of a specialist or an expert. Preparation for the assumption of office was through the mastery of abstract learning that bore only indirect relevance to the problems encountered in that office.[25] As C. K. Yang has pointed out, the "generalization" of the bureaucrat was bolstered not only by the nature of the examinations, but by philosophical rationalization and structural provisions, as well. He notes that the origins of the distinction between *ti* (essence) and *yong* (function) that loomed so large in the latter-day attempts by nineteenth-century Chinese modernizers to preserve traditional values while borrowing Western techniques "for practical purposes," originated as a rationalization for the distinction between the bureaucrat's preparation by mastery of the general solution (*ti*) and his functioning in office by reaching specific solutions (*yong*).[26] With regard to bureaucratic structure, the generalist office holder was assisted by "specialist" subordinates who were not themselves "members" of the bureaucracy, in that the majority of them could not aspire to the actual holding of office.[27]

In this latter regard, then, the actual division of labor in the traditional Chinese bureaucracy is parallel in some respects to that in the contemporary Western bureaucracy. Not only is the basic

[24] See Alvin Gouldner, "Cosmopolitans and Locals: Toward an Analysis of Latent Social Roles," *Administrative Science Quarterly* 9:2 (1967), 23-45.

[25] It is true that the examination system varied greatly during the long course of its history in China, and that at certain periods greater emphasis was placed on the ability of the candidate to handle specific cases of governance. Nevertheless, the primary focus of the examinations over the longer term was generalized, rather than specific.

[26] C. K. Yang, "Some Characteristics of Chinese Bureaucratic Behavior," in David S. Nivison and Arthur F. Wright, eds., *Confucianism in Action* (Stanford: Stanford University Press, 1959).

[27] Probably the most complete secondary account of the mutually dependent relationship between bureaucrats and their subordinates is that of Tung-tsu Ch'ü in his book, *Local Government in China under the Ch'ing* (Cambridge: Harvard University Press, 1962). See also Thomas A. Metzger, *The Internal Organization of Ch'ing Bureaucracy: Legal, Normative and Communications Aspects* (Cambridge: Harvard University Press, 1975). Some of the same information is available in a quite different form in the "Judge Dee mysteries" of Robert Van Gulik. See, for example, *The Emperor's Pearl* (London: Heinemann, 1963).

distinction as between "staff" and "line" positions analogous in the two settings, but there existed some of the same tensions as between conflicting sources of power and authority for the two types of position in both cases. Perhaps the most important distinction between the traditional Chinese and the contemporary Western bureaucratic organization, then, is the traditional Chinese bureaucrat's glorification of generalization and his concomitant devaluation of specialization—a set of values that appears to have been, in large measure, shared by the specialists, as well.[28] In the Western setting, on the contrary, it is specialization that is valued both by the specialist and by the generalist—to the point where, as I have noted, the functions of the generalist manager are themselves taken to be a form of specialized knowledge.

The functional specialization implicit in the division of labor results in a system of recruitment which, Weber argued, must be based on achievement. Similarly, promotion within the bureaucracy must be based on achievement and seniority. As a result, from the point of view of the official, employment in the organization "constitutes a career," in Weber's words.[29] The purpose behind these bases for recruitment and promotion is not only to insure the quality of the human resources available to the organization, but also to increase employee loyalty to the organization.

It is obvious that the goals of efficiency and loyalty, and the criteria of achievement and seniority will sometimes prove antithetical rather than complementary in practice. Anthony Downs has noted that bureaucratic organizations are normally able to attract talent only for a limited time. As a corollary to this he observed that bureaus come to suffer from an "age lump"—old organizations characteristically have aged members who, because of their seniority, occupy positions that would otherwise be filled by younger and, presumably, more talented recruits.[30]

[28] Joseph Levenson's discussion of the "amateur ideal" in the Chinese tradition is relevant here; *Confucian China and Its Modern Fate* (Berkeley and Los Angeles: University of California Press, 1966), I, 15-43. Because of the nature and content of the generalized knowledge that was the exclusive possession of the official class, the bureaucrat became "tradition-oriented" rather than future-oriented, as Ambrose Y. C. King notes in his article, "The Behavior Patterns of Traditional Confucian Bureaucrats," *Chinese Journal of Administration* 8 (1967), 49-55.

[29] Max Weber, *The Theory of Social and Economic Organization*, translated and edited by Talcott Parsons (New York: Free Press, 1964), p. 334.

[30] Anthony Downs, *Inside Bureaucracy* (Boston: Little, Brown, 1967), pp. 13, 20f.

Like its Western counterpart, the ideal Chinese bureaucracy advanced achievement and seniority as the bases for recruitment and promotion. There is, however, a longstanding disagreement among scholars as to the degree to which achievement *per se* served as the criterion for office holding.[31] As we have noted earlier, even those who minimize the actual amount of social mobility in the system concede that the widespread myth of the openness of the bureaucracy to men of ability exerted an effective shaping force on traditional China.

Wealth was clearly an important determinant of bureaucratic recruitment in traditional China, for the leisure required to master the classics and to prepare for the examinations presupposed a certain minimal surplus above the level of subsistence on the part of the family of the prospective scholar. The basis of wealth in the traditional economy was land—even merchants followed the indirect route from commercial profit through land ownership to officialdom. Thus, although the Chinese bureaucracy was primarily a functional structure (and was kept that way by means of the law of avoidance, which prevented an official from serving in his home region), the bureaucrat's land-based wealth contributed a protofeudal character to the structure.[32]

A further deviation from the ideals of recruitment by achievement and promotion according to seniority resulted from the gap —both in time and in numbers—between the achievement of a degree and the appointment to office. In other words, there were many more degree holders than officials, and there was often a

[31] As noted earlier, the definitive work on the subject is that of Ho Ping-ti, *The Ladder of Success in Imperial China* (New York: Columbia University Press, 1962). Ho sees a relatively limited amount of social mobility, but argues that it was nevertheless a significant determinant of the composition of the Chinese elite over the long run. Karl Wittfogel (*Oriental Despotism* [New Haven: Yale University Press, 1957], p. 348) tends to minimize the effect of the examination system on recruitment by achievement, and thus on social mobility within the system as a whole. Cf. Franz Michael, "State and Society in Nineteenth Century China," *World Politics* 7 (1955), 419-433.

[32] S. N. Eisenstadt's distinction between what he calls "functional" and "ecological" (that is, territorially based) structures is relevant here. See his book, *The Political Systems of Empires* (Glencoe, Ill.: Free Press, 1963). In the Chinese case some degrees were simply purchased, thus bypassing the indirect route described here, but as Michael points out in "State and Society," the purchased degrees were the lowest in status, and the majority of those who purchased degrees occupied the less prestigious and less desirable official posts.

delay of many years between the receiving of the degree and the appointment to office.[33]

In spite of these deviations from the ideal, however, it is true that there was a high degree of homogeneity of background and experience in the group from which the bureaucracy recruited its members, a homogeneity that was not matched by the recruitment base from which Chinese bureaucrats were drawn during the Republican period.[34] In the case of Europe and the United States, this homogenous base is more reminiscent of the political bureaucracies of England and France than it is of equivalent organizations in the United States.

Considering Mao's view of the manner in which labor is divided and personnel are recruited and promoted in organizations, one finds it often stated that the "redness"—the high level of political consciousness—that he has put forward as a criterion for recruitment and promotion is in some sense a modern analogue for the Confucian knowledge that constituted a prerequisite to office holding in traditional times. Mao partially confirmed this analogy in a discussion of cadres policy in 1938:

> Throughout our national history there have been two sharply contrasting lines on the subject of the use of cadres, one being to "appoint people on their merit," and the other to "appoint people by favoritism." . . . The criterion the Communist Party should apply in its cadres policy is whether or not a cadre is resolute in carrying out the Party line, keeps to Party discipline, has close ties with the masses, has the ability to find his bearings independently, and is active, hard-working and unselfish. This is what is meant by "appointing people on their merit."[35]

It is also, in effect, what he meant when he referred to "redness" as a criterion for appointment. The distinction he has drawn here

[33] Michael gives figures in "State and Society" indicating that there were an average of about a million degree holders in traditional times. He uses a figure of forty thousand office holders, as does Yang ("Some Characteristics"). These figures result in a ratio of thirty-six degree holders to each occupant of an office. Michael also suggests that a delay of twenty to twenty-five years was not unusual between passing examinations and achievement of office, and that, as a result, it was not uncommon for a scholar to be fifty years old at the time he assumed his first office.

[34] King, "Chinese Bureaucracy in the Transitional Society," *Chinese Journal of Administration* 9 (1967), 28-39.

[35] 1938e:493/II, 202.

—that between the use of some criteria of ability as opposed to purely ascriptive or affective criteria in appointing to office—is not the same as the distinction I have been making between the use of generalized or specialized knowledge as the measure of "merit." Nonetheless, it is clear from Mao's description of what constitutes merit that it is, in fact, generalized, rather than specialized knowledge that serves as his first criterion.

Before we conclude, however, that Mao saw a bureaucratic organization staffed by generalists who are assisted by specialist subordinates as an ideal, and that he borrowed this ideal from his perception of the Chinese bureaucracy in traditional times, it is important that we look further at his conception of the role that specialized, practical, or technical knowledge should play in determining a potential cadre's "merit." In 1937, a little more than a year before the passage just cited was written, he made a somewhat more complete statement of the criteria for choosing the "tens of thousands" of new cadres needed to extend the party organization "all over the country" as the anti-Japanese war effort proceeded:

> They must be cadres and leaders versed in Marxism-Leninism, politically far-sighted, competent in work, full of the spirit of self-sacrifice, capable of tackling problems on their own, steadfast in the midst of difficulties, and loyal and devoted in serving the nation, the class and the Party. Such cadres and leaders must be free from selfishness, from individualistic heroism, ostentation, sloth, passivity, and sectarian arrogance, and they must be selfless national and class heroes; such are the qualities and the style of work demanded of the members, cadres and leaders of our Party.[36]

Certainly the thrust of this long list is to emphasize that generalized knowledge and personal qualities, rather than specialized knowledge, are to be taken as prerequisites for office holding. On the other hand, the phrase, "competent in work," is included, as well, in the list. That this kind of competence was important to Mao, though certainly not paramount in recruiting new cadres, is further suggested in his complaint two decades later on the eve of the Great Leap Forward concerning those in the party who

[36] 1937p:255/I, 291.

had become "mindless politicians," lacking in expertise and, as a result, in danger of "gradually losing their redness."[37]

Pursuing somewhat farther Mao's attack on obscurantism in organizational behavior, it is clear that certain common stereotypes concerning his approach to technical knowledge may be incorrect. In associating Mao with the "red" side of the contradiction between redness and technical or managerial expertise in organizational life, there is a tendency to ignore the fact that he called for a synthesis of red and expert—the creation of "red experts"—rather than a simple triumph of red over expert.

The first evidence in Mao's writing of the dialectical cast to his opposition to obscurantism, and his consequent attention to the need for expertise, came in 1949, when he began to devote his attention to the new problems posed by the fast-approaching victory of the Communist revolution. "From now on," he wrote in February 1949, "the formula followed in the past twenty years, 'first the rural areas, then the cities,' will be reversed and changed to the formula, 'first the cities, then the rural areas.' "[38] Pursuant to this, Mao insisted that cadres acquire administrative skills. They were to learn to be "good at managing industry and commerce, good at running schools, newspapers, news agencies and broadcasting stations, good at handling foreign affairs, good at handling problems relating to the democratic parties and people's organizations, good at adjusting the relations between the cities and the rural areas and solving the problems of food, coal and other daily necessities and good at handling monetary and financial problems."[39] For the cadres to shoulder these new tasks, their ranks must be augmented, he argued, by thirty to forty thousand new members.[40] The new cadre and the old alike must "have a head for figures": "we must attend to the quantitative aspect of a situation or problem and make a basic quantitative analysis."[41] Finally, in calling for a new system of reports, Mao went so far as to engage in a bit of bureaucratic pettifoggery himself: "Each report should be limited to about a thousand words and, except in special

[37] 1958b:77.

[38] 1949a:1407/IV, 337. Cf. 1949b:1428/IV, 363.

[39] 1949a:1407/IV, 337. This call is addressed to cadres in the army; essentially the same tasks are set for party cadres in the Second Plenum report (1949b:1430/IV, 365).

[40] 1948c:1350/IV, 365.   [41] 1949c:1443/IV, 379.

cases, should not exceed two thousand words. When all questions cannot be covered in one report, write two. . . . The comprehensive report should be concise in content and succinct in wording and should point out the problems or controversial issues. It should be written and telegraphed early in every odd month."[42]

Mao's opposition to obscurantism was not always addressed simply to a lack of administrative skills. He was concerned, as well, with technical expertise. As early as 1943 he called on cadres to "master all of the skills involved in leading the masses in production."[43] This emphasis was redoubled when he returned to the question twelve years later. Speaking in July 1955, Mao said, "We are now carrying out a revolution not only in the social system . . . but also in technology . . . and the two revolutions are interconnected."[44] On the eve of the Great Leap Forward, a movement often taken as a resurgent agrarian primitivism, he spoke as follows on the stages of development in China since Liberation: "In seven years cooperativization has been accomplished and productive relations have changed. This was followed by the launching of rectification, and after that, by technological revolution."[45]

Avoiding obscurantism in the face of the technical revolution required, as Mao saw it, a vast educational effort of a new kind, for even in his own case he recognized a deficiency in technical knowledge. "Before August of last year," he said in 1959, "I devoted my main energy to revolution. Being basically not versed in construction, I knew nothing about industrial planning."[46] In the "Sixty Work Methods" he devoted considerable attention to the

---

[42] 1948a:1263/IV, 177. It is interesting, parenthetically, to compare these comments of Mao's with Lenin's discussion of the same subject at much the same point in the Russian Revolution. In "State and Revolution," written in August 1917, Lenin argued that because of the advance of technology, "the great majority of the functions of the old 'state power' have become so simplified and can be reduced to such exceedingly simple operations of registration, filing and checking that they can easily be performed by every literate person"; James E. Connor, ed., *Lenin on Politics and Revolution: Selected Writings* (New York: Pegasus, 1968), p. 228. Subsequently, however, as Moshe Lewin argues in his interesting study of *Lenin's Last Struggle* (New York: Pantheon, 1968), Lenin became a strong foe of the obscurantism he saw developing among his colleagues and, in the course of arguing for his own "cultural revolution," advocated examinations by which to insure the quality of the newly recruited cadres.

[43] 1943d:914/III, 132.   [44] 1955d:19.
[45] 1958d:93f. Cf. 1960d.   [46] 1959r:38.

problem of resolving the contradiction between redness and expertise, politics and technique, or, as he described it there, between "armchair politicians" and "pragmatists."[47] It is necessary that *everyone* learn technique and science, Mao argued,[48] and, employing a traditional term in a new context, called this educational effort a *xiucai*, or self-cultivation, for the proletariat.[49]

Finally, as we have seen, Mao called in 1963 for a tripartite "class struggle, struggle for production, and [struggle for] scientific experimentation."[50] In preparation for this, he spoke the following year of· the project then underway "carefully [to] sum up our experience and formulate comprehensive guiding principles, policies, and methods for the seven fields of work, that is, industry, agriculture, trade, education, military affairs, the government, and the party."[51]

As these comments suggest, Mao was by no means an advocate of "redness" alone as a prerequisite for office. As I have suggested, he advocated instead a synthesis between general (or political) and specific (or technical and managerial) knowledge within each office holder. He appears to have realized, however, that achieving such a synthesis is a problematic process. One of the "five fundamental principles for running socialist enterprises well" that he included in the "Constitution for the Anshan Iron and Steel Company" in 1960 was that of "close cooperation among work-

---

[47] 1958e:6f.

[48] Ibid., p. 5. It is worth noting that very similar arguments were being made in American education circles in 1958 in the aftermath of the successful Russian satellite launching the previous year.

[49] Ibid., p. 12. This was a decade before the term *xiucai* (cultivation of one's talents), and the closely related term, *peiyang* (to cultivate or develop) became terms of opprobrium, having taken on overtones of bourgeois selfishness because of their association with the term *xiuyang* (self-cultivation) in the title of Liu Shaoqi's book, *On the Self-Cultivation of Communist Party Members*. If the terms themselves do, in fact, possess such overtones of selfishness, it is not for etymological reasons, but because of their association with the selfish motivations that were presumed to have governed the socialization process of the traditional scholar-bureaucrat.

[50] 1963c. Cf. 1963d:70f.

[51] 1962a:177. Among the policy documents he mentioned as being completed were "the sixty articles for agricultural work, the seventy articles for industrial enterprises, the sixty articles for higher education, and the forty articles for scientific research." These comments are found in a section of the speech that explores at some length the problem of "understanding the objective world" (ibid., pp. 170-180).

ers, cadres, and technicians,"[52] suggesting that he saw such cooperation as difficult to achieve at times. The danger is one of fragmentation on the basis of a narrow professionalism, a problem to which we shall return shortly. At the same time, he was at pains to show that redness and expertise are not fundamentally unsynthesizable. "For Marx," he wrote later in 1960, "the progress of natural science and technology further strengthen the whole position of the Marxist world outlook and the materialist conception of history, and certainly does not shake it. . . . For the welfare of their peoples and in the interest of peace for the people of the whole world, the socialist countries should, wherever possible, master more and more . . . new techniques serving the well-being of the people."[53]

With regard to this first element of bureaucratic organization —the division of labor and the resultant basis for recruitment and promotion within the organization—Mao seems thus to have seen both good and undesirable features in both the Chinese and the Western ideal types. His solution was one that was weighted, however, more toward generalization than specialization. He advocated the creation of *duomianshou*, or "many-faceted individuals" who would encompass both the general and the special knowledge that he saw as requisite to proper performance in organizations.

THE HIERARCHICAL STRUCTURE OF ORGANIZATIONS

A second aspect of the bureaucratic organization as seen by Weber is the hierarchical structure within which lower and higher offices are related to one another. These relationships involve duty and authority, as Blau has observed:

> To be able to discharge his responsibility for the work of his subordinates, [the official] has authority over them, which means that he has the right to issue directives and they have the duty to obey them. This authority is strictly circumscribed and confined to those directives that are relevant for official

[52] 1960d.
[53] 1960e:18. On the following page appears the oft-cited sentence, "Marxist-Leninists have always maintained that in world history it is not technique but man, the masses of people, that determine the fate of mankind." Reading this sentence out of the context of the paragraphs that precede it has led many to what is, in my view, an incorrect interpretation of its meaning.

operations. The use of status prerogatives to extend the power of control over subordinates beyond these limits does not constitute the legitimate exercise of bureaucratic authority.[54]

It is in this context that Weber advanced the distinction between power and authority that we discussed in Chapter Three—one in which power is associated with individuals and authority with positions or roles.

As I have already noted, in contemporary practice the legitimacy of the official is often diminished by his or her inability to comprehend the technical subtleties of the work of his or her subordinates. This problem is in turn related to the more general question of the flow of information and authority within a bureaucratic organization. Anthony Downs sees the functioning of the organizational hierarchy as involving complementary vertical flows of information and authority. He notes that in actual practice there is at each level of the hierarchy a "leakage" of information flowing upward and authority flowing downward as a result of the conflicting interests that exist among the levels.[55] The result of this leakage is, in Downs' view, a "rigidity cycle" wherein control mechanisms are set up to minimize leakage, the organization becomes rigidified and unresponsive to change as a result of these new appendages,[56] and this ossification leads, in turn, to the formation of a new "breakout" organization, the purpose of which is to carry out the function of the original organization.[57]

[54] Blau, *Bureaucracy*, p. 29.

[55] Downs, *Inside Bureaucracy*, pp. 134f.

[56] Similarly, Crozier sees a bureaucratic "vicious circle," which results from the imposition of impersonal rules and an increased centralization to enforce these rules. These measures lead to the isolation of the strata in an organization, Crozier argues, and a resultant increase in the saliency of peer pressure for determining individual behavior. Such a trend is normally met by the organization's leaders with an increase of impersonal rules and centralized enforcement; *The Bureaucratic Phenomenon* (Chicago: University of Chicago Press, 1963), pp. 190ff. Both descriptions are reminiscent of the problem posed in Sartre's existential anthropological approach to the organization with which we began this discussion.

[57] Downs, *Inside Bureaucracy*, pp. 158f. He offers as an example of such a "breakout" organization the mechanism established to run a "campaign" in Soviet politics. A Chinese campaign structure would be an equally relevant example. Elsewhere Downs speaks of the "law of ever-expanding control," by which he means that monitoring bureaus used for control of a main bureau themselves come to require controlling agencies. "The problem of

It is in the hierarchical structure of the bureaucracy and the attendant nature of authority within bureaucratic organizations that the Chinese and the Western bureaucratic models differ most strikingly, and an understanding of this difference is crucial to our understanding of those aspects of bureaucratic organization against which Mao reacts most strongly. Unlike the Western case, where status and authority in a bureaucratic organization are limited, in Blau's words, to "those directives that are relevant for official operations," in the Chinese case the basis of the bureaucrat's authority was by no means so circumscribed.

While leaving open the question of the general validity of Karl Wittfogel's thesis concerning the unique nature of something called "oriental despotism," I would nonetheless agree with his observation that the Chinese bureaucracy held a monopoly of both status and power within the traditional Chinese system.[58] Whereas the Western bureaucrat operates in a setting filled with competing bureaucratic organizations, there was but a single such organization in the Chinese setting, and its officials enjoyed a status based not only on their organizational authority, but also on their nearly exclusive command of economic, cultural, social, and political authority.[59] Final political authority, it is true, rested in the emperor and his court, but, as Levenson has argued, the emperor was heavily dependent upon the bureaucracy for the exercise of that authority, and the throne and the bureaucracy came to exist in what he described as a state of tension in the partitioning of power and authority.[60] Thus, unlike the Western bureaucracy, which functions, according to Weber, to execute efficiently the orders of a political elite, in the Chinese case bureaucratic and political elite were one.

'guarding the guardians,'" he notes, "has no satisfactory solution" (ibid., pp. 150, 153).

[58] Wittfogel, *Oriental Despotism*, pp. 338, 368.

[59] Wittfogel notes that the overlapping nature of these types of authority is suggested in the overtone of the Chinese word *zhunzi*. Normally translated "gentlemen," it carries not only the meaning of social status and culturedness, but also of political power and, to a lesser extent, of wealth as well (ibid., p. 320). It is important to note, however, that the primary determinant of status among the Chinese elite was office holding. Michael notes this in connection with his demonstration that office holding also constituted the primary basis of gentry wealth in traditional China ("State and Society").

[60] Levenson, *Confucian China*, II, Part II, Chapters 2-5.

The result of this unitary hierarchy within the Chinese elite was to make the Chinese official highly conscious of position within that hierarchy. King remarks that the Chinese official invariably took into account relative hierarchical position before entering into personal relationships.[61] On the other hand, the relative geographical isolation of many of the individual officials serving as *xian* (county) magistrates meant that the preponderance of their social relations, though predicated upon a sense of hierarchy, actually took place outside of the official setting that was the source of that sense of hierarchy.

The question of hierarchy in organizations is of particular importance in the attempt to understand how Mao has come to see organizational life as a potential locus for the process of embourgeoisement. His reactions to the problem of hierarchy are perhaps best understood by grouping them under the rubrics of structure and operation. With regard to structure, Mao follows closely Lenin's solution to the dilemma created by a commitment to egalitarianism on the one hand, and a commitment to effective action on the other: namely, Lenin's principle of democratic centralism. Violations in either direction that would upset the delicate balance between democracy and centralism are criticized by Mao. Authority, which Weber ties closely to bureaucratic structure, Mao treats as separable from that structure, as we have seen. It is, however, the operational question of the misuse of authority within bureaucratic organizations that Mao saw as the most important among several causes of the embourgeoisement of members of those organizations. With regard to operation, then, Mao's critique of the hierarchical structure of bureaucracy is at least reminiscent of that of Western organization theorists. He, too, is troubled by the tendency in organizations toward rigidification and the blockage of information flow.

Integral to an understanding of Mao's use of the Leninist principle of democratic centralism is the leadership method that he refers to as the "mass line." His description of this method, quoted here *in extenso*, is of particular interest because of the parallels one finds with his earlier description of the process of cognition discussed above[62]—parallels that he makes explicit in the conclusion of the passage:

[61] King, "Behavioral Patterns."

[62] John Lewis has discussed these parallels in his *Leadership in Communist China* (Ithaca: Cornell University Press, 1963), p. 72.

In all of the practical work of our Party, all correct leadership is necessarily "from the masses, to the masses." This means: take the ideas of the masses (scattered and unsystematic ideas) and concentrate them (through study turn them into concentrated and systematic ideas), then go to the masses and propagate and explain these ideas until the masses embrace them as their own, hold fast to them and translate them into action, and test the correctness of these ideas in such action. Then once again concentrate ideas from the masses and once again go to the masses so that the ideas are persevered in and carried through. And so on, over and over again in an endless spiral, with the ideas becoming more correct, more vital and richer each time. Such is the Marxist theory of knowledge.[63]

Speaking with André Malraux in 1965, Mao made his point yet more succinctly: "We must teach to the masses clearly what we have received from them confusedly."[64]

Although it is clear that, as Ed Hammond has shown in his discussion of the mass line, Mao was building upon positions already taken by Marx, Lenin, and Stalin in constructing his principle of a mass line method of leadership,[65] nevertheless it is also important to point up the originality of his position, exemplified by the degree to which he stressed the authority of the nonparty masses both to originate policy and to criticize the party for its incorrect implementation of that policy.[66] The mass line

[63] 1943b:854/III, 119.

[64] 1965h:362.

[65] Edward Hammond, "Marxism and the Mass Line," *Modern China* 4:1 (January 1978), 3-26. Of particular interest is his citation of a passage in which Lenin speaks of the maintenance, testing, and reinforcement of the discipline of the proletarian party through its ability "to merge itself with the broadest masses of the toilers—primarily with the proletarian, but also with the nonproletarian toiling masses" (ibid., p. 13, citing Lenin, *Collected Works* XXXI, 24f).

[66] Mao has commented on both sides of the issue of the originality of the mass line. In early 1956 he spoke twice of the fact that the mass line was a uniquely Chinese contribution, one that could help the CCP avoid the problems encountered by the CPSU (1956c:34 and 1956d:12). On the other hand, at the end of the same year he described the mass line as having developed from the experience of the October Revolution and the Civil War in Russia (1956n:48). The last citation is from an article in which Mao was attempting to redefine the position taken in the article (1956d:12) in order to criticize Khrushchev for his methods in criticizing Stalin. He thus made a point of the continuity between Chinese and Soviet experience during Stalin's rule.

is a system of democratic centralism, to be sure, but a system of democratic centralism that has been extended beyond the boundaries of the party itself to include what we might refer to as the "clientele" of the party organization.

The mass line originated, or came to the fore, in Chinese communist practice at a time when guerrilla warfare was the principal project with which the party was engaged. One cardinal advantage of the guerrilla over the conventional soldier is the degree to which, as we have seen, he or she is able to take the initiative into his or her own hands and to act without waiting for orders to pass through a hierarchical structure and the procedures it presupposes. The mass line, like guerrilla tactics, is important precisely because it restores initiative to those who know the objective circumstances best, Mao argued.[67]

Because it is central to the correct functioning of organizations, the maintenance of links with the masses was a virtually incessant preoccupation for Mao. Writing in 1956, he applied this view to his analysis of Stalin's rule: "When any leader of the party or the state places himself over and above the party and the masses instead of in their midst, when he alienates himself from the masses, he ceases to have an all-round penetrating insight into the affairs of state."[68] Later in the same article he spoke of the danger as being more widespread:

> After the victory of the revolution, when the working class and the Communist party have become the leading class and party in the state, the leading personnel of the party and state, beset by bureaucratism from many sides, face the great danger of using the machinery of the state to take arbitrary action, alienating themselves from the masses and collective leadership, resorting to commandism, and violating party and state democracy. Therefore, if we want to avoid falling into such a quagmire, we must pay fuller attention to the carrying out of the mass line method of leadership, not permitting the slightest negligence.[69]

[67] This thought was very much at the forefront of Mao's mind, so it seems, in the period of collectivization when, as has been noted in passing above, he found the masses more willing to move ahead than were his senior colleagues in the party (see, for example, 1955g:207; 1956c:31, 34; and 1958p:89).

[68] 1956d:8.   [69] Ibid., p. 13.

Elsewhere he used a now-familiar metaphor to describe the degree to which cadres should integrate themselves with the masses: "Some can go to factories or villages just to look around; this may be called 'looking at the flowers while on horseback' and is better than nothing at all. Others can stay there for a few months, conducting investigations and making friends; this may be called 'dismounting to look at the flowers.' Still others can stay and live there for a considerable time, say, two or three years or even longer; this may be called 'settling down.' "[70] This idea of "dismounting to look at the flowers," or "squatting on a spot," is critical to the correct operation of the mass line. Writing in 1941, Mao counseled cadres to "direct their eyes downward," because, he said, citing his own earlier remark, without a thorough investigation, a cadre has "no right to speak." These investigations require, however, that the cadre approach the masses correctly— not, as he put it, as "imperial envoys."[71]

The principal reason for the intimate association between bureaucrats and their clients, in Mao's view, is encapsulated in his injunction to "be a pupil of the masses before you become their teacher."[72] His point is that functionaries within the organization will be more likely to be able to perform their functions if they are endowed with, on the one hand, a knowledge of the interests of their clientele and, on the other hand, a familiarity with the productive process, both of which are acquired as a result of participation in productive labor alongside the masses. Writing on the question in 1963, Mao cited a local party official who said: "Being good at labor is the only way to achieve good work; without joining in labor, one's work will be like duckweed floating

[70] 1957f:9. He reiterated the argument and the analogy in Point 25 of the "Sixty Work Methods" (1958e:8). In the "First Ten Points" he contrasted the good results of those who investigate by "going deeply into the basic levels" and "squatting at a point," against the superficial results of those who lack "determination to train their eyes on the lower levels" (1963d:69).

[71] 1941a:747/III, 11. He discussed in some detail the correct methods to be employed in "squatting on a spot" in both the "First Ten Points" (1963d:69) and the "Twenty-three Articles" (1965c:122). Cf. 1965a:442. During the Cultural Revolution he noted that there had been those who spent long periods at the basic level who had ended up identifying themselves with the wrong side in the two-line struggle in the countryside. For this reason he came to be critical of party work teams that had been sent, he argued, to stifle the Cultural Revolution (1966j:26; 1966l:449).

[72] 1949c:1442/IV, 378.

on water, unable to reach the bottom."[73] Yet another advantage of the cadre who "squats on a spot" is the fact, as Mao noted in 1965, that an outsider is often able to resolve contradictions that local leaders either fail to perceive or are unable to resolve.[74] The danger in this situation, however, is that the local leader will come to rely on the outsider rather than exercising his own initiative. "Local cadres are the main force," he noted in 1955, "and central cadres the auxiliary force."[75]

A new and somewhat different note was struck in discussions of the relationship between organizations and their clients when, in 1962, Mao spoke of the desirability of the masses "supervising" the work of organizations.[76] This relationship, wherein the organization and its functionaries are subordinated, in a sense, to the masses they are supposed to serve, is an extension of the mass line principle, and lay at the heart of organizational reforms introduced during the Cultural Revolution. As this latter movement drew to a close, Mao summarized its lessons regarding the mass line as follows: "The questions of relations between superiors and subordinates should be properly solved, and relations between cadres and the masses should be harmonized. From now on, cadres should go to the grass-roots level and make investigations; they should persist in the mass line, consult the masses on matters that have come up, and be their pupils."[77]

As is often the case in Mao's writings, it is easiest to understand his sense of the correct functioning of the mass line by studying what he regards to be instances of its violation. There are some six modes of behavior that he specifically criticizes, which fall under the general problem of violations of democratic centralism and the mass line. On the one hand, there are "commandism" and "arbitrary action," both of which are manifestations of excessive

[73] 1965c:68. He went on in this document to speak of "class struggle, production struggle, and scientific experiment" as the "three great revolutionary movements that build up a powerful socialist nation," and continued: "With cadres and masses joining hand in hand in . . . production labor and scientific experiments, our party will take another stride forward in becoming a more glorious, greater and more correct party; our cadres will be versed in politics as well as in business operations, become red as well as expert."

[74] 1965a:444.   [75] 1955d:11.

[76] 1962a:37. Such a system is said to enhance "full-scale democratic life both inside and outside the party."

[77] Cited as a "recent directive" in *RMRB* (19 November 1969).

centralization. On the other hand, excessive democratization is manifested in what he called "ultrademocracy," disregard of organizational discipline, "absolute equalitarianism," and "semi-anarchism."

Excessive centralization, for Mao, referred to a particular style of leadership in which the downward flow of information in the organization is monopolized by orders. The organization under such leadership comes to rely heavily on coercion to insure compliance. He listed commandism and arbitrary action as incorrect styles of work at several points.[78] Elsewhere he extolled the opposite behavior patterns: reliance on reason and persuasion, rather than the issuing of orders,[79] and the institution of planning at all levels to supplant arbitrary action.[80] The leader who implements the correct style is one who operates as a "squad leader," rather than as a tyrant.[81] He reiterated these qualities when speaking of the nature of the "revolutionary successors" he hoped would be produced in China: "They must be models in applying the party's democratic centralism, must master the method of leadership based on the principle of 'from the masses, to the masses,' and must cultivate a democratic style and be good at listening to the masses. They must not be despotic like Khrushchev and violate the party's democratic centralism, make surprise attacks on comrades or act arbitrarily and dictatorially."[82] He noted a natural tendency in organizations to resort to a commandist style under pressure from above to increase output, but argued that results attained by this method, though initially impressive, are short-lived and counterproductive over time.[83] As we have seen, com-

[78] 1944b:995/III, 217; 1945a:1086/III, 315. Cf. 1956d:86.

[79] See, for example, 1955g:27. In 1958 he denounced the use of "too many imperial edicts" from the Center in running local affairs (1958b:79). Elsewhere he commented, "administrative orders and the method of persuasion and education complement each other in resolving contradictions among the people" (1957d:87). See also 1959m:9.

[80] See, for example, 1955g:361. Cf. 1956e:27f.

[81] 1962a:165.

[82] 1964n:72ff. Two years later, at the onset of the Cultural Revolution, Mao argued that the malfeasance of certain party leaders had grown to be of such seriousness that a violation of party discipline and a launching of "surprise attacks on comrades" was called for.

[83] 1933a:110/I, 134. Cf. 1959k:30, where he refers to such methods as "blowing communist wind." Closely related to this commandist style is the tendency to engage in false reporting to satisfy one's seniors in the hierarchy, a problem with which we shall deal shortly (1958ww:134; 1958yy:140).

mandism and arbitrariness may result as well from the personality of the leader. Writing in 1956, Mao used Stalin as an example of this: "During the latter part of his life, Stalin took more and more pleasure in this cult of the individual, and violated the party's system of democratic centralism and the principle of combining collective leadership with individual responsibility. As a result he made some serious mistakes."[84]

The opposite horn of the dilemma that democratic centralism sets out to resolve is excessive democratization. Mao described the source of "ultrademocracy" as the "petty bourgeoisie's individualistic aversion to discipline."[85] It is manifested, he said, in the phenomenon of "self-made policy," in the formulation of which the Center plays no part.[86] The good cadre, on the other hand, is one who avoids the pitfall of ultrademocracy by being "resolute in carrying out the party line."[87] The second manifestation, the disregard of organizational discipline, involves the "failure of the minority to submit to the majority" and "criticism made without regard to organizational discipline," which thus "sometimes turns into personal attack . . . [and thereby] damages the party organization as well as individuals."[88] Approved behavior is that of the cadre who "keeps to party discipline."[89]

Absolute equalitarianism is another facet of the general problem of excessive democratization. Mao described it as follows: "Absolute equalitarianism, like ultrademocracy in political matters, is the product of a handicraft and small peasant economy—the only difference being that the one manifests itself in material affairs, while the other manifests itself in political affairs."[90] The method of correction proposed for this incorrect mode of behavior is essentially that of education. Members of the organization should be instructed that, while relative equality accords with the requirements of the "present circumstances of the struggle," absolute equalitarianism "is not required by the struggle; on the contrary, it hinders the struggle."[91]

[84] 1956d:8.

[85] 1929:86/I, 108. He listed "ultra-democracy" as an organizational failing once again in 1944b:924/III, 217.

[86] 1962d:24.   [87] 1938e:493/II, 202.   [88] 1929:87f./I, 109f.

[89] 1938e:493/II, 202. Elsewhere Mao spoke approvingly of the "iron discipline of the Communist party" (1959bb:84). Cf. 1956c:33.

[90] 1929:88/I, 111. He lists absolute equalitarianism again as an organizational failing in 1957h.

[91] 1929:88/I, 111.

A final form of excessive democratization in organizations is "semianarchism." Mao simply lists this failing without further comment in a 1945 "Resolution on Certain Questions in the History of our Party."[92] He returned to the question of anarchism in the broader context of the society as a whole in his 1957 discussion of the "Correct Handling of Contradictions among the People." There he spoke of the civil rights that are enjoyed by those who fall in the category of "the people." "By civil rights," he explained, "we mean, politically, the rights of freedom and democracy." He saw limits, however, to these rights: "But this freedom is freedom with leadership and this democracy is democracy under centralized guidance, not anarchy. Anarchy does not accord with the interests or wishes of the people."[93]

The proper exercise of democratic centralism is seen by Mao as a correct middle road between the two mistaken styles of excessive centralization and excessive democratization. In his "Sixty Work Methods," Mao used what he referred to as an "eight-line rhyme coined in 1953" to describe this middle course: "The immeasurable power is monopolized but the lesser power is dispersed. Decisions are made by the party committee and carried out by all quarters. The decisions carried out must not depart from principles. The party committee has the responsibility to check on work."[94] He explained these terms as follows: " 'Immeasurable power' . . . customarily refers to the arbitrary action of an individual. We borrow this phrase to indicate that the immeasurable power should be centralized in such collectives as the Central Committee and local party committees for the purpose of opposing dispersionism. . . . The 'principles' referred to in the third phrase mean the party which is the supreme organization of the proletariat, democratic centralism, the unity of collective leadership and the individual role (the unity of the party committee and the first secretary), the decisions of the Central Committee and the higher level."[95]

Defined thus in strictly organizational terms (and thus divorced somewhat from the earlier "dictatorship toward enemies, democracy toward the people" formula of the New Democracy period),

[92] 1944b:954/III, 177.   [93] 1957d:84.   [94] 1958e:9.

[95] Ibid. What is sought, clearly, is a balance between centralization and decentralization that provides for initiative at the lower levels but still retains supervisory powers at the center (1956l:27; 1958j:102; 1958yy:143; 1970b:15).

the system of democratic centralism is comparable in many respects to Weber's notion of the hierarchical structure of bureaucratic organizations where information and compliance flow upward and directives backed by office-based authority constitute the downward flow through the hierarchy. In discussing the dispersal of the "lesser powers," Mao speaks of the need to observe the division of labor and the chain of command: "In relaying to subordinate units any task . . . a higher organization and its departments should in all cases go through the leader of the lower organization concerned so that he may assume responsibility; in this way both division of labor and unified centralized leadership are achieved."[96] He spoke elsewhere of the need for reliable subordinates,[97] but cautions against becoming overly dependent upon them: "You should not rely on your secretaries or 'second row parliamentarians' to do everything. You should mainly do things yourselves with the assistance of others. You should not let the secretarial system become a general system. . . . Reliance on your secretaries for everything is a manifestation of your degeneration in revolutionary will."[98]

In some respects, however, Mao's view of the suitability of democratic centralism as a solution for the problems of excessive centralization seems to have declined during the course of the Cultural Revolution. A widely disseminated discussion of the role of democratic centralism in a Communist party—Liu Shaoqi's *On the Self-Cultivation of Communist Party Members*—came under fire, as did its author. One Red Guard periodical said that Liu's theory "fostered an organization system where at each level individuals incorporate the qualities of a slave (toward their superiors) and of a slave-owner (toward their inferiors)."[99] This so-called "slave mentality" was widely denounced in the Maoist press.

In the long run, Mao appears to have grown pessimistic about the likelihood that either organization structure or the personali-

[96] 1943b:855/III, 120.

[97] 1958e:9. "There must be a number two man and a number three man," he says. "When the first secretary is not at home, there must be someone else to assume command."

[98] Ibid., p. 11. Cf. 1971:42.

[99] *Jinggangshan* (Peking), 13 April 1967, translated in *JPRS* 42070 (3 August 1967), 36. Mao himself had criticized the overhierarchical effects of the system of ranks for cadres as producing "father-son" and "cat-mouse" relationships in the organization (1958uu:131). Cf. 1959b:190.

ties of those who are leaders of the organization are likely to work toward the extinction of commandism. In a speech in 1962 on the subject of democratic centralism, he began to talk of a new solution: supervision of the organization and its leaders by the "masses" outside of the organization.[100] In 1966, as if to legitimate his new position, he said, "I have always proposed that whenever a central organization does something bad, we should call on the local organizations to rebel and to attack the central."[101] During the course of the Cultural Revolution these latter methods of combatting excessive centralization were put into practice on a broad scale. They were subsequently institutionalized, to a degree, in the new Revolutionary Committees, on which sat representatives, at least at the outset, of the "revolutionary masses."

The second facet of Mao's view of the hierarchical nature of bureaucratic organizations to be considered here is its effect on inter- and intraorganizational communications. He regarded it as a natural tendency of organizations to suffer from ineffective internal communications as well as from ineffective communication with the environment surrounding the organization. There are a number of forms that a breakdown in communications may take in an organization. The problem may be structural. Particularly in a mass line style of operation, with its emphasis on decentralization, the maintenance of effective lines of communication is at the same time crucial and problematic.[102] On the other hand, the problem may be behavioral. He addressed himself to a number of such behavioral problems, the first being a breakdown in communication between levels in the organization, and between the organization and its clientele—a phenomenon that I interpret to be the referent of his use of the term, "bureaucracy." The second is a lack of frankness, honesty, and truthfulness in relationships within the organization; and the third is the use of obfuscating language in the process of communication.

[100] 1962a:159. Precedents for this position are found, as Roderick Mac-Farquhar (*Origins of the Cultural Revolution*, 1, *Contradictions among the People, 1956-57* [New York: Columbia University Press, 1975]) and Parris Chang (*Power and Policy in China* [College Park: Pennsylvania State University Press, 1976]) have argued, in Mao's turn to local level cadres to support his position on the pace of collectivization in the mid-1950s, and subsequently to nonparty intellectuals during the Hundred Flowers period.

[101] 1966e.

[102] Mao spoke of this problem in 1959, and suggested a monthly exchange of letters as a possible solution (1959e:153).

In speaking of the merits and shortcomings of bureaucratic organizations and behavior, Mao much more frequently used the compound *guanliao* than he did the compound *zuzhi*. *Zuzhi* is commonly translated with the English term, "organization." The common translations for *guanliao*, particularly in the official English versions of Mao's writings, are "bureaucrat," "bureaucratic," and "bureaucracy." The basic meaning for the compound, however, is probably better rendered with the English terms, "official," and "officialdom," since the character *liao* carries the meanings of "companion," "colleague," "official associate," and, by extension, "clique."[103] Thus the compound *guanliaozhuyi*, commonly translated "bureaucratism," and ordinarily used by Mao in a pejorative sense, is perhaps better rendered with the English term, "officialism."

Writing in 1945 a list of incorrect organizational behavior patterns, Mao headed the list with "bureaucracy,"[104] thus suggesting that, though it was an important mistaken mode of behavior, it was but one of several such modes found in organizations. Thus, whereas in European and American usage, the term tends to comprehend various types of behavioral and structural elements, its usage by Mao is considerably more limited and, at the same time, very much influenced by his impression of the behavior of previous generations of Chinese bureaucrat-officials.[105]

[103] *Mathews' Chinese-English Dictionary* (revised American edition), (Cambridge: Harvard University Press, 1966), p. 576. Mathews gives "an official, a mandarin," as the primary meanings for the character, *guan* (ibid., p. 524). Even more accurate, perhaps, would be to render *guanliao* into English with the British colloquialism, "old boy net," but that seems a bit too arcane to be widely understood.

[104] 1944b:995/III, 217.

[105] Another adverse pattern of behavior described by Mao as characteristic of men and women in organizations is "patriarchalism" (1944b:995/III, 217). This mistaken style of work is mentioned only once, and seems sufficiently close in meaning to what he refers to as "bureaucracy" that I think it appropriate to include it within that mode of behavior in the present discussion. Evidence of this proximity and of the influence on his treatment of organizational behavior from the behavior patterns of the traditional scholar-official is found in the only other reference to "patriarchalism" in the *Selected Works*. In his "Hunan Report" of 1927, Mao spoke of the "patriarchal-feudal class of local tyrants, evil gentry, and lawless landlords [which] has formed the basis for autocratic government for thousands of years and is the cornerstone of imperialism, warlordism, and corrupt officialdom" (1927:15/I, 27). It is evident as well in the synonyms he uses for "bureaucratism": "bureaucratic airs" (1958e:8; 1959c:218), the style of a "bureau-

157

In February 1950, Mao wrote the inscription, "don't get contaminated by the bureaucratic style of work," during an inspection tour through Heilongjiang Province.[106] The following year the *Sanfan*, or "Three Antis" Campaign was launched to attack "corruption, waste, and bureaucratism."[107] Schurmann interprets this campaign as having been aimed at specific individuals within the bureaucratic organizations, rather than at the organizations themselves. He refers to it as "the first eruption of the endemic Chinese Communist fear that bureaucratization could mean a reversion to traditional bureaucracy."[108]

By 1956 Mao was speaking of the necessity to "establish certain systems" to combat the particular danger to party and government, "beset" as he saw them by "bureaucratism from many sides."[109] A year later, however, it was rectification, rather than prophylaxis to which he addressed himself. Announcing that the party had decided upon "another rectification within the party to be started this year," he pointed out that "the main thing in this rectification movement is to criticize the following three errors in one's way of thinking and style of work—subjectivism, bureaucracy, and sectarianism."[110] The problem, he explained in 1961, was one of education: "Rigid bureaucrats should be reformed into creative bureaucrats. If after a time they can't become creative, then we should get rid of them."[111]

In his "Sixty Work Methods," written in 1958, Mao spoke of the problem of intraorganization communication as follows: "People's work and duties are at variance, but no matter how high the office of a person may be he should assume the posture of a common laborer when he appears among other people. He can

cratic overlord" (1958p:87), "lordly airs" (1961a:283), a "Guomindang" or "warlord" work style (1943e:88/III, 158f.), and, as we have seen, cadres who descend on local organizations as "imperial envoys" (1941b:758/III, 21).

[106] 1950a.

[107] Mao's comments in conjunction with this campaign link authoritarianism, commandism, and a bureaucratic work style (1950b:110; 1950d; 1950e; 1950f; 1951a; 1951b; 1952a; 1952b; and 1953b:102).

[108] Schurmann, *Ideology and Organization in Communist China* (Berkeley and Los Angeles: University of California Press, 1968), p. 318. He notes here that the methods used in this campaign were relatively crude and terroristic, and cites official Chinese figures to the effect that "4.5 percent of all state officials in China received some kind of punishment during the *sanfan* campaign."

[109] 1956d:13.   [110] 1957f:13.   [111] 1961b:240.

never put on airs and must get rid of the bureaucratic style. When someone under you puts forward a different view, you must not get angry as soon as you hear some view different from yours and regard this as lack of respect for you."[112] At that point in his career, Mao considered what he called "uninterrupted revolution" to be an appropriate means of insuring that this problem did not become aggravated. "Our revolution," he explained, "is like fighting battles. After winning a battle a new task is at once put forward. In this way, the cadres and the masses can be made to uphold their revolutionary enthusiasm to the full extent. They are less arrogant, since they have no time to display their arrogance even if they want to."[113]

In a certain sense, the theory of uninterrupted revolution as it was advanced in 1958 and 1959 was a theoretical summary of the preceding decade of a campaign approach to social change. Like the Hegelian owl of Minerva that flies only at twilight, the theory came only when the usefulness of the practice had ended, for the Great Leap Forward was, in an important sense, the last of the major transformational campaigns.[114] Thus the notion that the arrogant bureaucratic behavior found in organizations could be curbed merely by keeping up a frenetic and irregular pace of operations was relatively short-lived.

In the constitution that Mao wrote for the Anshan Iron and

[112] 1958e:8.

[113] *Ibid.*, p. 5. The distinction between Mao's use of the term, "uninterrupted revolution" (*buduan geming*) and his use of the term, "continuing the revolution" (*jixu geming*) is well covered by Stuart R. Schram in his article, "Mao Tse-tung and the Theory of the Permanent Revolution, 1958-1969," *China Quarterly* 46 (1971), 221-244. Cf. Starr, "Conceptual Foundations of Mao Tse-tung's Theory of Continuous Revolution," *Asian Survey* 11:6 (1971), 610-628.

[114] The Socialist Education Campaign impresses me as a pale shadow of earlier campaigns and was afflicted, as several observers have noted, with the need to overcome patterns of behavior for avoiding real change that had been learned by cadres and masses alike over the course of the campaigns of the previous decade. The Cultural Revolution, on the other hand, constituted a new type of movement, significantly different from the campaign style that preceded it. The campaigns that have followed the Cultural Revolution—those to criticize Lin Biao, Confucius, and the Gang of Four appear to have conformed to a unique pattern of their own. Cf. Gordon Bennett, *Yundong: Mass Campaigns in Chinese Communist Leadership* (Berkeley: University of California, Center for Chinese Studies, 1976); and Charles Cell, *Revolution at Work: Mobilizational Campaigns in China* (New York: Academic Press, 1977).

Steel Company in 1960, he prescribed the institution of "cadre participation in productive labor and worker participation in management."[115] By 1963 he was speaking of the "established system" of intraorganizational *xiafang* (downward transfer), whereby "cadres diligently participate in collective production labor."[116] He linked this system to the then newly inaugurated Socialist Education Movement, and suggested that "with cadres and masses joining hand-in-hand in productive labor . . . [our cadres] will no longer be toplofty, no longer bureaucrats and overlords, no longer divorced from the masses."[117]

Two years later, when he addressed himself again to the nexus between cadre participation in labor and the Socialist Education Campaign, he added his thoughts on the class implications involved. It is one of the clearest statements we have of Mao's view of the relationship between bureaucratism and embourgeoisement:

> Management also involves socialist education. If management personnel do not go into the shops and sections to take part in the three togethers and to learn one or more manual skills from the workers, then they are liable to spend their whole lives in sharp struggle against the working class. In the end, they will inevitably be overthrown by the working class as members of the bourgeoisie. If they do not master a skill and remain a dilettante for long, they cannot properly perform management functions.[118]

The solutions advanced seemed promising, but apparently proved ineffective in his eyes, for Mao continued to talk about the persistence of a bureaucratic attitude within organizations.[119] In 1964 he criticized members of the All-China Federation of Literary and Art Circles for having "acted as high and mighty

[115] 1960d. His earlier comments on the problem are found in 1955g:44f.; 1958e:8; 1958t:103; and 1958bb:350.

[116] 1963d:68. He further noted that "we hope to succeed within three years in having all the party secretaries in the rural party branches throughout the country devote themselves to participation in productive labor."

[117] Ibid., pp. 7of.

[118] 1965e:99f. Cf. 1965c:120. Earlier, as a first step toward making this linkage, he spoke of bureaucrats as the unwitting allies of the bourgeoisie because of their rigidity and arbitrariness (1961b:237, 243).

[119] He pointed it out to French visitors in 1964 as one of the paramount problems in the Chinese system (1964t).

bureaucrats" and for having "not gone to the workers, peasants, and soldiers";[120] and he criticized provincial party secretaries who were "unable to tolerate opposing views and criticism": "One province held a meeting which started off in a very lively manner, but as soon as the provincial party secretary arrived a hush fell on the proceedings and nobody spoke. . . . Those of you [party secretaries] who shirk responsibility or who are afraid of taking responsibility, who do not allow people to speak, who think you are tigers, and that nobody will dare to touch your arse, whoever has this attitude, ten out of ten of you will fail."[121]

The question arose once again during the Cultural Revolution. During that movement he wrote a document on the problem of bureaucratism listing twenty manifestations of this incorrect work style—a document that, because of its comprehensive treatment of the problem of organizational malfunctioning, we have already had and will have occasion to refer to again in this chapter.[122] During the Cultural Revolution, the system of intraorganizational *xiafang* was revivifed and reinforced. It was, in addition, supplemented by the establishment of so-called "May 7 Cadre Schools." These schools took their name from the date, and their program of instruction from the substance, of a letter written by Mao to Lin Biao in 1966, wherein he discussed the necessity for a diversification of talents among cadres—a diversification that he saw implementable only through practical experience.[123] He summarized his view of cadre *xiafang* in 1968 as follows: "Sending the masses of cadres to do manual work gives them an excellent opportunity to study once again; this should be done by all cadres except those who are too old, weak, ill, or disabled."[124]

While, as we have seen, Mao mentioned worker participation in management, this side of the vertical exchange of personnel within the organization was never stressed. Indeed, he ignored an important model for such exchanges—the Yugoslavian workers' councils—presumably for political reasons, leaving it to his suc-

[120] 1964k.   [121] 1962a:166f.

[122] 1967a. The date of this document is open to question. It appears in the 1969 *Wansui* collection undated, but is referred to by Stanley Karnow (*Mao and China* [New York: Viking, 1972], p. 90) as having been written in January 1967.

[123] 1966f.

[124] 1968j. He made particular reference elsewhere to the importance of medical personnel implementing such a system as being beneficial both to themselves and to the rural population (1965d; 1966k:6f.).

cessors to explore, a year after his death, the lessons contained in that experience.[125]

Other forms of behavior inhibit the free flow of communications within the organization, just as a bureaucratic style of work does. Writing in 1948, Mao noted that in some party committees "solutions to problems are decided not by party committee meetings but by one individual, and membership in the party committee has become nominal. Differences of opinion among committee members cannot be resolved and are left unresolved for a long time."[126] As a solution to this incorrect situation, Mao proposed that "all important problems . . . must be submitted to the committee for discussion, and the committee members present should express their views fully and reach definite decisions." Furthermore, "on important problems which are complicated and on which opinions differ, there must, in addition, be personal consultations before the meeting to enable the members to think things over, lest decisions by the meeting become a mere formality or no decision can be reached."[127]

Six months later, Mao returned to the problem: "Place problems on the table. . . . Do not talk behind people's backs. Whenever problems arise, call a meeting, place the problems on the table for discussion, take some decisions and the problems will be solved."[128] As a prerequisite to the success of such a system, Mao also noted, "nothing is more important than mutual tolerance, understanding, support, and friendship between the secretary and the committee members."[129]

A third reference to the problem is found in Mao's speech at the Chengdu Conference in March 1958. In this more recent treatment of the question of the need for frankness in intraorganizational relationships, the emphasis is on the inhibiting effect upon such frankness exerted by fear of reprisals. He says: "Muttering behind people's backs and not speaking up is no good. There should be a general agreement . . . expressed either sharply or tactfully, but expression is necessary. . . . It is dangerous to hide your feelings. Naturally, you must select the opportune moment to speak, and you must also consider the strategy."[130] He con-

---

[125] Discussion of Yugoslavian worker-management schemes began to appear in the Chinese press in association with Tito's visit to China in the late summer of 1977.

[126] 1948b:1234/IV, 267.   [127] 1948b:1235/IV, 268.   [128] 1949c:1330f./IV, 377.
[129] Ibid.   [130] 1958m:123.

cludes his consideration of this question by criticizing as "vulgar" the working style of those comrades who "do not dare to express themselves but only speak a part of their mind . . . because they fear they will not get along well and that they will lose votes."[131]

The treatment of the problem of frankness and honesty in the exchange of information within organizations was transformed somewhat in Mao's writings as a result of the aftermath of the Great Leap. In a letter addressed to production team leaders in November 1959, he dealt at some length with the "question of telling the truth": "When output quotas are fixed, we should make known the actual output quotas we can guarantee. We must not tell lies by fixing the output quotas at a level which is actually beyond our means to fulfill."[132] He went on to attempt to place the blame for untruthfulness where he felt it belonged. "It should be said that many lies are told due to the pressures of a higher level. When the higher level resorts to trumpet blowing, applying pressure, and making promises, it makes things difficult for the lower level."[133]

A third barrier to the smooth flow of communications within the organization, in Mao's view, is that caused by obfuscating language. He spoke of the need to build a "common language" through the exchange of information,[134] and criticized those who subverted the development of such a language by the inaccuracies, inelegance, and immoderation of their own prose.[135] One of the

[131] Ibid. One supposes that this criticism of Mao's might subsequently have lost some of its saliency, given the consequences for Peng Dehuai and his colleagues of having taken it to heart during the summer of the following year. On the other hand, at the same time that he was criticizing Peng for his "planned, organized, prepared, and purposeful" attack, he praised Li Zhongyun for his letter of criticism written directly to the Central Committee, thereby bypassing middle echelons (cf. 1959p:25 and 1959s:47f.).

[132] 1959m:9.

[133] Ibid. Cf. 1958ww:134; 1958yy:140.

[134] 1949c:1331/IV, 378. He returned to this question in the "Sixty Work Methods" a decade later in 1958, noting that "in order to speak a common language, there must first be essential information and knowledge" (1958e: 10).

[135] The *locus classicus* for this criticism is Mao's 1942 article, "Oppose Stereotyped Party Writing." There he cited some of the rules set forth by Lu Xun for good writing. Among them appear the following injunctions: "Observe more, and if you have observed only a little, then do not write." "Do not force yourself to write when you have nothing to say." "Do your utmost to strike out nonessential words, sentences, and paragraphs without the slightest compunction." "Do not coin adjectives or

"Sixty Work Methods" is devoted to this latter question. There Mao listed four shortcomings which result in his finding "reading documents a woeful job, since it consumes a lot of energy and gives little in return": "First, the concept is not clear and definite; second, the judgment is not pertinent; third, there is a lack of logic when concepts and judgments are used in reasoning; fourth, no attention is paid to polished phraseology."[136] Elsewhere he criticized those comrades "who are extremely fond of using party jargon in their articles." As a result of this failing, "their writing is neither vivid nor graphic. It gives you a headache to read it. They care little for grammar or phrasing, preferring something which is a cross between the literary and the colloquial. Here garrulous and repetitive, there archaically cryptic, it is as if they were deliberately trying to make their readers suffer."[137]

Finally, the development of a "common language" depends on the rate of exchange of information as well as its content. "Generally speaking," Mao said, "we must not make people accept within a few hours a big pile of material or viewpoints which these people are not given access to at ordinary times. . . . It is necessary to have some drizzle, and it is undesirable to have a downpour which yields several hundred millimeters of precipitation in a few hours."[138]

As each of these examples shows, Mao's view of communications within an organization is a pessimistic one. Left to itself, the flow of communications is likely to be interrupted, thus severing what are—for anyone who attempts to use organizations to accomplish his or her purposes, but particularly for Mao because of his espousal of a mass line style of work—the crucial links between

---

other terms that are intelligible to nobody but yourself" (1942b:844f./III, 66f. Cf. 1955g:328; 1956d:14). Good advice, one might add, for any writer. It is interesting to compare these rules with Deng To's comments, evidently written with Mao in mind, in his satirical piece, "The Great Empty Talk" (1961): "I wish to advise my friend, the Great Empty Talker, hereafter to read and think more, but talk less. And whenever there is occasion for you to speak, you had better retreat instead somewhere to take a rest in order not only to avoid wasting your own time and energy, but that of others as well"; cited in "China's Enemy Within," *Atlas* 13:2 (February 1967), 25.

[136] 1958e:11. Correcting these four faults will result, he contended, in "accurate, clearcut" documents and articles that are "lively in character." A subsequent "work method" makes this same point much more succinctly. It reads, *in toto*, "Learn some grammar and logic" (ibid).

[137] 1955g:328.   [138] 1958e:10.

the strata within the organization itself. Interruption of these links, Mao argued, disrupts the operation of the organization, undermines the legitimacy of its leaders, brings about a deterioration of their political consciousness, and may ultimately cause them to form a new bourgeois class antagonistic to the lower echelons of the organization and to its clientele.

THE TENDENCY TOWARD ROUTINIZATION

Weber conceived of the operation of the bureaucratic organization as governed "by a consistent system of abstract rules," and as consisting of "the application of these rules to particular cases."[139] The purpose of this system of rule application is to provide for uniformity of operation through routinization. Subsequent observers have noted that an unintended consequence of this system is to focus the attention of the bureaucrat on what might be called "tactical" decisions rather than "strategic" ones. As a result, the bureaucratic organization has a natural tendency toward ossification—toward an inability to adapt to a changing environment.

The generalization espoused by the Chinese bureaucrat in place of specialization resulted in a situation not wholly unlike that of the Western bureaucrat's application of abstract rules to specific situations. In the Chinese setting, however, the general precepts were so abstract as scarcely to constitute "rules," much less a "consistent system." Moreover, the purpose of this mode of operation was not necessarily to promote uniformity or routinization, but rather to preserve the abstractions themselves, since they were seen to be intrinsically "true" and valued because of their relationship to Confucian doctrine.[140]

No doubt because of the irregularities of guerrilla operations

[139] Weber, *The Theory of Social and Economic Organization*, p. 330.

[140] Yang notes the paucity of rules for the functioning of the basic level in the bureaucracy ("Some Characteristics"). This paucity was partially compensated for by the existence of descriptions of experiences by retired officials and "expert" subordinates. Even these, however, were not used in any sense as "precedents" for solving specific cases, as would be the case in Western jurisprudence. Rather, in King's terms, the individual officials were highly "situation oriented," taking both the solutions for specific problems and the ethical standards to be applied in reaching those solutions from the specific situation rather than from abstract principles ("Behavioral Patterns").

out of which the post-Liberation bureaucracy originated, Mao's description of overroutinization as an adverse mode of behavior in organizations appears only in 1955 and beyond. Because overroutinization was not a characteristic of the operation of the traditional Chinese bureaucrat, his treatment of the problem seems more a response to the operation of modern bureaucracy in China than to traditional bureaucratic patterns.

He first took up the question in an introductory note in *The Socialist Upsurge in China's Countryside*. There he contrasted the "immense enthusiasm" of the people for socialism with the outlook of those "who only know how to follow the routine paths." The latter group "cannot see this enthusiasm at all. They are blind. All is dark before them."[141] He goes on to elaborate on the behavior of these individuals "who can only travel the well-trodden paths": "Let something new appear and they invariably disapprove, they rush to oppose it. Later, they admit defeat and do a bit of self-criticism. But next time something new appears, they do the same things again, and in the same sequence. This becomes their regular routine in regard to anything and everything new."[142] As a result of his love of routine, an individual afflicted with "rightist obtuseness" such as this stands "truth on its head, . . . confusing black with white." What is more, he is "always passive. He can never get going at a critical moment. Someone always has to give him a poke in the back before he will move forward."[143]

Though criticisms of the problem of overroutinization in organizations appears relatively late in Mao's writings, the solution advocated there harks back to earlier discussions of the need to establish revolutionary priorities rather than routine as a means of overcoming the problem of a small organization confronting a large number of tasks. In 1949, Mao likened this process to playing the piano: "In playing the piano all ten fingers are in motion; it won't do to move some fingers only and not others. But if all ten fingers press down at once, there is no melody. To produce good music, the ten fingers should move rhythmically and in coordination. A Party committee should keep a firm grasp on its central task and at the same time, around the central task, it should unfold the work in other fields."[144] Priorities among tasks are to be established not solely by those at the Center, but also by those in charge at the local level, with a view toward the local

---

[141] 1955g:44.   [142] Ibid., p. 45.   [143] Ibid.
[144] 1949c:1332/IV, 379.

"history and circumstances of the struggle."[145] The implication here is clear, then, that with such a basis for the establishment of priorities among tasks, routinization is both impossible and undesirable.

Much the same kind of argument was raised in Mao's subsequent assault on overroutinization. In the 1960 constitution for the Anshan Iron and Steel Works, he called for the "reform of outdated and irrational rules and regulations."[146] There are at least five examples in Mao's writings of his attempts to set down new "rules and regulations"—"work methods" (*gongzuo fangfa*) as he called them.[147] In each case, the "rules and regulations" were a reiteration of and elaboration upon the principles of the mass line—open-ended methods, that is, rather than specific rules to be applied without variation to all cases. In one of these sets of prescribed methods—that written in 1958—he spoke of the necessity of fitting "new methods to new political conditions," and elaborated on the reform of those "rules and regulations accumulated over the past eight years [that] . . . have become obstacles to further raising mass enthusiasm and developing productivity."[148] The process of reform should involve sending "responsible comrades to the basic-level units in all places to find out what rules and regulations there have restricted the enhancement of mass enthusiasm and the development of productivity. In accordance with the actual conditions of those places . . . the rational part should be preserved, while the irrational part should be revised or abolished. Some new rules and regulations which meet the need should also be laid down for enforcement in the unit concerned."[149]

Routine is a critical element of any organization. Mao recognized that fact, but at the same time took routinization to be a potential corrupting force on the organization and its participants. Much of his concern, then, was to limit the rules and regulations which, if allowed to proliferate, could lead to overroutinization.

THE FORMALISTIC IMPERSONALITY OF OFFICIALS

"The ideal official," wrote Weber, "conducts his office . . . [in] a spirit of formalistic impersonality, '*Sine ira et studio*,' without

---

[145] 1943b:856/III, 121.
[146] 1960d. Cf. 1958e:7; 1958uu:130.
[147] 1943b; 1949c; 1958e; 1959n; 1960d.
[148] 1958e:1, 7.
[149] Ibid., p. 8.

hatred or passion, and hence without affection or enthusiasm."[150] Blau comments on this aspect of the bureaucratic ideal type as follows: "The exclusion of personal considerations from official business is a prerequisite for impartiality as well as for efficiency. The very factors that make a government bureaucrat unpopular with his clients, an aloof attitude and a lack of genuine concern with their problems, actually benefit these clients. Disinterestedness and a lack of personal interest go together."[151]

This quality of formalistic impersonality is a particularly difficult one to realize in practice. Because it is so seldom found in actual organizational settings, contemporary observers have come to focus attention on the effect on the organization of the informal, personalistic relationships that predominate. Pursuing this line of investigation, Philip Selznick differentiates what he terms an "organization" from what he refers to as an "institution."[152] The organization, as he treats it, is a "technical instrument" for the achievement of specific goals. "It is a tool, rationally designed for specific technical ends, and, like any tool, expendable."[153] "Institution," on the other hand, is the term Selznick employs to describe the effects of personalistic relationships. It is "more nearly a natural product of social needs and pressures, a responsive, adaptive organism."[154] Alvin Gouldner makes much the same argument, using the term "rational model" in place of Selznick's "organization." Unlike Selznick, who sees organizations and institutions as sequential stages in the development of a single bureaucracy—organizations gradually institutionalize, in his terms—Gouldner sees the two types of structure as coexistent in every organization. The "natural-system model" portrays the emergence of informal groups within the organization, which displace the organization as a whole as the locus of primary loyalties for its members.[155]

[150] Weber, *The Theory of Social and Economic Organizations*, p. 340.

[151] Blau, *Bureaucracy*, p. 30.

[152] Philip Selznick, *Leadership in Administration* (Evanston, Ill.: Row, Peterson, 1957), pp. 5, 21.

[153] The paraphrase of Selznick's idea is that of Sheldon Wolin, *Politics and Vision* (Boston: Little, Brown, 1960), p. 412.

[154] Selznick, *Leadership in Administration*, p. 21. Wolin's discussion of the conceptual origins and logical consequences of arguments like those of Selznick is instructive (*Politics and Vision*, pp. 412ff.).

[155] Alvin W. Gouldner, "Organizational Analysis," in Robert K. Merton et al., eds., *Sociology Today: Problems and Prospects* (New York: Basic Books, 1959), pp. 400-428.

Crozier sees validity in this type of analysis, but warns against regarding either type of model as exclusively associated with one or another level within the bureaucratic hierarchy. It is not true, he argues, that impersonal rationality is exclusively manifested by the upper reaches of the organization, or that empathetic and informal affectivity is exclusively the characteristic of the lower levels. Workers and officials alike, in the bureaucratic settings that he has observed, operate rationally as well as emotionally.[156] In a similar vein, Downs notes that informal groups by no means work exclusively to the detriment of the goals of the organization; they may, in fact, come into being in order to implement these formal goals more effectively.[157]

The ideal bureaucrat in traditional China also operated impersonally. As part of the relationship of tension in which Levenson depicted the throne and the bureaucracy as existing, there were regulations that aimed at instilling a degree of impersonality in the bureaucrat. Primary among these regulations was the "law of avoidance," by which the official was prevented from serving in his home district. The purpose of this law was to sever as completely as possible the particularistic ties of the official to the primary groups to which he owed his loyalty, and thereby to insure maximal objectivity in the execution of his duties.[158]

In actual practice, however, the law of avoidance and other similar regulations were only partially successful in molding the behavior of the official. King lists "particularistic orientation" as one of the behavior patterns characteristic of the traditional bureaucrat, and notes that officials were "particularly susceptible to pressures from their primary groups."[159] Certainly if one looks

[156] Crozier, *Bureaucratic Phenomenon*, p. 212.

[157] Downs, *Inside Bureaucracy*, p. 63f.

[158] These regulations resulted in a complex situation in which loyalties of the official to his home were balanced against his need for cooperation and information from the locality to which he was assigned. This situation necessitated his cultivating good (and, presumably, personal) relations with the local gentry; it eventuated as well in balancing in his staff of "expert" subordinates those from the locality in which he served (the clerks and runners) and those from his own home locality, who were thus personally employed and personally loyal to the official (cf. Ch'ü, *Local Government*).

[159] King, "Behavioral Patterns." H. G. Creel sees the emphasis on informal, affective relationships as a common link between the traditional Chinese bureaucracy and views of contemporary Western bureaucracy such as those of Selznick and Gouldner, as described above; "The Beginnings of Bureaucracy in China: The Origin of the *Hsien*," *Journal of Asian Studies* 23:2 (1964), 155-184.

at the question from the side of the relatives of the official, one finds that they appear to have expected some benefit from their familial connection with officialdom.

It would seem that the degree of impersonality typically manifested by the Chinese bureaucrat was inversely proportional to the status of those to whom he related. He would be much less likely to treat his peers or superiors in an impersonal way than he would be to deal thus with his inferiors.[160] The same could be said, no doubt, of the imperfect official in a Western setting, as well, but the purpose of advancing impersonality as a goal is different in the two cases. In the Western organization impersonality is encouraged to maximize efficiency and equity. In the Chinese case, impersonality was advanced as an ideal in an effort to curb the growth of the independence of the bureaucracy *vis-à-vis* the throne.

Although very much aware of the problems involved in maintaining a tension of checks and balances between the power of the "throne" and that of the bureaucracy in the administration of the contemporary Chinese state, Mao nevertheless came down hard on the side of abandoning the impersonality of officials (as that impersonality was manifested by the traditional bureaucrat in China), and of substituting for it an intimate relationship between bureaucrat and client. But while he spurned the manifestations of "formalistic impersonality" as found in the haughty demeanor of the former occupants of the *xian* magistracies, he advocated something rather closer to the Weberian idea of impersonality. He did this despite the intimacy of the connections between official and masses that he advocated, arguing that intimacy must be based on other than personalistic considerations.

It was his abiding conviction that organizational behavior, if left to itself, is likely to result in the opposite of an intimate relationship between bureaucrat and client. This hypothesis concerning the behavior of bureaucrats is not only among the most important elements in his theory of organizations, but in a certain sense, it encompasses the theory as a whole. Thus, writing in 1945, Mao commented, "The reason why such evils as dogmatism,

---

[160] Frederic Wakeman, Jr. has elucidated this point with a hypothetical legal altercation, the outcome of which is determined on the basis of personal, affective relations between the local magistrate and one of the disputants; "High Ch'ing: 1683-1839," in James B. Crowley, ed., *Modern East Asia: Essays in Interpretation* (New York: Harcourt Brace and World, 1970), pp. 13ff.

empiricism, commandism, tailism, sectarianism, bureaucracy, and an arrogant attitude in work are definitely harmful and intolerable, and why anyone suffering from these maladies must overcome them is that they alienate us from the masses."[161] I have touched already on the dangers Mao saw in "officialism"—a rupture of the connection between the leaders and the lower echelons within the hierarchical structure of an organization. Equally or even more undesirable, in his view, are the consequences of a severance of the linkages between the members of an organization and the masses outside, who constitute its clientele.

As we have seen, the maintenance of close contacts with the masses serves several important purposes for the organization: among the most important is that of gathering the information requisite to the policy-making process. If linkages between the organization and its clientele are close, the organization will meet with greater success in mobilizing support from the masses because it will be aware of mass demands;[162] moreover, compliance will be more likely if instructions are taken to the basic level and conveyed by personal example, rather than merely being issued as orders.

The distinction between impersonality and personal involvement is made more difficult by the postulate in Mao's theory of knowledge that contends that each new individual, each new problem, must be approached, at least in the perceptual stage, as *sui generis*. Personalistic relations are to be encouraged because they enable the cadre better to perceive the subjective as well as

[161] 1945b:1096/III, 315. Similarly, among the "contradictions among the people" that Mao listed in 1957 was that "arising from the bureaucratic style of work of certain government workers in their relations with the masses" (1957d:81).

[162] Mao offered a specific instance of this, citing the case of the Dingzhou municipal government, whose excessive concern over the expansion of the Red Army and mobilization for the transport corps caused them to overlook the problems of their constituents: "The problems facing the people of Dingzhou City were that they had no firewood, no salt was on sale because the capitalists were hoarding it, some people had no houses to live in, and rice was both scarce and dear. . . . But the Dingzhou municipal government did not discuss any of these matters. . . . The result was that very little was achieved in regard to the expansion of the Red Army and mobilization for the transport corps" (1934b:132/I, 148). An additional, and, in a certain sense, an opposite danger inherent in ignoring mass demands is that the organization may come to "lag behind the masses." Such was the situation as Mao saw it in the move toward cooperativization in 1955 (1955d:2).

the objective conditions confronting him. Speaking with André Malraux in 1965, Mao related the question of the links between officials and masses to the problem of egalitarianism: "The revisionists mix up cause and effect. Equality is not important in itself; it is important because it is natural to those who have not lost contact with the masses. The only way of knowing whether a young cadre is really revolutionary is to see whether he really makes friends with the workers and peasants."[163]

Personal intimacy without the attendant favoritism appears, then, to have been the solution Mao advocated for the dissociation of officials from those they are supposed to serve—a dissociation that he saw as potentially corrupting to the individual bureaucrat and destructive of the effectiveness of the organization.

EFFICIENT OPERATION AS THE GOAL OF THE ORGANIZATION

According to Weber, "experience tends universally to show that the purely bureaucratic type of administrative organization . . . is, from a purely technical point of view, capable of attaining the highest degree of efficiency."[164] "The fully developed bureaucratic mechanism compares with other organizations exactly as does the machine with non-mechanical modes of production."[165] It is this conception of the organization to which Selznick refers as involving "a certain bareness, a lean, no-nonsense system of consciously co-ordinated activities. It refers to an expendable tool, a rational instrument engineered to do a job."[166]

As we have seen, however, the goal of efficient execution of purposes set by policy makers at the head of (or outside of) the bureaucratic organization is seldom realized in practice. The emergence of "institutions" or "natural systems" within the organization is accompanied by the development of separate and often conflicting sets of goals, primary among which are the security and self-enrichment of individual members of the organization.

Downs deals at some length with the problems that organizations encounter because of this tendency toward goal displacement. He notes that the ascendency of organizational goals over

[163] 1965h:373.
[164] Weber, *Theory of Economic and Social Organization*, p. 337.
[165] Gerth and Mills, eds., *From Max Weber*, p. 314.
[166] Selznick, *Leadership in Administration*, p. 5.

personal goals is lowest among individuals at the lowest levels of the organization, and tends to increase with status.[167] He also notes that officials can usefully be categorized on the basis of the mix of personal and organizational goals that they hold, arguing that this mix is the result of the personality, position, and time in job of the individual official.[168]

Clearly, a prime prerequisite for efficiency must be adaptability, and, as we have seen, the displacement of goals that tends to occur within an organization results in a sharp decline in the adaptability of the organization. Bennis makes this point, contending that the bureaucratic form of organization "seems most likely to founder on its inability to adapt to rapid change in the environment."[169]

The efficient achievement of externally determined goals was by no means the primary objective of the Chinese bureaucracy. Indeed, that organization had its own substantive goals. The aim of the Confucian order was harmony, and the function of the bureaucracy was to effectuate, or at least to maximize this state.[170] Since the bureaucracy was not conceived of merely as a "rational instrument," or an "expendable tool," but rather as an agent for the maintenance of social stability, the pursuit of security and self-aggrandizement by the individual official was not *ipso facto* antithetical to nor destructive of the goals of the organization. King puts it thus:

> In Weber's model the ideal-type bureaucrat should be a de-humanized machine to carry out the "political will," but in the Confucian model, the ideal type of bureaucrat should not be a man without passion or enthusiasm, but a man with courage and the will to fight against the "political will" (Emperor's will) in order to carry out the mandate of heaven. . . . [Bureau-

---

[167] Downs, *Inside Bureaucracy*, pp. 67f. Crozier makes essentially the same observation, noting that both commitment and subordination are in fact low in contemporary bureaucracies, whereas both are assumed to be high in the ideal model (*Bureaucratic Phenomenon*, p. 199).

[168] Downs, *Inside Bureaucracy*, pp. 88f., 98f. He sees five such types, moving from those whose goals are purely personal to those who espouse a maximum number of the organization's goals. He refers to the types as climbers, conservers, zealots, advocates, and statesmen.

[169] Warren G. Bennis, *Changing Organizations* (New York: McGraw-Hill, 1966), p. 9. Downs relates this tendency toward rigidity to what he calls "sunk costs"—the "cost of shifting a pattern which will not be incurred if one avoids change" (*Inside Bureaucracy*, p. 173).

[170] Among others, Yang makes this point ("Some Characteristics," p. 138).

crats] refused to accept the idea that bureaucracy was merely a "subservient administrative machine," but wanted to turn the bureaucracy into a dynamic political body.[171]

Elsewhere King speaks of the bureaucratic ideal in China as being an "ethocracy," and describes the ideal bureaucrat in such a system as "service-oriented" and "public will minded" rather than self-oriented. In practice, on the other hand, he finds undeniable "the fact that idealistic scholar-officials were the minority in officialdom."[172]

In general, Mao shared with his Chinese progenitors a low regard for efficiency as the primary goal for organizations.[173] The low value that he placed upon efficiency *per se* has earned him the disregard of those students of Chinese development who mistakenly see him as an antipragmatic ideologue. While he did not attack efficiency as counterproductive of itself, he was nonetheless quick to sacrifice efficiency where necessary to achieve other transformational goals that he regarded as more important.

A more accurate appraisal of his position can be achieved by considering the problems Mao raised in his critique of organizational behavior that bear on the question of efficiency as an organizational goal or purpose. Most closely related to the question of efficiency itself is his attack on officials for their tendency toward prodigality with scarce resources. At a broader level, he attacks bureaucrats for their tendency to overlook not so much the goal of efficiency alone, but rather the goal of efficiency tempered with the political considerations that he posed for contemporary Chinese officialdom—for their tendency to supplant these considerations with individual, personal goals. For Mao, this failing manifests itself in the various forms of individualism, and, in the realm of theory, in the error of subjectivism.

One discovers Mao's view of organizational behavior as characterized by prodigality through his frequent injunctions in favor of the opposite virtue of frugality. Because of the fact that China is a poor country, "diligent and frugal operation ought to be the policy of . . . all our enterprises. . . . [A] policy of economy [is] one of the basic policies of socialist economics."[174] Other refer-

---

[171] King, "Behavioral Patterns." [172] Ibid.

[173] It is true, nonetheless, that he spoke early on of the need for cadres to adopt "efficient methods" in their work (1933a:109/1, 133).

[174] 1955g:67. Subsequently he spoke of three campaigns aimed at frugality:

ences make it clear that Mao had human as well as material resources in mind when he spoke of frugality. Reiterating the
slogan, "better and fewer troops, simpler administration," in 1942,
Mao went on to argue that it represents a policy which is beneficial not only from the point of view of organizational efficiency,
but also from the point of view of military tactics.[175]

He took up the question of excessive personnel in his essay,
"On Ten Major Relationships," written in April 1956: "Both the
political party of the proletariat and proletarian dictatorship will
wither away in the future, but they are indispensable at present.
. . . But we must oppose bureaucracy and overexpansion of organizations. I suggest that the party and government organs be re-
trenched on a large scale and cut away by two-thirds."[176] In the
same vein, he had spoken earlier of the need to cut down the
time spent in overlong and too-frequent meetings. "Talks,
speeches, articles, and resolutions should all be concise and to the
point. Meetings should also not go on too long."[177]

Perhaps the greatest single failing of men and women in organizations, in Mao's view, is their tendency to manifest individualist tendencies. The term individualism covers, for Mao, a
wide range of behavior patterns, several of which I will discuss
here. It is crucial to understand what he meant by individualism,

---

"During the *sanfan* (or three-antis) movement in 1952, we fought against
corruption, waste, and bureaucracy, with the emphasis on combatting corruption. In 1955 we advocated the practice of economy with great success
. . . but at that time economy was not yet applied in earnest as a guiding
principle in all branches of the national economy, or in government offices,
army units, schools, and people's organizations in general. This year [1957]
we are calling for economy and the elimination of waste in every sphere
throughout the country" (1957d:127).

[175] 1942d:882/III, 100f.; 1942e:896/III, 115.

[176] 1956e:29. A decade later, just prior to the major thrust of the Cultural
Revolution, Mao argued against overstaffed committees. "There must not
be too many members. When there are too many members . . . they will
make telephone calls and prepare reports and returns. I am alone here and
am doing quite well. At present many ministers have secretaries. All of
these secretaries should be eliminated. I had no secretary before I came to
Yan'an. . . . We did not have such mammoth organs in the past" (1966j:29;
cf. 1956e: 25; 1958e:7; and 1963b:323).

[177] 1949c:1444/IV, 380. Cf. 1945a:1343/III, 268; and 1958e:9f. In the "First
Ten Points" he suggested that meetings be held "at the work sites and in
the paddy fields" to "cut down drastically . . . the time they consume"
(1963d:68).

175

for individualism, as we have already begun to see, was a crucial element in his definition of bourgeois class status.[178]

Individualism was, for Mao, a quality to be avoided or overcome by cadres in organizations.[179] Ideal cadres "must be free from selfishness, from individualistic heroism, ostentation, sloth, passivity, and sectarian arrogance, and they must be selfless national and class heroes; such are the qualities and the style of work demanded of the members, cadres, and leaders of our party."[180] This listing of the adverse aspects of individualism suggests something of the definitional range of Mao's use of the term and the concept. I want to explore this range by considering more closely certain of these diverse qualities.

Among the first of the faults found under the general rubric of individualism is the quality that Mao, in the passage just cited, referred to as "individualistic heroism,"[181] and which he contrasted with the condition of being "selfless national and class heroes." Heroic action is clearly an antidote to the routinized behavior characteristic of the members of an organization, as we have seen, but it serves only to compound the damage if it is aimed at individual glorification. Thus revolutionary successors "must be modest and prudent and guard against arrogance and impetuosity; they must be imbued with the spirit of self-criticism and have the courage to correct mistakes and shortcomings in their work. They must never . . . claim all the credit for themselves and shift all the blame on others. . . . They must be revolutionaries who wholeheartedly serve the overwhelming majority of the people of China and the whole world."[182]

A second form of individualism that Mao criticized is the characteristic which he called "independence."[183] He spoke critically of the cadre who is unresponsive to the directions he or she receives from above, and to the interests of his or her subordinates and clients,[184] but on the other hand praises the cadre who "has the ability to find his or her bearings independently."[185]

Another three qualities associated with the notion of individual-

[178] Mao linked membership in the bourgeoisie with the qualities of arrogance and complacency, the economic roles of exploiters and small producers, the philosophical world view of idealism, and the pursuit of individualistic goals in 1963k.

[179] 1957g. Cf. 1956d:13f.   [180] 1937d:267/I, 291.
[181] 1944b:995/III, 217. See also 1958l:113.
[182] 1964n:27.   [183] 1944b:995/III, 217.
[184] 1959j:172.   [185] 1938e:515/II, 202.

ism seem sufficiently closely related to one another to merit their treatment conjointly. Each of them constitutes a grouping of individuals for the pursuit of their common interests when those interests do not coincide with those of the party. Included are the behavior patterns that Mao termed "guild mentality," the "mountain stronghold mentality," and factionalism.

Manifestations of guild mentality, which Mao criticized in 1945 as an incorrect mode of behavior,[186] involves the formation of an individualistically oriented interest group, the nucleus of which is determined on the basis of occupation. In 1959 he spoke disparagingly of this tendency in terms reminiscent of claims laid against the structure of our own society. Addressing himself in a letter to Zhang Wentian[187] he said, "the adage says: Things are aggregated into like categories, but men gravitate to their group. . . . You have completely forgotten the excellent words and the best ways of Marxism, and so you joined the Military Club, which is really a combination of the civilian and the military, like two pieces of jade complementing each other."[188]

In 1960 Mao's response to the tendency toward guild mentality was to call for "cooperation" between workers, technicians, and cadres.[189] In a letter to Lin Biao in 1966 he advocated, as we have noted, the developing of "many-faceted individuals" as a solution to the problem. He spoke there of five areas of social and political life—politics, military affairs, agricultural production, industry, and culture—and argued that everyone should be familiar with each of those spheres of activity that lie outside of his or her own *métier*.[190]

A footnote in the *Selected Works* offers the following definition of the "mountain-stronghold mentality": "[It] was a tendency to form cliques and arose mainly out of the circumstances of the protracted guerrilla war in which rural revolutionary bases

---

[186] 1944b:995/III, 217.

[187] Zhang Wentian was at the time an alternate member of the Central Committee and former ambassador to the Soviet Union. He had acted as foreign minister during Zhou Enlai's absences from the country. Accused of membership in the Peng Dehuai "anti-party group" he disappeared from view in 1959; Union Research Institute, *Who's Who in Communist China* (Hong Kong: Union Research Institute, 1965), pp. 41ff.

[188] 1959u:54f. A very early criticism of professionalism in the military is found in 1929:84f./I, 106f. He similarly criticized the medical profession for its professionalism (1954c:13; 1964b).

[189] 1960d; cf. 1957i.   [190] 1966f:56f.

were scattered and cut off from each other. Most of these bases were first established in a mountain region. Each tended to regard itself as a compact unit, like a single mountain stronghold, so this wrong tendency became known as mountain-stronghold mentality."[191] Mountain-stronghold mentality, then, is a tendency toward the formation of individualistically oriented interest groups, the nucleus of which is, at least in part, determined on a geographical basis.[192] Regionalism or localism has been a perennial problem in China, and was thus a form of individualism that was of particular concern for Mao. He touched on this question again in a 1958 instruction: "It is not absolutely necessary for a province to be ruled by a person from the same province. It matters not where he hails from—the south or the north—and what nationality he belongs to; the only question which must be considered is whether he has communism and how much communism he has. . . . There should be provinciality, but there should not be provincialism."[193]

A third, more generalized type of individualistically oriented group behavior is what Mao referred to as "factionalism," "sectarianism," or "small-group mentality." Speaking of the latter of these, Mao noted, "Some comrades consider only the interests of their own small group and ignore the general interest. Although on the surface this does not seem to be the pursuit of personal interests, in reality it exemplifies the narrowest individualism and has a corrosive and centrifugal effect."[194] Similarly, he defined sectarianism as a failure to "subordinate the partial interests of some of the party members to the interests of the whole party," and to "regard the leading body of the party as the concentrator of the will of the whole party."[195] Elsewhere he criticized a "closed-door attitude" toward nonparty members as constituting a form of sectarianism.[196] The problems to which sectarianism gives rise, he argued, involve drawing incorrect distinctions both

[191] 1944b:953n/III, 176n.

[192] Independence being a positive quality in Mao's view, he took pains to distinguish between what he regarded as legitimate and illegitimate independent kingdoms (1956c:32). As had been the case with Gao Gang and Rao Shushi, the "Peng-Huang-Zhang-Zhou anti-party group" was accused, among other failings, of this sort of illegitimate regionalism (1959w: 67).

[193] 1958i:30. [194] 1929:95/I, 112.

[195] 1944b:980/III, 209.

[196] 1941c:767/III, 33; and 1942a:779/III, 43f.

in judging the work of existing cadres and in recruiting new cadres—that is, distinctions on the basis of narrow, individualistic criteria.[197] Elsewhere he denounced the use of criteria such as these, calling it "favoritism" and "one-sidedness."[198]

In place of each of these individualistically oriented groupings, Mao advocated that the only distinctions drawn be those based on broad and impersonal criteria. Writing in 1949, he called on party committees to "draw two lines of distinction," the one between "revolution and counterrevolution," and the other "between right and wrong" within the revolutionary ranks.[199] This conception of the proper distinctions to be drawn was reflected, as well, in his subsequent treatment of the difference between antagonistic and nonantagonistic contradictions.

A fourth manifestation of individualism in organizational behavior is the tendency to launch personal attacks rather than principled criticism. Mao classified as a "manifestation of petty-bourgeois individualism" the tendency to substitute personal attack, which "damages the party organization as well as individuals," for the correct form of intraparty criticism, which constitutes "a weapon for strengthening the party organization and increasing its fighting capacity."[200]

Another form of personal attack is retaliation. Those who are wronged seek revenge either within or outside of the organization. "Such retaliation arises from purely personal considerations, to the neglect of the interests of the class and of the party as a whole. Its target is not the enemy class, but individuals in our own ranks. It is a corrosive which weakens the organization and its fighting capacity."[201]

In place of the tendency toward personal attack and retaliation, Mao advocated paying attention "to uniting and working with comrades who differ with you." We should be good, he continued, "at uniting in our work not only with comrades who hold the same views as we but also with those who hold different views. There are some among us who have made very serious

---

[197] 1944b:980/III, 209. Other criticisms of sectarianism appear in Mao's writings during the course of the antirightist campaign of 1957. See 1957f: 13; 1957g. Cf. 1959u:54f.

[198] 1944b:995/III, 217. Cf. 1956p:13 and 1957f:18f.

[199] 1949c:1444f./IV, 381.   [200] 1929:92/I, 110.

[201] 1929:95/I, 112. In a similar vein, he denounced elsewhere in the same article the quality of "punitiveness" he found in the behavior of members of organizations (1929:92/I, 110).

mistakes; we should not be prejudiced against them but should be ready to work with them."[202] This alternative is embodied in the "unity-criticism-unity" formula that he reiterated in his speech at the Tenth Plenum,[203] and which was repeated with great frequency during the course of the Cultural Revolution. The point to be remembered in launching critical attacks, Mao argued on several occasions, is to differentiate "between the nine fingers and the one finger"—remembering, that is, that those who merit critical attack constitute only a small percentage of the group as a whole.[204]

The other side of the coin of personal attack and retaliation is the equally undesirable quality that constitutes the fifth manifestation of individualism in organization, namely, self-justification. A denunciation of self-justification is found in his speech at the Lushan Plenum.[205] Elsewhere he suggested that there are circumstances in which self-justification is appropriate: he argued that unmerited abuse should be resisted, while, on the other hand, abuse that is merited should be accepted.[206]

A sixth manifestation of individualism is found in the closely related qualities that he referred to as "passivity" and the "employee mentality." He spoke of "some comrades" who "do not realize that they themselves are makers of the revolution. They think that their responsibility is merely to their individual superiors and not to the revolution. This passive mentality of an 'employee' is also a manifestation of individualism."[207] This "passive mentality" is reflected in a reduced output. "Some comrades," Mao argued, "become passive and stop working whenever anything goes against their wishes."[208]

Elsewhere Mao associated the passivity that arises from individualism with what he called "right conservatism." Asking rhetorically why all areas could not move toward cooperativization with the same speed as a certain model area, he answered his own question: "I can only see one reason—unwillingness to take the trouble, or, to put it more bluntly, right opportunism."[209] He

---

[202] 1949c:1444/IV, 380.   [203] 1962e:90.
[204] 1958e:9. Cf. 1959d:22.   [205] 1959r:28f.
[206] 1958e:9.   [207] 1929:96/I, 113.
[208] Ibid. Elsewhere he spoke of "slacking at work due to indifference or perfunctoriness" as being a "manifestation of bureaucracy" (1933a:118/I, 134).
[209] 1955g:12. Elsewhere he defined right conservatism as "the failure to

later derided "those who drag their feet" as having "the world outlook of the cowards and lazybones," and as lacking "the least ambition of the Marxist-Leninists."[210]

The desirable alternative qualities to this passivity and lack of initiative—diligence[211] and industriousness[212]—can be inculcated, to a degree at least, through education.[213] Even more effective in this regard is the periodic exchange of functions between the cadres and the rank and file in an organization.[214]

A final manifestation of individualism encountered in organizational behavior is "pleasure-seeking." In 1929, pleasure-seeking took the form of Red Armymen who "always hope that their unit will march into big cities. They want to go there not to work, but to enjoy themselves."[215] Thirty-five years later the similar fault was manifested differently: "The life of sitting on sofas and using electric fans will not do," Mao said in 1966.[216] In both cases, however, his countersuggestion was the same: "We must keep to our style of plain living and hard work."[217]

As I have argued in the foregoing sections, the traditional Chinese bureaucrat was a generalist, where his Western counterpart is a specialist.[218] Both operated in an essentially hierarchical structure, though there was, generally speaking, a single such structure in the Chinese milieu rather than many competing structures, and thus organizational authority for the Chinese bureaucrat was coterminous with cultural, political, economic, and social authority. Whereas in the Western organization operations aim at uniformity and routinization—often at the expense of the ability to innovate—the operation of the Chinese bureaucracy was essentially situation-oriented, with no particularly strong urge toward routinization.

In both organizational settings, impersonal relations are seen as desirable goals, but in both cases, as we have seen, affective relations are likely to occur, and may in fact contribute to the viability

---

carry out something which should be done and is within our means to accomplish" (1956a:97).

[210] 1959cc:173f. Cf. 1955d:8 and 1955f:27.

[211] 1955g:67.   [212] 1938e:514/II, 202.

[213] 1929:96/I, 113.   [214] 1960d.

[215] 1929:96/I, 113.

[216] 1966i:24ff. Cf. 1959y:57 and 1964q:387.

[217] 1949c:1444/IV, 380.

[218] The British bureaucrat is an exception to this generalization.

of the organization. The models are also similar in their advancement of achievement and seniority as the basis for recruitment and promotion. In both settings, position within the organization constitutes a career. The Chinese model is unique in the gulf that existed between the particular type of achievement upon which recruitment was based and the actual requirements of the office.

Finally, the goals of the two organizational models are not only dissimilar in content, they are dissimilar in kind. Whereas the Western bureaucracy is conceived of as a purely instrumental structure designed to carry out efficiently the will of others, the Chinese bureaucracy had essentially two substantive goals: the first, to promote social stability; the second, to maximize its political power *vis-à-vis* that of the throne. In actual practice, officials in both organizations tended to pursue their own goals of personal security and aggrandizement, though I have suggested that this tendency proves more destructive to the goals of the Western organization than it did to those of the traditional Chinese bureaucracy.

Comparing these generalizations with the model that we are now able to construct of the ideal organization from Mao's point of view, we find that this latter construct differs significantly from both its Chinese and its Western precursors. Mao appears, in his consideration of organizations, to be attempting to avoid what he regarded as the undesirable qualities of both of the organizational archetypes as he had observed them, directly or indirectly, during the course of his career.

One must also add that his conception of an ideal organization is informed by yet a third set of organizational principles—those governing military organizations. As Weber pointed out, however, military and civilian bureaucratic organizations are closely related through their common roots in rational discipline.[219] In the case of the Chinese communist movement, furthermore, the effort has been not only one of militarizing civilian bureaucracies, but also, throughout the course of the Chinese communist revolution, one of "civilianizing" the military—reducing to a minimum, in short, the distinctions between the two organizational types. One is therefore justified, I think, in subordinating the military influences on Mao's organizational theory to the influences of the primarily civilian paradigms described above.

[219] Gerth and Mills, eds., *From Max Weber*, pp. 253ff.

As I have shown, recruitment into an ideal organization was not, for Mao, to be based exclusively upon the expert performance of a specialized function. On the other hand, it seems clear that he would have regarded as equally unsatisfactory recruitment based on the command of certain general principles external to the functioning of the office, to the exclusion of competence for the specific tasks involved. He found, in short, the excessive specialization of the Western ideal-type organization and the excessive generalization of the traditional Chinese ideal-type organization to be equally undesirable, and the correct solution to lie in a balance or synthesis of the two.

With regard to the question of hierarchy, Mao accepted the need for a hierarchical type of organization, though in doing so he espoused and expanded upon Lenin's principles of democratic centralism, which are analogous to, but at the same time a significant deviation from, Weber's conception of the relationships involved in a hierarchical structure. Like Weber's successors, Mao is concerned with the problem of information flow, but this concern is no doubt triggered more by his knowledge of the problem as it manifested itself in the operation of traditional Chinese bureaucratic organization and in a setting of guerrilla warfare than by his awareness of the similar problem in Western organizations.

Routinization is central to the rational-legal bureaucracy, relatively peripheral to the situation-oriented traditional Chinese bureaucracy. Mao saw more danger than benefit in routinization, and thus hedged it about with restrictions in his conception of an ideal organization. His pragmatic emphasis on practice over theory led him to prefer a situation-oriented approach, in many respects closer to the traditional Chinese bureaucracy than to the routinized operation of the Western organization. Moreover, like Western observers, he saw routinization as antithetical to revolution. As I shall show, he appears to have regarded the converse of that statement to be true as well: counterroutinization in organizational life was, for Mao, a form of revolution.

Both the Chinese and the Western organizational ideal types feature an impersonal, disinterested approach to his client by the functionary. As we have seen, however, impersonal behavior of functionaries is scarcely ever found in actual bureaucratic practice, and may, in fact, be harmful rather than beneficial to the achievement of the goals of the organization. Mao's view of the place of impersonality in the bureaucrat's performance of his duties appears to have been an attempt to avoid the pitfalls shared by Chinese and Western models. He rejected both the haughty demeanor toward inferiors that was characteristic of the Chinese bureaucrat's impersonal execution of his duties, and the pettifogging performance of the rational-legal functionary, advocating instead a close, peer-like relationship between bureaucrat and client. At the same time, this relationship is to be an impersonal, selfless one, the empathy between bureaucrat and client being based not on their qualities as individuals, but on their common membership in that body known as "the people," or "the masses."

Finally, Mao rejected efficiency as a primary organizational goal. Qualitative goals concerning the direction of development must always be given at least equal consideration alongside what might be viewed as the primarily quantitative goal of efficient operation. In this case, Mao's view appears to me to have constituted a synthesis of the Western and traditional Chinese models of organization. Clearly Mao's goals were different from those of the traditional Chinese rulers—conflict replaced stability as a first value, and goals were not seen as fixed, but rather as emerging from ongoing practice. Nevertheless, he shared with his predecessors the sense that the manner in which the goal is achieved is equally important as the speed and economy with which it is achieved, if not more so. Furthermore, the contemporary Chinese bureaucracy, like its traditional and Western counterparts, tends to put forward goals of its own to rival those of its leaders. Just as the traditional Chinese bureaucracy sought to increase its resources of political power in order to enhance its prestige and perquisites, and just as Western organizations are seen to pursue their own goals of security and self-aggrandizement, so contemporary Chinese bureaucrats were seen by Mao as having individualistic goals of their own that tend to conflict with, rather than enhance, the pursuit of the goals of the leadership. The tendency toward the pursuit of individualistic goals is doubly dangerous from Mao's viewpoint; not only does the organization cease to perform the functions for which it was established, but in addition, its pursuit of these individualistic goals tends to corrupt —to cause the embourgeoisement of—the functionary.

Presenting Mao's views of organizational life in this composite fashion obscures somewhat the degree to which those views changed during the course of his career. The change is most strikingly evident if one compares the Leninist enthusiasm of his

1943 injunction to "Get Organized!"[220] with the pessimistic tone that pervades his post-Liberation "Twenty Manifestations of Bureaucracy."[221] Thus it is important to realize that, while Chinese and Western organizational practice came to serve as negative examples that helped to shape Mao's early views on the subject, his experience with the bureaucratic tendencies within the party, state, and military organizations that he had helped to found came to serve him as the principal negative examples on the basis of which he constructed his later views. Whereas he initially regarded organizations formed under communist auspices and supervision as able to avoid the pitfalls of bureaucratization, this view changed during the late 1950s and early 1960s. At that point he came to regard the party itself as having fallen victim to bureaucratization, and thus in need of thoroughgoing reform. The experience of the Cultural Revolution—a profound movement of a new type, which aimed at the stemming of the tide of bureaucratization—appears to have convinced Mao of the validity of his negative assessment of bureaucratic organizations, to have demonstrated to him the magnitude of the task of reversing the trend of bureaucratization, but not to have changed his fundamental conviction as to the necessity for organization to achieve revolutionary goals.

AUTHORITY AND CLASS IN ORGANIZATIONAL LIFE

The organization is thus a crucial factor in the determination of the class structure of a society, in Mao's view as I have reconstructed it here. Similarly, Ralf Dahrendorf has treated organizational authority as the critical variable in his definition of social class. There are important differences, however, between Mao's and Dahrendorf's views, and it will help to clarify our understanding of Mao's view to compare the two here.

Dahrendorf sets forth in his book, *Class and Class Conflict in Industrial Society*, a "completion" of Marx's *Capital* in the form of an extrapolated chapter on social classes.[222] Following this he takes issue with Marx's contention that property relations are the basis on which the composition of social classes is determined. In their place he suggests the substitution of authority relations in

---

[220] 1943e.   [221] 1967a.

[222] Ralf Dahrendorf, *Class and Class Conflict in Industrial Society* (Stanford: Stanford University Press, 1959), pp. 9-18.

"imperatively coordinated associations." This latter term Dahrendorf borrows from Weber, who defined it as a collectivity whose "members are, by virtue of a prevailing order, subject to authority relations."[223]

Authoritative positions within these associations, Dahrendorf argues, give rise to "orientations of behavior" that constitute "latent interests." When these interests become "articulate and conscious" to individuals within the collectivity, they are referred to as "manifest interests."[224] On this basis, then, he redefines the concept of class as follows: "By *social class* shall be understood such organized or unorganized collectivities as share manifest or latent interests arising from and related to the authority structure of imperatively coordinated associations. It follows from the definitions of latent and manifest interests that classes are always conflict groups."[225]

It will help us to grasp the difference between Dahrendorf's view of the relationship of organizational authority and class to that of Mao, as I have depicted his views in the preceding pages, to consider the impulse that gave rise to each of the two arguments. Dahrendorf has set out to explain how the individual members of a society form themselves into groupings on the basis of common traits. In doing so he hypothesizes a definition of these groupings based on the occupancy or nonoccupancy of roles of authority within the associations that comprise the society. Mao, on the other hand, appears to have begun with a quite different project in mind—namely, to formulate an explanation for the tendency he observed in certain individuals to change their behavior in significant ways when they wield authority within organizations, a change of behavior that seemed to Mao to place them in a different societal grouping from that to which they previously belonged.

As a consequence of the difference between these two projects, the structures of the two explanations differ in kind from one another. On the one hand, Dahrendorf has constructed certain

---

[223] Weber, *Theory of Social and Economic Organization*, p. 153.

[224] Dahrendorf, *Class and Class Conflict*, pp. 237f.

[225] Ibid., p. 238. Emphasis in original. In a somewhat similar vein, Franz Schurmann makes the point that bureaucracies give rise to class distinctions in socialist and capitalist systems alike. *The Logic of World Power: An Inquiry into the Origins, Currents and Contradictions of World Politics* (New York: Pantheon, 1976), p. 45.

analytical structures—the "imperatively coordinated association," the social role, the class—which bear only an analytical relationship to one another. Mao's explanation, on the other hand, deals *both* with analogous analytical structures *and* with concrete structures—specific organizations and specific individual members of those organizations.

Closely related to this difference in the structure of the two arguments is the difference in the use of the concept of authority by the two men. Dahrendorf employs Weber's concept of authority—"legitimate power"—where the legitimacy is seen as residing in social roles rather than in individuals. As I have pointed out in the previous chapters, to the extent that an analogous definition of authority can be found in Mao's writings, it is prestige rather than legitimacy that combines with power to form authority, and prestige is associated, in Mao's view, with individual behavior as well as with role behavior in classes, parties, and institutions. In addition, as we have seen, the importance of the element of power is concomitantly elevated in Mao's concept of authority.

The idea of a social role figures in Mao's explanation of change of class status only in a very minor way. His emphasis was almost invariably upon performance of a role, rather than upon the role itself. Because it lacks, or deemphasizes, the concept of a social role, Mao's explanation lacks the definitional inevitability of Dahrendorf's. For Dahrendorf, those who occupy positions of authority constitute a "bourgeois" class by definition; for Mao their class status depends not on the mere occupancy of the authoritative roles, but rather upon how those roles are performed. It is possible, in Mao's schema, for there to be proletarian as well as bourgeois wielders of authority.

Finally, Mao seems unwilling to reduce the basis for class distinctions to a problem of authority alone. Mishandled positions of authority within organizations are an important cause of embourgeoisement for Mao—in the latter stages of the development of his thought on the subject, the most important cause, I would argue—but he was not willing to use mishandled authority as the lowest common denominator to which every case of political, economic, and ideological backsliding must ultimately be reduced.

187

Chapter Six

ON PARTICIPATION AND
REPRESENTATION

> Our aim is to create a political situation which
> is centralist and yet democratic, disciplined and
> yet free, ideologically united and yet individu-
> ally content, and dynamic and lively.[1]

Proposed solutions to the problem of the potential corruption of those who take part in organizational life were set forward at one point early in the Cultural Revolution, by means of an historical example—that of the Paris Commune of 1871. The *dazibao* written in late May 1966 by a young philosophy teacher at Beida—an act that marked the initiation of the active phase of the Cultural Revolution—was described two months later by Mao as having been a "declaration of a Chinese Paris Commune of the 1960s."[2] Less than a month later, the "Sixteen Point Decision" of the Central Committee regarding the conduct of the movement spoke of the need for implementing a general election system modeled after that in the Paris Commune to choose delegates to the "organs of power" in the Cultural Revolution.[3]

In their discussions of the experience of the Paris Commune that appeared prior to the Cultural Revolution, Chinese writers, Mao among them, had tended to stay rather close to the treatment given that historical episode by Marx, Engels, and Lenin. Thus, although credit was given for the precedent set by the Communards, the emphasis in most allusions to the events of 1871 was upon the failures rather than upon the successes of the Commune.[4]

---

[1] 1957g.   [2] 1966i:24.   [3] 1966m:123.

[4] See, for example, 1963j:11. In other pre-Cultural Revolution references to the Paris Commune, Mao referred to it as marking the beginning of a century of international proletarian revolution (1964n:123), as a "dress rehearsal" for the Russian and Chinese revolutions (1960e:1f.), and as an example of the dictatorship of the proletariat (1956n:126 and 1959r:42), the principles of which are "permanent and indestructible."

In 1966, however, articles commemorating its ninety-fifth anniversary presented a view of the Commune that was both more comprehensive and more positive.[5]

Marx had observed that the Commune raised the possibility of creating an institution that would alleviate, by means of mass participation, the alienation of state from society typical of political systems of the capitalist stage and of those stages that had come before.[6] The particular measures of which he took note in this connection were the system of direct election and recall of officials, the combination of executive and legislative functions in a single "working, not a parliamentary body," and the provision that officials receive workingmen's wages for carrying out their duties. Lenin subsequently argued that these measures had demonstrated that it is impossible for the proletariat simply to seize control of the existing state machinery. What is necessary instead, and what the Communards succeeded in creating, he went on to argue, was a new governmental form—the "proletariat organized as the ruling class" or, borrowing a phrase from Marx's "Critique of the Gotha Program," the "revolutionary dictatorship of the proletariat."[7] What Lenin extolled and what the Chinese took as a model for the reform of their own institutional life is an apparent paradox: that of a system which might best be termed a "participatory dictatorship." It is within the context of Mao's faith in the possibility of realizing an apparently paradoxical system such as this that the development of his ideas of participation and representation must be read and understood.[8]

[5] The most important of these articles is Zheng Zhisi, *"Bali gongshe de weida jiaoxun"* (The Great Lessons of the Paris Commune) *HQ* 4 (1966), translated in *PR* 9:14 (1 April 1966), 23-26; 9:15 (8 April 1966), 17f., 25; and 9:16 (15 April 1966), 23-29.

[6] Karl Marx, *The Civil War in France*, in Robert C. Tucker, ed., *The Marx-Engels Reader* (New York: W. W. Norton, 1972), p. 555; cf. Lenin, *State and Revolution*, in James E. Connor, ed., *Lenin on Politics and Revolution: Selected Writings* (New York: Pegasus, 1968), p. 208.

[7] Lenin, *State and Revolution*, pp. 214, 218.

[8] I have explored in greater detail the Chinese use of the Paris Commune as an organizational model in the Cultural Revolution and during the period leading up to it in the article, "Revolution in Retrospect: The Paris Commune through Chinese Eyes," *China Quarterly* 49 (1972), 106-125. See also Maurice Meisner, "Images of the Paris Commune in Contemporary Chinese Marxist Thought," *Massachusetts Review* 12:3 (1971), 479-497.

From "Mass Line" to "Mass Criticism"

Before we can fruitfully explore the nature of the Paris Commune model of political participation and political representation as it helped to shape Mao's thought on these questions, we need to retrace our steps briefly. In the preceding chapter I discussed at some length Mao's treatment of the principle of the mass line from the point of view of the correct functioning of the organization. We turn here to a reexploration of this crucial principle, this time taking into account the relationship between those inside and those outside of the organization. Seen from this latter point of view, the principle of the mass line constitutes the basis for a system of political participation.

We have observed the close links that Mao drew between the operation of the mass line and the process of cognition as he described it in the article, "On Practice."[9] Like the latter process, the mass line involves three stages. Opinions are first gathered "from the masses," next these "scattered and unsystematic" ideas are "concentrated" or "centralized" (*jizhong*), and thereby transformed into systematic ideas, and finally these systematic ideas are taken back and explained "to the masses," so that the masses "embrace them as their own, hold fast to them and translate them into action."[10] Although one might initially be tempted to label these stages with more familiar terms—plebiscite, policy making, and political education, for example—such labels obscure the fact that Mao believed the process to be a dialectical one. Such a conception proceeds from the assumption of a dialectical interaction between leaders and masses, and between policies and the political reality those policies are designed to transform. Because he saw this relationship as dialectical, each of the elements in the process—leaders, led, policies, and political reality—emerge qualitatively altered as a result of the operation of the mass line.

It is the first of these stages, gathering ideas from the masses, that is basic to an understanding of Mao's view of political participation. Although, as we have seen, obliging a cadre to engage in direct contact with the masses whom he or she is appointed to serve has positive effects on curbing that cadre's natural tendencies toward alienation from the masses, self-seekingness, and a bureaucratic style of work, this is not the central reason for Mao's insist-

[9] The description of the mass line is found at 1943b:854/III, 119. The description of the process of cognition is found at 1937e:259-273/I, 295-309.
[10] 1943b:854/III, 119.

ence on the implementation of the mass line. Rather, the mass line is necessary primarily because without it the polity could not operate, and its development could not be realized: "Politics must follow the mass line. It will not do to rely on leaders alone. How can the leaders accomplish so much? The leaders can cope with only a fraction of everything, good and bad. Consequently everybody must be mobilized to share the responsibility, to speak up, to encourage other people."[11] Implicit here is the vesting of at least a limited amount of authority in "the masses"—a point that we have made earlier in another context. As a source of policy initiatives, the masses were seen by Mao as possessing an authority which, because of the indispensability of these initiatives, can at certain points become greater than that of the party itself.[12] Just as the material world presents itself as a "realm of necessity"—a series of constraints beyond which perception cannot move until that world has been transformed—so the authority of the masses lies in the constraints they are able to impose on the policies put forward by their leaders. In the same way that the observer's conceptions are limited by his or her perceptions of the material situation which he or she observes, so the leader's policy options are limited, in mass line theory, to those which he or she has discovered among the views, interests, and opinions of the masses that he or she has observed. The authority is, to be sure, a limited one, and we will discuss those limitations shortly, but at the same time, it is not a negligible one.

The second stage of the process—that of "concentrating" or "centralizing" the ideas of the masses—is a crucial, yet an ambiguous one. Although the function of the leader in this description is made to sound minimal—indeed, at one point Mao spoke of the role of leadership in this stage of the mass line as being that of a "processing plant" dealing with the raw material of mass views[13] —in fact, as we have seen in analyzing the correlative stage in the formation of ideas, the function is actually both broadly conceived and crucial to the successful outcome of the interaction.

[11] 1965g:102.

[12] Initiative, as we have seen, is an aspect of Mao's concept of power, and hence authority. He treated the implementation of democracy and the augmentation of initiative at the basic level as directly proportional (1937d: 256/I, 292, and 1938e:494/II, 204). It is the exercise of this initiative that he saw as requisite to the functioning and development of a polity, as we have seen in the passage just cited.

[13] 1962a:164.

As in the case of the formation of concepts, the preconceptions of the leader are crucial here, for it is clearly these preconceptions that make possible the "systematization" spoken of by Mao as a part of the process.[14]

The third stage of the mass line process—that of taking newly formulated policy back to the masses, explaining it, and helping to effect its implementation—is a process of education that commits the cadre not only to being responsive to the interests of the masses he or she serves, but to engaging with them in an ongoing relationship of developing interdependency. We shall explore this educational process more fully in the next chapter.

As much as any element of what has come to be called the "Yan'an way" or "Yan'an syndrome" in Chinese communist praxis,[15] the mass line appears to be a product characteristic of the particular circumstances of the base areas during the revolution, depending for its optimal functioning on the face-to-face interaction possible under those circumstances.[16] The mass line

[14] Hints as to the nature of the process of "centralization" in the mass line are found elsewhere in Mao's writings. In the same article in which he set forward the description of the mass line cited above, he spoke of the necessity for establishing priorities—rather like the process of distinguishing principal and nonprincipal contradictions in the process of cognition—as follows: "It is part of the art of leadership to take the whole situation into account and plan accordingly in the light of the historical conditions and existing circumstances of each locality, decide correctly on the center of gravity and the sequence of the work for each period, steadfastly carry through the decision, and make sure that definite results are achieved" (1943b:856/III, 121). Elsewhere he spoke explicitly of the fact that the process of centralization of mass views requires "comprehensive guiding principles, policies and methods" (1962a:177).

[15] See Mark Selden, *The Yenan Way in Revolutionary China* (Cambridge: Harvard University Press, 1971), especially pp. 208-270, and Chalmers Johnson, "Chinese Communist Leadership and Mass Response: The Yenan Period and the Socialist Education Campaign Period," in Ho Ping-ti and Tang Tsou, eds., *China in Crisis* (Chicago: University of Chicago Press, 1968), I, 397-437.

[16] As we discovered in treating the effects of mass line operations on the organization, Mao devotes considerable attention to methods of communicating between cadres and the masses at the basic level (see, for example, 1959j:172). In 1955 he suggested that, although direct contact with the masses was requisite to the operation of the mass line, that it was possible to generalize on the basis of "limited contact." By "contact" in this instance, he explained, he meant a responsible person stationed at the basic level for seven to ten weeks (1955f:28). He summarized his views on the general question in 1963: "What is important is whether or not our comrades can

as formulated in 1943 contains no provision for a hierarchical relationship among leaders or for a chain of command within an organization. Just as second-hand perceptions are relatively less reliable than those gained through direct experience, so second-hand reports of the interests and opinions of the masses are a relatively less reliable basis for policymaking. Equally dangerous, particularly from the point of view of the leaders, is the inevitable situation within a large organization wherein the leaders' praxis consists exclusively of issuing orders to their subordinates in the process of carrying out the "to the masses" side of the formula. These dangers were realized as a result of the move, during the Civil War, from the relatively intimate scale of the base areas to the vast scale of the nation as a whole—a move that was marked by the introduction of a highly complex chain of command within the party, state, and army organizations. The alienation of the organization from its clients, at least where the upper echelons of the organization are concerned, thus results not only from the malfeasance of cadres who choose to ignore the principles of the mass line, but also from the problem of sheer size, a problem for which the principles of the mass line offer no solution.

If the mass line is a means whereby mass initiative can be brought into play in political life, the idea of mass criticism calls forth a somewhat different type of expression from the masses, and expands proportionately the authority that Mao saw invested in them. The idea of the legitimacy of mass criticism of organizations and their leaders appeared early in Mao's writings. In 1929 he spoke of mass criticism as being one of several means of curbing a tendency toward the "purely military viewpoint" among army cadres.[17] Mass criticism appears, in these early treatments, to serve a complementary role to that of the mass line, if it is not actually integral to it. Certainly the return to the masses, once the new policy has been implemented, to observe the verification or invalidation of the policy that results from that implementation, carries within it a potential for criticism of the cadre by the masses. Beyond that, however, the function of mass criticism is seen as correcting mistakes not only in the policies made by the

---

get close to the masses, whether or not they are able to concentrate the diverse opinions among the masses, form systematic opinions and obtain unified recognition among leading cadres through fermentation and discussion" (1963:69).

[17] 1929:84f./I, 106f.

leadership, but also in the cadres' performance of their job in a more general sense—including, importantly, violations of the consultative and educative functions of the mass line resulting from the proliferating and lithifying bureaucratic structures.[18] The extension of the authority of the masses in the concept of mass criticism derives from the idea that it is the interests of the people whom the organization and its leaders are constituted to serve, and thus that it is the people who are best able to determine when that goal is not being achieved.

The nature of mass criticism as an expansion of the mass line will become clearer as we look briefly at three instances in which it was implemented in the post-Liberation period. The first instance in which mass criticism figured importantly began in 1955, at which time a debate arose within the Central Committee regarding the appropriate pace of socialist transformation in the agricultural sector. While some argued for a deliberate pace that would permit consolidation at each stage, Mao and others made the case that it was desirable to capitalize on the forward thrust already generated by the initial stages of the movement, and that prolonged periods of consolidation would not only destroy that thrust, but would foster the development of counterproductive expectations and habits among the peasants, which would then require subsequent reform.[19]

---

[18] In 1941 he advised his colleagues that they "must listen attentively" to the views of nonparty members and "let them have their say." If their views are correct, they should be learned from; if wrong, the cadre should wait until all is said and then "patiently explain it to them." The CCP works in the interests of the nation and the people, he concluded, and thus the party "should be supervised by the people and never go against their will" (1941c: 767f./III, 33f.).

[19] In mid-summer 1955 Mao addressed a conference of secretaries of provincial, municipal, and autonomous region committees of the CCP on the subject of agricultural cooperation. He opened his remarks as follows: "A new upsurge in the socialist mass movement is imminent throughout the countryside. But some of our comrades are tottering along like a woman with bound feet and constantly complaining, 'You're going too fast.' Excessive criticism, inappropriate complaints, endless anxiety, and the erection of countless taboos—they believe this is the proper way to guide the socialist mass movement in the rural areas" (1955d:1). Five months later, in an editorial note in the *Socialist Upsurge* collection, he suggested that the problem of "combatting rightist conservative ideas about the speed of socialist transformation of agriculture . . . has already been solved" (1955g: 9). See also Thomas Bernstein, "Leadership and Mass Movement in the

The rapid pace of cooperativization was maintained, but not, apparently, without Mao's alienating those of his colleagues who had argued for a more moderate approach. He was confident, however, that their view was wrong, and that his position on this question and other more general issues was shared by the masses. His comments in the *Socialist Upsurge* collection abound with examples drawn from the articles it contained proving, in Mao's view, that his colleagues' opinion—that "the speed at which the cooperatives have been developing has gone beyond the understanding of the masses and the ability of the officials to lead"— was incorrect. "The people . . . demand cooperatives. The officials . . . have gone from 'not understanding to understanding,' " he said, citing one such example.[20] Later in the same document he spoke of 1955 as having been a year of "dispelled illusions" for many people. The people in question were those who held conservative views about the pace of collectivization, and their illusions were "shattered by the criticism of the Sixth Plenary Session (Enlarged) of the Seventh Central Committee" in October. He continued:

> This should be a serious lesson to all communists. Since the people have this enormous enthusiasm for socialism, why were many of the leading organizations completely unaware of it, or only slightly aware of it, just a few months ago? Why was there such a difference between what the leaders thought and what the great mass of the people thought? Taking this as a lesson, how should we handle similar situations and programs in the future? There is only one answer. Don't lose touch with the people; be adept at recognizing their enthusiasm from its very essence.[21]

He took a more cautious position the following month (January 1956), but still based himself firmly on the opinion of the masses: "To speed up cooperativization is good, but we should not speed it up excessively. . . . We should not try to advance anything before the overwhelming majority of the people are satisfied with the advance. . . . What I mean is that we should always make over ninety percent of the people delighted."[22]

Soviet and Chinese Collectivization Campaigns of 1929-30 and 1955-56: A Comparison," *China Quarterly* 31 (1967), 1-47.

[20] 1955g:13.   [21] 1955g:151.   [22] 1956a:96f.

Starting with this assessment of the views of the masses, Mao turned from the mass line to mass criticism as a means of bringing pressure to bear on his recalcitrant colleagues. "We should lead the masses, yet the masses are more progressive than we are," he noted later.[23] The Hundred Flowers Campaign of 1956 and early 1957 was the occasion for this initial turn toward mass criticism.[24] There are conflicting interpretations of Mao's intentions in this campaign. Some have argued that the call for mass criticism was a ruse designed to reveal sources of opposition to the party who might then be dealt with in the Anti-Rightist campaign that followed it.[25] Others view Mao as having been naive as regards the depth of opposition to the CCP, and as having unleased a torrent of criticism that quickly exceeded his expectations both by its breadth and by its depth.[26]

It is my view of the period that Mao intended to use mass criticism as a lever to elicit the support of his colleagues. I think it is also clear in retrospect that he underestimated the level of opposition or, perhaps better, that he overestimated the degree to which he and the intellectual community, that sector of the masses

[23] 1958m:51.

[24] The evolution of Mao's use of the phrase, "Let a hundred flowers bloom, let a hundred schools of thought contend," is an interesting one to follow. In 1952 he wrote an inscription for the *Tianjin Ribao* in which he combined the first half of that phrase with the phrase, "sweeping away the old to make way for the new" (1952c). The essentially cultural thrust of this use of the phrase was repeated when it again appeared, four years later, in a speech before the Politburo. There he suggested that the "hundred flowers" applied to the realm of art and the "hundred schools" to the realm of literature (1956c:33; cf. 1956g). By January 1957 he had added the idea that the "weeding out of poisonous weeds" must accompany the blooming of the hundred flowers, and that the advantage of the contending of the hundred schools was the exposure of "evil elements" (1957a:49, 52). Later in the same meeting of local party leaders, and the following month in his "Correct Handling" speech, he expanded on these latter points, arguing that it is only through conflict and struggle that truth is revealed (1957b:57). "Plants raised in hothouses are unlikely to be sturdy," he said on the latter occasion (1957d:117).

[25] See, for example, Edward E. Rice, *Mao's Way* (Berkeley and Los Angeles: University of California Press, 1972), p. 148.

[26] This is an important aspect of the interpretation of the movement found in Roderick MacFarquhar, *The Hundred Flowers Campaign and the Chinese Intellectuals* (New York: Praeger, 1960). His more recent views on the period are contained in *The Origins of the Cultural Revolution* 1, *Contradictions among the People, 1956-57* (New York: Columbia University Press, 1975).

to which the campaign was primarily addressed, shared a common view of post-Liberation Chinese politics—a view which differed from that of his Central Committee colleagues. In any event, the "great blooming and contending" of mass criticism was soon terminated, an event marked by the publication in June 1957 of his February "Correct Handling" speech. The published version of the speech contained a list of criteria for distinguishing legitimate from illegitimate mass criticism, a list that is clearly the product of what were, in Mao's view, the excesses of the movement and that, as we have noted earlier, had it been incorporated in the original speech, would certainly have precluded the "blooming and contending" of the preceding four months.[27]

A second instance of the expansion of the mass line toward mass criticism is found in the Socialist Education Campaign of 1963-1965. Adherents within the party of what were later characterized, during the Cultural Revolution, as the "two lines," "capitalist" and "socialist"—lines that in retrospect are seen by Chinese writers as having had their origins in the early stages of collectivization—were deeply divided with regard to the goals and methods of the Socialist Education Campaign.[28] Those later said

[27] The criteria were described as being those "for distinguishing right from wrong in words and action," and read as follows:

(1) Words and actions should help to unite, and not divide, the people of our various nationalities.

(2) They should be beneficial, and not harmful, to socialist transformation and socialist construction.

(3) They should help to consolidate, and not undermine or weaken, the people's democratic dictatorship.

(4) They should help to consolidate, and not undermine or weaken, democratic centralism.

(5) They should help to strengthen, and not discard or weaken, the leadership of the Communist party.

(6) They should be beneficial, and not harmful, to international socialist unity and the unity of the peace-loving people of the world (1957d:119f.).

[28] The "struggle between two roads and between two lines," which pervades so much Chinese writing on contemporary history, particularly since the Cultural Revolution, is a theme we shall consider in the final two chapters. Its pervasiveness no doubt accounts for the response of a person who has spent many years during the post-Liberation period as a resident of Beijing. To the question, "What is the mass line?" her response was immediate: "If it is a line, then there are two of them." Her dialectical insight is an important one, though it is interesting that, whereas both the capitalist and the socialist *roads* are known by their respective names, the antithesis of the mass *line* is not commonly referred to by a specific term. The char-

to have been following the "capitalist road" saw little to be gained from a new campaign, particularly one that took as its initial target the malfeasance of basic level cadres, since adherents to this line were initially wary of upsetting the delicate balance that had been reestablished in the management of the countryside in the post-Great Leap Forward period of retrenchment. In their view, any such campaign, if it were to be carried out at all, should be conducted under the close supervision of the party.[29]

Followers of what is retrospectively referred to as the "socialist road," by contrast, sought to correct the errors of the basic-level cadres, who were regarded as having been responsible for certain of the setbacks in the aftermath of the Great Leap Forward, and to root out the revivals of "capitalism" in rural production—reliance on monetary incentives, overemphasis of private plot production, and a return to the individual household as the basic accounting unit. To achieve these ends, and because he had come increasingly to regard the party as an illegitimate agent since it was itself in need of rectification, Mao proposed the use of novel methods that would short-circuit the party apparatus and subject it to pressure from without. Specifically, he proposed the revival of Poor and Lower-Middle Peasant Associations as the vehicle for conducting the campaign, suggesting that "where basic-level organizations have atrophied or become paralyzed," all power should be placed in the hands of these associations and the masses "boldly unleashed."[30] In one of his clearest statements on mass

acteristics of such an antithesis are clear enough, nonetheless, as we discovered in discussing violations of the mass line in the previous chapter.

[29] Positions taken by the adherents of the two lines are said to be found in the four documents issued by the Central Committee to guide the campaign. The first and the last were retrospectively attributed to Mao, the second and third, respectively, to Liu Shaoqi and Deng Xiaoping, who were subsequently accused of being the leading "capitalist roaders." These attributions were made during the Cultural Revolution in the article, "The Struggle between the Two Roads in the Chinese Countryside," *RMRB, HQ,* and *JFJB* (23 November 1967), translated in *PR* 10:49 (1 December 1967), 11-19. The documents in question are translated and analyzed in Richard Baum and Frederick C. Tiewes, *Ssu-ch'ing: The Socialist Education Movement of 1962-66* (Berkeley: University of California, Center for Chinese Studies, 1968). Additional analysis is found in Richard Baum, *Prelude to Revolution: Mao, the Party and the Peasant Question* (New York: Columbia University Press, 1975).

[30] In the "First Ten Points" (1963d:65), the "organizations of poor and lower-middle peasants" were to "assist and oversee" the work of the com-

criticism, he concluded, in the same document, "We must let the people fully express themselves. Cadres must be supervised both from above and from below. The most important supervision is that which comes from the masses."[31] The subsequent attempt of his opponents to keep the campaign exclusively under the control of party work teams was regarded by Mao as an attempt on their part to emasculate the threatening use of mass criticism against them, and thus as proof of their illegitimacy.

The third and most important instance of the use of mass criticism was the Cultural Revolution. Mao would appear to have learned a number of lessons from the failure of the Socialist Education Campaign to mobilize effective popular political action. Among them, as we have seen, was the necessity for his return to the "first line" of party decision making and execution. As a consequence of the lesson of this personal experience, he came to re-emphasize the importance of power as an element of authority. In addition, he appears to have learned that the mobilizational campaign, an instrument upon which he had come to rely in his attempt to stem the tide of routinization, could itself become routinized, and that new mobilizational devices were thus necessary. With regard to the nature of political participation, he seems to have learned that mass criticism was a potentially effective means of controlling and correcting the ossification of party and state organs, but that its very effectiveness elicited strong reactions from functionaries in the organs being criticized. Thus, just as he apparently came to realize his own need for political power, he realized as well that, in order that mass criticism be effective, the political power of the masses must be reinforced. It was with these lessons in mind that Mao began to think of what a "Chinese Paris Commune of the 1970s" might look like.

Particularly during the middle phases of the Cultural Revolution, emphasis was placed on the seizure of political power by "revolutionary rebels" within organizations, manifesting the view that without power to reinforce it, criticism was either impossible or else it became routinized and ineffective. It soon became clear that the problem with power seizure, however, lay in the double

mune and brigade administrative committees, but they were not to supercede these committees. In the subsequent "Twenty-three Articles" (1965c: 124f.), the more radical position cited in the body of the text was set forward.

[31] 1963d:65.

nature of the tasks it was assigned to perform. Rebels were required to act both as critics and as administrators—functions that frequently proved mutually exclusive in practice. To the extent that the rebels were successful critics, they tended to fail as administrators. To the extent that they succeeded in exercising administrative power, they tended to neglect their critical function.[32] What this suggested is that the type of legitimacy which rests with the masses, in Mao's view, is at least potentially at variance with experience as a criterion of legitimacy. What makes the masses legitimate—that is, their ability to initiate and evaluate—they retain as a quality only so long as they remain outside of the organization itself. Once inside, they vitiate that peculiar legitimacy and, moreover, they lack the experience and knowledge requisite to administer effectively. The immediate solution to this problem—the summons of the army to enter the movement to provide a lever of power and a standard of legitimacy—was only a partially successful solution to the dilemma. Mass participation in administration was routinized in the "three-in-one revolutionary committees," set up as an alternative to, rather than a realization of, the Paris Commune model, but this participation appears more token than genuine, in most instances.[33]

The essence of the Commune—the element that presented itself to Mao in 1966 as a possible solution to the central problem in the Chinese state and party—was the destruction of an alienated bureaucracy whose functionaries were becoming corrupted as a result of this alienation. The idea that the clientele of the bureaucracy could replace the bureaucrats by rotating among themselves the task of sitting behind the bureaucrats' desks was an appealing

[32] Mao alluded to this problem in his long (and rambling) conversation in July 1968 with "responsible persons of the Beijing Red Guard Congress" (1968f).

[33] Army or militia representatives far outnumbered either the mass representatives or the retained cadres who were, nominally, to constitute two-thirds of the membership of these committees. See Richard Baum, "China: The Year of the Mangoes," *Asian Survey* 9:1 (1969), 1-17. The number of representatives of the masses—model workers, peasants, and the like—on the party Central Committee increased at each of the two subsequent Congresses. Whereas 29 percent of the Ninth Central Committee (elected in 1969) were mass representatives, 40 percent of the Tenth Central Committee (elected in 1973) were individuals who fit this category. See Gordon A. Bennett, *China's Eighth, Ninth and Tenth Congresses, Constitutions and Central Committees: An Institutional Overview and Comparison* (Austin: Center for Asian Studies, University of Texas, 1974).

one, for it promised to reduce the amount of time that each individual is subject to the organization's corrupting influence.[34] To have brought the masses into the organization in this fashion may have been a relatively accurate reconstruction of the Paris Commune, but it was in conflict with what Lenin had taken that experience to exemplify. Participatory it may have been, but it was not effective as a dictatorship. Revolutionary Committees, which replaced the Commune-like organs of power in early 1967, were a compromise, but they succeeded in placing mass critics back outside of the organization, where their critical role could more effectively be exercised.

Mao spoke of the Cultural Revolution at its height as follows: "Never before has a mass movement been aroused so extensively and penetratingly as it is at present."[35] The unprecedented level to which political participation in the form of mass criticism was raised during the Cultural Revolution appears to have had lasting, if not necessarily permanent, effects on the Chinese political system. The upsurge of public criticism of official malfeasance at the local level which accompanied certain phases of the campaign to criticize Lin Biao and Confucius in 1974, the labor unrest in Hangzhou in the summer of 1975, and the demonstration in the Tian'anmen Square in April 1976 all seem to suggest that the masses (or at least certain sectors of the masses), having learned during the Cultural Revolution the utility and effectiveness of public enunciation of their criticisms, were quick to use this tactic when they felt that certain of the achievements of the earlier movement were in jeopardy.[36]

[34] "The most fundamental point of reform of state organs," he said at the midpoint of the Cultural Revolution, "is to establish ties with the masses. Institutional reforms must be adapted to the establishment of ties with the masses. There must not be any effort to promote bureaucracy" (1967i). I have discussed at considerable length elsewhere the organizational experiments during the Cultural Revolution that involved rotation in office; Starr, "Mao Tse-tung's Theory of Continuing the Revolution under the Dictatorship of the Proletariat: Its Origins, Development and Practical Implications," Ph.D. dissertation, University of California, Berkeley, 1971.

[35] 1967k.

[36] I have discussed this aspect of the post-Cultural Revolution political situation in "China in 1974: 'Weeding through the Old to Bring Forth the New,'" *Asian Survey* 15:1 (1975), 1-12, and in "From the Tenth Party Congress to the Premiership of Hua Kuo-feng: The Significance of the Colour of the Cat," *China Quarterly* 67 (1976), 457-488.

Limits to Participation

Alongside his heavy emphasis on the importance of mass participation in political life, Mao also posed limits on participation. These limits affect who may legitimately participate, the forms that this participation will take, the issues regarding which participation is appropriate and, finally, the rhythm of participation. The first of these limitations—that which determines who the legitimate participators are within a political system—is perhaps best approached by investigating what Mao meant in his use of the term "the masses" (*qunzhong*).

Whereas the term "the people" has been explicitly (albeit flexibly) defined by Mao, his use of the term "the masses" is considerably more ambiguous. It is difficult to find a word that he used with greater frequency, and yet he offered no definition for it. In most instances the ambiguity is not particularly problematic to an understanding of his meaning, since the context suggests a reading of "most of the people." Where "the masses" is to serve, as it does in the case of the mass line and mass criticism, as a determinant of legitimate participation, an ability to assess the precise composition of the group referred to by that term is more critical.

In some instances Mao used the term "the masses" virtually synonymously with the term "the people." We have alluded to the evolution of the latter term in the previous chapter; however, that evolution merits reinvestigation and amplification here, since crucial qualitative differences exist in the nature of the political participation appropriate to the people and that appropriate to their enemies. The use of the term "the people" derives from Mao's description of that form of government which he called a "people's democratic dictatorship." He touched upon this concept in his report to the Second Plenum of the Seventh Central Committee in March 1949, and elaborated upon it in a speech two months later commemorating the party's twenty-eighth anniversary.[37] It grew out of the idea first of a "people's republic," and then a "New Democracy" as forms of government appropriate for eliciting cooperation from a broad spectrum of political groups outside of the Communist party itself.[38] The dividing line

[37] 1949b:1326ff./IV, 372f.; and 1949d:1357-71/IV, 411-423.

[38] Mao described the New Democracy in 1940 as the third of three types of state systems: "(1) republics under bourgeois dictatorships; (2) republics under the dictatorship of the proletariat; and (3) republics under the joint dictatorship of several revolutionary classes." This latter form "is the

between participants and nonparticipants—those enjoying democratic rights and those subject to dictatorship—in the New Democracy was based on attitudes toward the Japanese presence in China. Those prepared consistently and resolutely to resist Japanese aggression were regarded as members of the revolutionary classes and were to enjoy democratic rights. Those who wavered in their resistance or whose interests allied them with Japanese imperialism were to be subjected to dictatorship.

When coalition government in postwar China was ruled out of the question—an event signaled by the breakdown of American-supported negotiations between the Guomindang and the CCP[39] —the concept of New Democracy gradually evolved into that of a people's democratic dictatorship, wherein the dividing line between revolutionary and counterrevolutionary classes was based on opposition to the Guomindang government. This new dividing line encompassed a somewhat narrower group in the initial stages of the Civil War than had been included under New Democracy, but as the war-induced corruption and military ineptitude of the Nationalist government became more widely known in China, more and more Chinese changed their attitude, thereby joining the ranks of "the people."

Mao's description of the people's democratic dictatorship in June 1945 took the form of a series of responses to criticisms of the party by its opponents. Among them was the criticism of the dictatorial nature of the party's policies. Mao's response was to argue that the experience of the Chinese revolution pointed up the necessity for exercising dictatorship over reactionaries and permitting freedom only to the people.

---

transitional form of state to be adopted in the revolutions of the colonial and semi-colonial countries" (1940a:636/II, 350). The New Democracy was to be based on a system of popularly elected people's congresses from the basic level to the national level, and a system of "really universal and equal suffrage, irrespective of sex, creed, property or education" to insure "proper representation for each revolutionary class according to its status in the state" (ibid., p. 352).

[39] The events of this confusing period are ably recounted in Herbert Feis, *The China Tangle* (Princeton: Princeton University Press, 1953), and, from the viewpoint of one of the participants, in Barbara Tuchman's *Stillwell and the American Experience in China* (New York: Macmillan, 1971). Cf. Tang Tsou, *America's Failure in China* (Chicago: University of Chicago Press, 1963), and U.S. Department of State, *The China White Paper*, edited by Lyman Van Slyke, 2 vols. (Stanford: Stanford University Press, 1967).

Who are the people? At the present stage in China they are the working class, the peasantry, the urban petty bourgeoisie and the national bourgeoisie. These classes, led by the working class and the Communist Party, unite to form their own state and elect their own government; they enforce their dictatorship over the running dogs of imperialism—the landlord class and the bureaucrat-bourgeoisie, as well as the representatives of these classes, the Guomindang reactionaries and their accomplices—suppress them, allow them only to behave themselves and not to be unruly in word or deed. If they speak or act in an unruly way, they will be promptly stopped and punished. Democracy is practiced within the ranks of the people, who enjoy the rights of freedom of speech, assembly, association and so on. The right to vote belongs only to the people, not to the reactionaries. The combination of these two aspects, democracy for the people and dictatorship over the reactionaries, is the people's democratic dictatorship.[40]

As we have seen earlier, Mao's use of the category "the people," defined on the basis of attitudes toward principal projects of the political system, continued at least through the "Correct Handling" speech of 1957. Though the principal projects themselves changed during that period, the division of the society into friends and enemies, the image of that division as being one between the vast majority and a tiny minority, and the view that democracy was appropriate among the people, dictatorship appropriate toward enemies, remained throughout this period.

At the same time that Mao was developing these ideas, a number of his colleagues were constructing a system of "socialist legal institutions" modeled after those of the Soviet Union.[41] From the writings available to us, we have no indication that Mao interested himself particularly in this project. He spoke of the Soviet legal system in 1956, but it was to criticize rather than to praise it: Stalin had failed, he argued, to develop "democratic procedures in the political life of the country" and to perfect a socialist legal system.[42] The following month he spoke favorably of the legal system that had been established in China as having been "enacted

[40] 1949d:1364/IV, 417f.

[41] The use of Soviet models in the Chinese legal system during this period is discussed by Jerome Alan Cohen, *The Criminal Process in the People's Republic of China* (Cambridge: Harvard University Press, 1968).

[42] 1956n:49.

by the workers": the laws "protect the workers' interests, productive power, and the economic base. We therefore must abide
by them."[43]

The bulk of Mao's commentary on legal matters is set in the
context of his distinction between people and their enemies.[44]
Writing on the campaign to criticize Hu Feng[45] in 1955, he reiterated the distinction between methods appropriate for dealing
with problems among the people and among enemies of the people, and concluded thus: "[Among the people] it is criminal to
restrict freedoms, to stifle people's criticisms of the mistakes and
weaknesses of the party and government, and to suppress free
academic discussions; this is our system. . . . [With enemies of the
people] it is criminal to allow counterrevolutionaries to say and
do whatever they like and it is legitimate to practice dictatorship;
this is our system."[46]

It is in the context of this distinction that Mao addressed the
question of rights in a socialist system in his speech on the correct
handling of contradictions among the people. In that speech,
"democracy" is treated as having three aspects: the first aspect is
that of the "democratic methods" of political education to be
used among the people—persuasion, criticism, and self-criticism.
Second, democracy involves political participation: the principles
of democratic centralism and the mass line are to be implemented
by party and state organs. The third aspect of democracy is the
enjoyment by the people of certain freedoms and democratic
rights: "Our constitution lays it down that citizens of the People's
Republic of China enjoy freedom of speech, of the press, of
assembly, of association, of procession, of demonstration, of religious belief, and so on."[47] Questions of freedoms and rights, for

[43] 1957b:61. He reaffirmed this position a decade later, when he commented that "even under a proletarian dictatorship the masses should be
allowed to petition, demonstrate, and litigate" (1966l:450).

[44] This point is developed by Stanley B. Lubman, "Mao and Mediation:
Politics and Dispute Resolution in Communist China," *California Law
Review* 55:5 (1967).

[45] Hu Feng was a Marxist literary critic and writer active in the communist movement after 1925. Although he occupied various positions in the
post-Liberation government in China, he criticized the "sterility" of literary
criticism under the CCP in 1954 and was, as a result, the object of an
intensive campaign in the summer of the following year.

[46] 1955b:52.

[47] 1957d:84. In order to mobilize popular support during the anti-Japanese
war he was considerably more inclusive in his treatment of rights, arguing

Mao, must always be considered in a specific political context; otherwise their pursuit as ends in themselves will result in the creation of a system that would be indistinguishable from a bourgeois democracy. Nowhere is this made clearer than in a letter that Mao wrote to Peng Dehuai in June 1943 criticizing Peng for his "Talk on Democratic Education," in which he proceeded "from the definitions of democracy, liberty, equality, and fraternity, rather than from the needs of the current anti-Japanese struggle."[48] As is the case in the particular instance that occasioned his criticism, Mao argued that the specific political context within which rights and freedoms must always be understood is provided by the determination of the principal contradiction confronting the political system at any given historical period—a determination which, at the same time, divides friends from enemies.

The first and most important limitation on participation is thus based on this distinction between people and enemies. "The masses" as a social category is not more encompassing than the category "the people"; enemies of the people are not regarded as being members of the masses. On the other hand, it is also true that not everyone who is a member of the masses participates in

---

that even landlords who were prepared to resist Japanese imperialism should be granted democratic rights (1940f:726/II, 447). In 1961 he spoke of the fundamental right of workers to administer the country, their own enterprises, and culture and education within the political system. They are deprived of these rights when administrative positions in these fields are seized by right opportunists (1961a:266; cf. his critical comments on worker self-government in Yugoslavia two years later, 1963h:30). The revised state constitution, adopted at the Fourth National People's Congress in 1975 —the last revision prior to Mao's death the following year—devoted four of its thirty articles to the "fundamental rights and duties of citizens." In addition to those freedoms alluded to in the passage cited here, the constitution provided as well for the freedom to strike, and the freedom to disbelieve in religion and to propagate atheism. Moreover, "the citizens' freedom of person and their homes shall be inviolable." The constitution also provided for certain rights: the right to vote, to stand for election, to work to be educated, and to lodge complaints for malfeasance by members of state organs. Working people have the additional rights of rest and of social welfare in old age and when ill. Women are guaranteed equal rights with men. Importantly, however, this list of freedoms and rights is preceded by the statement that the "fundamental rights and duties" of citizens are to support the leadership of the party and the socialist system; Chapter III, Constitution of the People's Republic of China," in *PR* 18:4 (24 January 1975), 17.

[48] 1943c:7-9.

the political system on an equal footing, and it is this attempt to draw distinctions among the masses that brings us to the second limitation on who participates in the political process according to Mao. A cadre putting the mass line into practice at the basic level is not encouraged simply to conduct a plebiscite among the members of the masses he or she encounters there, with the majority view being the one that is subsequently "centralized." Certain opinions and views count for more than others, as Mao suggested when he pointed out in 1962 that the basis of centralization in the mass line is the centralization of *correct* opinions.[49]

There are two interconnected axes along which the masses are divided, the correctness of their opinions evaluated, and, thereby, the potency of their participation determined. One of these axes —quite expectedly, given what we have seen to be the definitions of legitimacy advanced by Mao—is that of class. Those with a "good class background"—members of the proletariat and the poor and lower-middle peasant classes—should speak with a more potent voice than members of other classes. The other axis, a more ambiguous distinction, but no less important given the attention accorded it by Mao, is that between "advanced" and "backward" elements among the masses. The two axes are obviously cross-cutting, since he regarded certain classes as advanced, others as backward in a particular historical period. They are distinguishable as well because, as we have seen, an individual's class status may, under certain circumstances, be affected by the advanced or backward opinions he or she holds. Opinions are not always determined exclusively by class status in Mao's view.

The most important characteristic of this latter contradiction between advanced and backward elements among the masses is its permanence. As he explained in 1959,

> At the end of the transition period, after classes have been totally destroyed, politics will completely be relationships within the ranks of the people. By that time there will still be ideological struggles among the people, political struggles and revolutions. . . . But the nature of the struggles and revolutions will not be the same as in the past. They will not be class struggles, but struggles between the advanced and the backward

[49] 1962a:164. It is in this passage that he went on to describe the party's leading organs as no more than a "processing plant" for these correct opinions.

within the ranks of the people, and struggles between the advanced and the backward in science and technology.[50]

The advanced, as he defined that group succinctly in early 1966, are those who "do the work of the backward."[51] Elsewhere he offered some additional distinguishing characteristics: "In a socialist society there are still the advanced and the backward, people who have faith in collective undertakings, are diligent and earnest, full of vigor and vitality, and people that strive for fame and fortune, look out for themselves, and are gloomy and moody [—] people who would like to preserve backward production relationships and social institutions."[52] In dealing with advanced and backward elements in a particular situation, his advice to cadres is that they "unite with the advanced elements," then "unite with the middle to bring along the backward."[53]

Weighting the influence of advanced elements in the process of political participation insures that the ideas on which mass line policy is based are correct. As he phrased it in 1955, "In any society at any point in time there are advanced and backward people whose views are contradictory to and contending with each other. Advanced views always prevail over backward ones. It is therefore impossible and undesirable to have 'uniformity of public opinion' [as Hu Feng had advocated]. The only way to make progress is to promote what is advanced so that it can prevail over what is backward."[54]

Participation should thus vary among individual members of the political system according to their respective positions within that system. It should vary, as well, for each individual over time, and this variation constitutes a second type of limitation on participation posed by Mao. The rhythm of this variation was determined, in large measure, by the use of the "campaign" or "movement" (*yundong*) in the post-Liberation period. Mobilizational campaigns were seen as an effective device not only for accomplishing particular goals, but also for conducting political

[50] 1959c:221. Cf. 1956d:10f.; 1958e:6, and 1963b:321. He explained the permanence of this contradiction by an analogy: just as the varying heights of a set of sons cannot be evened up, so advancedness and backwardness are qualities that resist evening up. Only Bukharin would disagree, Mao contended (1961a:297).

[51] 1966b:30.   [52] 1961a:273.

[53] Earlier his advice was that cadres "keep watch over the advanced and the backward in order to bring along the majority in between" (1958e:4, 7).

[54] 1955b:51.

education and for contravening a tendency toward routinization in the political system.[55] Mao spoke frequently of specific campaigns, but had relatively little to say on the concept of the campaign as a political style. He did, however, allude to the goals of the campaign style of politics when he described, in a passage we have already had occasion to study, his own theory of "permanent revolution": "I stand for the theory of permanent revolution. Do not mistake this for Trotsky's theory of permanent revolution. In making revolution one must strike while the iron is hot—one revolution must follow another, the revolution must continually advance."[56] He went on in the same passage to suggest that what he had in mind by "revolutions" here were actually a succession of campaigns, each building on the accomplishments of the preceding one. "After Liberation in 1949 came the Land Reform; as soon as this was completed there followed the mutual-aid teams, then the low-level cooperatives, then the high-level cooperatives. After seven years the cooperativization was completed and productive relations were transformed; then came the Rectification. After Rectification was finished, before things had cooled down, then came the Technical Revolution."[57]

The mobilization characteristic of the first stages of a campaign involves a quickening of the pace of political participation. Mobilization of the vast majority of the population, Mao wrote in 1939, is the only way in which the goals of the revolution can be realized—a lesson he attributed to Sun Zhongshan and the 1911 Revolution:[58] "Armed resistance requires the mobilization of the people, but there is no way of mobilizing them without democracy and freedom."[59]

The level of enthusiasm and activity of this initial stage of the mobilizational campaign is not easily maintained, however.[60] As

---

[55] Gordon A. Bennett, *Yundong: Mass Campaigns in Chinese Communist Leadership* (Berkeley: University of California, Center for Chinese Studies, 1976) is the most complete study of campaigns and the campaign style. Cf. Starr, *Ideology and Culture: An Introduction to the Dialectic of Contemporary Chinese Politics* (New York: Harper and Row, 1973), pp. 155-161; and Charles Cell, *Revolution at Work: Mobilizational Campaigns in China* (New York: Academic Press, 1977).

[56] 1958d:94.   [57] Ibid.

[58] 1939c:529/II, 244.   [59] 1937c:236/I, 267.

[60] Mao took cognizance of this fact, and in so doing suggested some of the methods appropriate for the mobilization process when he called for mass meetings among industrial workers during the initial stages of the

others have observed, during the course of the campaigns prior to the Cultural Revolution there emerged a pattern of a varying intensity of political participation—widespread and vigorous participation in the initial stages, gradually tapering off as the campaign wound down.[61] This pattern resulted finally in the deterioration of the capacity of a campaign successfully to arouse the desired level of enthusiasm and participation. Campaigns themselves had become routinized,[62] a problem that led Mao at the latter stages of the Socialist Education Campaign to urge his colleagues "boldly [to] unleash the masses; we must not be like women with bound feet—we must not bind our hands and feet."[63]

Great Leap Forward, to explain to them the "tasks, reasons, and methods" appropriate to the movement (1958rr).

[61] G. William Skinner and Edwin Winckler, employing a typology of power and the response each type elicits, derived from the work of Amitai Etzioni, discuss the cyclical pattern of campaigns. Etzioni suggests that coercive power (which involves the use of force) elicits a response of alienation; remunerative power (which involves the use of money, goods, and services) elicits a response of calculated involvement; and normative power (which involves the manipulation of values and the symbols that stand for those values) elicits a response of commitment. Skinner and Winckler suggest that each of the major campaigns in the Chinese countryside between Liberation and the Cultural Revolution began with the employment of normative power, during which slogans, patriotic appeals, and ideological lessons would take the place of a predominantly remunerative power mix left over from the previous campaign. Normative appeals would initially elicit a positive response from the peasantry. When this positive response began to diminish, prior to the time that the goals of the campaign had been fully realized, coercive power would be used to reinforce commitment. Coercion, however, produced the opposite effect; alienation would begin to take the place of commitment. To counteract the alienation, remunerative power would be employed, with the result that alienation was curbed and a calculating involvement would take its place. The cycle would begin again as the regime set forth toward a new goal with a burst of normative appeals. G. William Skinner and Edwin A. Winckler, "Compliance Succession in Rural Communist China: A Cyclical Theory," in Amitai Etzioni, ed., *A Sociological Reader on Complex Organizations* (New York: Holt, Rinehart and Winston, 1969), pp. 410-438. Etzioni's typology is found in his book, *A Comparative Analysis of Complex Organizations* (New York: Free Press, 1964). Charles Cell (*Revolution at Work*) takes issue with Skinner and Winckler's analysis of the campaign sequence.

[62] Doak Barnett has discussed the effect of the cyclical pattern of the political campaign on organizational behavior in *Cadres, Bureaucracy and Political Power in Communist China* (New York: Columbia University Press, 1967), pp. 69f.

[63] 1965c:21. It was an analogy which, as we have seen, he used for the same purpose during the debate over the pace of collectivization.

A third limitation on participation derives from the forms Mao regarded appropriate for the exercise of political action by the masses. Those who have studied the question of political participation in China find numerous problems in using this term, because of its heavy load of American and Western European connotations.[64] The *sine qua non* of meaningful participation in the eyes of some observers is the presence in a political system of an active and institutionalized political opposition, ordinarily taking the form of an opposition political party. It is, however, precisely when it becomes institutionalized that Mao denied the legitimacy of political opposition. The minority view must be protected, he pointed out on numerous occasions, because, quite simply, "the minority's opinions often are correct."[65] Such views can only be protected, however, when they are individually held. The organization of a minority opposition smacked, to Mao, of the activity of secret cliques: "We must bring democracy into play and encourage others to talk. This is the way it should be within and without the party. . . . Meanwhile, we forbid the organization of secret cliques. We do not fear open opposition, but object to secret opposition."[66]

Despite these important limitations on its meaning, Mao used the term "democracy" frequently. He defined it in a straightforward way in 1965 as "allowing the masses to manage their own affairs."[67] In opposition to the viewpoint of Sun Zhongshan, who had seen the need for a period of "political tutelage" prior to the introduction of democratic forms in China, Mao began at an early point in his career to argue that the Chinese peasantry was ready for democratic government, and that the exercise of democracy was the most effective form of political education.[68] "Our demo-

[64] The most important treatment of the subject is James Townsend's book, *Political Participation in Communist China* (Berkeley and Los Angeles: University of California Press, 1967).

[65] 1962a:182. See also 1964e:339 and 1966m:121.

[66] 1962a:182. There have been, it is true, minority political parties in China since the time of Liberation, which have served as a loyal but largely ineffectual opposition. Mao spoke of them in 1956 as providing a vehicle for "democrats" to "state their own views" (1956e:29). In the early months of the Cultural Revolution he suggested that it was the function of the democratic parties to absorb those who would otherwise be illegitimate members of the CCP (1966o:72). The function of, as well as the restrictions on, the participation of these parties in the political system are made clear in his discussion in 1957 of the "mutual supervision" of the democratic parties by the CCP and of the CCP by these parties (1957d:121f.).

[67] 1965g:102.   [68] 1939f:551/II, 270.

cratic tradition has a long history," he wrote in 1958. "Promoting democracy at our base, with neither money, grain, weapons, nor outside aid, we had no choice but to rely on the people. The party had to become one with the people, the troops with the masses, and the officers with the soldiers."[69]

Operating on the basis of a democratic centralist system, the implementation of this principle of democracy involves a limited use of the franchise. Direct elections are conducted, but only at the basic level in China, and even there voting as an aspect of participation is confined to the validation of a preselected slate of candidates for office in a local People's Congress.[70] Mao expressed on a number of occasions his distrust of balloting as a form of political participation. Writing in 1967 he said, "I don't believe in elections. . . . I was elected by Beijing but aren't there quite a few people who have never seen me? If they haven't even seen me how can they elect me? It's nothing more than their having heard of my name."[71]

Much more important than elections as a means of popular participation in the recruitment of leaders is the informal selection processes that take place within the face-to-face environment of the small group. Leaders in these groups are chosen from among activists who demonstrate their commitment and effectiveness in campaigns, and are subsequently placed in leadership positions. It is highly unlikely that a genuinely unpopular individual can survive in this difficult and demanding position, the successful execution of which depends so completely on the activist's ability simultaneously to gain the confidence of his superiors and his subordinates.[72]

A fourth and final set of limitations on political participation involves the question of political issues. Participation is by no means equal with regard to every issue. Having a tendency in our

[69] 1958p:87.

[70] John P. Burns, "The Election of Production Team Cadres in Rural China: 1958-1974," paper prepared for the Workshop on the Pursuit of Political Interests in the People's Republic of China, Ann Arbor, Michigan, August 1977.

[71] 1967b:100. This distaste is reflected in the 1975 constitution, which substituted for the word "elected" the considerably more ambiguous phrase, "elected through democratic consultation" (Constitution of the People's Republic of China, Chapter I, Article III).

[72] Mao discussed at some length the dynamics of small-group operation in 1938 (1938a:130ff.).

own political life to regard a political issue as more critical the greater the number of individuals it affects, we regard national issues and national elections as more important than local issues and local elections. It is almost always by breadth of affect rather than depth of affect that we determine the importance of an issue. This criterion is a perfectly valid one, but it is not the only one that can be employed. If, instead of the number of people affected, we were to consider the degree to which any one person is affected, the evaluation of the relative importance of issues might well have a different result. Using this criterion, it might prove that the more local the issue, the more deeply it affects the individual, and thus the more thoroughly involved politically the individual is likely to become with regard to that issue.

Mao's concept of participation makes much of this latter criterion of salience. The more local the question at issue, the greater the degree of participation is likely to occur, and the broader the range of alternative views that will be tolerated. Because their experience is broader and thus more significant, and because the policy outcome will affect them more directly, the members of a production brigade have a far greater voice in determining, for instance, the distribution of their year's profits than· they do in determining the nation's foreign policy. Political participation, as Mao treats it, thus seems to require a face-to-face directness of contact between individuals and an immediate salience of issues to be genuine and meaningful. His strong emphasis on participation as a means of curbing the arbitrary and alienating exercise of political authority translates into practice, therefore, in a very limited, but not negligible level of popular involvement.

These limits on the conduct of the mass line and mass criticism are not, however, unproblematic. "Support of the socialist system" and "support of the leadership of the party"—phrases that define the perimeters of legitimate dissent—are ambiguous ones, subject to varying interpretations. Once again, the need for authoritative definitions becomes critical, as those who operate within the system and engage in criticism are clearly well aware.

INDIRECT PARTICIPATION: THE ROLE OF REPRESENTATION

Although they are closely related to one another, interest group analysis and class analysis are generally regarded as alternative, rather than as complementary modes. Class analysis is seen as treating interests as a function of social class—and therefore mutually exclusive—requiring a revolution to alter the relationship between dominant and subordinate interests. Interest group analysis, by contrast, regards each individual as holding a congeries of interests, only some of which are determined by his or her economic position; this analysis views conflicting interests as mutually reconcilable, even if only temporarily so, and sees a pluralist society that guarantees the coexistence of conflicting but complementary interests as an optimal situation.[73]

As we have seen in tracing the evolution of Mao's concept of class, although he initially interpreted Marxism to mean that an individual's interests arise exclusively from his or her economic position,[74] he subsequently came to see individuals, particularly in a revolutionary situation, as able to transcend the attitudes and interests associated with their economic position, to take on new attitudes and interests, and thereby, in effect, to change their class status. Interests have a role to play, therefore, in determining one's class as well as the reverse, as Mao treated the question.

In making a revolution, he found, it was clearly in the class interest of the proletariat to struggle to end the domination of the bourgeoisie and its foreign imperialist allies, but it was also in the interest of a number of other classes to do so. Shared interests that linked classes together were the basis of the tactic of a united front, which played such an important role in Mao's concept of the New Democracy. It is from the concept of a united front, in turn, that the category "the people" emerged, along with the idea

[73] A statement of this latter position is found, for example, in Earl Lathan, *The Group Basis of Politics* (Ithaca: Cornell University Press, 1952). See also Henry W. Ehrman, ed., *Interest Groups on Four Continents* (Pittsburgh: University of Pittsburgh Press, 1960).

[74] Prior to his introduction to and assimilation of Marxist categories, Mao spoke of the need to form a "great union of the popular masses," as we have noted. This union was to be constructed, he argued, on the basis of small groups or unions of, among others, students, women, primary school teachers, policemen, and rickshaw pullers, each of whom were seen as having distinguishable interests on the basis of which the union was to be formed. His sense of class divisions as demonstrated in this article is only minimally developed (1919a:80, 85). Eight years later, in making a "class analysis" of Chinese society, he assumed a more rigid position regarding the relationship between economic position and political interests (1926). In his comments on the Soviet text on political economy he spoke disparagingly of the actions of "vested interested groups" in a socialist system in much the same way he would later speak of the actions of a new bourgeoisie (1961a:267, 273).

that there are a broad range of interests shared by members of this category.

In schematized and simplified form, the system of interest articulation or representation in a Leninist theory of the party is straightforward. In each historical period there are advanced and backward classes. The interests of the advanced class, if effectively served, will cause society to move forward. In the period of the decline of capitalism and the rise of socialism, the proletariat is the advanced class. Composed of its most advanced members and acting as the vanguard of this class, the Communist party represents and acts upon the interests of the proletariat. Because other interests in the society are relatively less advanced, to represent them would cause retrogression, or at least bring about a slower pace of forward movement.

Because of China's peculiar situation of being semifeudal and semicapitalist at the outset of the Chinese Communist revolution, the problem of identifying the advanced class was never resolved. Projects such as industrialization and the transformation of the peasantry—which, in a Marxist view, are to be completed during the capitalist stage of development, and which, when completed, will help society to advance beyond the capitalist stage—had not been completed in China at the outset of the revolution. Thus, not only in terms of numbers and skills, but also in terms of a not yet completed historical role, the interests of both the bourgeoisie and the peasantry needed to be served in order to complete the revolution and to begin economic construction.[75]

Despite China's anomalous historical situation, Mao nonetheless saw the Leninist principle of democratic centralism as providing an appropriate framework for a system of representation. Responding to a question from a British journalist who found "democratic centralism" to be a self-contradictory term, Mao said,

> We must look not only at the term but at the reality. There is no impassible gulf between democracy and centralism, both of which are essential for China. On the one hand, the government we want must be truly representative of the popular will; it

[75] This shift of emphasis from the Leninist schema is found in Mao's 1960 discussion of Lenin's theory of the party, to which he appended a statement on the importance of representation of mass interests (1960e:4f.). Much earlier, in 1934, he noted that the party must "safeguard" and never "neglect or underestimate" the interests of the masses (1934b:122/I, 147).

must have the support of the broad masses throughout the country and the people must be free to support it and have every opportunity of influencing its policies. This is the meaning of democracy. On the other hand, the centralization of administrative power is also necessary.[76]

The problem of representation is further complicated by the fact that not all interests in the society can be associated exclusively with one or another class. Indeed, there are a number of axes or contradictions along which participants in the Chinese political system divide, some of them legitimate, some illegitimate in Mao's view, and each of them creating, in effect, a pair of or sets of interests. Those interests that are legitimate require representation, for however much he may have extolled face-to-face political interaction, Mao was well aware that a political system incorporating several hundred million participants must inevitably involve indirect as well as direct political participation.

Elsewhere I have described these axes or contradictions on the basis of which the Chinese political system is divided as including cliques based on personal loyalties, factions based on shared ideological positions, classes, interest groups based on organizational affiliation, regional groups, age cohorts, and gender and ethnicity groupings.[77] Of these eight axes or types of contradictions, Mao denied, as we have already seen, the validity of the first two. Cliques based on personal loyalties constitute a deviation from correct organizational behavior and require elimination, not representation. Similarly, factions based on shared (and conflicting) ideological positions are precisely what he had in mind when he denounced "secret cliques" and "secret opposition"—a denunciation made with Peng Dehuai and his colleagues in mind, but one that has taken on even greater significance in the wake of what he regarded as having been the defection of Liu Shaoqi and Lin Biao.

Mao regarded the remaining six contradictions as, at least to some degree, legitimate features of political life and, as such, as meriting representation in the political process. We have already discussed at considerable length the role of class analysis in Mao's thought. Clearly the most important axis or contradiction along which the society is divided is that which separates the classes, and any investigation of social problems must begin by an explora-

[76] 1937i:354/II, 57.
[77] Starr, "From the Tenth Party Congress," 479-487.

tion of this contradiction. It is, however, not the only axis; there are other contradictions that tend to cross class lines, and that are also important for resolving social problems, in his view. The first of these concerns organizational affiliation. Writing in 1962, he noted the existence of seven "fields" within the political system: industry, agriculture, trade, education, military affairs, the government, and the party. Among these fields, he pointed out, "the party leads everything." Nonetheless, the implication is strong in the passage that there are potential contradictions among these seven sectors which do not coincide with class divisions, and which call for legitimate representation of the interests involved.[78]

With regard to regional groupings, Mao was of two minds. On the one hand he saw, no doubt in light of his personal experience of the centrifugal tendencies of the transitional years of warlordism in China, dangers in conceding too much to regional interests.[79] On the other hand, he could not but recognize the intense diversity of China's regions and the need that interests deriving from this diversity be given representation. He summarized his position in 1958 as one of supporting "regionality but not regionalism."[80]

Age cohorts as a contradiction within society requiring representation came to the fore in Mao's thought in the relatively

[78] 1962a:179. Mao's sectoral analysis of Chinese society at this point is reminiscent of efforts by American social scientists to come to grips with the problem of constructing an interest group analysis of socialist systems. See, for example, H. Gordon Skilling's article, "Group Conflict and Political Change," in Chalmers Johnson, ed., *Change in Communist Systems* (Stanford: Stanford University Press, 1970), pp. 215-234; and Michel Oksenberg, "Occupational Groups in Chinese Society and the Cultural Revolution," in *The Cultural Revolution: 1967 in Review* (Ann Arbor: University of Michigan, Center for Chinese Studies, 1968), pp. 1-44. A conference was held in Ann Arbor during the summer of 1977 on the "Pursuit of Political Interest in the People's Republic of China." Among the many useful papers prepared for this conference that treat the general question of interest group analysis as applied to China are Bernard M. Frolic, "A Preliminary Discussion of the Pursuit of the Political Interest of Chinese Workers"; Donald J. Munro, "The Concept of 'Interest' in Chinese Thought"; and Andrew J. Nathan, "The Structural Analysis of Political Conflict Groups." The conference was held under the auspices of the Social Science Research Council.

[79] In the wake of the experience of the purge of Gao Gang and Rao Shushi he spoke of the danger of regionalism in 1956, and argued for what he called "national balance" (1956c:33).

[80] 1958i:84.

recent period. As early as 1939 Mao spoke of the youth movement as forming a "vanguard" in the revolution,[81] but it was in the mid-1960s that the problem of "cultivating revolutionary successors" to his own generation most occupied his mind.[82] The Cultural Revolution demonstrated both the greatest strength and the greatest weakness of the younger generation: its freedom from corruption,[83] and its lack of experience.[84] The importance of recognizing differences of interest based on age, and representing these interests, remained strong in Mao's thought.

The position of women in the political system has been a question to which Mao devoted attention throughout his career. Among the earliest of his writings are a series of articles devoted to the injustices of the system of arranged marriages that then prevailed, his attention to the problem having been captured by the suicide of young women who chose that act as their only means of rebellion against the system.[85] The CCP, he said in 1965, was the first political party to address women directly, and as a result of that, women felt involved and participated actively in the revolution.[86] His solution to the problem of the unequal treatment of women was to encourage their entry into the work force with equal pay and equal employment opportunities. This move, he commented in 1958, would ultimately "break the paternalistic system."[87] Legal equality, he acknowledged, is only the first step toward the emancipation of women: "from there on, everything still remains to be done."[88]

[81] 1939c:529/II, 245. In 1955 he spoke of youth as the most docible and least conservative group in society, and thus argued that "we must not lump them together with everybody else and overlook their special characteristics" (1955g:292). On the other hand, he made it clear earlier that youth were not to be regarded as a class or a stratum unto themselves (1939j:604/II, 521f.).

[82] See, for example, 1964i, 1964j, 1964l, 1964m, and 1964t.

[83] 1958s:94.

[84] As early as 1939 he commented on the lack of experience of young people (1939e:4). He spoke to Malraux in 1965 of the need to "put young people to the test" (1965h:366).

[85] 1919b. See also his reference to the unequal burden of authority borne by peasant women by virtue of their subservience to their husbands (1927: 31/I, 44).

[86] 1965h:361. "Times have changed," he commented the year before, "and today men and women are equal. Whatever men comrades can accomplish, women comrades can too" (1964a).

[87] 1958jj; see also 1955e:9 and 1955g:274, 286.

[88] 1965h:361.

The last of these contradictions or axes—that of ethnicity—is one that Mao, perhaps with an eye toward the problems encountered by his Soviet counterparts over this issue, gave considerable thought. The Chinese ethnic composition is, of course, far different from that of the Soviet Union: ethnic minorities comprise only about five percent of the Chinese population. Nonetheless, one of the "ten major relationships" that Mao set forward in 1956 as requiring the attention of the political system was that between the Han majority and the national minorities.[89] "Respect and equality" were the bases he set forward for the treatment of minority nationalities, and he consistently advocated bringing representatives of the ethnic minorities into public life at the Center as well as in the local areas.[90]

These, then, are the interests that Mao regarded as having a greater or lesser claim to representation as the socialist system develops. The principal form that the articulation and aggregation of these interests took in the early post-Liberation period was the Chinese People's Political Consultative Conference.[91] This body, composed of more than five hundred members, included representatives from all of the major political parties and groups in China, and those mass organizations that had thus far been established. It first met in September 1949 and adopted a Common Program that served the new state in lieu of a constitution during its early years. Following the adoption of a new constitution in 1954, the equivalent institution is the National People's Congress, whose delegates represent both organizations and regions. The size of this body, the infrequency and the brevity of its meetings

[89] 1956e:28f.

[90] The rationale behind Mao's continued acknowledgment of the legitimacy of the separate interests of the minority nationalities was not always entirely clear. The fact that the minority nationalities in China occupy areas that are both strategically important because of their proximity to the nation's land borders, and economically important because of the natural resources located there, are obviously not irrelevant in the determination of this policy (see, for example, 1955e:24, where he called for correct treatment of ethnic minorities because of the resources located in their territories). In selecting leaders for these areas Mao pointed out in 1958 that national origin should be irrelevant: "The question is whether they have communism and how much" (1958i:84). See also his comments on the position of blacks in American society (1963f and 1968c).

[91] Various forms of representative assemblies preceded the formation of the CPPCC in 1949. Mao speaks of these at 1928a:54/I, 71 and 1937f:319/II, 17.

(there were nearly a thousand delegates at the Fourth National People's Congress, which met for five days in 1975, having last met twelve years earlier) all suggest that, however closely its members may represent the interests of the society as a whole, it lacks real power in the political system to act upon these interests.

Two questions need to be asked when evaluating an instance of representation against our own notions of this concept: do those who are acting as representatives speak for themselves, or do they speak for their constituencies; and are the interests for which they speak acted upon? In the Chinese case, representation is the means by which the mass line is expanded from the limited realm of face-to-face relationships to operate on a broader scale. Representation is thus subject to the same constraints that apply to individuals or groups operating within the mass line. Opinions or interests are acceptable—and thus representable—if they fall within the limit of broad support for the system and the party's leading role within that system.

With regard to the degree to which elected officials feel constrained to speak for those whose interests they nominally represent, the norm, as well as the actual implementation of that norm, vary with different organizations. As we have seen, direct election of representatives is rare both in the party and in the state structures. The People's Congresses at each level, for instance, elect representatives to the congresses at the next level. The members of the higher level organs represent only very indirectly the interests of their constituencies.

At the lower levels—in a commune People's Congress, for example, the level of representation is likely to be higher, since the members are not only directly elected by their constituents, but are also in daily contact with them. Mao set forward in 1959 his own detailed view of how such congresses should operate:

The representatives should include men and women, the old and the young, and the positive and negative elements (excluding landlords, rich peasants, counterrevolutionaries, and bad elements, but including well-to-do middle peasants). They are to discuss some problems and elect commune administrative committees. It is suggested that such representatives' meetings should be held four times a year, with each meeting lasting one or two days, and, at most, three days. The first secretary of the commune should master his ability to preside over this kind of meeting.[92]

Another form for the aggregation and articulation of interests is the so-called "mass organization." Mass organizations in China are, generally, interest-based, not class-based. Two important examples of these organizations are the Women's Association and the Communist Youth League. These organizations are seen as having a threefold purpose: not only do they serve as vehicles for tapping the views of their members and acting on those views, but they also serve as a vehicle for the political education of their members, and as a source for identifying and recruiting new leaders into the political system. Leaders of these organizations are regarded as speaking for their constituencies in state and party circles, and sit on representative assemblies at various levels.

Since before Liberation, but particularly during and after the Cultural Revolution, use has been made of "three-in-one combinations" as a means of implementing representation in political structures. An early precursor of this formula is the "three-thirds" system of government building in the period of the New Democracy. Government organs were to be staffed with equal numbers of personnel drawn from the CCP, from "non-Party left progressives," and from "intermediate sections who are neither left nor right."[93] The middle stages of the Cultural Revolution saw the three-in-one combination advanced as a model for new organs of power after the seizure of power and following the abandonment of the Paris Commune model as infeasible. The three elements of the combination were the People's Liberation Army (or in many instances the militia), the revolutionary rebels from within the organization, and those former cadres who were regarded as potentially reformable. Together, representatives of these three elements were to form revolutionary committees.[94] More re-

---

[92] 1959i:169.   [93] 1940e:700/II, 418.

[94] "There are three elements in the basic experience of the revolutionary committee. It embraces representatives of the revolutionary cadres, representatives of the armed forces, and representatives of the revolutionary masses, constituting a revolutionary 'three-in-one' combination. The revolutionary committee should exercise unified leadership, eliminate duplication in the administrative structure, follow the policy of 'better troops and simpler administration,' and organize a revolutionized leading group which links itself with the masses" (1968d:10).

cently, the use of the three-in-one combination has involved representation of a different set of interests, calling for leadership positions to be divided between representatives of the young, the middle-aged, and the old.[95]

In sum, then, we have found Mao, in his work on the organization and operation of a revolutionary regime, to have devoted considerable attention to the problem of participation. It is clear that he viewed mass participation positively, seeing it as necessary as a source of initiative in the political process and as a means for curing illegitimate tendencies of organizational life. Pursuant to this positive view of participation, he came to advocate mass participation and criticism of the party, state, and army to a considerably greater extent than Lenin had initially envisaged in his theory of democratic centralism. It is equally clear, on the other hand, that Mao's theory of participation contained relatively narrow limits within which it may legitimately operate. Political dissent is tolerable, indeed requisite, for the system's proper functioning, but the boundaries of that legitimate dissent are stringent and ever-changing, and as a result may come to serve as an inhibiting force upon its free expression. Furthermore, he regarded mass participation in the decision-making process and in the criticism of policy and performance as more significant, on balance, than mass participation in the recruitment of leaders. He also saw the greatest strength of mass participation as lying within the basic-level unit, and with regard to questions that most directly concern the daily lives of members of these units. Finally, he treated political participation as requisite not only for the correct functioning of the political system, but also for the political education of the participants. It is to an exploration of that process of political education that we turn next.

[95] The principle of the three-in-one combination of young, middle-aged and old was incorporated in the 1975 constitution. ("Constitution of the People's Republic of China," Chapter I, Article 11).

Chapter Seven

ON POLITICAL EDUCATION

We must educate a lot of people—the sort of
people who are the vanguard of the revolution,
who have political farsightedness, who are prepared for battle and sacrifice, who are frank,
loyal, positive and upright; the sort of people
who seek no self interest, only national and
social emancipation, who show, instead of fear,
determination and forwardness in the face of
hardships; the sort of people who are neither
undisciplined nor fond of limelight, but practical, with their feet firmly on the ground.
If China possesses many such men, the tasks of
the Chinese revolution can easily be fulfilled.[1]

To the problem of retrogression and embourgeoisement in a
socialist society Mao proposed four solutions: three therapeutic,
the fourth prophylactic. In the preceding chapters we have considered at some length two of the therapeutic solutions: organizational reform and mass participation. We turn now to a discussion
of the remaining two solutions. Both are included in the project
of political education, since that project is seen as having a dual
goal. Although the principal purpose of education is to create a
new generation of "revolutionary successors," immune, to the
greatest extent possible, to the corrupting effects of political life,
a secondary purpose is the reeducation of individuals who have
succumbed to those corrupting effects. We have discussed at some
length the mass line as a process of political education whereby
the cadre is informed of the interests and opinions of the masses,
and the masses, in turn, are instructed in the policies or "lines"
that are developed pursuant to those interests and opinions. In
this chapter I shall focus particularly upon the ethical lessons that
Mao believed should be inculcated as a part of the process of
political education. Next, I shall treat the goals of these forms of

[1] 1937j:11.

political education and the agents to whom this project is entrusted. The third section of the chapter will take up the question of the setting within which the educational process takes place. Finally, we will investigate Mao's ideas with regard to the process of reeducation.

POLITICAL ETHICS

Mao's clearest statement of those skills and qualities that he saw as appropriately inculcated by the educational process is found in the description of the characteristics requisite for revolutionary successors that he wrote in 1964. He listed five characteristics, quoted here in somewhat abbreviated form:

> They must be genuine Marxist-Leninists. . . .
>
> They must be revolutionaries who wholeheartedly serve the overwhelming majority of the people. . . .
>
> They must be proletarian statesmen capable of uniting with and working together with the overwhelming majority. Not only must they unite with those who agree with them, but they must also be good at uniting with those who disagree and even with those who formerly opposed them and have since been proved wrong in practice. . . .
>
> They must be models in applying the party's democratic centralism, must master the method of leadership based on the principle of "from the masses, to the masses," and must cultivate a democratic style and be good at listening to the masses. . . .
>
> They must be modest and prudent and guard against arrogance and impetuosity; they must be imbued with the spirit of self-criticism and have the courage to correct mistakes and shortcomings in their work. Successors to the revolutionary cause of the proletariat come forward in mass struggles and are tempered in the great storms of revolution.[2]

Categorizing these characteristics, we might view the goals of the political educational process as involving the inculcation of a body of knowledge: Marxism-Leninism; two sets of skills: the ability to unite with the majority and the ability to practice the

---

[2] 1964i. A somewhat different version of the same five characteristics is found in 1964h. See also 1964n:26f.

mass line; and two ethical principles: service to the people and selflessness. Looking at them in a somewhat different light, what we find here in a slightly altered form is a restatement of Mao's criteria of legitimacy—criteria that we treated earlier under the threefold headings of stand, viewpoint, and method. Revolutionary successors must take the class stand of the proletariat, work on the basis of the viewpoint of service to the people, and employ the Marxist-Leninist methods of democratic centralism and the mass line.

The ethical principles that are added here appear only implicitly in his earlier discussions of legitimate authority, but must be considered in conjunction with those discussions because it is clear that without a clear-cut set of ethical imperatives, even the political actor exercising legitimate authority can become corrupted. Taking the corpus of Mao's writings as a whole, we find five ethical principles that constitute, I think, the elements of his definition of political morality. These principles are selflessness (or a collective spirit), self-reliance, persistence, honesty, and faith. The clearest statement of his commitment to these principles is found in a series of three articles excerpted from his works, distributed separately during the last decade or so, and referred to as the "three well-read articles." The pedagogical method employed in these articles is of particular interest, since it follows the principle commonly employed by Confucian predecessors of teaching moral lessons through the use of model figures.[3] Each of the three articles—"In Memory of Norman Bethune," written in 1939,[4] "Serve the People," written in September 1944,[5] and "The Foolish Old Man Who Removed the Mountains," written in June 1945[6]—uses an individual who incul-

---

[3] Despite his own use of it, the method of imitating models is one that Mao has occasionally described as counterproductive: "There are two methods of learning: one is merely to imitate, and the other is to apply the creative spirit. Learning should be combined with creativity" (1958j:26). He is speaking here of the use of the Soviet model in China. On the other hand, one of the "Sixty Work Methods" advocates the use of model units for emulation as a "very good leadership method" (1958e:4). Donald Munro has pointed out the conflict between education that uses emulatory models and education that stresses creativity. "Egalitarian Ideal and Educational Fact in Communist China," in John M. H. Lindbeck, ed., *China: Management of a Revolutionary Society* (Seattle: University of Washington Press, 1971), pp. 256-304.

[4] 1939l.   [5] 1944c.   [6] 1945b.

cates certain ethical qualities to serve as model for instructional purposes.

Norman Bethune was a Canadian doctor who came to China in 1938 at the head of a team of medical specialists. He stayed on in the base areas until, in November of the following year, he died of blood poisoning contracted while operating on wounded soldiers.[7] Mao wrote a eulogy the following month, emphasizing certain of Bethune's exemplary qualities. Among them was his strong commitment to his skills—not an ethical attribute, clearly, but instructive nonetheless of Mao's attitude toward technical skill: "The art of healing was his profession and he was constantly perfecting his skill. . . . His example is an excellent lesson . . . for those who despise technical work as of no consequence or as promising no future."[8] In addition, Mao lauded him as a man who put his principles (particularly that of proletarian internationalism) into practice. Most important, however, is Bethune's selflessness:

> Comrade Bethune's spirit, his utter devotion to others without any thought of self, was shown in his great sense of responsibility in his work and his warmheartedness towards all comrades and the people. Every communist must learn from him. . . . We must all learn the spirit of absolute selflessness from him. . . . A man's ability may be great or small, but if he has this spirit, he is already noble and pure, a man of moral integrity and above vulgar interests, a man who is of value to the people.[9]

A particularly important aspect of that selflessness exemplified in Bethune is the quality of modesty, one of the ethical principles subsequently stressed, as we have seen, as requisite for revolutionary successors. By contrast, Mao pointed out, "there are not a few people who think of themselves before others. When they make some small contribution, they swell with pride and brag about it for fear that others will not know."[10] He subsequently devoted a nineteen-point directive to the question of overcoming conceit and instilling modesty among cadres, in which he spoke of conceit as "derived from individualism," and as based on a "bourgeois idealist world view."[11]

Selflessness as manifested in a concern for others is a characteristic illustrated as well by the example of Zhang Side, who is

[7] 1939j:621f./II, 328. [8] Ibid. [9] Ibid.
[10] Ibid. [11] 1963k:88.

eulogized in the article, "Serve the People." Zhang served as a member of the Guards Regiment of the Central Committee, and was killed in 1944 when a charcoal kiln near which he was working collapsed, crushing him. Mao took the occasion of Zhang's death to comment on the new ethic of service in the base area: "We have the interests of the people and the sufferings of the great majority at heart, and when we die for the people, it is a worthy death. . . . Our cadres must show concern for every soldier and all people in the revolutionary ranks must care for each other, must love and help each other."[12]

A third example of selflessness or a collective spirit is found in Yu Gong, the "foolish old man" of the third article. The article recounts a Chinese fable in which Yu Gong and his sons set out to solve the problem of two mountains that "obstruct the way" in front of their home by undertaking to remove them. Relying on their own resources, Yu Gong realizes that their only recourse is to accomplish the task shovelful by shovelful. Eminently practical, he has boundless faith as well: "When I die my sons will carry on; when they die there will be my grandsons, and so on to infinity."[13] The denouement of the fable is particularly interesting: touched

[12] 1944c:906/III, 228. A similar note is struck in Mao's remarks at a meeting marking the first anniversary of Lu Xun's death, where he praised his "readiness to sacrifice himself." He was, Mao went on, completely fearless of enemy intimidation and persecution and utterly unmoved by enemy enticement." This was the third of three qualities that Mao regarded as deserving of emulation in Lu Xun; the first two were his political vision and his militancy (1938b:14f.).

[13] 1945b:1002/III, 322. A fourth model figure, much less well publicized than the first three, is found in Mao's letter to Xu Teli in 1937, commemorating the latter's sixtieth birthday. There he lauded Xu as follows: "'Age,' 'declining physical and mental abilities,' and 'hardships and obstacles' have all surrendered to you, in spite of the fact that they have served as excuses for the timidity of many people. You know a great deal but always feel a deficiency in your knowledge, whereas many 'half-buckets of water' make a lot of noise. What you think is what you say or what you do, whereas other people hide filthy things in a corner of their minds. You enjoy being with the masses all the time, whereas some others enjoy being without the masses. You are always a model of obedience to the party and its revolutionary discipline, whereas some others regard the discipline as a restraint for others, but not for themselves. For you, it is 'revolution first,' 'work first,' and 'other people first,' whereas for some others it is 'limelight first,' 'rest first,' and 'oneself first.' You always pick the most difficult things to do, never avoiding your responsibilities, whereas some others choose easy work to do, always shunning responsibilities" (1937b:5).

by the old man's perseverance, "God was moved and he sent down two angels, who carried the mountain away on their backs." "Our god," Mao hastens to add, "is none other than the masses of the Chinese people."

Yu Gong's selflessness—his sense of the greater importance of the collectivity—is manifested in his realization that, while he himself is unlikely to benefit from his efforts, those who come after him—his sons and grandsons—will not only continue his work, but will live to reap its reward. While his is a limited sense of the collective because it is restricted to his own descendants, it nevertheless serves to illustrate the positive aspects of working for the benefit of others, which must replace the narrow pursuit of selfish and self-interested goals.

The very strong emphasis that Mao placed on the value of self-lessness is occasioned by the fact that, if it is possible to pinpoint a single quality which he regarded as epitomizing the bourgeoisie and bourgeois society, that quality is self-seeking individualism. Given what we commonly assume to have been the very low level of development of individualism in China in the pre-Liberation period,[14] it is somewhat surprising to find Mao devoting such considerable attention to the overcoming of that quality. Indeed, a case could be made to support the contention that bourgeois individualism only began to be introduced into China during the May Fourth period (1919),[15] and had scarcely penetrated beyond the intelligentsia and a small segment of "treaty port" society by the time of Liberation.

Mao was, of course, a member of the May Fourth generation himself. Evidence of his own emergent sense of individualism is found in a number of his pre-Marxist works, where struggle is seen as directed toward individual, rather than social or political liberation.[16] His treatment of individualism as a problem and his

[14] See Donald J. Munro, *The Concept of Man in Contemporary China* (Ann Arbor: University of Michigan Press, 1977), 52f., 55, and 178f.

[15] Concerning the details of which, see Chow Tse-tsung, *The May Fourth Movement* (Cambridge: Harvard University Press, 1965).

[16] In one of his articles dealing with the suicide of a young woman protesting her arranged marriage, he lauded the object of her action, which he saw as the desire to follow her individual will. "The goal of struggle," he said, "is not 'to be killed by others,' but 'to aspire toward the emergence of a true personality'" (1919b:336). The same themes occur in the article on physical education, where physical training is seen as an integral part of individual self-realization and as producing a genuine morality and virtue (1917:154).

advancement of selflessness and collectivism, however, appears to me to have been occasioned less by a concern for a preexisting and pervasive individualism in the society, and more by a concern that, in the process of accomplishing those developmental projects in a socialist society that would otherwise have been accomplished under bourgeois auspices, there is the danger of the emergence of individualism. This concern is made particularly clear in his treatment of the cooperativization of agriculture, where the appeal to the peasants to join the cooperative was made on the basis of the furthering of their individual interests,[17] while at the same time an attempt was made to encourage them to see these individual interests as linked together in the "mutual benefit" of the collective.[18] Clearly the balance was a delicate one, for with no emphasis on individual interests, the move toward cooperatives would have been slower, or might, in some instances, not have been made at all. With an excessive and prolonged emphasis on individual interests there was a danger that "spontaneous capitalistic tendencies" would be fostered among the poor and lower-middle peasants.[19] "Giving consideration to the whole is the supreme ethic," Mao wrote in 1958.[20] "Public interests come first and private interests come later," he said three years later. "The individual is an element of the collective. When collective interests are increased, personal interests will subsequently be improved."[21]

The most important lesson to be learned from the example of the "foolish old man" is that of self-reliance, the second of the five moral principles comprising Mao's political ethic. The lesson of self-reliance is taught here, however, in a somewhat indirect way. The redefinition of the *deus ex machina* in the fable as symbolizing the masses of the Chinese people may solve the immediate problem of theism, but whether Yu Gong is assisted by beings natural or supernatural, it does undercut somewhat the impact of

[17] 1955d:15.
[18] Ibid., p. 12.
[19] 1955g:302f.
[20] 1958zz:139.
[21] 1961a:290. Elsewhere he used the analogy of a machine to describe what he called the "collectivist's view of work": collective work is "constructed like a huge machine with its wheels, screws, steel frames, and other parts of different size and shapes, each being indispensable. As a collectivist, one should respect each person's work and each person's achievement. For the perfection of the revolutionary work one must coordinate one's own work with that of others. . . . As for an individual, he or she is no more than a small screw in the revolutionary works" (1963k:90f).

the ethical lesson to suggest that the act of following the principle of self-reliance will be rewarded with help that renders one dependent on others to accomplish a major task.

Despite this ambiguous aspect, however, the denouement of the fable does suggest that, while the value of self-reliance is applicable to the individual, it applies to him or her within the context of a collectivity—a point that is suggested in Mao's substitution of the masses for the fable's God and angels. Not only must individuals direct their action toward the welfare of others and be prepared to engage in that action relying on their own resources, but they must also act together with others in such a way as to promote collective achievement. Self-reliance is propounded by Mao not only as an individual virtue, then, but also as an ethical principle to be realized at every level of society. He put forward self-sufficient agricultural units as models for others to follow,[22] praised self-reliant industrial units for their initiative,[23] emphasized local and regional self-sufficiency as a national developmental policy,[24] and regarded China's national self-reliance and freedom from foreign assistance as being among her most important achievements.[25]

A third value in Mao's ethical system exemplified by Yu Gong is that of persistence. China's developmental tasks are well symbolized by the mountains that "obstruct the way" at Yu Gong's doorstep, and given the limited capital resources available for accomplishing those tasks, to undertake them "shovelful by shovelful" seemed the only feasible alternative. Apart from a brief period of euphoria during the Great Leap Forward, when much more emphasis was placed on the immediate wonders that could be worked by the "God" of the fable—by the collective efforts, that is, of the masses of the huge Chinese population—than on the dogged labors of Yu Gong and his sons, the more consistent

[22] See, for example, 1955g:14 and 1958hh:3. The most important example of this in recent years is the Dazhai Production Brigade, to which example Mao called the nation's attention in 1964 (1964v). See Mitchell R. Meisner, " 'In Agriculture Learn from Dazhai': Theory and Practice in Chinese Rural Development," Ph.D. dissertation, University of Chicago, 1977.

[23] See, for example, 1956e:26; 1958e:12; and 1958dd:3.

[24] 1956c. See also Jon Sigurdson, "Rural Industry and the Internal Transfer of Technology," in Stuart R. Schram, ed., *Authority, Participation and Cultural Change in China* (Cambridge: Cambridge University Press, 1973), pp. 199-232.

[25] 1958x:16.

theme has been that of the necessity for persistence in accomplishing the task of China's economic development.[26]

The fourth of the ethical principles that we have found in the fable about Yu Gong is that of faith. "What is important," Mao said in 1965, "is to begin action with faith."[27] Yu Gong's faith is vested in his progeny; Mao advocated the vesting of faith elsewhere. Two "cardinal principles," he indicated in 1955, are faith in the masses and faith in the party.[28] Faith in the goals of development—that is, faith in socialism and communism—is also requisite.[29] Finally, it is necessary to have faith in victory: "Faith in victory is the first element of victory—in fact, it may mean victory itself."[30] "Revolution," he said to Malraux just prior to the Cultural Revolution, "is a dream of passion; we did not win the people over by appealing to reason, but by developing hope, trust, and fraternity."[31]

Honesty, the last of the elements of a Maoist political ethic, is one that does not figure prominently in the stories of the model figures contained in the "three well-read articles," but is nonetheless critical, in Mao's view. Although treated separately from the context of opposition to individualism, the value placed on honesty is not wholly divorced from the attempt to create a value structure that will serve as an alternative to the selfish individualism Mao saw as the defining characteristic of the bourgeoisie, since dishonesty is frequently encountered as an attempt to further selfish causes. Mao's theory of knowledge and his espousal of the mass line method of policy formulation both necessitate, as we have seen, the unencumbered exchange of accurate information between subordinates and leaders, and between members of an organization and the clients of that organization. Dishonesty constitutes a break in these crucial communication links. As a result, honesty becomes a particularly important element of a socialist morality: "Those who are honest and dare to tell the truth are, in the final analysis, beneficial to the cause of the people, and they themselves also have nothing to lose."[32]

The ethical system that Mao espoused thus comprised the values of a selfless collective spirit, self-reliance, persistence, faith, and honesty. Consistent with his epistemological principles, he argued that these ethical principles must be borne out in

[26] See, for example, 1955g:67.   [27] 1965f.

[28] 1955d:7, 18.   [29] 1958m:120.   [30] 1965f.

[31] 1965g:360.   [32] 1959m:9.

practice. As theoretical abstractions alone they are without meaning. Moreover, he pointed out that a dialectician must insist on the unity of motive and effect, and motives can be judged only on the basis of their effects in social practice.[33]

THE GOALS AND THE AGENTS OF POLITICAL EDUCATION

The project of political education, as Mao saw it, is threefold. The first aspect of the project—that of reeducating those who grew up under the pre-Liberation regime—has become decreasingly important as the first quarter century of the People's Republic has drawn to a close and the second begun, since only a small and declining percentage of the population lacks the experience of the post-Liberation system of political education. The second aspect of the project is that of educating anew a young generation of men and women in such a way as to make them, to the maximum extent possible, immune to the possibility of corruption. Such an education aims at inculcating not only the ethical principles discussed above, but also the knowledge of Marxism-Leninism and the skills in relating to the masses that are seen as requisite for "revolutionary successors." Finally, the third aspect of the project of political education is the reeducation of those whose immunity has failed them and who have succumbed, at least to some degree, to the economic, political, or ideological causes of corruption and class deterioration inherent in political life.

A problem with this threefold project of political education lies in the fact that the agents who are, in many cases, entrusted with carrying it out are intellectuals, whom Mao regarded as especially vulnerable themselves to the corrupting influences that create new bourgeois elements in a socialist system. His view of intellectuals is highly ambiguous, even contradictory. Indeed, with some selectivity, one could even make a case from Mao's speeches and writings for his being profoundly anti-intellectual. On at least five occasions in the post-Liberation period he voiced the idea that it is not the educated but the unschooled who are the innovators in history. "Ever since ancient times," he said at Chengdu in 1958, "the people who founded new schools of thought were all young people without too much learning. They had the ability to recognize new things at a glance and, having

[33] 1942c:825/III, 88. He uses the ethic of service to the people as his example here.

grasped them, they opened fire on the old fogeys."[34] Earlier in the same speech he explained the background of his feelings: "Professors—we have been afraid of them ever since we came into the towns. We did not despise them, we were terrified of them. When confronted by people with piles of learning we felt that we were good for nothing. For Marxists to fear bourgeois intellectuals, to fear professors while not fearing imperialism, is strange indeed. . . . We must not tolerate it any longer."[35]

There is an autobiographical ring to Mao's remarks here. Although he began his own career as an intellectual, he found himself on the fringes of the intellectual community of the May Fourth movement. During his brief sojourn in Beijing just prior to the May Fourth Incident, he found that the leading intellectuals in the movement for cultural reform had, as he put it, "no time to listen to an assistant librarian speaking in the southern dialect."[36] He spoke of the transformation he experienced in becoming a revolutionary, a passage quoted here *in extenso* not only for what it tells us about Mao's attitude toward intellectuals, but also because it is among his clearest descriptions of the process of a change of class:

> I began life as a student and at school acquired the ways of a student. . . . At that time I felt that intellectuals were the only clean people in the world, while in comparison workers and peasants were dirty. I did not mind wearing the clothes of other intellectuals, believing them clean, but I would not put on clothes belonging to a worker or a peasant, believing them dirty. But after I became a revolutionary and lived with workers and peasants and with soldiers of the revolutionary army, I gradually came to know them well, and they gradually came to know me well too. It was then, and only then, that I funda-

[34] 1958m:119. Cf. 1958p:89; 1958s:92; 1958u:119f.; 1964c:334; and 1965j:53. "The more books one reads, the stupider one becomes, knowing almost nothing," he concluded in 1965 (1965a:439).

[35] 1958m:116. Not all intellectuals are to be tarred with the same brush, however. In 1964 he pointed out that intellectuals differ in their willingness to accept socialism: technical personnel are best in this regard, scientists next. "Those who study liberal arts are the worst," he concluded (1964r: 401).

[36] The comment is from Mao's autobiographical account contained in Edgar Snow's *Red Star over China* (New York: Grove Press, 1968), p. 151. See Stuart R. Schram's treatment of this period in Mao's life in his biography, *Mao Tse-tung* (Baltimore: Penguin, 1967), pp. 47-50.

mentally changed the bourgeois and petty-bourgeois feelings implanted in me in the bourgeois schools. I came to feel that compared with the workers and peasants the unremolded intellectuals were not clean and that, in the last analysis, the workers and peasants were the cleanest people and, even though their hands were soiled and their feet smeared with cow dung, they were really cleaner that the bourgeois and petty-bourgeois intellectuals. That is what is meant by a change in feelings, a change from one class to another.[37]

A portrayal of Mao as an unmitigated "Know-Nothing," however, is a selective and thus an inaccurate one, as I have indicated above. "The working class," he said in 1940, "should welcome the help of the revolutionary intellectuals and never refuse it. For without their help the working class itself cannot go forward nor can the revolution succeed."[38] The criterion by which the acceptability or nonacceptability of intellectuals is to be measured is "whether or not they are willing to integrate themselves with the workers and peasants and actually do so," he said elsewhere.[39] Thus, over the short run, the solution that Mao proposed is to "unite with and remold" bourgeois intellectuals;[40] the longer-range solution is for the workers and peasants to become intellectuals themselves. "Intellectuals are indispensable," he commented in 1958. "The proletariat must cultivate its own talents. They must be up to a certain cultural standard, have scientific knowledge, and be trained in polished phraseology."[41]

[37] 1942c:808/III, 73. His remarks were addressed to an audience of bourgeois intellectuals at the Yan'an Forum on Art and Literature.

[38] 1940c:686/II, 404. Cf. 1940f:726f./II, 448, where he said, "bourgeois-liberal educators, men of letters, journalists, scholars, and technical experts should be allowed to come to our base areas and cooperate with us in running schools and newspapers and doing other work. We should accept into our schools all intellectuals and students who show enthusiasm for resisting Japan, give them short-term training, and then assign them to work in the army, the government, or mass organizations; we should boldly draw them in, give them work and promote them."

[39] 1939c:530/II, 246.

[40] 1956h:89. Cf. 1951f:97f. and 1954d:8. The disadvantage of having taken this necessary course was, as he commented in 1966, the creation of an academic system manned and controlled by non-Marxists (1966c; 1966d:375). "Bourgeois intellectuals are with us when it's sunny, but away when it is dark," he commented in 1962. "Their dark side has not yet been dispersed and we must do further analysis" (1962d:24).

[41] 1958e:12. A much earlier version of the same argument is found in 1939i:582f./II, 303.

There are problems inherent even in this longer-range solution, however, and these problems pose themselves with particular strength when the task of political education is turned over to intellectuals. Even worker-peasant intellectuals are subject to corruption and at times require transformation. The problem lies in an intellectual's relationship to his or her knowledge: "Some people consider knowledge as their own possession and wait to get a good price for it in the market. When the price is not high enough for them, they will refuse to sell their knowledge. They are expert only, but not red."[42] The intellectuals are "beginning to have children," Mao explained to André Malraux in 1964. "Their thinking is anti-Marxist. At the time of the Liberation we welcomed them even when they had been involved with the Guomindang, because we had too few Marxist intellectuals. Their influence is far from disappearing. Especially among the young."[43]

It is no doubt because of this ambiguous attitude of his toward intellectuals that so much of Mao's effort in the sphere of political education was directed toward the deinstitutionalization of the education process and its reintegration with the society as a whole. By such deinstitutionalization he hoped to mitigate or control the potential ill effects of the use of intellectuals as the agents of political education.

THE SETTING FOR POLITICAL EDUCATION

"Of course some things can be learned at school; I don't propose to close all the schools," Mao assured his colleagues at Chengdu in 1958. "What I mean is that it is not absolutely necessary to attend school. The main thing is whether your direction is correct or not and whether you come to grips with your studies."[44] Mao's education reforms can accurately, if summarily, be described with the title of Ivan Illich's book, "deschooling society." It is precisely the institutional isolation of the school from the society which

[42] 1961a:257. "Intellectuals have always been quick in altering their perception of things," he said in 1967, "but because of the limitations of their instincts, and because they lack a thorough revolutionary character, they are sometimes opportunistic" (1967:458f.).

[43] 1965h:365. The principal hindrance to technical innovation, he commented three years earlier, are the " 'academic lords' who are in control of scientific and research institutions and suppress newborn forces" (1961a: 275).

[44] 1958m:120.

Illich deplores that Mao has attempted to alter in the Chinese education system.[45] Emblematic of this goal of deinstitutionalization of education is his comment that "philosophy should be liberated from the classrooms and books of philosophers and turned into a sharp weapon in the hands of the masses."[46]

In his "May 7 Instruction" in 1966, contained in a letter to Lin Biao, Mao called for a "revolutionization" of education[47]—a call that was echoed in the "Sixteen Point Decision" of the Central Committee inaugurating the Cultural Revolution.[48] It was not the first time that Mao had uttered a call for revolutionization. His earlier attempt, made in conjunction with the Great Leap Forward, had gone largely unheeded, however. The revolution in education aimed first at cutting through the faults of the unhappy melange of traditional Chinese, European, American, and Soviet models on the basis of which the Chinese education system of the 1950s had been created. Second, it was an attempt to return to those principles of establishing education institutions that had first emerged from the guerrilla experience of the CCP in the pre-Liberation period.

Mao's first recorded thoughts on the reform of the Chinese education system are found in an article written in 1917 on the subject of physical education. There he saw three aspects to the process of education: the moral, the intellectual, and the physical. He berated the existing school system particularly for its failure to attend to the third of these aspects, arguing that China needed a strong population to salvage itself from its weak position in the world, and that, as they were then constituted, the schools not only failed to contribute to the physical well-being of their students, but they actually undermined that well-being by the demands they placed on the students in their academic work.[49] In

[45] Ivan Illich, *Deschooling Society* (New York: Harper and Row, 1970). It is interesting to note that more recently Illich has come to a somewhat different position: "For all its vices," he writes, "school cannot be simply and rashly eliminated" (Ivan Illich *et al.*, *After Deschooling, What?* [New York: Harper and Row, 1973], pp. 9f.). His argument here is that so long as education is treated as a commodity in the society, the existing system protects children from self-interested educational entrepreneurs.

[46] 1963d:69.   [47] 1966f:104.

[48] 1966m:124. In both this and the previous instance, the call for revolutionizing the education system was linked directly with the necessity for putting an end to the domination of the education system by "bourgeois intellectuals."

[49] 1917:154. His concern over the adverse effects of academic work on

setting up a university in Yan'an for workers and peasants who had joined the Red Army, Mao enunciated anew his principles of the purpose of an education system: it must instill a correct political orientation, give the students the experience of hard work, and insure their integration with the masses of workers and peasants.[50] He elaborated on these principles two decades later in setting forth a series of "principles of educating youth":

1. Teach them to grasp Marxism-Leninism and to overcome petty-bourgeois consciousness.

2. Teach them to have discipline and organization and to oppose anarchism and libertarianism in organization.

3. Teach them to penetrate resolutely into the lower levels of practical work and to oppose looking down on practical experience.

4. Teach them to become close to the workers and peasants, to serve them resolutely, and to oppose the consciousness of looking down on workers and peasants.[51]

The revolution that sought to break down the existing, institutionalized education system and to reestablish these pedagogical principles touched upon every aspect of the education system: curriculum, faculty, students, and the management of the schools.[52] The impulse toward deinstitutionalization was especially clear in Mao's proposals for reform of the curriculum. Courses, he argued, should be made relevant to the practical tasks facing the society as a whole. To insure this relevance, work and study should be combined either by relocating the school in a factory or other workplace, or by constructing productive workshops as adjuncts

---

physical well-being continued into the post-Liberation period. See, for example, 1953d and 1964c:203.

[50] 1939d:146 and 1939e:3f.   [51] 1960c.

[52] In 1968 Mao summarized his plan for the revolution in education as follows: "It is necessary to shorten the length of schooling, revolutionize education, put proletarian politics in command, and take the road of the Shanghai Machine Tools Plant in training technicians from among the workers. Students should be selected from among workers and peasants with practical experience and they should return to practical work in production after a few years' study" (1958e). Four years earlier he had proposed education reforms that included the shortening of the school year and reduction of the number of subjects taught, an increase in recreation, open-book examinations, and the integration of work and study (1964c: 200-211).

to the schools.[53] Once students have completed their schooling, they should be encouraged, through a regular system of downward transfer (*xiaxiang*) to apply their newly acquired skills where they are most needed.[54] Instructors should themselves take part in practical work at the basic level,[55] and should be assisted in the classroom by teams of workers, peasants, and soldiers in order to insure that their instruction remains relevant and politically correct.[56] Students are to be recruited from among workers and peasants with practical experience, to avoid the development

[53] He voiced the rationale behind this reform as early as 1942 in phrases reminiscent of his description of the requisites for the process of cognition: "What sort of knowledge is the students' book-learning? Even supposing all their knowledge is truth, it is still not knowledge acquired through their own personal experience, but consists of theories set down by their predecessors in summarizing experience of the struggle for production and of the class struggle. It is entirely necessary that students should acquire this kind of knowledge, but it mut be understood that, as far as they are concerned, such knowledge is in a sense one-sided, something which has been verified by others but not yet by themselves" (1942a:774/III, 39). Cf. 1939c: 532/II, 248, where he speaks disparagingly of Confucius' lack of expertise and ability to teach practical skills such as plowing and vegetable raising, and the need for schools in the base areas to teach these and other skills by means of practical experience. In his earlier and unsuccessful efforts at revolutionizing the Chinese education system, a primary point was the introduction of part-work, part-study schools that would help to link up "textbook science with practical experience" (1958e:12; 1958ee; and 1958mm). In 1961 he raised the idea again, praising its implementation by the Jiangxi Labor University (1961d:9f.). In those fields where no factories were directly related to the work in that field, students were counseled to "regard the whole of society as their factory" (1964s:23).

[54] Extolling this practice as early as 1955, Mao commented favorably on an informal system of *xiaxiang* in Henan Province: "All people who have had some education ought to be very happy to work in the countryside if they get the chance. In our vast rural areas there is plenty of room for them to develop their talents to the full" (1955g:378). The directive in 1968 establishing the formal system which, with some modifications, continues in operation at the present time, reads as follows: "It is absolutely necessary for educated young people to go to the countryside to be reeducated by the poor and lower-middle peasants. Cadres and other city people should be persuaded to send their sons and daughters who have finished junior or senior middle school, college or university to the countryside. Let us mobilize. Comrades throughout the countryside should welcome them" (1968n). The language is interesting, since in his reference to the persuasion needed in the case of parents and to the necessity for rural comrades to welcome the transferred students, Mao pointed to two of the ongoing problems in the *xiaxiang* system.

[55] 1964q:385.   [56] 1968g; 1968h.

and perpetuation within the education system of a protoclass consisting of the children of the well-educated and well-placed.[57] Finally, pursuant to the principle of self-reliance and in further-ance of the goal of deinstitutionalization, schools should be locally, rather than centrally, managed wherever possible.[58]

The institutionalization of education—its exclusive relegation to the classroom and its control by professional educators and administrators—was thus opposed by Mao on three analytically distinguishable but related grounds. First, he believed that the institutionalization of education depoliticizes the learning process, whereas he saw the linking of the inculcation of information and skills to the conveying of political principles, techniques, and values as being the only means of resolving the contradiction between red and expert in the political system. Second, the confinement of education to the classroom results, he argued, in a kind of learning that is irremediably divorced from its practical applicability—an outcome that not only causes an estrangement of the education system from the process of economic development, but, more fundamentally, conveys to the student a mistaken sense of the relationship between theory and practice. Finally, the institutionalization of education places, for instructional purposes, the least corrupted members of the society in the hands of the most easily corruptible, hardly a situation designed to solve the problem of embourgeoisement in a socialist society.

There are two aspects to Mao's policy of deinstitutionalizing the education system. On the one hand, as we have seen, it is a

[57] The point was made as early as 1956 (1956j). This aspect of the Cultural Revolutionary education reforms was largely abandoned with the new admissions procedures announced in October 1977, which placed great emphasis on examination scores in the admissions decision. The procedures were described in the report of a National Conference on Admissions Procedures held in October (NCNA, 20 October).

[58] In his "Hunan Report," Mao praised the fact that he found the peasants "enthusiastically establishing evening classes, which they call peasant schools." He contrasted these with the "foreign-style schools" established by county education boards, which he saw as "not suited to the needs of the peasants" (1927:39f./1, 53f.). In the early post-Liberation period he praised the locally run and locally financed *minban* (popularly run) schools. These schools were vigorously opposed by those in the central government interested in regularizing the education system through central control. During the Cultural Revolution he reasserted his position, arguing that "in the countryside, the schools should be managed by the poor and lower-middle peasants—the most reliable ally of the working class" (1968g).

call to open the school system to participation by members of the society at large. The obverse aspect of this policy—one that he supported with equal enthusiasm—was the transformation of society as a whole to become a kind of education institution. Thus, far from limiting the function of political education to a reformed school system, he advocated instead that a range of social and political institutions—the family, the small group in neighborhood or workplace, mass organizations,[59] mobilizational campaigns,[60] the media, and the cultural realm all join in the task of political education.[61]

Mao's views concerning the cultural sphere—the realm of art, literature, and the performing arts—serve as a useful example of his efforts to extend the process of political education beyond the confines of the school system. In the forum held in Yan'an to deal with questions of art and literature in 1942, Mao made the point that the appropriate goal of the cultural sphere is political. Insisting that the audience for art and literature should be the masses of workers and peasants,[62] he went on to define the goals to be achieved by the artist and writer: "Revolutionary literature and art should create a variety of characters out of real life and help the masses to propel history forward. . . . Writers and artists concentrate . . . everyday phenomena, typify the contradictions and struggles within them and produce works which awaken the

[59] At 1961a:274 he spoke of one function of the trade union as being that of political education.

[60] He described the Cultural Revolution, for example, as "a movement in which the masses, by being given free rein to express themselves will educate themselves politically" (1966m:120). The question of the duration of the effects of this educational experience was raised in the discussion concerning political participation in the preceding chapter.

[61] As a part of the campaign to cultivate revolutionary successors, for example, Mao advocated that members of the older generation recount their experience of pre-Revolutionary society and of the revolution itself, so that the young might learn the political lessons inherent in this experience in a more direct and vivid fashion (1963b: 321).

[62] 1942c:812f./III, 76f.: "Our literature and art are first for the workers, the class that leads the revolution. Secondly, they are for the peasants, the most numerous and most steadfast of our allies in the revolution. Thirdly, they are for the armed workers and peasants, namely, the Eighth Route and New Fourth Armies and the other armed units of the people, which are the main forces of the revolutionary war. Fourthly, they are for the labouring masses of the urban petty bourgeoisie and for the petty-bourgeois intellectuals, both of whom are also our allies in the revolution and capable of long-term cooperation with us."

masses, fire them with enthusiasm and impel them to unite and struggle to transform their environment."[63]

Another forum on art and literature was conducted two decades later, this time under the joint auspices of Lin Biao and Jiang Qing, Mao's wife. In the report of that meeting, which was said to have been extensively edited by Mao before its publication, the definitions of the audience and the mission of art and literature were substantially unchanged. What was new in this report was the substitution of the phrase "by the masses," where the Yan'an Forum Talks had spoken of art and literature "for the masses."[64] Rather than as passive recipients of art and literature produced for their edification, the masses were portrayed here as combining the functions of creator, audience, and critic, thereby cutting through the bureaucratic structure into which the artistic establishment had grown in the post-Liberation decades.[65] An integral connection between art and literature and the process of political education is advocated throughout the report.[66]

REEDUCATION

"Our aim in exposing errors and criticizing shortcomings, like that of a doctor curing a sickness, is solely to save the patient, and not to doctor him to death."[67] So Mao described one of the basic

[63] Ibid., 818/III, 82. Earlier he spoke of the successful use of the performing arts in the military and political training of guerrilla forces (1938a: 127ff.).

[64] 1966a:12. Despite the statements regarding Mao's role in formulating this document, the subsequent fall of both the individuals with which it is primarily associated—Lin Biao and Jiang Qing—raises questions concerning the degree to which Mao concurred with its conclusions.

[65] Ibid., pp. 14f. The "rules of artistic creation" set forward here include hard work, freedom from bureaucracy, reliance on first-hand material, freedom from fear of failure, implementation of the mass line, submission of works of art to the test of practice, and the summing up of creative experience in order to grasp its laws. The important and intriguing question of Mao's views on the relationship between contemporary art and literature and China's cultural heritage we shall reserve for the following chapter.

[66] Three unsatisfactory types of artistic work are set forward: (1) those that are correct in political orientation but low in artistic level; (2) those that have a mistaken political orientation but are high in artistic level; and (3) "poisonous weeds which lack both a correct orientation and artistic merit" (ibid., p. 12). In the wake of the arrest and criticism of Jiang Qing as a member of the Gang of Four in October 1976, these views were criticized as too restrictive of the realm of art and literature.

[67] 1942a:785/III, 50.

principles of the rectification campaign of 1942. This view of dissident elements in the party and in society as patients suffering from a potentially curable disease is one of the unique and most important features of Mao's concept of political education. Donald Munro has referred to it as a basic commitment on Mao's part to the idea of the "malleability of man."[68]

Mao addressed himself to the question of human nature in his Yan'an Forum talks in 1942. Arguing against a literary theory based on the principle of a universal human nature, he said, "Is there such a thing as human nature? Of course there is. But there is only human nature in the concrete, no human nature in the abstract. In class society there is only human nature of a class character; there is no human nature above classes."[69] His position here follows that of Marx, who argued that those characteristics which link all men and women together—what he called their "species being"—were fully realizable only after classes had been overcome by the establishment of a communist society. Until that time, the most important human characteristics are determined by class, and thus are not universally shared.[70]

So long as Mao conceptualized classes as being determined primarily on the basis of an individual's relationship to the means of production, his argument that human nature is class-determined was logically sound within the Marxist framework. As we have seen, however, he did not hold to that position. Rather, he came to argue that experience, behavior, and attitude are just as important as economic position in determining one's class. Put in another way, what he appears to have done is to have abstracted from the historical experience of the proletariat and the bourgeoisie certain characteristic modes of behavior and points of view of members of those two classes. Taking these behavior patterns as modal types, he then contended that the class of an individual can be ascertained by categorizing his or her behavior and outlook as falling within one or the other type. He went beyond that to suggest that there is a universal, human tendency for

[68] Donald Munro, "The Malleability of Man in Chinese Marxism," *China Quarterly* 48 (1971), 609-640.

[69] 1942c:827/III, 90.

[70] See, for example, Marx's discussion of species being and alienated labor in the "Economic and Philosophical Manuscripts" of 1844 in Robert C. Tucker, ed., *The Marx-Engels Reader* (New York: W. W. Norton, 1972), pp. 60-64.

individuals to move in a retrograde direction between these two behavioral categories if they are left to themselves. As he pointed out to Malraux in 1965, "Humanity left to its own devices does not necessarily reestablish capitalism . . . but it does reestablish inequality. The forces tending toward the creation of new classes are powerful."[71] As Mao saw it, there is, thus, a universal human tendency toward the reestablishment of political and economic inequality, presumably through the pursuit of individual self-interest. It is the universality of this tendency toward corruption —its givenness, if you will—that makes reeducation such a critical part of his view of the process of political education.[72]

He reiterated in 1956 his argument on the necessity of avoiding "doctoring to death" those in need of political reeducation. In doing so he suggested another rationale behind his position—that of the possibility of rendering a mistaken judgment. Using a different metaphor he said, "The head of a man does not grow like the leek, and once it is cut another will not come up. If a head were wrongly cut, there would be no way to correct the mistake."[73] On the other hand, he did not hold to a position of universal salvageability, and insisted that, while a hesitancy to execute the unsalvageable criminal should lead to a thorough investigation or his or her crimes and a full-scale attempt at reform, it should not paralyze the ability to eliminate those who are irredeemably counterrevolutionary.[74] His position of caution was inspired, at

[71] 1965h:373.

[72] "Permitting people to make revolution," he argued in 1956, presupposes a necessity to correct mistakes (1956e:32). Elsewhere he contended that the idea that mistakes can be eliminated entirely is anti-Marxist and metaphysical (1958l:113).

[73] 1956e:31. This concern is manifested in his frequent comments on the danger of false arrest in the campaigns to suppress counterrevolutionaries in the early post-Liberation years. See, for example, 1951c and 1951d:9f.

[74] In 1956 he told his colleagues in the Politburo, "we should take affirmative action in regard to the suppression of counterrevolutionaries. In the past, we have killed, locked up, and controlled two to three million such persons, and this was extremely necessary. . . . Now the counterrevolutionaries are fewer. We should take affirmative action to see if there are still any counterrevolutionaries, and this year decide upon having some of them killed. . . . We cannot be lax and lenient; we must carry out this bitter task" (1956c:34). Later in the same month, in the "Ten Major Relationships," he investigated the relationship between revolution and counterrevolution, and had this to say: "Who were executed? They were those elements laden with blood debts whom the common people hated most.

least in part, by what he took to be the negative lesson of Stalin's prewar purges in the Soviet Union.[75] It was based, as well, on the very practical grounds that excessive purging diminishes the party's base of support—it constitutes, to use his phrase, an instance of "lifting a rock to drop it on one's own feet."[76]

If there are, in fact, those who are unsalvageable—that sector of the "die-hards," as he referred to them in 1940, who fail to change for the better and become "something filthy and contemptible"[77]—they are few in number. Categorizing cadres at the outset of the Cultural Revolution, he argued that even the worst category—"antisocialist, antiparty rightists"—"should be given a way out so that they can turn over a new leaf."[78]

The redemption of those who are redeemable—the vast majority, as Mao saw it—is to be brought about by means of political education. "Of one thing we may be sure," he said in 1955, "working people, given proper political education, can overcome their shortcomings and correct their mistakes."[79] The process is public —that is, it requires the participation of others and takes place in

---

The common people would voice their disapproval if these despots were not executed but dealt with leniently. . . . The suppression of counterrevolutionaries in society from now on should see to it that fewer of them are arrested or executed. The majority of counterrevolutionaries should be handed over to agricultural producers' cooperatives so that they may . . . reform themselves through labor" (1956e:30f.).

[75] "The Soviet Union killed too many people," he said in 1961. "We will not make Stalin's mistake . . ." (1961b:241). The remainder of this last sentence, ". . . but we will also not make Khrushchev's more civilized mistake of dismissing the Central Committee," is intriguing in post-Cultural Revolutionary retrospect.

[76] 1956e:32.

[77] 1940d:695/II, 413. "The attitude of communists towards any person who has made mistakes in his work should be one of persuasion in order to help him change and start afresh and not one of exclusion, unless he is incorrigible" (1938e:488/II, 198).

[78] 1966m:123. Two months later, in October 1966, he applied the same argument to Liu Shaoqi and Deng Xiaoping: the two should "be allowed to make mistakes and make revolution as well. They should [be] allowed to mend their ways" (1966o:70ff.). Elsewhere I have treated Deng's first return to power (Starr, "China in 1975: The Wind in the Bell Tower," *Asian Survey* 16:1 [1976], 42-60), and his subsequent fall therefrom ("From the Tenth Party Congress"). Mao proposed a similar prescription of reeducation for Lin Biao just prior to his attempted escape and consequent death (1971:27).

[79] 1955g:198.

a public setting.[80] This setting is almost invariably that of the small group (*xiaozu*) of fellow workers, fellow residents, or fellow members of an organization. The "public" involved is thus a group of cohorts who know the individual well.

Mao characterized the process of reeducation with two slogans, both of which are intended to emphasize what he saw as the dialectical framework within which the process is to take place. The first of these slogans is "struggle-criticism-transformation," the second, "unity-criticism-unity." Struggle and criticism are the two crucial elements of the process of reeducation. The first slogan stresses the goal of the process, which is the transformation or reform of the deviant individual. The second slogan, approaching the process from the point of view of the group as a whole, emphasizes the fact that everyone in the group, including the individual to be reeducated, must begin from the unified position of a desire to resolve the contradiction. The process of criticism will inevitably divide the group, but the end result of the process is the achievement of "a new unity on a new basis."[81]

Struggle is often necessary in order to persuade the deviant individual that there are faults to correct, contradictions to be resolved. "The first thing to do," Mao said in 1942, pursuing his medical analogy in a way with which a member of the medical profession would be likely to take issue, "is to give the patient a good shakeup by shouting at him, 'You are ill!' so as to administer a shock and make him break out in a sweat, and then to give him sincere advice on getting treatment."[82] The shock is administered by the process that Mao referred to as struggle. The method involved is a dialectical one, he explained, which takes account of both accomplishments and shortcomings.[83] The necessity of struggle in the process of political reeducation is emphasized when he described the task of remolding dissident elements: "Our experi-

[80] 1955a. "All comrades who have committed mistakes but have awakened and are willing to make progress not only must be observed, but also must be helped."

[81] 1962a:171. Mao reviewed the 1942 rectification campaign in this passage, and traced the origin of the slogan "unity-criticism-unity" to that campaign. "As long as the attitude is to unify and help," he said elsewhere, "sharp criticism will not split the party; it will only unite the party" (1958m:123).

[82] 1942b:790/III, 58.

[83] 1964o:403. There are a few individuals who are not of a dual, but of a single nature and are, therefore, irredeemable, he argued. His examples are Jiang Jieshi and Hitler (1959c:211).

ence shows that remolding is not easy. One cannot be remolded well if he is not subject to struggle over and over again."[84]

The prescription that follows the shaking up of the patient invariably calls for a healthy dose of criticism and self-criticism. The rules for this procedure, as we have seen, are that personal attack is to be avoided and principled criticism adhered to,[85] that self-criticism be engaged in *pari passu* with criticism itself,[86] and that the process is to take place in a "democratic atmosphere" of mutual help and mutual support.[87] Equally important, as he subsequently pointed out to Red Guards during the Cultural Revolution, is that the process not terminate prior to its dialectical resolution. "Struggle-criticism-quit" was a practice that he found unacceptable, even though prevalent, among Red Guard organizations.[88] What is frequently needed for the successful completion of the process—for the transformation called for by the slogan—is what Mao referred to as a "change in the objective circumstances."[89] Because the setting in which reeducation is first attempted is also the setting in which the contradiction originally arose, successful transformation in many cases requires removal from that setting to put the individual in closer touch with productive labor and with the masses. It is with this idea in mind that reform through labor, May 7 Cadre Schools, and some instances of the system of *xiafang* are conceived as necessary adjuncts to the process of reeducation.

Political education, then, is a twofold project in a mature socialist political system, which aims at both prophylaxis and cure. It seeks to imbue the young with a set of values, skills, and theories that will permit them to perform as legitimate political actors and to avoid the economic, political, and ideological corruption that

---

[84] 1961a:253. He went on to speak of this process as being among the "main tasks" of the dictatorship of the proletariat. Elsewhere he averred that to ignore struggle in favor of unity is anti-Marxist-Leninist (1958l:107).

[85] 1929:88/I, 110. [86] 1967h; 1967m.

[87] 1962a:186. He described this atmosphere as follows: "We must refrain from wanton accusations of others. . . . It is best that a person makes his own accusations. . . . If after a person has blamed himself several times and no one agrees with him, then we can drop it. . . . We do not propose to pull anybody's queue, to accuse anyone, or to brandish a big stick. Our purpose is to ease everybody's mind and encourage free expression of opinion" (cf. ibid., p. 160).

[88] 1968f. [89] 1959v:62.

is a possible outcome of that performance. At the same time, political education is also designed to correct for that corruption —a corruption that Mao came in his later years to see as an almost inevitable concomitant of political and economic activity, even in a socialist system.

In the same way that Mao attempted to redefine the political realm to incorporate almost every phase of life—a redefinition that presupposes rendering public most of those aspects of life which, in our own society, we conceive of as private—so "political" education has been redefined, as we have seen here, to include virtually every aspect of the socialization process. An intentional aspect of deinstitutionalizing education is thus its politicizing. Because the society itself must be politicized, to break down the institutional barrier that separates the education system from the society is to extend this politicization into the schools, as well. While this politicization is deplored by visiting Western academics—an understandable position which, in all likelihood, is shared by some Chinese academics—it is the result of an intentional choice on Mao's part, a choice taken with a reasonably clear view, I think, of the costs involved. The gains to be made through a depoliticized education system are outweighed, in his opinion, by the costs incurred in the alienation of the educated from the society whose development they are expected to serve.

Chapter Eight

ON POLITICAL HISTORY

> China's present new politics and new economy
> have developed out of her old politics and old
> economy, and her present new culture, too, has
> developed out of her old culture; therefore we
> must respect our own history and must not lop
> it off. However, respect for history means
> giving it its proper place as a science, respect-
> ing its dialectical development, and not eulo-
> gizing the past at the expense of the present or
> praising every drop of feudal poison.[1]

Given the subject matter of the bulk of Mao's writings, one
might well take him for an historian rather than for a political
thinker. Not only do his speeches and essays abound with historical examples, but most of his pre-Liberation writing and much of
what he wrote after Liberation is devoted to the chronicling of
the history of the revolution in which he was participating, and
which he subsequently led and helped to shape.[2] Far from merely
recounting the events in which he participated, however, Mao's
historical writing is analytical in nature. It is based upon a philosophy of history, it is written with certain clear-cut purposes in
mind beyond that of merely recording contemporary events, and
it follows certain methodological principles.

Basic to his concept of history is Mao's sense of the transitoriness of particular individuals, institutions, or modes of thought
seen in the context of the vast span of historical development. In
1956, for example, he commented, "of all the things in this world,

---

[1] 1940a:668/ii, 381.

[2] This emphasis led Howard Boorman to compare Mao with such actor-
historians as Thucydides, Julius Caesar, Leon Trotsky, and Winston Church-
ill; "Mao Tse-tung as Historian," in Albert Feuerwerker, ed., *History in
Communist China* (Cambridge: MIT Press, 1968), p. 306. "The recorded
views of such event-making individuals," Boorman argues, "are of intrinsic,
albeit uneven, value because the men had personal knowledge of the events
described—because they were, in short, actors before they were authors."

there are none which are not the products of history. That is point number one. The second point is that everything which is produced by history will also be destroyed by history."[3] It is Mao's failure to allude in contexts such as this to the idea of the "end of pre-history" that tempts one to label his conception of history "Chinese" rather than "Marxist."[4] Nevertheless he did place this idea of historical flow in a dialectical framework that he derived from his study of Marx. "Isn't the historical process the unity of opposites?" he asked rhetorically some years later. Responding to his own question, he continued, "modern history is continually divided from one into two; it is a history of uninterrupted struggle."[5] Moreover, like Marx, who argued that history "shows that circumstances make men just as much as men make circumstances,"[6] Mao, too, saw a dialectical interrelatedness between human action and the constraints of material givens, even though he was occasionally inclined to emphasize the importance of human action.[7]

[3] 1956e:75. This comment is reminiscent of his remark to Edgar Snow in 1965 cited earlier: "Man's condition on earth was changing with ever-increasing rapidity. A thousand years from now all of us, he said, even Marx, Engels, and Lenin, 'would probably appear rather ridiculous'" (1965b:222).

[4] One is reminded of two lines in Mao's 1956 poem, entitled "Swimming": "Standing at a ford, the Master once said:/ 'Thus life flows into the past'" (1956f.).

[5] 1965j:54.

[6] Marx and Engels, *The German Ideology*, in Robert C. Tucker, ed., *The Marx-Engels Reader* (New York: W. W. Norton, 1972), p. 129. Marx amplified this epigram as follows: "History does not end by being resolved into 'self-consciousness' as 'spirit of the spirit,' but . . . in it at each stage there is found a material result: a sum of productive forces, a historically created relation of individuals to nature and to one another, which is handed down to each generation from its predecessor; a mass of productive forces, capital funds and conditions, which, on the one hand, is indeed modified by this new generation, but also, on the other, prescribes for it its condition of life and gives it a definite development, a special character" (ibid., pp. 128f.).

[7] On the one hand, he argued that "conditions must be ripe" before any action is taken (1955e:20), and that in the Chinese revolution "everything arose out of a specific situation: we organized peasant revolt, we did not instigate it" (1965h:360). On the other hand, he averred that it is not technique "but the masses of men that make history" (1960e:19; a much earlier version of the same comment is found at 1938d:437/II, 143: "Weapons are an important factor in war, but not the decisive factor; it is people, not things that are decisive"). The two positions are combined in an unexpected

Another aspect of Mao's philosophy of history appears to contravene Marx's views in an important way. As we have seen in discussing the evolution of Mao's concept of class, he introduced the idea that a socialist or semisocialist society can produce its own class enemies and that, unless effectively opposed, these class enemies can overturn the socialist system and "restore capitalism," thereby reversing the forward course of historical development. Marx, a child of his age as well as a shaper of it, believed firmly in the inevitability of progress, and expressed this belief in his concept of the dialectic, where the resolution of any stage of conflict and change must be qualitatively better than the conflicting elements that gave rise to it. Although there might be setbacks and delays in the revolution that brought about a new stage, the idea of an actual reversal in the process and the possible return from one historical stage to its antecedent stage seems to me to be genuinely foreign to his thought.[8] By divorcing the dialectic from this idea of inevitable progress, Mao created a more flexible tool that he believed more accurately reflected social reality, and expanded (or clarified, depending on one's interpretation of Marx's own views) the role of the human actor in bringing about desirable or progressive ends in social and political change. Mao's view of historical development, then, sees a perpetual, dialectical flow of events in which men and women and the material world within which they act interrelate and transform one another. Historical development is not necessarily a forward-moving process, however, and effective human action is thus required to prevent its reversal through the "restoration" of an earlier socioeconomic stage.

Mao's philosophy of history, then, was firmly rooted in and thus wholly consistent with his concept of contradiction and the

---

way in a comment he made in 1939: "If anyone asks why a Communist should strive to bring into being first a bourgeois-democratic society and then a socialist society, our answer is: we are following the inevitable course of history" (1939a:523/II, 238). A masterly treatment of the false dichotomization of "voluntarism" and "determinism" in the study of Mao's thought is Andrew G. Walder's article, "Marxism, Maoism and Social Change," *Modern China* 3:1 and 2 (1977), 101-118 and 125-160.

[8] A contrasting interpretation of Marx's concept of historical development is found in Joseph W. Esherick's article, "The 'Restoration of Capitalism' in Mao's and Marxist Theory," *Modern China* (forthcoming). Esherick finds historical antecedents in Marx's work for Mao's views concerning the possibility of a retrogressive movement between stages.

theory of knowledge that grew out of that concept. It was with this philosophy of history as a basis that he depicted the events in which he himself took part, and reinterpreted the course of Chinese history prior to the beginning of his career as a revolutionary.

Political history served a number of purposes for Mao. First, and perhaps most fundamentally, he saw political history as a particularly effective vehicle to communicate the lessons of political theory. Because theory must derive from practice, theoretical lessons can thus be accurately conveyed only in their historical context.[9] History is thus the recounting of the interaction of theory and practice in the past, and as such, serves as a source of instructive examples.[10] He referred incessantly to the importance

[9] Mao cited Stalin, writing of himself in the third person, on the mistake of citing a dialectical thinker without reference to historical context: "What significance can Semich's reference to the passage in Stalin's pamphlet, written in the period of the *bourgeois* democratic revolution in Russia, have at the present time, when, as a consequence of the new historical situation, we have entered a new epoch, the epoch of *proletarian* revolution? It can only signify that Semich quotes outside of space and time, without reference to the living historical situation, and thereby violates the most elementary requirements of dialectics, and ignores the fact that what is right for one historical situation may prove to be wrong in another historical situation." The citation is from Stalin's "The National Question Once Again"; the passage is found at 1940a:631/II, 346. Lest his own readers make the same error, Mao consistently reedited his own writings to conform with current theoretical positions. Stuart Schram's textual notes in his *Political Thought of Mao Tse-tung* (New York: Praeger, 1969), and Jerome Ch'en's comments in the introduction to his *Mao Papers: Anthology and Bibliography* (New York: Oxford University Press, 1970), are helpful in ascertaining the nature of these alterations.

[10] Thus, in 1941 he complained about party members' lack of attention to history: "Although a few Party members and sympathizers have undertaken [the study of history], it has not been done in an organized way. Many Party members are still in a fog about Chinese history, whether of the last hundred years or of ancient times. There are many Marxist-Leninist scholars who cannot open their mouths without citing ancient Greece; but as for their own ancestors—sorry, they have been forgotten" (1941b:755/III, 19). Three years earlier he had called on his colleagues to avoid "lopping off our history. We should sum up our history," he continued, "from Confucius to Sun Zhongshan and take over this valuable legacy. This is important for guiding the great movements of today" (1938e:499/II, 209). We will have occasion to return to this passage for a closer investigation later in this chapter. Precisely thirty years later he found it necessary once again to direct a similar comment to his colleagues: "Historical experience merits attention" (1968m).

of learning from past experience: either positive lessons to be emulated or negative lessons to be avoided in current and future praxis. Thus his writing is filled with instructive historical allusions that add to the richness of the preconceptions of the political actor as he or she deals with current problems.

A second function of history in Mao's political writing is to provide a pattern of development by means of which one's own past can be rendered orderly, disparate societies can be compared, and the future course of development can be predicted. Following Marx, he argued that historical development is best conceived of in terms of broad stages characterized by the dominant relationship between the means of production and the relations of production.[11] Once dates have been assigned to these stages in the history of a given society, it is possible to determine which were the progressive and which the conservative or reactionary forces operating at any particular point in that history.

Finally, political history is important in Mao's thought as a means for establishing the uniqueness and importance of China. By far the majority of his historical references are to events in China's past, and they ordinarily serve to recall to mind and to reinterpret individuals and events that contributed to China's rich historical legacy.

The latter two functions are in a sense contradictory, however. He seeks to make history serve to place China in the context of the social, political, and economic development of the world as a whole, while, on the other hand, he attempts to make it serve to set China apart by virtue of the unique achievements of her own past. This contradiction constitutes a problem of historiography that greatly occupied the attention of Chinese intellectuals during the period in which Mao was reaching intellectual maturity. Confronted during the half century following the Opium War with a Western culture that was both dissonant with and threatening to Chinese culture, Chinese intellectuals sought various ways in which to resolve the dissonance and cope with the threat. Some advocated the total rejection of things Western; others, by contrast, advocated the total abandonment of their own

[11] Among Marx's earliest statements of this pattern of history marked by stages of development of the means and relations of production is that found in *The German Ideology*, where he described three such stages: that of tribal ownership, that of "ancient communal and State" ownership, and that of "feudal or estate" ownership. Tucker, ed., *Marx-Engels Reader*, pp. 115-118.

heritage and the wholesale "Westernization" of their society.[12] Most, however, sought some middle road, attempting to create some viable combination of Chinese and Western elements to preserve their heritage, while at the same time speeding the process of the modernization of their society and reducing its impotence in the face of Western threats to Chinese sovereignty.

Following a lead suggested in lectures by Joseph Levenson shortly before his untimely death, we might characterize those solutions as either eclectic, syncretic, or synthetic, depending upon the way in·which the exponents of each solution attempted to combine Western and Chinese elements. Eclectic modernizers gave no thought to the logical and practical inconsistencies between the elements they proposed to paste together. Typical of this solution is the "select the best from East and West" slogan advanced in the latter days of this period.[13] Eclecticism is a solution hardly attended to, much less espoused by, Mao, except perhaps in his earliest writings, where the eclecticism appears to be more the result of his naivete than of a considered choice.[14]

Those for whom consistency was a greater concern sought a syncretic combination of Chinese and Western elements, seeking the requisite logical framework to effect this combination in one tradition or the other. While some Chinese intellectuals looked for and found a connecting logic in Western philosophy,[15] other

[12] Apropos of these solutions, Mao commented in 1956, "we must not be like the Empress Dowager Ci Xi, who blindly rejected all foreign things. Blindly rejecting foreign things is like blindly worshiping them. Both are incorrect and harmful" (1956h:87). Elsewhere he attributed these solutions to the nature of the response to the Western presence: "Ever since Qin Shi Huang, the Chinese people have never respected foreigners, calling them barbarians. By the end of the Qing dynasty, when foreigners attacked and entered China, the Chinese were frightened, became slaves, and felt inferior. Arrogant before, we are now too humble. Let us have the negation of the negation" (1958u:123).

[13] Levenson used this phrase to describe, among others, the ideas of Cai Yuanpei—ideas which, in this context, Levenson saw as syncretic, rather than eclectic; *Confucian China and Its Modern Fate* (Berkeley and Los Angeles: University of California Press, 1966), I, 109-114.

[14] See, for example, 1919a. The denunciation in late 1975 of eclecticism as a solution to problems in the education system, and, by extension, as a *modus operandi* of Deng Xiaoping, is instructive in this connection. See, for example, Ji Peng, "Eclecticism Represents Revisionism," *HQ* 2 (1976), translated in FBIS (PRC) 1:26 (6 February 1976), E6-E9.

[15] Hu Shi, for example, believed that pragmatism served as the connecting link. He found this philosophical school during his study in the United

syncretists sought it in Chinese thought, some of them lighting upon the Neo-Confucian idea that all things possess both a spirit or essence (*ti*), and a function (*yong*). By separating essence from function, members of this group found it possible to argue that while Chinese ideas could continue to serve as the spirit or essence of Chinese culture, Western implements and ideas could simultaneously be borrowed and used exclusively for their functional contribution.[16] Mao initially rejected this solution on the grounds that he regarded Marxism, itself a "foreign" import, as appropriately serving as the spirit or essence in any such combination.[17] Predicated perhaps upon the successful "Sinification" of Marxism, he subsequently suggested that the *ti/yong* formula might be an appropriate one if one were to take the party's "general line" to be the essential, and Western technique to be the functional.[18]

Despite this conditional acceptance of a syncretic combination of Eastern and Western ideas, Mao's commitment to the dialectic led him ultimately to espouse a synthetic rather than a syncretic

States, and devoted his thesis research to locating the same principle in Chinese thought. See his *Outline of the History of Chinese Philosophy* (Shanghai: Commercial Press, 1919). I have discussed at greater length the relationship of Mao's thought to the pragmatism of John Dewey and his Chinese pupils in the paper, "On the Possibility of a Pragmatic Ideology: Epistemological Principles of John Dewey and Mao Tse-tung," paper for the Seminar on the Comparative Study of Communist Societies, University of California, 1975. As I have shown there, Mao was for a variety of reasons consistently hostile to Hu Shi and his approach. See, for example, 1940a: 664/II, 378; 1954d:7; 1955c; 1958s:95; and 1959e:155.

[16] The figure most closely associated with the phrase "Chinese learning for the fundamental principles (*ti*), Western learning for practical application (*yong*)," is Zhang Zhidong, excerpts from whose *Exhortation to Study* (1898) are found in Teng Ssu-yu and John K. Fairbank, eds., *China's Response to the West* (New York: Atheneum, 1963), pp. 166-174. Levenson's discussion of the failure of the *ti/yong* solution is instructive. See *Confucian China* I, 59-78.

[17] "Some people advocate 'Chinese learning as the substance, Western learning for practical application.' Is this idea right or wrong? It is wrong. The word 'learning' in fact refers to fundamental theory. Fundamental theory should be the same in China as in foreign countries. There should be no distinction between Chinese and Western things in fundamental theory" (1956h:85f.; cf. 1958s:96).

[18] 1965j:51. Stuart Schram discusses the evolution of Mao's political thought during the Cultural Revolution in terms of the *ti/yong* formula. "The Cultural Revolution in Historical Perspective," in Schram, ed., *Authority, Participation and Cultural Change in China* (Cambridge: Cambridge University Press, 1975), pp. 1-108.

resolution. In 1940 he described the process as one of "assimilating" Western ideas: "We should not gulp any of this foreign material down uncritically, but must treat it as we do our food —first chewing it, then submitting it to the working of the stomach and intestines with their juices and secretions, and separating it into nutriment to be absorbed and waste matter to be discarded —before it can nourish us."[19] He took up the theme again in 1956, arguing as follows: "We must learn good things from foreign countries and also learn good things from China. We must master both Chinese and foreign things and combine them into an organic whole."[20] That the resolution he had in mind is synthetic and not syncretic in nature is made clear as the passage continues: "When two things combine, their form is changed. It is not possible for them to remain completely unchanged. Chinese things will change. . . . Foreign things also change."[21] Nonetheless, as he argued in the midst of the same passage, "however much they change, Chinese things will always have their own characteristics." The new synthesis must bear the "character of the times" as well as the "national character."[22]

His commitment to achieving a synthesis of the domestic and the foreign is reflected in Mao's discussion of the problems of historiography and his search for the correct historical method. A correct method, he suggested in 1961, in the course of criticizing a Soviet textbook on political economy, requires the "integration of logic and history": "Logic is derived from history. Although the book is crammed full of [historical] materials, if they are not analyzed, there is no logic and you cannot recognize the laws. This is no good. However, it is likewise no good not to have [historical] materials. Then people will read about logic

---

[19] 1940a:667/II, 380. As we have seen earlier, the process of digestion is used elsewhere by Mao to represent the dialectic. See also 1956e:82, where he said, "We must learn analytically and critically. We cannot be so one-sided as to copy all things from foreign countries for mechanical application."

[20] 1956h:88. The context is a speech to music workers on the relationship between Western and Chinese culture.

[21] Ibid. Among the most frequently cited fields in which such a synthesis is possible is that of medicine, where Mao advocated the combination of Chinese and Western techniques to create a novel and unique set of medical practices and *materia medica*. See, for example, 1954a; 1954b; 1954c:13; and 1958ss. Another example that he put forward of this synthetic combination is that of a particular smelting process (1958qq:8).

[22] 1956h:88.

only, but not history."[23] The logic and laws he has in mind here are those of the class struggle. As he pointed out in 1964, "if one does not discuss history from the point of view of class struggle, his perceptions of history will not be very clear. It is only by using class analysis that it can be analyzed clearly."[24] He referred to it in 1966 as the "1958 method of studying history," and noted that it was a method that professional historians in China were not wholly reconciled to. He referred to these reluctant historians as the "emperor-king school" because of their proclivity to focus in their historical studies upon "emperors, kings, generals, and prime ministers." Their reluctance notwithstanding, class analysis was nonetheless the only correct and acceptable method, in Mao's view.[25]

Class analysis is integral, as well, to a second methodological point made by Mao in his discussion of history. A crucial task of the historian—a task that, as we have seen earlier, has important epistemological implications, as well—is the determination of historical epochs. Citing Lenin, Mao described the correct method for determining an epoch as requiring "a concrete analysis of the concrete situation with regard to the overall class contradic-

[23] 1961a:304.

[24] 1964q:392. He made much the same point in 1951 in discussing the film "The Life of Wu Xun," and the implications for Chinese historiography of the film's positive treatment of what Mao took to be a reactionary individual (1951e:364).

[25] 1966d:376. The year 1958 was the point at which this method of class analysis was widely debated in historical circles in China. The opposition among historians to the imposition of class analysis as the sole legitimate historiographic method is touched upon in Albert Feuerwerker and Harold Kahn's article, "The Ideology of Scholarship: China's New Historiography," in Feuerwerker, ed., *History in Communist China*, pp. 2-4, and is discussed in some detail in a pair of articles by Merle Goldman, "Party Policies toward the Intellectuals: The Unique Blooming and Contending of 1961-62," in John W. Lewis, ed., *Party, Leadership and Power in China* (Cambridge: Cambridge University Press, 1970), pp. 268-303, and "The Role of History in Party Struggle, 1962-1964," *China Quarterly* 51 (1972), 500-519. See also Arif Dirlik, "The Problem of Class Viewpoint versus Historicism in Chinese Historiography," *Modern China* 3:4 (1977), 465-488. Mao's only other historiographic comment was an eminently practical one. In a conversation with his nephew, Mao Yuanxin, he touched on the subject of the need for efficiency in all fields of learning in order to accomplish what needed doing in the minimum time. With regard to history, he suggested that the focus should be on the modern period: "There has been over three thousand years of history, and what are we going to do when there has been ten thousand years?" (1966b:29).

tions and class struggle, putting forward strictly scientific definitions, and thus bringing the essence of the epoch thoroughly to light. . . . An epoch . . . presents the question of which class holds the central position . . . and determines [the] main content and main direction of development [of that epoch]."[26] This project of defining periods or epochs in the history of their own society has engaged most of the efforts of Chinese historians since Liberation. It is to the results of that work that we turn our attention next.

History as Pattern

If establishing the grounds for China's uniqueness was one of Mao's objectives as a Marxist historian, then it is important to understand the reasons behind his rejection of Marx's own provision for this uniqueness. Very much an empiricist in his work, as he understood that term (starting, as he put it, from "actual economic fact"[27]), Marx devised a schema of historical development by stages, working both backward and forward from his own time. He studied capitalist society in detail, and the feudal past from which it had emerged. Based on historical research, he then speculated on the stages from which feudalism had developed, and advanced tentative and sketchy hypotheses about the stage that he predicted would follow capitalism. Because he based his work on his interpretation of the historical development of Western Europe, particularly that of England and Germany, he was reluctant to extrapolate from that work the hypothesis that the pattern he had discerned was universally applicable outside of that milieu. Indeed, he suggested that what he knew of India, Russia, and China seemed to indicate a variant form of historical development, a pattern he referred to either as the "Asiatic mode of production," or elsewhere as "Oriental despotism."[28]

---

[26] 1960e:35.

[27] Marx, "Economic and Philosophical Manuscripts," in Tucker, ed., *Marx-Engels Reader*, p. 56.

[28] Among other places, Marx set forward his ideas on "Oriental Despotism" in a pair of articles on British rule in India written for the *New York Daily Tribune* in the summer of 1853. There he spoke of the necessity for irrigation in certain societies as having resulted in the "interference of the centralizing power of Government." "These two circumstances—the Hindu, on the one hand, leaving, like all Oriental peoples, to the Central Government the care of the great public works, the prime condition of his agri-

One finds no reference in Mao's writings to China as an Oriental despotism, or as having experienced a unique "Asiatic" mode of production. The reason for this neglect, I believe, lies in the importance he attached to showing that China is not aberrant, but that its development fits the pattern of development of the advanced nations, on which Marx based his central theoretical principles. As Levenson pointed out, one of the principal reasons for the appeal of Marxism for Chinese intellectuals of the May Fourth period was that it provided a schema which, although of Western origin and professing a scientific basis, could incorporate China in world history in such a way as not to leave her at a permanent disadvantage in the process of development. Marxism could accomplish this because, unlike other Western theories of development that had been presented to the Chinese, Marxism postulated a stage beyond that which the West had then achieved.[29] If China was to be shown as unique, in some sense, it could not merely be by virtue of having run unrivaled on a track of its own, Mao believed. Rather, it must be a uniqueness derived from China's having followed the same course that was followed by the West, but having followed it with greater rapidity or greater success.

To reject the possibility that China had followed a unique and aberrant course is to take up the challenge of fitting the more than three millennia of Chinese history into Marx's self-consciously Europocentric four-stage historical schema. If one focuses on the fact that approximately half of the income of the official class derived from investment in land,[30] and that despite open recruitment and the law of avoidance there was a certain level of con-

---

culture and commerce, dispersed, on the other hand, over the surface of the country, and agglomerated in small centers by the domestic union of agriculture and manufacturing pursuits—the so-called *village system*, which gave to each of these small unions their independent organization and distinct life." The two articles and one other brief excerpt are included as a text entitled "The Consequences of British Rule in India," in Stuart R. Schram and Hélène Carrère d'Encausse, eds. *Marxism and Asia* (Baltimore: Penguin, 1969), pp. 115-119. See also George Lichtheim, "Oriental Despotism," in *The Concept of Ideology and Other Essays* (New York: Vintage, 1967), pp. 62-93, and Karl Wittfogel, *Oriental Despotism* (New Haven: Yale University Press, 1957).

[29] Levenson, *Confucian China*, I, 134ff.

[30] The figure is that of Franz Michael, "State and Society in Nineteenth Century China," *World Politics* 7 (1955), 419-433.

tinuity and geographical stability among "gentry" families, then the characterization of traditional Chinese society as feudal is seen to have a basis in fact. To depict the society from which it emerged as a slave society and to fix the historical point of that transition, however, is a more difficult exercise.[31] Recent archeological finds have suggested to Chinese historians, on the basis of the fact that the Shang dynasty tombs that have been unearthed contain a number of bodies presumably buried simultaneously, the hypothesis that the bodies were those of slaves and, proceeding from that hypothesis, the conclusion that the Shang dynasty was part of the period of slave society.

Mao's comments on this problem in the periodization of Chinese history are contained in the article, "The Chinese Revolution and the Chinese Communist Party," written in 1939, which set down certain guidelines for subsequent historical research. There he implies that the period of slave society ended with the collapse of the Shang, since he refers rather vaguely to the subsequent feudal period as having begun "with the Zhou and Qin dynasties."[32] He characterized the feudal period in China as one in which the principal contradiction was that between the peasantry and the landlord class, and spoke of the "unparalleled" history of peasant uprisings during this period—uprisings which, despite their number and vigor, lacked the leadership requisite to the successful overthrow of the feudal system, and which thus contributed instead only to the periodic change of ruling houses.[33]

The Marxist schema of historical periods thus proved to be a not unmanageably Procrustean bed into which to fit the span of Chinese history prior to the modern period. On the other hand, the more recent years posed problems for Chinese Marxist historians that were at once both more urgent and more difficult to resolve without substantial modification of that schema. The theoretical challenge here was to find an explanation for the possibility of the emergence of a socialist society prior to the full-blown development of capitalism in China. The problem was not

[31] Albert Feuerwerker treats the sources and the debates among Chinese historians on the dating of the beginning of the feudal period in his article "China's History in Marxian Dress," in Feuerwerker, ed., *History in Communist China*, pp. 28-31.

[32] 1939j:586/II, 307. Stuart Schram has pointed out to me that the original text of this article asserts unambiguously that the feudal period dates from the beginning of the Zhou dynasty.

[33] 1939j:588/II, 308.

easily resolved, primarily because of the emphasis Marx placed on the idea that the developmental achievements realized under capitalism were prerequisite to the emergence of socialism. Although unquestionably a detrimental system when compared with socialism, capitalism nonetheless had important positive features, in Marx's view. Both industrialization and urbanization were projects to be accomplished under capitalism, as was the creation of the proletariat as a "universal class" that could then, because of the nature of its exploitation, represent the exploitation of humanity as a whole.[34] In speaking of this latter project, Marx tended to emphasize the unique and necessary formative effects of the industrial workplace in the creation of a proletarian class. Mao, by contrast, emphasized the general fact of exploitation as the necessary and sufficient condition for the creation of a proletariat. He was thus able to transfer "proletarian" characteristics to other segments of the population by redefining the nature of the exploitation involved, and particularly by moving the locus of this exploitation from the town to the countryside.

Mao's resolution of the theoretical problem—his explanation for the possibility of moving directly to the project of socialist transformation after the victory in the Civil War—involved three principal elements: first was his treatment of Chinese society in the century preceding Liberation as having been "semi-feudal and semi-colonial"; second, he treated the events of 1911 as having constituted the opening stages of an abortive bourgeois-democratic revolution; finally, he evolved the concept of the New Democracy as a unique political form for bridging the transition from bourgeois-democratic to proletarian-socialist revolution.

Although the feudal period continued on into the twentieth century, by Mao's reckoning, its character was fundamentally altered by the imperialist penetration into the Chinese economy, society, and polity. He dated this penetration from the Opium War of 1840, and argued that it changed the society into a semi-feudal and semi-colonial one. The imperialist presence in China was two-faceted. On the one hand, it "hastened the disintegration of feudal society and the growth of elements of capitalism, thereby transforming a feudal into a semi-feudal society."[35] Having accorded to imperialism this limited positive role in China's his-

[34] Marx makes this point in *The German Ideology*. Tucker, ed., *Marx-Engels Reader*, p. 162.
[35] 1939j:593/II, 312.

torical development, he went on to show in considerable detail how the other facet of the imperialist presence was detrimental. It succeeded in "imposing . . . ruthless rule on China, reducing an independent country to a semi-colonial and [in the case of Japanese imperialism after 1931, a] colonial country."[36]

The 1911 Revolution marked the beginning, in Mao's view, of China's bourgeois-democratic revolution and the awakening, among the Chinese masses, of a new political consciousness.[37] There are problems in treating the events of 1911 in this way, since, as Mao was well aware, the bourgeoisie was only one among several social classes and groups that participated in the movement; their commitment to democratic reforms was, in many instances, a tenuous and ultimately ineffectual one; and the results of these events were "revolutionary" as much because of the internal collapse of the dynastic system as because of a unified program for replacing that system effectively enforced by a band of committed revolutionary actors. Nevertheless, by 1927 Mao had labeled the 1911 Revolution an unsuccessful bourgeois-democratic revolution, arguing that "the national revolution requires a great change in the countryside"—a change which that movement had failed to bring about.[38]

In his estimation, the May Fourth Movement of 1919 succeeded in altering the character of the bourgeois-democratic revolution in China, in that it created a "powerful camp" of participants in that revolution who had not previously been involved. This powerful camp consisted of "the working class, the student masses and the new national bourgeoisie."[39] Yet this movement, too, proved to be a failure, in that it left China still under the joint domination of feudalism and imperialism.[40]

Mao's view of the failings of the 1911 Revolution helps to account for the ambiguity of his treatment of Sun Zhongshan. On the one hand he spoke of Sun as the founder and leader of the first bourgeois-democratic revolutionary movement in China, and thus as having been responsible for its limited but not negligible

---

[36] Ibid.   [37] 1919a:84.

[38] 1927:16/I, 26. Returning to the question a decade later, Mao assessed the 1911 Revolution as follows: "Was not the Revolution of 1911 a success? Didn't it send the emperor packing? Yet it was a failure in the sense that while it sent the emperor packing, it left China under imperialist and feudal oppression, so that the anti-imperialist and anti-feudal revolutionary task remained unaccomplished" (1939c:528/II, 243).

[39] 1939a:522/II, 237.   [40] 1939c:528/II, 243f.

achievements.[41] On the other hand, in less public circumstances, Mao derided Sun for his political ignorance and his lack of a commitment to democracy.[42] Through all his comments, however, it is clear that Mao regarded himself as Sun's successor, the political leader who succeeded in completing the revolutionary projects that Sun began, but having misconstrued, failed to carry through during his lifetime. Furthermore, Mao suggested, as he did with regard to other figures in Chinese history, that although Sun suffered from inevitable shortcomings, those shortcomings "should be explained in terms of history so that they can be understood."[43]

The failure of the 1911 Revolution accounts as well for the fact that Mao continued to regard the mission of the Chinese Communist party during the late 1920s and early 1930s as being that of completing the unsuccessful bourgeois-democratic revolution that Sun had begun. This belief led him to assume positions that seem bizarre in the light of orthodox Marxism: "China is in urgent need of a bourgeois-democratic revolution, and this revolution can be completed only under the leadership of the proletariat," he wrote in the fall of 1928.[44] He explained this novel stance by underscoring the dual purpose of this revolution: it must accomplish both the defeat of imperialism in China "so as to complete the national revolution," and the prosecution of an agrarian revolution "so as to eliminate the feudal exploitation of

[41] In 1956 Mao commemorated Sun on the occasion of his ninetieth anniversary as a "great revolutionary pioneer" whose "bitter struggle" and "magnificent contributions" should be honored (1956k:19f.).

[42] At a forum on Central Committee work in 1964 Mao spoke of Sun's political theory as having little substance—"full of water and very little oil," as he put it. He continued: "He was so undemocratic and so ignorant that when he was defining communism for the rightists, he would draw a *taiji* diagram first, and then draw a smaller circle inside it, and write the word, 'communism.' On the outside circle he would draw still another circle, which he would call socialism. Finally, he would draw a large circle and write his words 'principle of people's livelihood.' He would say that both socialism and communism are included in 'my Three People's Principles'" (1964w:408). In 1957, at a conference of local-level party committee secretaries, he went so far as to link Sun's name with those of Jiang Jieshi and Kang Youwei, suggesting the publication of the collected works of the three to serve as instructive negative examples (1957b:57).

[43] 1956k:20. "We should not judge our forerunner too harshly," he concluded here. See also 1956m:44 and 1964u:75.

[44] 1928a:48/1, 64. Cf. 1928b:76f./1, 97.

the peasants by the landlord class." These two projects could only
be undertaken with the participation of the working class and its
political party; they could only be achieved under the leadership
of that class and its party. He held to this position until, in 1935,
he concluded that the Japanese invasion of China had brought
about the beginning of a new stage in the revolution—one in
which the contradiction with Japanese imperialism had come to
overshadow the contradiction with imperialism generally, had
altered class relations within China, and had "demoted the domestic contradictions between classes and between political groupings
to a secondary and subordinate place."[45]

In 1935, immediately after the Long March, Mao called for the
formation of a "people's republic."[46] Two years later he spoke of
the republic as an "alliance of all revolutionary classes." "As to
its future," he said, "it may move towards socialism."[47] By 1939
he was referring to this new stage as that of the New Democracy
—a stage that was a bourgeois-democratic revolution of a new
type, the unique character of which was determined by the fact
that it was taking place in the wake of the October Revolution in
Russia. Its novelty lay in the fact that, although led by the proletariat and aiming at the overthrow of imperialism and feudalism,
it sought the active participation of a range of "revolutionary"
classes and groups, and it did not aim at the overthrow of capitalism in China, since capitalism was "capable of contributing to the
anti-imperialist, anti-feudal struggle."[48] The result of this revolution was to be the establishment of a "joint dictatorship of the
revolutionary classes," under which the tasks of the political, economic, and social development of China would be carried out and,
ultimately, the "revolution . . . carried forward to the second
stage, in which a socialist society will be established in China."[49]

[45] 1937c:232/I, 263. Cf. 1935:146/I, 169. In the latter citation—a passage
devoted to the discussion of the "people's republic" that served as the
forerunner of the New Democracy which he described five years later, he
denounced the view that the bourgeois democratic revolution had been
completed as a Trotskyite position. "We are exponents of the theory of
the transition of the revolution, and not of the Trotskyite theory of 'permanent revolution,' " he said two years later. "We are for the attainment of
socialism by going through all the necessary stages of the democratic republic" (1937d:254/I, 290).

[46] 1935:142-147/I, 165-170.   [47] 1937c:243/I, 275.   [48] 1939j:610f./II, 327.

[49] 1940a:632/II, 347. Looking back on the period in 1964, Mao had this
to say about the policy of the New Democracy: "It was impossible for us

Slave society, feudalism, semi-feudalism and semi-colonialism, bourgeois-democratic revolution, and New Democracy are thus the periods into which Mao divided Chinese history prior to Liberation. Nowhere in his recent writings, however, do we find a systematic answer to the question of the periods of epochs into which the post-Liberation period is to be divided. There are, nonetheless, scattered references to periods and transition points that help us to reconstruct the epochs into which he saw these three decades of Chinese history as correctly divided. The end of the period of New Democracy appears to have come in 1953, when Mao set forward the "general line for the transition period." This line called for the gradual socialist industrialization of China, and the socialist transformation of agriculture "over a fairly long period."[50] Nominally, at least, the period of the transition to socialism extended through the completion of the collectivization of agricultural production, though the point at which the period of transition ended and the period to which he refers as that of

---

to set up a bourgeois dictatorship, and we could only establish a New Democracy under proletarian leadership wherein we had a people's democratic dictatorship under the leadership of the proletariat. For some 80 years in China, all democratic revolutions under bourgeois leadership had failed. The democratic revolution which we led was bound to triumph. This was the only road, there was no other." In the same passage, he chided Stalin for his failure to understand this fact about the Chinese revolution (1964q:388). Schram and Carrère d'Encausse make the following observation on the basis of their comparison of the original and the 1951 texts of the 1940 article, "On New Democracy": "[In the original version] he includes among the classes which should participate in the united front not the 'national bourgeoisie,' as in the current version, but simply the bourgeoisie. In other words, he includes the big bourgeoisie as well, and even the 'comprador' bourgeoisie, provided it is 'patriotic.' It is also interesting to note a sentence (which has naturally disappeared from the current edition) regarding the possible hegemony of the bourgeoisie in the revolution" (Schram and Carrère d'Encausse, *Marxism and Asia*, p. 251).

[50] 1953a. Two other references to the beginning of the transition period are contained in documents published for the first time during the Cultural Revolution in conjunction with the campaign against Liu Shaoqi. Both were intended to show Liu's failure to recognize the shift in epochs and his efforts to prolong the period of New Democracy. In 1955 Mao commented on the end of the alliance with the bourgeoisie, suggesting that it had come as a result of the forging of a "worker-peasant alliance" "on the basis of socialism" during the course of the cooperativization movement. "This new worker-peasant alliance has caused the bourgeoisie to be isolated at last and capitalism to die out in China" (1955e:16).

"socialist construction" began is particularly unclear, at least in part because the latter phrase, "socialist construction," is used not only to describe a discrete period but also, more generally, to describe certain tasks of construction that were actually begun during the period of transition.[51] The first unambiguous statement concerning the new period came in 1957, when Mao noted that the "present period" was that of socialist construction.[52]

This system of periodization—New Democracy giving rise to socialist transformation, which in turn gives rise to the period of socialist construction—was interrupted by two trends in the evolution of Mao's historiography during the post-Liberation period. The first involves the treatment of major campaigns as historical periods unto themselves; the second is the use of the concept of a "two-line struggle" to interpret recent history. The Great Leap Forward was taken at its inception to be a campaign that would abbreviate the process of socialist construction. It was thus often treated in Mao's writing at the time as a historical period unto itself.[53] Similarly, the Socialist Education Campaign and the Cultural Revolution were treated by Mao as such major social and political undertakings as to cast their particular stamp on the periods in which they took place.[54] Second, during the course of

[51] In June 1953 he spoke of a "new epoch of construction" as having begun (1953e), but two years later he continued to talk of the preparatory work needed prior to undertaking socialist construction (1955d:10 and 1955e:16, 25). In early 1956 he dated the end of the period of New Democracy as having taken place at Liberation, and blurred the distinction between the period of transition and that of construction (1956b:291f.). Subsequently, during the course of that year, he spoke of the contribution of the "Ten Major Relationships" in achieving "better, faster, more economical results in socialist construction" (1956e:21), of the role of intellectuals in the socialist construction (1956h:89), and the necessity to rally all sectors of the population to accomplish the tasks of socialist construction (1957b: 54).

[52] 1957d:80f.

[53] The fact that the campaign superceded earlier periodizations is suggested in Mao's chiding his colleagues good-naturedly for their eagerness to "enter communism first," suggesting not that it would be impossible, but rather that it would be unseemly for China to enter communism before the Soviet Union (1958yy:145).

[54] In 1963 he described the Socialist Education Movement as the "first great struggle" since the land reform, suggesting at the same time that since it was more than a mere mobilizational campaign, the educational effort might well take decades to complete (1963a:314). Late in the Cultural Revolution he put that movement into perspective by referring to it as a

the Cultural Revolution, a long-standing tendency to speak of modern history in terms of a "two-line struggle" between those advocating taking a "capitalist road" and those holding to a "socialist road" in the development of Chinese society was, as we have seen, strongly emphasized.[55] As a result, political history after 1921 was recast in terms of the various instances of mistaken or nefarious individuals attempting to redirect the development of the party and the nation in a retrogressive direction.[56] Whatever the ambiguities in periodization introduced by the tendency to think in terms of campaigns or conflicts, however, the draft of the revised state constitution, which first circulated in China in 1970, and which was adopted in 1975, clarified the historiographical picture in its opening statement: "The People's Republic of China is a socialist state of the dictatorship of the proletariat."[57]

---

continuation of the struggle against the Guomindang and the bourgeoisie (1968b). Periodizations of the movement itself are found at 1967n:458 and 1967j:4f.

[55] It was at a working conference at Beidaihe in 1962 that Mao posed the conflict within the party leadership over developmental goals and priorities in terms of a struggle between two roads. He said, "socialist society is a fairly long historical stage. During this historical stage, classes, class contradictions, and class struggle continue to exist, the struggle between the road of socialism and the road of capitalism goes on, and the danger of a capitalist restoration remains" (1962c). The following year he cited Stalin on the subject: "There you have two paths, the capitalist path and the socialist path; the path forward—to socialism, and the path backward—to capitalism. . . . The so-called third path is actually the second path, the path leading back to capitalism" (1963h:18).

[56] In 1956 Mao discussed six examples of errors within the party, but did not link this to the idea of a two-line struggle. Included in the list of six were Chen Duxiu, Li Lisan, the first Wang Ming line, Zhang Guotao, the second Wang Ming line, and the Gao-Rao incident (1956d:17f.). In 1959 the list was repeated, this time including only five. Chen Duxiu and Zhang Guotao had been dropped and the "Peng-Huang-Zhang-Zhou" antiparty clique added (1959bb:82). By 1971 the list was expanded to ten—a number that remained fixed until the dismissal of Deng Xiaoping in 1976—and the linkage was explicitly made between each erroneous line and the "capitalist road." The ten struggles were those against Chen Duxiu, Qu Qiubai, Li Lisan, Lo Zhanglun, Wang Ming, Zhang Guotao, Gao Gang and Rao Shushi, Peng Dehuai *et al.*, Liu Shaoqi, and Lin Biao (1971:33f.). Recently the struggle against the Gang of Four has been added to this list to make the number of struggles eleven. See Hua Guofeng, "Political Report to the Eleventh National Congress of the CCP," *RMRB* (23 August 1977), translated in *PR* 20:35 (26 August 1977), 25.

[57] The draft was translated in U.S. Department of Commerce, *Foreign*

Socialist construction was regarded as complete, and China had begun the historical epoch of socialism—an epoch that Mao had come to regard, as we have seen, as a "very long historical period."

Apart from providing an orderly description of Chinese history and a means of drawing comparisons between the practice of the Chinese revolution and that of revolutions in other societies, the subperiods into which the post-Liberation years have been divided are epistemologically and politically crucial to an understanding through analysis of the cleavages in society. Just as is the case in Marx's treatment of the broader historical periods in which relations of production determine the class conflicts that impel history forward, so, in analogous fashion, the projects that dominate the subperiods following Liberation, leading up to and during the socialist state, determined for Mao the dividing lines along which attitudes will be distinguished and social and political divisions in the post-Revolutionary society determined and "correctly handled."

Historical Nutriment, Historical Waste

With justifiable pride, Mao spoke in 1940 of the "splendid old culture" that had been created during China's feudal period. "To study the development of this old culture," he continued, "to reject its feudal dross and assimilate its democratic essence is a necessary condition for developing our new national culture and increasing our national self-confidence."[58] Making use of the "democratic essence" of the past would make the difference, he pointed out in 1942, between "crudeness and refinement, between roughness and polish, between a low and a high level, and between slower and faster work" in the field of art and literature.[59] Moreover, as he pointed out some years later, rejecting the history and culture of feudal China would not meet with the approval of the masses.[60]

Broadcast Information Service (People's Republic of China) (5 November 1970), B1-B5. The version officially adopted by the Fourth National People's Congress, substantially unaltered from the earlier draft, was published in *RMRB* (18 January 1975) and translated in *PR* 18:4 (24 January 1975), 12-25.

[58] 1940a:667f./II, 380. Much the same argument appears at 1945a:984/III, 305, and, twenty years later, in 1965j:53.

[59] 1942c:817/III, 81.   [60] 1956h:85.

On the other hand, it was perfectly possible to go too far: while "one cannot help being fond of antiques, . . . one also cannot be too fond of them," he said in 1958.[61] It was for their tendency to be "too fond of antiques" that Mao chided his colleagues in the realm of art and literature on a number of occasions during the revolutionary years and in the post-Liberation period. Like the historians to whom he referred as members of the "emperor-king school," artists and writers, in his estimation, too frequently depicted the lives of members of the feudal ruling classes in too sympathetic a manner, failing to extract the "democratic essence" from the reactionary dross.[62] Old plots and old characters, he argued, should be replaced by new and realistic ones. Old styles of writing should give way to simple, direct, and accessible language.[63] And the old works of art themselves may be read and appreciated, but they must be apprehended as history, and not for their affective qualities alone.[64]

[61] 1958b:79.

[62] In 1944 he commented that "the old opera (and all the old literature and art which are divorced from the people) presents the people as though they were dirt and the stage is dominated by lords and ladies and their pampered sons and daughters" (1944a:77f.). See also his comments in 1963 expressing disapproval of the continued presence of traditional themes on the stage (1963i:462). The forum on art and literature held in 1966 criticized Stalin for his "uncritical" use of traditional and foreign forms—particularly in the ballet—and praised the new model revolutionary operas, which were said to have inherited the Beijing opera traditions in a critical way and have really "weeded out the old to let the new emerge" (1966a:12, 14).

[63] An interesting version of this argument is found in Mao's letter to the publishers of a collection of his poetry which, by contrast with his prose style, is uniformly written in a classical and thus relatively inaccessible style. He suggested that because of its style his poetry should not serve as a model for the young. On the other hand, he did not stand in the way of its publication (1957c).

[64] In 1964 he commented that he had "read *Hong Lou Meng* [Dream of the Red Chamber] four times but I have not been influenced by it because I regarded it as history" (1964q:391). Cf. his comments on the work in a letter to the Politburo in 1954 (1954d). One of his favorite classical novels, the *Shui Hu Zhuan* (Water Margin Novel) was used at his instigation in 1975 as the source of a series of negative historical lessons regarding the error of capitulationism. His comments on the work are contained in 1975c. Since his death it has been reported that Jiang Qing and her colleagues in the Gang of Four distorted Mao's intentions and attempted to use the campaign for their own purposes. His pungent reaction to Jiang Qing's speech on the subject at a conference to study the Dazhai model, held in September 1975, is said to have been: "Shit. Wide of the mark" (Hua Guofeng, "Political Report," p. 28).

By what method is it possible to "weed through the old," rejecting the worthless and salvaging the worthwhile in this rich feudal
culture that sets the Chinese revolution apart among socialist
revolutions? In his report to the Sixth Plenum of the Sixth Central
Committee in 1938, a seminal document in Mao's efforts to "Sin-
ify" Marxism, he suggested an answer to this question—an answer
which he subsequently abandoned, but which nonetheless suggests
the importance he assigned and continued to assign to the dialectical assimilation of the positive aspects of the past. "The assimilation of this heritage," he wrote, "itself turns out to be a kind
of [method] that is of great help in the guidance of the revolutionary movement."[65] This statement, juxtaposed with his reference earlier in the same paragraph to the need for the use of a
"Marxist method" in evaluating the Chinese heritage, appears to
suggest that, in his view at the time, Marxism and Chinese history
taken together would provide a complementary pair of methods
for the guidance of the revolution. More recent editions of this
report omit the term "method," recasting the sentence entirely to
read, "This [summary of the past and acceptance of its legacy]
is an important help in guiding the great movements of today."[66]
His revised view is thus that Marxism alone, albeit Marxism which
has taken on a "national form," provides all of the necessary
methodological tools for understanding the lessons of the past.

The methodological problem is much the same for the artist or
writer as it is for the historian: since theory can grow only from
practice, and since the experience of one individual, one society,
or one historical epoch offers only a limited range of experience,
it is necessary to turn to history and to the old culture in order to
circumvent this limitation and to amplify one's store of perceptions and preconceptions. Experience teaches through negative as
well as through positive examples. Precisely how the historian or
writer distinguishes positive from negative in historical experience, however, depends on whether he or she takes what the
Chinese refer to as a "historicist" position or a "class viewpoint."
As we have seen, history is to be viewed as the development of
class struggle through time, a development that results, in turn,

[65] 1938f:172. Schram's translation uses the word "methodology" for the
bracketed "method"; however, he has subsequently pointed out to me that
the latter, and not the former, is the correct translation.

[66] 1938e:499/II, 209. The official English translation omits even the word
"help."

from the evolution of the material world conceived of as a set of factors of production, and products of that productive process. Among the various classes that have played a role in this historical development, the proletariat, for Marx, occupied a unique position. As we have seen, it was his view that, by virtue of its characteristics as a class and of the nature of the exploitation it experienced, it became a universalized class, capable of representing the oppression and alienation of mankind as a whole. With the ascendency of the proletariat following the socialist revolution, history as it had unfolded thus far would come to an end, and a wholly novel epoch begin. Given this view of the unique character of the proletariat, the question that then faces the Marxist historian is what positive weight, if any, to assign to other classes in earlier historical epochs.

The "class viewpoint" position on this question holds that because of the progressive nature of historical evolution, what has come before is inevitably inferior to what exists at present, and should be treated as such—as a source, that is, of exclusively negative lessons for current praxis. Mao assumed this viewpoint in cautioning historians who attended too much to antiquity that they ran the risk of advocating the emulation of the backward rather than the progressive, since "things of antiquity are always a little backward."[67] The most important effect of the commitment to the "class viewpoint" position in Chinese historiography is an increased emphasis on writing history from the point of view of the masses rather than from that of the ruling classes. It has unavoidably been the case that, because history has heretofore relied primarily on written records, the deeds and ideas of the literate segment of society have been more fully recorded than the deeds and ideas of the vast majority of the members of society, who were nonliterate. The turn to "mass history" helps to account for the emphasis that has been placed on archeology in the post-Liberation period in China. The material unearthed is used as graphic and tangible supplement to the written historical record, in order to depict the society as a whole rather than merely the historical experience of its elites.

The historicist position, by contrast, sees both positive and negative forces at work in each historical period, and treats pro-

[67] 1958b:79. Elsewhere he said, "I consider that human history advances. One generation is not as good as another—people who went before are not as good as those who follow later" (1958d:93f.).

gressive forces from earlier epochs as the bearers of potentially useful lessons for the present. Mao's own treatment of history has closely approximated the position of the historicist rather than that of the class viewpoint, though it is important to note that his espousal of the former position is by no means a denigration of the importance of class analysis in history. As he made clear, the historicist risks mistaking those qualities or characteristics that are, in their historical setting, positive in nature, for characteristics that are universally or permanently positive. It is this danger against which, as we have seen, Mao cautioned in his call for selectivity in the use of the past on the basis of a class analysis. We have seen an example of his use of the historicist and class viewpoint positions in his treatment of Sun Zhongshan: from a class viewpoint, Sun is seen as a member of the bourgeoisie, who was thus severely limited in his ability to understand socialism and to lead a revolution. From the historicist position, his achievements as a member of the nascent Chinese bourgeoisie within his bourgeois-democratic setting were important, progressive, and worthy of commemoration.

An even more important example of these two methods of historical analysis is found in the evolution of Mao's treatment of Confucius. It is an example that will serve, as well, as an introduction to the more general problem of Mao's treatment of the relationship between traditional Chinese culture and the process of political, social, and economic development—a problem that will occupy our attention in the concluding chapter.

The rationale behind the anti-Confucius campaign of 1974 has yet to be fully explicated,[68] and Mao's position with regard to the criticisms raised in that campaign has yet to be completely clari-

[68] An official explanation was advanced by Hua Guofeng in his "Political Report." There the Gang of Four was accused of distorting the campaign and using it for its own nefarious purposes—among them the launching of an attack on Zhou Enlai. Secondary treatments of the campaign include my own article, "China in 1974: 'Weeding Through the Old to Bring forth the New,'" *Asian Survey* 15:1 (1975), 1-12; Wang Gungwu, "Juxtaposing the Past and Present in China Today," *China Quarterly* 51 (1975), 1-24; Parris Chang, "The Anti-Lin Piao and Confucius Campaign: Its Meaning and Purpose," *Asian Survey* 14:10 (1974), 871-886; Thomas W. Robinson, "China in 1973: Renewed Leftism Threatens the 'New Course,'" *Asian Survey* 14:1 (1974) 2-5; Peter Moody, "The New Anti-Confucius Campaign in China: The First Round," *Asian Survey* 14:4 (1974); and Merle Goldman, "China's Anti-Confucian Campaign, 1973-74," *China Quarterly* 63 (1975), 435-462.

fied. The campaign was conducted without his commenting publicly on the issues it raised. In fact, a careful reading of his
previous comments on Confucius reveals a fairly consistent position, which is essentially at variance with the principal criticisms
of Confucius raised during the campaign. He cited Confucius on
several occasions in listing those of little formal learning who, at
a young age, made a major contribution to their societies.[69] He
spoke frequently and without particular disapproval of the Confucian bent of his own early education,[70] though late in his life he
did use the nature of his education to discredit Lin Biao's attempt
to impute to him a unique genius. His critical comments on
Confucius were generally mild in tone, and were put in the context of the historical limitations within which Confucius necessarily operated, given his class and his historical epoch.[71] Indeed,
as late as 1964 he commented that "Confucius was raised among
the masses and he understood their sufferings. . . . Do not discard
the tradition of Confucius."[72]

In two of his comments on Confucius it is possible to find suggestions of the subsequent campaign, but they are discernible
only, I would suggest, in the retrospective light of the campaign
itself. Both of the comments touched upon the important question
of Confucius' social position. The first of them is found in his
1961 reading notes on the Soviet textbook on political economy,
where he commented that Confucius never achieved the official
position which he sought and that, as a result, he became a
"knowledge manager," leading a kind of parasitic life by teaching
and collecting poetry.[73] Three years later he spoke of Confucius
as having been a figure allied neither to the exploiters nor to the
exploited of his era: "Confucius said that 'the benevolent person
is humane and loves people.' But which people did he love? All
the people? Not on your life! Did he love the exploiters? Not
completely . . . otherwise why was it that he failed to attain high
office? . . . [Moreover] he almost lost his life when the people
of Kuang wanted to kill him."[74]

---

[69] 1958m:48f.; 1958s:93; and 1964c:334.

[70] 1964q:385, 389; 1964r:400; 1971:36; and n.d.:434.

[71] He spoke of the propagandization of Confucianism by the feudal ruling class that "made us feel inferior" (1958s:92), of the fact that Confucius
(like Lenin) had shortcomings (1959r:37f.), and that, despite the exemplary
brevity of Confucius' curriculum, which produced "men of great virtue,"
that curriculum was lacking in practical knowledge (1964c:204f., 210).

[72] Ibid., p. 208.   [73] 1961a:307.   [74] 1964q:385.

When read today, these comments on Confucius' social position can be interpreted as presaging the first step in the campaign to criticize him, which began late in 1973. That first step involved a change in the hitherto correct interpretation of Confucius' class status. Whereas he had previously been regarded as a representative of the then newly emergent feudal class—the class that subsequently took over his precepts as a form of state ideology—the new interpretation treated him as a figure associated with the decadent slave-owning class, and thus as a retrogressive, not a progressive figure in his own time. The question of why his thought then prevailed throughout the protracted feudal period was neither raised nor answered. This new interpretation made it possible to attack him even from a historicist point of view.[75] As the representative of a defunct social class, he advanced arguments concerning the "restoration of rites," "revival of states that were extinct," and the "restoration of families whose line of succession had been broken," which could be reinterpreted and denounced as those of a reactionary attempting to impede the forward development of the society.

In depicting Confucius as a retrogressive, not a progressive figure in his own time, the literature of the campaign suggested that he had no positive lessons to contribute to the present day. He was now regarded as a part of the waste, not the nutriment of China's past. If, indeed, Mao concurred in this reevaluation (and we can only affirm such concurrence by assuming that a major political campaign required his approval before it could proceed), the question arises of what caused him to change his evaluation of this major figure from Chinese history. Historians often operate on the working assumption that pre-Opium War Chinese culture was fundamentally Confucian in nature. One would assume that the post-Liberation effort among Chinese historians to augment "elitist" history with the history of other social strata would reveal important non-Confucian strains in popular culture running as a counterpoint to the Confucianism of the scholar-gentry class. On the contrary, however, the attempt during the recent campaign to discredit and extirpate Confucianism from Chinese culture seems to suggest that Confucian ideas are seen as having penetrated deeply, and indeed as dominating

[75] A two-volume collection of the major articles critical of Confucius was published by Foreign Languages Press in 1974 under the title *Selected Articles Criticizing Lin Piao and Confucius*.

the culture of the precapitalist period in China at both the elite level and the mass level. As we shall see, Mao seems at several points in his writings to have agreed with this point of view.[76]

One particularly interesting feature of the anti-Confucius campaign was the widespread distribution of fully translated (from *wenyen* to *putonghua*—from the literary to the colloquial language) and annotated editions of excerpts from Confucius' writings. One effect of this publication program was doubtless to broaden substantially the familiarity of the Chinese population as a whole with Confucian ideas. A plausible explanation for what at first might appear to be a counterproductive effort is that old ideas—the superstructure of the old society—cannot be overcome dialectically without an actual struggle with the new ideas. Although the Confucian culture may have lost much of its viability as a contemporary mode of thought, nonetheless certain elements of that culture, divorced from the canon within which they had originated, still carried weight in the current culture. It was not enough that these ideas simply pass out of circulation, for their negative residue would be likely to linger on after them. Rather, they needed to be revived in order to be actively struggled against, and thus transformed and superseded dialectically.

That elements of the cultural past, when correctly assimilated, have a necessary role to play in the revolutionary present and future is an idea that is very much a part of Mao's views of cultural transformation as an aspect of political development. It is to this broader question of the pattern of political development that we now turn, not only as a means of explicating that aspect of Mao's political thought, but also—political development being, in a certain sense, a dominant theme in Mao's thought—as a means of summing up what has been said about that political thought in the preceding chapters.

[76] See, for example, 1940a:655/II, 369, where he said, "China also has a semi-feudal culture which reflects her semi-feudal politics and economy, and whose exponents include all those who advocate the worship of Confucius, the study of the Confucian canon, the old ethical code and the old ideas in opposition to the new culture and the new ideas." Cf. 1958s:92.

Chapter Nine

ON POLITICAL DEVELOPMENT

> The development of socialist society is a proc-
> ess of uninterrupted revolution.[1]

Mao's political thought is fundamentally developmental in character. Basic to that thought, as we have seen, is the idea of positive or progressive change over time, which results from conflict and struggle correctly handled and resolved. Thus we shall find that to discuss Mao's concept of political development—including in that concept both the goals toward which change is directed and the process by means of which the goals are achieved—is, in a sense, to summarize his political ideas.

Among the goals toward the realization of which the political development of China must be directed, in Mao's view, are a set of short-range objectives and a number of longer-range goals. In the shorter term, Mao's concept of the goals of development encompassed certain rather specific changes in the character of Chinese society and politics, a number of which were achieved during his lifetime. In this narrow sense, Mao's developmental goals did not differ all that significantly from those espoused by several generations of Chinese modernizers, reformers, and revolutionaries over the course of the last century. Like their successful Japanese contemporaries, who put forward the slogan *"fukoku kyōhei"*—a rich country and a strong military—those Chinese in the nineteenth century who, in the face of the threat of Western imperialism were concerned for the future of their country, saw as a desirable goal the creation of a strong and wealthy China, capable of expelling the foreign presence, of fending off future threats from the outside world, and of compelling the respect of and equal treatment by other nations.

Mao was a member of that generation of Chinese who, somewhat paradoxically, were initially attracted to Japan as a model of successful adaptation to the challenge of the West, only to

[1] 1964n:9.

275

find themselves galvanized into revolutionary action by a reactive nationalism when the miracle of Japanese modernization resulted in a new imperialist threat even more direct than that China had experienced at the hands of Japan's Western mentors. Like other members of that generation, Mao believed in the need for China to acquire sufficient wealth and power to assert her independence from foreign intervention—to "stand up," as he phrased it on numerous occasions, most notably on that of his proclamation of the founding of the People's Republic of China in October 1949: "Our nation will no longer be an insulted nation; we have stood up."[2]

Following the May Fourth movement of 1919, a new aspect of the goal of increased national power rose to the fore, namely, the unification of what had become a country devoid of an effective central government. The goal of national wealth, too, had taken on a new meaning for Mao by the early decades of the twentieth century. Rather than regarding the acquisition of national wealth exclusively as a means to fend off foreign intrusions, he had come to see economic development as necessary to alleviate the poverty and malnutrition of substantial numbers of the Chinese population, a situation that was the result of decades of rebellion, war, disunification, mismanagement, and corruption. Mao's view of the use of national wealth to correct the economic situation in which China found itself was, of course, based upon the socialist principles he had come to espouse: national wealth must not only be increased; more importantly, it must be equitably distributed. Thus transformed, *fukoku kyōhei*—the achievement of national unity and independence, and the alleviation of poverty—were the principal short-term developmental goals toward which Mao saw the political and economic development of China as necessarily directed at the time of Liberation.

Mao's longer-range goals of the political and economic development of China he viewed as a series of contradictions, some of which he regarded as resolvable during the socialist period, others of which he believed to be much more permanent, and thus susceptible only to "correct handling" during the socialist stage. A by no means exhaustive list of these more permanent contradictions would include the contradiction between tradition and modernity, that between a technical rationale and a political rationale, and that between town and country—between urban

[2] 1949e.

and rural, industrial and agricultural development. Mao's treatment of these contradictions forms the heart of his theory of political and economic development, and will occupy our attention in the sections which follow.

Mao conceived of the process of realizing these developmental goals as one of revolution. In arriving at the use of the terms development and revolution as synonymous—in coming, that is, to see development as necessarily involving a process of "uninterrupted" or "continuing" revolution, he substantially modified, and in some sense attenuated, the definition of revolution which, with a self-conscious antitraditionalism, he put forward in 1927: "A revolution is not a dinner party, or writing an essay, or painting a picture, or doing embroidery; it cannot be so refined, so leisurely and gentle, so temperate, kind, courteous, restrained and magnanimous. A revolution is an insurrection, an act of violence by which one class overthrows another."[3] Mao subsequently learned that one class is not successfully overthrown merely by a single act of violence, but that the influence of the overthrown class remains strong long after that act of violence is successfully terminated. Moreover, he came to believe that the revolutionaries themselves may, in the process of managing the postinsurrection political system, become so corrupted as to assume a role analogous to that of the overthrown class enemy. As a result, as his career drew to a close, he came to view revolution as a sustained effort to destabilize and deinstitutionalize the political system created in the wake of the seizure of state power. This view of development as deinstitutionalization and the creation of political instability contrasts sharply with—indeed, is the antithesis of—the definitions of development commonly employed by Western, and particularly American, political scientists.[4] Mao's view of development has been rejected with considerable fervor by the political leaders of the Soviet Union, which, for a time in the early post-Liberation years, had served Mao as a developmental model. We will return to a discussion of this view of the developmental process in the concluding section of this chapter, following an exploration of the long-term contradictions, toward whose correct handling and ultimate resolution this process is directed.

[3] 1927:17/I, 28.

[4] I have in mind particularly the work of Samuel Huntington, who defines political development in terms of institutionalization; *Political Order in Changing Societies* (New Haven: Yale University Press, 1968).

TRADITION AND MODERNITY

Although the phrase is ordinarily associated with its appearance in an article Mao wrote for the inaugural issue of the theoretical journal, *Hongqi*, in 1958, he actually began to speak of the Chinese people as "poor and blank" as early as 1956.[5] The later, more familiar, passage reads as follows: "Apart from their other characteristics, China's six hundred million people are, first of all, poor, and secondly, 'blank.' That may seem like a bad thing, but actually it is a good thing. Poor people want change, want to do things, want revolution. A clean sheet of paper has no blotches and so the newest and most beautiful words can be written on it, the newest and most beautiful pictures can be painted on it."[6] This view of the Chinese population as a *tabula rasa*, available for and open to transformation and mobilization, is one that followed naturally from the optimism engendered in Mao's mind by the relative lack of resistance encountered in the process of the socialist transformation of agriculture.[7] It is a point of view that can also be seen to follow from a rather too mechanically materialist reading of Marx's conception of the relationship between the "economic base" and the "superstructure" in a social system, a reading wherein the superstructure of culture and political forms is seen as transformed automatically, in a sense, when the economic relationships in the society are altered by a revolution.[8]

[5] The first reference occurs in a speech on intellectuals that Mao delivered to a Central Committee conference in January 1956 (1956a:99). He used virtually identical language to make the same point at a Supreme State Conference two years later (1958d:11).

[6] 1958q.

[7] An optimism that is perhaps best exemplified, as we have seen, in his editorial comments in the volume, *The Socialist Upsurge in China's Countryside* (1955g).

[8] Such a reading is based on texts such as the passage in *The German Ideology*, for example, where Marx says, "The ideas of the ruling class are in every epoch the ruling ideas: i.e., the class which is the ruling material force of society is at the same time its ruling *intellectual* force. The class which has the means of material production at its disposal, has control at the same time over the means of mental production"; Robert C. Tucker, ed., *The Marx-Engels Reader* (New York: W. W. Norton, 1972), p. 136. Later in the same work he spoke of the state as "nothing more than the form of organization which the bourgeoisie *necessarily* adopt, both for internal and for external purposes." "Whenever," he continues, "through the development of industry and commerce, new forms of intercourse have been evolved . . . the law has always *been compelled* to admit them among the modes of acquiring property" (ibid., pp. 150, 152. Emphasis added).

If this was, in fact, Mao's initial understanding of Marx's concept as it applied to the Chinese case, it was reflected in an interesting way in the introductory chapter to Franz Schurmann's important book, *Ideology and Organization in Communist China.* There Schurmann argued that "at certain times in a country's history things change so radically that the old patterns no longer reappear to reconstitute unity."[9] Applying this principle to the Chinese revolution, he said: "In traditional China, the trinity of ethos, status group and modal personality was represented by Confucianism, the gentry and the *pater familias.* . . . By 1949, the revolution had destroyed all three."[10] Following this line of argument, he suggested that "social systems take time to build up; once destroyed, long periods of time must elapse before one can say that a new social system has arisen." In the interim, during the course of building the new social system, "organization must . . . do for society what earlier had been done by the social system." As for the defunct ethos of the prerevolutionary society, he argued, "ideology has been substituted."[11] Thus Schurmann, like Mao, depicted the Chinese revolution as having created a kind of blank sheet on which the revolutionaries might write the "most beautiful words" of their own ideology. Neither Mao nor Schurmann persisted in this position, however.

In writing a supplement to his book in 1968, Schurmann commented that, were he to retitle the work, he would choose to call it, "Ideology, Organization and Society in China." The change was occasioned by what he referred to as the "resurgence of the forces of Chinese society," which he had come to realize had not, after all, been destroyed by the revolution.[12] Similarly, prior to

[9] Franz Schurmann, *Ideology and Organization in Communist China* (second edition, enlarged) (Berkeley and Los Angeles: University of California Press, 1968), p. 2.

[10] Ibid., p. 7.

[11] Ibid., pp. 7f. An antecedent of Schurmann's argument is found in a passage from Mao's 1940 article, "On New Democracy." There he spoke of "communism" as being "at once a complete system of proletarian ideology and a new social system." The feudal ideology and social system have "only a place in the museum of history," and the capitalist ideological and social system "resemble a dying person who is sinking fast" (1940a:646f./II, 344). The important difference between Mao's and Schurmann's formulation is that by describing this new ideology and social system as "communist" rather than "socialist," Mao implies that its realization presupposes a period of transition.

[12] Schurmann, *Ideology and Organization,* p. 504.

the Cultural Revolution, Mao ceased to use the phrase "poor and blank," and even in using it in the early 1960s he returned to an earlier formulation whereby it was China as a country, rather than China as a population, that was regarded as being "blank," and blankness was thus taken to mean "devoid of technological and economic development."[13]

The evolution of Mao's concept of the cultural superstructure suggested by the alteration and subsequent abandonment of this phrase, is an interesting and important aspect of his view of the handling and resolution of the contradiction between tradition and modernity in the process of political development. In 1940 he described the relationship between base and superstructure as follows: "Any given culture (as an ideological form) is a reflection of the politics and economics of a given society, and the former in turn has a tremendous influence and effect upon the latter; economics is the base and politics the concentrated expression of economics."[14] By the mid-1950s he had modified in an important way this rather orthodox reproduction of Marx's and Lenin's position on the subject. In 1956, speaking on the question of the role of intellectuals in the political system, he said, "When the superstructure is not in conformity with the economic base and cannot promote economic development, it loses its designed function. . . . The superstructure . . . must function to promote the development of the productive forces."[15] He reiterated this point of view two years later in the "Sixty Work Methods": "The superstructure certainly must conform to the economic base and the need for the development of productivity."[16]

In 1961 he devoted considerable attention to the problem of the superstructure in the process of commenting on a Soviet textbook on political economy. In his commentary he criticized Stalin for having devoted insufficient attention to the superstructure, contending that adequate analysis presupposes giving full attention to both base and superstructure.[17] The relationship he depicted there is a simple one, indeed a return to an earlier formulation, since no mention is made of the need for development: "The superstructure adapts itself to production relationships, and production rela-

[13] "Have we not," he asked in 1964, "on the basis of a poor and blank nation, attained an impressive level in such areas as socialist revolution and socialist construction after fifteen years of endeavor?" (1964u:94f; cf. 1965g:101).

[14] 1940a:642/II, 340.   [15] 1956a:96.   [16] 1958e:7.
[17] 1961a:260.

tionships adapt themselves to productive forces."[18] If the population is no longer treated here as "blank," at least it is assumed to be educable: where economic conditions have been changed, he said, "the world outlook of the peasants will change little by little until the process is complete."[19]

The Socialist Education Campaign, which began two years after these notes were written, was an effort to speed the process of this change of outlook. The obstacles encountered during the course of that movement seem to have led Mao to the point of view that, without radical action, the superstructure was likely to remain out of phase with the economic base over a long period. Moreover, because the superstructure can affect the base just as the base affects the superstructure, there was even the possibility that the unregenerated superstructure might bring about the degeneration of the transformed economic base. Thus, by the opening stages of the Cultural Revolution, Mao was calling for mass revolutionary action to refute the old and wrong, affirm the new and correct, and thus actively to "transform the superstructure to conform to the economic base and to strengthen the socialist system thereby."[20]

Mao's concept of a "cultural revolution" did not originate in the mid-1960s. Writing on the New Democratic revolution in 1940, he spoke of the need for a revolution on the cultural front to parallel that on the political front: "Reactionary culture serves the imperialists and the feudal class and must be swept away. Unless it is swept away, no new culture of any kind can be built up. There is no construction without destruction, no flowing without damming and no motion without rest; the two are locked in a life-and-death struggle."[21] One of the points he made in the passage from which this citation is drawn was that the cultural efforts of the Communist party in the new united front were a continuation of and complement to those of the cultural revolution of the May Fourth period. The May Fourth movement, he argued, was an instance of a bourgeois culture in conflict with a feudal culture. In the wake of that movement, the bourgeois culture could no longer maintain a leading position in the cultural revolution. This

[18] Ibid., p. 280.   [19] Ibid., p. 253.   [20] 1966m:118.

[21] 1940a:655/II, 369. His treatment of the concept of a cultural revolution is not unlike Lenin's. See, for example, Lenin's article, "Better Fewer, But Better" (4 March 1923), translated in Moshe Lewin, *Lenin's Last Struggle* (New York: Pantheon, 1968), pp. 156-174.

was true because bourgeois culture in China owed its existence to the imperialist presence, and the political necessity of the time had become that of attacking imperialism as well as feudalism. At that point—a point marked by the assumption of a revolutionary role by the Chinese Communist party—the cultural revolution was transformed, becoming one of a socialist culture in conflict with bourgeois and feudal culture: "Prior to the May Fourth Movement, China's new cultural movement, her cultural revolution, was led by the bourgeoisie, which still had a leading role to play. After the May Fourth Movement, its culture and ideology became even more backward than its politics and were incapable of playing any leading role."[22]

"Culture" (*wenhua*) is used in these passages in the rather narrow sense of a formally learned body of knowledge. A culture in this narrow sense, he argued, both "reflects" and "serves" the economic order of the society of which it is a part.[23] A similar use of the term is found in his comment in the summer after Liberation concerning the efforts to transform the prerevolutionary culture: "The work of reforming education in long-established schools and of reforming the old social culture should be carried out methodically and carefully. . . . On this question, procrastination and reluctance to carry out reforms is incorrect; but rashness or attempts to carry through reforms precipitately is also incorrect."[24] In this narrow sense it was, in fact, possible to think of the majority of the Chinese population in the mid-1950s as being blank—that is, devoid of a formally acquired culture, be it feudal, bourgeois, or socialist. Very shortly thereafter, however, it seems to have become evident to Mao that while much of the Chinese population may have lacked a formally acquired knowledge of the principles of Confucianism or of an imported set of bourgeois-liberal principles, nonetheless they could not be considered to be blank. Indeed, to understand what filled them and constituted an obstacle to their mobilization and transformation required broadening the definition of culture to incorporate more than formal principles formally acquired.

By 1961 Mao gives evidence of having begun to conceive of the cultural superstructure as covering a broad range of ideas and habits, and of coming to believe that its transformation was therefore a very long-range and extensive project. The transition period must involve the transformation of "all social relations,"

[22] 1940a:659/II, 372.   [23] 1940a:656/II, 370.   [24] 1950b:109.

he argued, including in that term "the relations of production and the superstructure, and the relations of the different sectors, such as economy, politics, ideology, and culture."[25] Five years later he had come to the point of arguing that the transformation of the culture required a revolution of its own—a cultural revolution—but here "culture" was taken to include "the old ideas . . . customs and habits of the exploiting classes," as well as formal culture in the old, narrower sense of that term. Against this structure of ideas, customs, and habits, he argued, the proletariat must, by revolutionary means, put forward the "new ideas, customs, culture, and habits" of their own class.[26] In this broader sense of the term culture, then, the Chinese population was by no means blank: each member possessed to some degree or another "old ideas, culture, customs, and habits" which were not by any means automatically transformed as a result of the revolutionary seizure of power or of the socialist transformation of the economy. It was on the basis of this broader definition of culture, then, that the Great Proletarian Cultural Revolution was conceived and launched.

This broader range of ideas that Mao ultimately came to regard as being resistant to rapid transformation he had alluded to as early as 1927, when he found Hunanese peasants to be bound by superstitions that could be traced back to their origins in the "great traditions" of Chinese culture, but which had, through centuries of assimilation into the popular culture, become only distantly associated with these formal systems of thought. "The gods? Worship them by all means," he told the peasants then. "But if you had only Lord Kuan and the Goddess of Mercy and no peasant association, could you have overthrown the local tyrants and evil gentry?" "My words," he concluded, "made the peasants roar with laughter"—a particularly effective means for dispelling superstition.[27] The solution to the problem of these old ideas, superstitions, customs, and practices, as he saw it in 1940, was to wipe them out: "Only by destroying the old and the rotten can we build the new and the sound."[28]

[25] 1961a:248.   [26] 1966m:117f.

[27] 1927:33/I, 46f. Elsewhere in the same report he spoke of the targets of the movement as being "patriarchal ideas and institutions" and "bad practices and customs in the countryside" (1927:14/I, 25).

[28] 1940d:690/II, 408. "Our method," he said in 1961, "is to lift the lid, break down superstition, and let the initiative and creativity of the laboring people explode" (1958s:95).

The same solution was reflected in his remarks fifteen years later, but a new sense of the magnitude of the task was injected: "Before a brand-new social system can be built on the site of the old, the site must first be swept clean. Old ideas reflecting the old system invariably remain in people's minds for a long time. They do not easily give way."[29] Political education was required: communists must "patiently educate the great mass of the peasants— who are still burdened with many of the habits and ideas of the old society—and explain things to them in vivid terms which they can easily understand."[30] In conjunction with his remarks reasserting the salience of class struggle in a socialist society in 1962, he observed that, whereas the socialist transformation of the ownership of the means of production in the countryside had been largely effective, it had not brought about the expected destruction of old ideas and habits. "The effects of ideological consciousness are long lasting," he reflected.[31] Speaking to André Malraux on the eve of the Cultural Revolution, he cited Lenin on the subject: "Lenin wrote, 'The dictatorship of the proletariat is an unrelenting struggle against all the forces and traditions of the old society.' Unrelenting," he repeated, emphasizing the word.[32]

This sense of the need for an unrelenting struggle, taken in the context of his revival of the concept of class conflict, and his formulation of a new theory of continuing the revolution under the dictatorship of the proletariat, suggests that whereas Mao once saw the destruction of the prerevolutionary culture (in the broader sense in which he used that term) as being a simple act of

[29] 1955g:302.

[30] Ibid., p. 253. Elsewhere in the same document he suggested that these old ideas are held with differing degrees of persistence by the various sectors of the peasantry: "At a given time, a section of the society is very stubborn and refuses to abandon its old ways. At another time, these same people may change their attitude and approve the new" (ibid., p. 128). In 1961 he identified this sector of the population as the middle and rich peasantry, whose "private viewpoints have greater depth" and are thus more difficult to alter (1961a:256).

[31] 1962d:23.

[32] 1965h:372. Nine years earlier he had cited another part of the same passage from Lenin: "Certain rotten, poisonous ideological survivals of the old society may still remain in people's minds for a very long time. 'The force of habit of millions and tens of millions is a most terrible force'" (1956d:9). The reference here, however, was to the cult of the individual, which Mao identified as being "one such force of habit of millions and tens of millions."

"sweeping clean the site," he subsequently came to view the struggle between tradition and modernity in a socialist society as intimately related to the class struggle, protracted in duration, and dialectical in nature. The idea that the conflict between tradition and modernity is dialectical in turn suggests that the old culture is to be transformed and superseded, rather than merely destroyed or swept away. In the same way that he regarded the old culture in the narrow, formal sense as having its "feudal dross and democratic essence," so he came to regard the prerevolutionary culture in the broader sense as in need of "assimilation," to preserve those elements that could be taken to be its "nutriments."

If revolutionary ideology, in Schurmann's terms, constitutes a new ethos, then Mao's concept of this aspect of the process of transition during the socialist stage seems to have been one of a dialectical interaction between this new ethos and the ethos inherited from the old society. The new culture, the eventual product of this period of transition—being the dialectical supercession of both of its constituent elements—will be neither an unadulterated revolutionary ideology nor an unaltered traditional ethos, even though it will contain elements of them both.[33] Mao's references in the late 1960s to the necessity for "many cultural revolutions"[34] were thus, among other things, an acknowledgment that the conflict between tradition and modernity in a socialist society is a very long-term contradiction that it may be possible to handle correctly, but not necessarily to resolve finally during the short run of political development in the socialist stage.

TECHNIQUE AND POLITICS

In 1960 Mao observed that "Marxist-Leninists have always maintained that in world history it is not technique but man, the masses of people, that determine the fate of mankind."[35] Comments such as this, taken out of context, together with the virtually total omission of mention of technology in Mao's pre-Liberation writings, have contributed to this image of Mao as a sort of twentieth-century Luddite, determined to replace technique with a primitive

---

[33] I have made this argument in the context of a discussion of its implications for contemporary Chinese politics in the book, *Ideology and Culture: An Introduction to the Dialectic of Contemporary Chinese Politics* (New York: Harper and Row, 1973), especially pp. 10ff.

[34] 1967e.   [35] 1950e:19.

but pure political faith. This image is not only biographically incorrect, but also, and more importantly for our present purposes, it misrepresents his concept of political and economic development.

Mao was frank about his own ignorance of technical matters. "I don't understand industry," he commented in 1958. "I know nothing about it, and yet I do not believe that [such knowledge] is unattainable. It seems to be incomprehensible at the beginning, but becomes comprehensible after a few years of study."[36] Given the circumstances of the guerrilla bases in which Mao spent the first quarter century of his revolutionary career, it should come as no particular surprise that he devoted virtually no attention to problems of the technological development of China in his writings of that period, and remained "able to ride in an airplane, but unable to fly one," as he described himself in 1958.[37] By the late 1950s he manifested considerable concern over the problem of altering this situation. As he explained in 1959, "prior to August of last year I devoted my main energies to revolution. Being basically not versed in construction, I knew nothing about industrial planning."[38] Ignorance of technology, however, by no means meant rejection of it. Indeed, he insisted on the necessity of mastering it: "We cannot transform what we do not know about," he commented in 1961.[39] Committed as he was to the transformation of his society, the implication was clear that becoming technically knowledgeable was the obvious next step.

Virtually from the outset Mao regarded the relationship between technical knowledge and political correctness as dialectical. Unlike the Chinese peasants whose old ideas and habits first inspired in him a feeling for the necessity of "sweeping the site clean," he regarded those with technical ability as possessing something of value to the process of development. The contradiction as it presented itself at the time of Liberation was a clear-cut one: those who possessed technical knowledge were almost invariably unfamiliar with the principles of Marxism-Leninism, whereas party cadres who were well versed in political principles were almost invariably technically ignorant.

Writing of this contradiction between "redness" and expertise in 1958, Mao made his dialectical treatment of the contradiction clear: "The ancients said, 'The virtuous and the able: it is impos-

[36] 1958s:96.

[37] 1958v:110.

[38] 1959r:38.

[39] 1961b:240.

sible to combine the two into one.' I feel that the two can be combined into one."[40] On two other occasions during the same year he referred to redness and expertise as a unity of opposites, and called for a "technical revolution" as the means to resolve this contradiction and thereby to further national development.[41] "The call for a technical revolution," he explained, "aims at making everybody learn technique. . . . In the past we were capable of fighting and carrying out the agrarian reform. Now it is not enough to possess these capabilities alone. We must learn new skills, understand our functions in the real sense, and know science and technology. Otherwise, it is not possible for us to exercise good leadership."[42]

A part of the resolution of the contradiction lay, then, in training politically reliable cadres in the necessary technical fields. This more recent position is mirrored in Mao's pre-Liberation call for cadres to "master all the skills involved in leading the masses in production."[43] Because the production of which he spoke at that point was agricultural production, not industrial or technical production, the skills involved were of a very different sort, but the thrust of the argument was the same: without a knowledge of the productive processes cadres were incapable of acting as effective leaders.[44] In 1956 he spoke of the need for

[40] 1958vv:126.

[41] 1958e:5f. In May of that year he likened his view of the necessity for a synthesis of politics and technology to that embodied in Lenin's call for "soviets plus electrification" as constituting the road to communism (1958v:115). His call for a technical revolution is found, as well, in his speech on agricultural cooperativization in 1955, where he said, "we are now carrying out a revolution not only in the social system, the change from private to public ownership, but also in technology, the change from handicraft to large-scale modern machine production, and the two revolutions are interconnected" (1955d:19). Speaking on the question of intellectuals in January of the following year, he alluded to China's dependence on foreign technology: "Although we have a large amount of land and a large population, how many automobiles, tanks, and airplanes have been manufactured by us? . . . Some comrades say imprudently, 'As revolutionaries, we can do without them.' They are wrong. Now we are undertaking technological revolution and cultural revolution with the purpose of revolutionizing ignorance. We cannot do without them and rely on us boorish fellows alone" (1956a:98).

[42] 1958e:5.　　　　　　　　　　[43] 1943d:866/III, 133.

[44] The role of the effective "red" leader, he pointed out in 1958, is that of "handling the relationships between people—of promoting the mass line" (1958v:111).

400,000 new technical cadres, arguing that much of their training could be completed on the job.[45] Two years later, he asked the party secretary of the chemical department of a rubber factory whether he was an "outsider or an expert." Upon learning that the secretary was an outsider, Mao replied, "it is time that the outsider should become an expert."[46]

As we have seen earlier, the other side of the resolution of the contradiction involved both the political education of those who already possessed expertise, and the reform of the education system so as to produce graduates who combined political knowledge and experience with their technical abilities. There was, meanwhile, a problem of communication that needed to be resolved: experts must learn to present information to political leaders in an easily assimilable form—a "gentle rain"—in order to avoid "washouts."[47] "In order to speak a common language," he said, referring to the same problem on another occasion, "there must first be essential information and knowledge."[48]

In proposing the possibility of the long-term resolution of the contradiction between technical and political expertise, Mao took implicit issue with a position such as that advanced by Jacques Ellul.[49] Mao would have agreed with Ellul's argument that technical decisions—decisions based, ultimately, that is, on grounds of efficiency alone—have a tendency to take on a life of their own, limiting the possibility of further political choice once the initial decision in favor of a technical rationale has been made. On the other hand, he did not share Ellul's pessimism concerning the possibility of correcting for this tendency—of putting "politics in command," to use a much-quoted phrase of his from the period of the Great Leap Forward.[50]

---

[45] 1956e:24; cf. 1956b:293, where, during the same year, he called for an emphasis upon training cadres in technological and scientific skills.

[46] 1958nn:4.   [47] 1958c:81.   [48] 1958e:10.

[49] Ellul's argument is found in his book, *The Technological Society*, translated by John Wilkinson (New York: Alfred A. Knopf, 1967).

[50] In his "Sixty Work Methods," written in 1958, Mao spoke of "ideology and politics" as the "supreme commander and the soul." "Those who pay no attention to ideology and politics and are busy with their work all day long will become economists and technicians who have gone astray and are dangerous. Ideological work and political work guarantee the accomplishment of economic work and technical work and they serve the economic foundation. . . . As long as we are a bit slack with ideological and political work, economic and technical work will surely go astray" (1958e:6).

Based on this concept of the relationship between technique and politics, he disagreed explicitly with those who argued (as, in 1960, he accused Tito of arguing) that technological developments had rendered obsolete certain aspects of Marx's and Lenin's views on the development of socialist society. In the hands of socialist economies, technological developments can only redound to the benefit of the people, Mao argued. Moreover, in the hands of capitalists, technological development "means pushing to a new stage the contradiction between the development of the social productive forces and the capitalist relations of production." It must, therefore, bring about the "further rousing of the revolution of the people in those countries" and the consequent speeding of the demise of capitalism and imperialism.[51] Finally, he disagreed with the idea that, because of its late start, China must accept a permanent handicap in competition with the Soviet Union and the West. "We cannot follow the old path of technological development of other nations in the world by crawling behind them step by step," he said in 1964. "We must break the conventional rules and adopt so much as possible the most advanced technology, so that within a not too long historical period it will be possible to build China as a modern socialist great power."[52]

Technological development and political mobilization must thus go hand in hand in the process of development: merely adding farm machinery in the countryside, for example, is insufficient unless an effort is made simultaneously at "raising the consciousness of the peasants and remoulding the ideology of people."[53] While the ultimate resolution of the contradiction between redness and expertise was seen by Mao as being far off, the short-term handling of the contradiction was, he believed, feasible, as is usefully summarized in this brief excerpt from the Anshan Iron and Steel Company constitution, which he wrote in 1960, and to

[51] 1960e:16ff.

[52] 1964u:94f. It is comments such as this and the foregoing that led Stuart Schram to conclude that the policies of Hua Guofeng and his associates during the period following Mao's death were "close to the center of gravity of Mao's own thinking over the last twenty years of his life"; "Mao's Thoughts: The Revised Version," *Far Eastern Economic Review* (7 October 1977), p. 58. Although I have difficulty with the idea of a "center of gravity" in the thought of a dialectician, I would agree that there is ample justification in Mao's treatment of technological and economic development for many of his successors' policies in those areas.

[53] 1961a:262.

which we have alluded earlier: "Keep politics firmly in command; strengthen party leadership; launch vigorous mass movements; institute the system of cadre participation in productive labor and worker participation in management, of reform of irrational and outdated rules and regulations, and of close cooperation among workers, cadres, and technicians; and go full steam ahead with the technical innovations and technical revolution."[54]

TOWN AND COUNTRYSIDE

"The greatest division of material and mental labor is the separation of town and country," Marx wrote in *The German Ideology*. "The antagonism between town and country begins with the transition from barbarism to civilization, from tribe to State, from locality to nation and runs through the whole history of civilization to the present day."[55] The resolution of this historically crucial contradiction in society is a third long-range goal in Mao's theory of political and economic development. The process of handling and resolving this contradiction, in his view, involves the parallel development of both town and countryside combined with the attempt to break down the differences between the two. In formulating a plan to accomplish this, Mao initially followed, then subsequently rejected, the prior experience of the Soviet Union, deeming it unsuitable for Chinese circumstances. More recently, he came to treat the Soviet developmental experience as fundamentally flawed, and thus as illegitimate even as applied in the Soviet Union itself. He came to see its usefulness to China as that of a negative lesson rather than a model to be emulated.

Writing in 1961, Mao formulated a model from the order in which tasks had been taken up in the Chinese revolution: "First and foremost, create public opinion and seize power. Then resolve the question of ownership. Later develop productive forces to a large extent. This, in general, is the rule."[56] After the seizure of power, in the case of urban and rural development alike, the pattern of ownership was transformed first, then economic development begun.

[54] 1960d.

[55] Marx and Engels, *The German Ideology*, in Tucker, ed., *Marx-Engels Reader*, p. 140. The comment was echoed by Lenin in 1919; Robert C. Tucker, ed., *The Lenin Anthology* (New York: W. W. Norton, 1975), pp. 478f.

[56] 1961a:269. Cf. ibid., p. 259. Much the same order appears in 1956m:44.

The change in ownership in the urban sector followed a policy, as Mao described it in retrospect in 1963, of "utilizing, restricting, transforming, and eliminating" the private capitalist sector in the economy.[57] A distinction had been drawn, as he noted in 1961, between what he called "bureaucrat capital" and "national capital." The former was confiscated outright; the latter, because it was held by those allied with the Communist party in the period of the New Democracy, was subjected to the policy of utilization, restriction, and transformation.[58] Following the change in ownership, industrial development was carried out under economic plans formulated by what he described in retrospect as a "groping process."[59] Although beneficiaries, as he acknowledged, of more than two decades of administrative experience behind them when they came to power,[60] the communists found that their experience was largely irrelevant to the problems they faced after entering China's urban areas, and their reliance on the experience of their Soviet mentors was thus heavy during this initial period of "leaning to one side."

Despite the "groping" involved, certain principles of industrial development that continue to be associated with a "Maoist model" nonetheless grew out of the experience of the 1950s. Among the most important of these was an emphasis on diversification over specialization in enterprises,[61] and on decentralization over cen-

---

[57] 1963h:15. He regarded the following of this policy, as opposed to one of "laissez-faire and fostering and encouraging" private capital, as "an important criterion for determining whether a country is developing towards socialism or towards capitalism." Yugoslavia was his negative example in this instance.

[58] By his estimation, bureaucrat capital "constituted some 80 percent of the fixed assets of industry and transportation in the country." It was a dual struggle against the comprador bourgeoisie, on the one hand, and against the "big bourgeoisie" on the other. The first aspect of the struggle constituted a part of the national revolution, and had been begun under the Guomindang. The second aspect was a part of the socialist revolution and was begun afresh after Liberation (1961a:252).

[59] 1959a:194.   [60] 1955f:29.

[61] Visiting the Wuhan Iron and Steel Works in 1958 to observe the commissioning of a new blast furnace, he asked his guides how much copper the works produced. He then "suggested that the company should also go in for a little chemical industry, a little machine-building industry, a little building materials industry, a little of everything so that it can be turned gradually into an integrated complex." He observed that, "apart from industry, big enterprises should take up agriculture, trade, education and culture and a militia" (1958ii).

tralization of management decisions. The policy of decentralization was to be pursued, both in order to take advantage of natural
economic affinities within China's geographical regions,[62] and because of the strategic benefit to the defense of China that would
result from having the nation's industrial capacity widely dispersed throughout the country, rather than concentrated in a
few areas and thus easily crippled by an enemy attack.[63] A third
important principle in Mao's concept of the process of industrial
development that derived from this period was that of reliance
on moral rather than material incentives to increase the productivity of the work force.[64]

A similar pattern—one of attention first to the system of ownership, then to the development of production—was followed in
the transformation of Chinese agriculture in the immediate post-
Liberation years. Many of the elements of this development policy
had been laid out during the early years of the revolution. In
his article, "Our Economic Policy," written in 1934, Mao was
already speaking of the possibility of increasing agricultural production, of the necessity of attending to problems of insufficient
farm animals, fertilizer, seeds, and irrigation and of the need to
augment rural labor power by making it possible for women to
join in agricultural production. All of these measures presupposed,
however, the initial upsurge of peasant enthusiasm attendant upon
settling what he referred to as the "ownership problem."[65]

In part because of the unexpected rapidity of the movement
through the preliminary stages of collectivization, Mao's class line

[62] During a visit to an import and export commodities exhibition in
Tianjin (on the same inspection tour referred to in the previous note), he
commented, "Localities should build up independent industrial systems.
First, coordinization zones, and then provinces in which the situation
permits, should establish their own different and relatively independent
industrial systems" (ibid.).

[63] Decentralization of command was a principle learned during the revolutionary war years, he observed in 1966, and should be applied to industrialization in the post-Liberation period, as well. "This country of ours is
made up of 28 'countries.' There are large 'countries' as well as small
'countries.' . . . Each province must fight its own battle" (1966d:378).

[64] Writing in 1960, he spoke of the pre-Liberation years as having been
a period when "in work everyone was industrious and in warfare all were
courageous. There was absolutely no reliance on material incentives, but
rather a reliance on the drumbeat of revolutionary experience." To rely on
material incentives was to invite the creation of a bourgeois spirit among
the workers, he argued (1960a:233. Cf. 1961:281).

[65] 1934a:117/1, 142f.

in agricultural development changed radically during the course of the first post-Liberation decade. In the summer of 1950 he called for a new policy toward the rich peasant: "a change from the policy of requisitioning the surplus land of the rich peasants to one of preserving a rich peasant economy in order to further the early restoration of production in the rural areas."[66] Five years later he reversed himself and called for the elimination of the rich peasant economy in the countryside "so that all the rural people will become increasingly well off together," and so that the situation could thereby be avoided under which "the polarization in the countryside will be aggravated day by day."[67] Looking back on this period in 1963, he noted that the policy of relying on the poor peasant for revolution and the relatively better off peasants for production had been a mistaken one. "Reliance on the poor and lower-middle peasants should be the long-range class line of the party," he concluded.[68]

Cooperativization was seen by Mao not only as a necessary step in regulating the ownership system in the countryside, but also as a prerequisite to the modernization of agricultural production through the introduction of mechanization.[69] It was necessary, he argued, to move rapidly from mutual assistance teams to lower-level cooperatives, and from lower-level to higher-level cooperatives, both in order to take advantage of the peasants' enthusiasm which had been generated by the land reform, and in order to avoid their becoming entrenched in the small producer relationships engendered by the first stages of the process of socialist transformation. Rapid movement toward higher-level cooperatives was also seen as desirable because of the need to rationalize the irregular land-owning patterns that were maintained (albeit in new hands) after the land reform, and that inhibited the introduction of mechanized farm equipment.

Although Mao is often regarded as responsible for the "gigantism" typical of the initial stages of the formation of communes, a close reading of his comments at the time suggests that this is

---

[66] 1950b:108.　　　[67] 1955d:26f.　　　[68] 1963d:62.

[69] Refuting the idea advanced in the Soviet textbook on political economy that mechanization of agriculture must precede cooperativization, he reiterated his earlier point that "we must first alter the relations of production before we can possibly develop social productive forces on a grand scale. This is a universal law" (1961a:289). During the Cultural Revolution, Liu Shaoqi was accused of having embarked upon the capitalist road in agricultural policy by advocating that cooperativization await mechanization.

an erroneous interpretation of his position. In December 1958—
prior to the time when the communization movement was regarded by many of his colleagues as having been mistaken in conception or execution or both—Mao commented that the advent
of the people's communes as a stage beyond the higher-level cooperatives had not been planned in advance. "The appearance of
the people's commune was not foreseen at the Chengdu conference in April and in the Party Congress in May. Actually it had
already appeared in Henan in April, but remained undiscovered
through May, June, and July. It was not discovered until August."[70] At the Lushan Conference the following summer, where
his colleagues took him to task for the excesses of the communization movement, he accepted responsibility for having "shot the
cannon" that began the movement, agreed that the cannon had
not been "shot carefully" enough, and that the movement had
proceeded too rapidly in some areas. At the same time he explained the circumstances under which the cannon had been fired:
"I did not claim the right of inventing the people's communes,
but I had the right to suggest. In Shandong, a reporter asked me:
'Is the commune good?' I said, 'good,' and he immediately published it in the newspaper."[71] "Hereafter," he concluded, sounding
rather more like a harassed American politician than the chairman
of the Chinese Communist party, "newspaper reporters should
leave me alone."[72] Despite these somewhat excessively modest disclaimers, however, he remained convinced of certain positive
features of the communes.

Among the advantages he saw in this organizational form over
the cooperative that it replaced was, in fact, its greater size, which
made possible "undertakings on a large scale and by many people."[73] More important than this advantage, as he saw it, however,
were a number of other features. First, the commune would serve
as a basic-level governmental organ, thereby linking state and
society in a smaller unity than had been possible before. In this
connection, gigantic communes were not an advantage, since they
often exceeded the size of the townships whose governmental
functions they were to take over. Second, like the multipurpose
industrial complex, the commune would make possible the integration of a diverse range of productive activity not possible in
the smaller-scale cooperatives. Third, the commune would form

[70] 1958yy:140.
[72] Ibid.
[71] 1959r:41.
[73] 1958yy:140.

the basis for the expansion of the civilian militia in the countryside, thereby contributing to national defense. Finally, and perhaps most important, he regarded the commune as constituting a
new form for the transition from socialist ownership by the collective to ownership by the whole people, and thus to communism.[74]

There is, moreover, no convincing evidence that Mao was
unalterably opposed to the subsequent transfer in 1959-1960 of
certain accounting and planning functions initially carried out by
the commune administration to the production brigades and production teams. Although he subsequently criticized those who had
proposed a return to the individual household as the basic-level
accounting and planning unit in the countryside, his only comment on the decentralization that took place during the period of
retreat following the Great Leap Forward was that the local units
themselves, whether brigade or production team, must be satisfied
with the decision ultimately taken.[75]

The separate development of the industrial and agricultural
realms, however, did not in itself contribute to the ultimate resolution of the contradiction between the two, and it is in the effort
to come to grips with this contradiction that Mao found himself
diverging from his Soviet mentors and seeking for new solutions
of his own. The policy of "leaning to one side" had been enunciated prior to Liberation,[76] and was substantiated with the conclusion of the Sino-Soviet pact during Mao's visit to Moscow in
the winter of 1949-1950.[77] His publicly expressed views during
this early period are well summarized in an excerpt from his speech
to the Fourth Session of the Chinese People's Political Consultative Conference in 1953: "We must learn from the Soviet Union.
We are going to carry on our great national construction. The
work facing us is hard and we do not have enough experience.
So we must seriously study the advanced experience of the Soviet
Union."[78]

From his speeches and writings one can date Mao's shift away
from this point of view fairly precisely. In July 1955 he reiterated
the necessity of learning from Soviet experience, referring par-

[74] 1958uu:132. Cf. 1958tt.   [75] 1959f:160f.; 1959h:166f.

[76] 1949d:1362f./IV, 415, 417.

[77] Mao's comment on the niggardliness of Soviet aid to China in conjunction with this pact is found at 1964d.

[78] 1953b:101f.

ticularly to the relevance of that experience to the process of cooperativization in China.[79] By December of that year, however, he suggested that "we should not always compare ourselves with the Soviet Union [since it is apparent that] we will be faster than the Soviet Union."[80] The following April he issued the document entitled "Ten Major Relationships,"[81] which he described two years later as having set out an indigenous alternative to the Soviet model of development.[82]

If he subsequently came to regard this document as having been a kind of declaration of independence from the Soviet model of economic and political development, it was nonetheless a cautiously worded one. One of the fundamental planks of the Soviet model, a plank the Chinese had adopted during their first five-year plan, was the emphasis on developing heavy industry first, using accumulation from the agricultural sector to finance the requisite capital investment. In the discussion of the first of the "ten major relationships"—that between agriculture and industry —the emphasis on heavy industry remains. At the same time, however, the relationship between agriculture and industry as a whole is cautiously but fundamentally altered: "Our conclusion is as follows: one way of developing heavy industry is to develop light industry and agriculture somewhat less. There is another way, which consists in developing light industry and agriculture somewhat more. . . . The second method, i.e., developing heavy industry on a foundation of satisfying the needs of the people's livelihood, will provide a more solid foundation for the development of heavy industry, and the result will be to develop it more and better."[83] As the year went on, Mao continued to develop the idea that China needed an economic and political development plan of its own that would correspond more directly to the particular characteristics of the Chinese situation. The Chinese and Russian revolutions were alike in fundamental principles, he ar-

[79] 1955d:19f.   [80] 1955f:29.

[81] 1956e. The relationships he discussed there were those between industry and agriculture, coastal and inland industry, economy and national defense, the state and production units, central and local control, Han and minority nationalities, party and nonparty, revolutionaries and counterrevolutionaries, right and wrong, and China and other countries.

[82] 1958j:101.

[83] 1956e:64f. Whereas here he accused "some socialist countries" of taking the first road, two years later he made it clear that it was the Soviet Union he had in mind in leveling this charge (1958uu:129).

gued in August; their differences lay in "form and style."[84] There was a danger, he suggested four months later, in "mechanical borrowing" from the Soviet Union.[85]

The most complete statement of Mao's views on the divergence between the patterns of Chinese and Soviet economic and political development is found in his 1961 reading notes on the Soviet text on political economy. There he summarized the Chinese use of the Soviet model during the early post-Liberation years as having been necessary at the time, even though "we always had a feeling of dissatisfaction with it." In these notes he dated from the winter of 1955-1956 China's decision to pursue its own policies, and attributed this decision to the realization that the Soviet Union had started in 1917 with a more fully developed industrial infrastructure, and, even taking account of war-induced setbacks, had developed that industrial infrastructure at a pace that the Chinese regarded as unacceptably slow, and on a basis of agricultural capital that the Chinese regarded as unacceptably exploitative of the peasantry.[86]

As the Sino-Soviet dispute deepened in the mid-1960s, Mao became more and more outspoken on the subject of the inappropriateness of the experience of the Soviet Union, and on the errors of the Soviet leadership of and advice to the Chinese revolutionaries during the course of their own revolutionary struggle. Stalin's methods, he said, had they been followed by the Chinese revolutionaries, would have led to failure.[87] Stalin "knew nothing at all about peasants."[88] Indeed, Stalin was finally persuaded to

---

[84] 1956h:84. Cf. 1958j:103, where he described the two nations as following a similar basic line but differing with regard to "details."

[85] 1956m:40. The internal economic situation—the progress in cooperativization and the results of three years' experience with the Soviet-inspired first five-year plan—contributed importantly to a reassessment of the relevancy of Soviet experience for China's development. See Victor D. Lippitt, "The Great Leap Forward Reconsidered," *Modern China* 1:1 (1975), 92-115. It is important to note, however, that there were political reasons, as well, for this reassessment. The Twentieth Party Congress of the CPSU, at which Stalin was denounced by Khrushchev, took place in February, two months before the publication of the "Ten Major Relationships." Mao's response to the Soviet Party Congress, contained in the two editorials "On the Historical Experience of the Dictatorship of the Proletariat," should thus be read in conjunction with the documents dealing primarily with the Chinese economy (see 1956d and 1956n).

[86] 1961a:310.   [87] 1958j:102.

[88] 1965h:358.

take the outcome of the Chinese revolution seriously only as the result of China's participation in the Korean War, having regarded it up to that point as another Yugoslavian revolution, and Mao as another Tito.[89] Not only did the deepening of the split between the Soviet Union and China cause Mao to be more outspoken on Stalin's errors, it also resulted in his treating the economic and political development of the Soviet Union as a model of a different sort. Because, following Stalin's death, it had fallen under the control of revisionists and, consequently, had experienced a restoration of capitalism,[90] Soviet experience was now worthy of study not as a positive developmental model, but rather as a negative example.[91]

With the gradual abandonment of the Soviet model in the late 1950s, Mao came more and more to emphasize the agricultural sphere in framing the concept of an alternative developmental scheme for China. By 1958, at the height of that uniquely Chinese movement, the Great Leap Forward, he suggested that this shift of emphasis had been so great that "in time" it would be necessary to redirect the focus of leadership from agriculture back to industry once again.[92] In the wake of the economic setbacks of 1959-1961, however, developmental priority remained with the agricultural sector, now by necessity rather than by choice.[93]

While a policy for the assignment of priorities between agriculture and industry may constitute a means of handling the contradiction between town and countryside, it does not necessarily contribute toward the resolution of that contradiction. Mao's constant concern in attempting to resolve it was that the relationship between town and countryside, between urban and rural workers, might, if not correctly handled, become exploitative, and the contradiction deteriorate into an antagonistic one. Both because of the reliance upon agricultural capital to finance industrial devel-

[89] 1962e:89.

[90] In 1966 Mao said that capitalism "has been or is being" restored in the Soviet Union (1966p:437f.). By 1970 the doubt was removed, and the restoration was spoken of as having already taken place (1970a:7).

[91] 1962a:181.   [92] 1958ll.

[93] 1959o:183. The order of priorities listed here—agriculture, light industry, heavy industry—is one which, except for brief periods, has remained in effect since 1959. They were reiterated by Zhou Enlai in his speech to the Fourth National People's Congress early in 1975, *RMRB* (18 January 1975), translated in *PR* 18:4 (24 January 1975), 23, and have been reaffirmed by Mao's successors.

opment and because of the continuing coexistence of the two systems of ownership—collective ownership in the countryside, state ownership in the industrial sector—he saw the danger of the peasantry coming to perceive itself as exploited, and the worker-peasant alliance upon which, over the short run, development of the national economy was based, collapsing into a class conflict.[94]

What the resolution of this conflict calls for, as Mao saw it, is a dialectical supersession such that the fundamental differences that divide town from countryside will ultimately be overcome. There are, in his view, virtues to be found in both elements of the contradiction. While the urban sector is progressive, the rural sector has both the strength of numbers and the strength of natural virtue which, as we have seen, he consistently regarded as resident in the peasantry. The ultimate resolution of the contradiction must thus rest in the creation of new economic entities, which are neither exclusively industrial nor exclusively agricultural, and in the consequent possibility of replacing village and city with new residential-work units that retain the positive characteristics of both the rural and the urban environments. Although the realization of this resolution is clearly distant, the initial steps already taken point in that direction. As we have seen, both the future of industrialization and the continuing strength of the commune, in Mao's view, lies in the possibility of diversification. Diversified industry that adds agricultural production as an adjunct is seen as a step toward surmounting the urban-rural contradiction. Similarly, the ability of the commune to engage in industrial production of a modest sort is seen as another such step.[95] Reducing

[94] In 1950 he argued that the alliance between workers and peasants must be maintained by peasants contributing to the process of industrialization and workers aiding the peasantry in completing land reform (1950c:93). By 1955 he argued for the need for an equal pace in the socialization of agriculture and industry in order to prevent the possibility that the peasantry, perceiving itself as obliged to contribute an unequal share to the developmental process, might break its ties in the worker-peasant alliance and cast its lot with the bourgeoisie, reestablishing, in the process, a capitalist system in the countryside (1955e:14f.). In 1961 he noted the dangers of a dual system of ownership, stating that it "cannot endure over a long period in a socialist system" (1961a:261).

[95] Mao noted, in 1961, that the "backyard furnaces," widely taken to be an exemplary folly of the Great Leap Forward, had, in fact, produced useless pig iron. Over the longer run, however, he saw them as a positive first step in introducing industrial production into the rural setting, using the commune as the organizational vehicle for this introduction (1961a:285).

the gap in living standards between town and countryside by increasing the educational and economic opportunities available in the rural areas is yet another step in the same direction, he argued.[96] Finally, the systematic use of *xiaxiang* to bring urban-educated youth into the countryside for short-term or permanent residence was also treated as contributing toward the final resolution of this contradiction.

What is significant in Mao's treatment of each of the contradictions discussed here—that between tradition and modernity, between technique and politics, and between town and countryside—is that the long-term developmental goals he posited do not involve the eventual suppression of the one side of the contradiction by the other side. He did make it clear that he saw one side of each of these contradictions as more progressive than the other, but he regarded the less progressive side in each case as having its positive points, as well. Consequently, what his developmental scheme does call for is the eventual creation of a new synthesis that is neither exclusively traditional nor exclusively modern, but contains elements of both; that is neither exclusively technical nor exclusively political, but contains elements of both; that is neither exclusively urban nor exclusively rural, but contains elements of both. The means by which these syntheses are to be achieved—the process of economic and political development—is one of active encouragement of struggle and conflict, active deinstitutionalization: a process that Mao came to refer to as that of "continuing the revolution under the dictatorship of the proletariat."

CONTINUING THE REVOLUTION

Mao's theory of continuing the revolution under the dictatorship of the proletariat was never set out as a series of integrated arguments in essay form. Rather, it was first alluded to in the closing stages of the Cultural Revolution, at which time a compendium of quotations from his earlier writings was published which, taken collectively, was said to comprise this theory.[97] These quotations,

[96] Ibid., p. 313.

[97] The collection was published under the title, "Chairman Mao on Continuing the Revolution under the Dictatorship of the Proletariat," *PR* 12:39 (26 September 1969), 3-10. The theory was summarized in the article, "Advance along the Road Opened up by the October Socialist Revolution," *HQ*, *RMRB*, and *JFJB* (6 November 1967), translated in *PR* 10:46 (10 November 1967), 9-16.

many of which have been cited in the preceding pages, underscored the persistence of classes and class conflict in a socialist society, spoke of the resultant protraction of the socialist stage, and characterized it as a period of mounting, rather than diminishing, struggle. They referred to the Cultural Revolution as a necessary part of this mounting struggle, and asserted the necessity for a series of such movements in the future.

This theory of continuing the revolution under the dictatorship of the proletariat constitutes Mao's statement of his view of the process of political development in socialist society, by means of which its long-term contradictions are to be resolved, and the emergence of new antagonistic class contradictions in the society is to be controlled. The theory constituted a new, but not unprecedented, development in the evolution of Mao's political thought and, coming at the end of his career as a political actor and thinker, serves as a kind of political testament, reasonably clear in its intent, but extremely difficult to carry out.

The precedents for his theory of continuing the revolution under the dictatorship of the proletariat are found in Mao's earlier treatment of the Chinese revolution as a "protracted" one, and subsequently in his discussion during the period of the Great Leap Forward of the necessity for a revised, non-Trotskyist theory of "permanent" or "uninterrupted" revolution as a guide in the period of the transition to socialism.

Immediately following the Long March, Mao spoke of the fact that, in his view, the Chinese revolution was likely to be protracted. "The uneven political and economic development of China," he said, "gives rise to the uneven development of her revolution. . . . The transformation of this unevenness into a general evenness will require a very long time."[98] Three years later he devoted a series of lectures to the subject of the "protracted war," pointing out there that the war of resistance against Japan must necessarily be protracted, since a quick victory was impossible.[99] In his directive, "On Policy," in 1940, he asserted that correct policy must be based on two lessons learned during the period of the Jiangxi Soviet—namely, that success in the

---

[98] 1935:138f./I, 162f. The passage concludes: "We must be prepared to devote to the already protracted revolutionary war led by the Chinese Communist Party the longer time necessary to dispose of the domestic and foreign counter-revolutionary forces finally and thoroughly. The kind of impatience that was formerly displayed will never do" (ibid.).

[99] 1938d.

Chinese revolution depended upon acknowledgment of its bourgeois-democratic character, and upon the recognition of its protracted duration.[100] Although this view of the Chinese revolution
and the war of resistance against Japan as being protracted contributed the idea of long-enduring struggle to what later became
his theory of continuing the revolution, the idea that the revolution must continue even after national liberation—an idea that
Mao subsequently accused Khrushchev of having failed ever to
grasp[101]—apparently became clear in his own mind only during
the post-Liberation period itself.

In advocating a theory of permanent or uninterrupted revolution, Mao took particular pains to dissociate his version of this
theory from that of Trotsky. Indeed, writing in 1937, as we have
seen, he pointed out that he and his colleagues were "exponents
of the theory of the transition of the revolution, and not of the
Trotskyite theory of 'permanent revolution.' We are for the attainment of socialism by going through all the necessary stages
of the democratic republic."[102] In fact, he did disagree with Trotsky's assessment that the bourgeois-democratic revolution had
essentially been completed in China at the time.[103] On the other
hand, Mao returned once again to the term permanent or uninterrupted (*buduan*) revolution at the time of the Great Leap Forward,[104] and despite his protestations to the contrary, his use of
the term resembled rather closely at least one aspect of that of
Trotsky. Trotsky had described his theory of permanent revolution as having three facets.[105] The first aspect treated the necessity
for moving directly from one stage of the revolution to the next
—from bourgeois-democratic to socialist revolution—without
permitting the society to stabilize itself as a bourgeois democracy.
The third facet of his theory treated the necessary relationship
between specific national revolutions and the international revolu-

[100] 1940f:720/II, 441.

[101] 1965h:373. Khrushchev's problem, Mao said, was his tendency to con-
fuse the idea of a revolution with that of a struggle for national liberation.

[102] 1937d:254/I, 290.

[103] An assessment found in Trotsky's *Problems of the Chinese Revolution*
(New York: Doubleday, Doran and Co., 1937).

[104] Stuart Schram investigated the documents of this period in his *La
Révolution permanente en Chine* (Paris: Mouton, 1963). He returned to
the question in his article, "Mao Tse-tung and the Theory of the Permanent
Revolution, 1958-1969," *China Quarterly* 46 (1971), 221-244.

[105] Leon Trotsky, *The Permanent Revolution* (New York: Pioneer Publishers, 1965), pp. 7-9.

tion. It is the second aspect of Trotsky's theory of permanent revolution, however, that closely approaches what Mao had in mind in advancing his own theory in the late 1950s. Trotsky described this second aspect as that of keeping a society in permanent upheaval—not permitting it, as he put it, to achieve a new state of equilibrium—until all of the revolutionary tasks had been completed.

In spite of his disclaimers to the contrary, Mao's statement of his views in 1958 bears a striking resemblance to this second aspect of Trotsky's concept: "I stand for the theory of permanent revolution. Do not mistake this for Trotsky's theory of permanent revolution. In making revolution one must strike while the iron is hot—one revolution must follow another, the revolution must continually advance."[106] As we have discussed earlier, the "revolutions" that he listed to illustrate his point were the land reform, the formation of mutual aid teams, the move first to lower-level cooperatives, then into higher-level cooperatives, the rectification campaign, and the technical revolution. He returned to the idea of permanent revolution some weeks later in the "Sixty Work Methods," suggesting there that even the accomplishment of this series of movements did not mark the end of the uninterrupted revolution; "for a fairly long period to come, the method of airing of views and rectification must be used continuously each year to solve problems."[107] While certain of Mao's colleagues stressed the idea that this new theory of permanent revolution might provide a rationale for the movement during the Great Leap Forward from the socialist stage directly into the stage of communism, there is no evidence to suggest that Mao himself ever took this idea seriously.[108] Although the concept of uninterrupted revolution disappeared from Mao's writings for some years after the setbacks following the Great Leap Forward, the idea of intentional destabilization of the society as a means for realizing revolutionary goals more rapidly and effectively constitutes the link

[106] 1958d:94. A useful discussion of the relationship between Mao's and Trotsky's theories, which emphasizes the differences between them, is found in James Peck, "Revolution vs. Modernization and Revisionism," in Victor Nee and James Peck, eds., *China's Uninterrupted Revolution* (New York: Pantheon, 1976).

[107] 1958e:5. Cf. 1958m:117.

[108] In fact, in December 1958, as we have noted earlier, he commented that it would not be right for China to enter the stage of communism before the Soviet Union (1958yy:145).

that connects his comments on permanent revolution in the late 1950s and his theory of continuing the revolution that emerged a decade later.

The shift from the term "uninterrupted revolution" to the term "continuing (*jixu*) the revolution" is significant. Although in writing about the more recent term some years ago[109] I used the phrase "theory of continuous revolution," to translate it as "theory of continuing the revolution" is actually more faithful, and conveys a sense of the fact that the Chinese term *jixu* in this phrase serves a function analogous to that of a transitive verb, whereas the term *buduan* serves a function analogous to that of a predicate adjective. Thus, whereas the earlier term, "uninterrupted revolution," constituted a statement concerning what could be taken to be a natural characteristic of the revolution, the term "continuing the revolution" conveys the idea that action is required on the part of revolutionaries in order to insure its prolongation. This idea of the necessity of positive action in order to maintain the destabilization of the social system is an integral part of the more recent theoretical formulation.

The phrase "continuing the revolution" appeared in the preamble to the constitution of the Chinese Communist party drafted by Mao and adopted at its Ninth Congress in 1969. Speaking of a socialist society as covering a long period, and as characterized by a series of contradictions, the constitution said, "These contradictions can be resolved only by depending upon the Marxist theory of continuing the revolution and on practice under its guidance."[110] The passage continued by citing the Cultural Revolution as an example of this theory and its application. A closer look at certain aspects of that movement gives a clearer indication of what Mao had in mind in putting forward this theory as the appropriate mode for the political development of Chinese society during the course of the socialist stage.

The Cultural Revolution can be seen to exemplify the theory of continuing the revolution in four ways. First, and most important, it was a movement in which a new legitimacy was accorded to direct, popular action in pursuit of the resolution of old conflicts in the society. Youthful rebels in schools, factories, and govern-

---

[109] Starr, "Conceptual Foundations of Mao Tse-tung's Theory of Continuous Revolution," *Asian Survey* 11:6 (1971), 610-628.

[110] 1968l:170. The formula is not substantially modified in the current party constitution; *PR* 20:36 (2 September 1977), 16.

ment agencies were moved to act on certain long-standing griev-
ances when and only when such action was legitimated by the
Center, and specifically, by Mao himself. His swim in the Yangtze
River in July 1966, his big character poster and letter endorsing
the action of the Red Guards, written the following month, and
finally, his appearance at a rally of young rebels in the uniform
of the People's Liberation Army with a band inscribed "*hong-
weibing*" (Red Guards) on his arm, all signified his approval of
their actions. The issues on the basis of which they acted, however, were not merely the ephemeral consequence of Mao's ex-
hortations, but rather were issues that derived from their own
concrete experience of institutional life in post-Liberation China.
Whereas the legitimation of their actions came from Mao, the
reasons for their rebellion lay in their own perceptions of an
elitist school system, of unresponsive and bureaucratic leaders,
and of an emergent new class of self-interested cadres. It was
because they were moved to act on issues that touched their own
lives that the movement subsequently proved so difficult to regu-
late and control from the Center.

A second aspect of the Cultural Revolution germane to an
understanding of its relationship to Mao's theory of continuing
the revolution lies in the fact that it encompassed, ultimately, not
only the occasionally willful and often excessive actions of young
students attacking remnants of feudal culture in their society, but
also the implementation of carefully conceived systems of organizational reform and of reforms to the education system, which
were designed to correct the causes of and thus to avoid the
recurrence of the problems to which the movement as a whole
was responding. Although these reforms were, in some cases, ineffective even where implemented, and, in other instances, impossible to implement because they met with strong resistance from
powerful interests unwilling to relinquish the authority they held,
the reforms nonetheless focussed attention on and began the process of dealing with the problem of miswielded authority as a cause
of embourgeoisement.

Third, the Cultural Revolution was concerned with the exercise
of political power. It demonstrated the necessity for those who
supported a policy of continuing the revolution to possess sufficient power to impose that policy on those who were its targets.
Herein lay a paradox implicit in the theory, since it was this self-
same power which, miswielded, had caused individuals to become

targets. While their power had corrupted them, that same power subsequently protected them from attack unless a superior power could be brought to bear upon them. Mao, as propounder of this theory, traded heavily on his own charismatic legitimacy and on the ideological legitimacy (and, in some instances, the coercive power) of the People's Liberation Army as sources of the power required first to attack the corrupted power holders, and then, having "seized power," to release the latent conflicts at every level in the society.

Finally, the Cultural Revolution as a discrete movement was seen by Mao from early on as insufficient in and of itself. Although it could serve as an example of a policy based on the theory of continuing the revolution, it alone was not coterminous with the implementation of that theory. Many cultural revolutions were necessary—one every seven or eight years, he suggested as the Cultural Revolution began,[111] one every thirty to fifty years, he suggested more conservatively after the movement had progressed for nearly a year.[112]

These aspects of the Cultural Revolution suggest what Mao meant by a developmental policy based on the theory of continuing the revolution. It is a concept of political development that, first of all, assumes the givenness and permanence of conflict in society. Second, it is based on the idea that this conflict can be "handled" correctly in such a way as to make the most of its creative potential toward the gradual resolution of the very long-term contradictions in a socialist society in transition toward communism. The responsibility for this correct handling cannot, however, be consigned to stable institutions, since their very stability makes them resistant to the semianarchic aspects of the conflict, which Mao viewed as requisite to the process. This resistance, in turn, makes these institutions a corruptive environment for those who function within them. The theory of continuing the revolution thus prescribes, instead, periodic revolutions that are to be made from the bottom up and from the top down, simultaneously—revolutions which give vent to the conflicts that naturally exist within the society, but which at the same time manage that conflict in such a way as to maximize its contribution toward the achievement of certain developmental goals.

These views are suggested in a number of Mao's comments

[111] 1966g:96.　　　　　　　　　　[112] 1967n:459. Cf. 1967e; 1969:94.

prior to and following the Cultural Revolution—comments that evoke the confidence and optimism he felt in the face of chaos. In 1958 he spoke of the possibility that disorder might result from the period of socialist construction: "if disorder results it won't be all that great, there will just be a spell of disorder and then things may well move toward order. The appearance of disorder contains within it some favorable elements, we should not fear disorder."[113] On the eve of the Cultural Revolution he commented in a letter that the movement from "great upheaval" to "great peace" was a cyclical one, and beneficial for the society.[114] A month later, as the movement was getting underway, he advocated "letting the chaos go on" for a few months, contending that it did not threaten the stability of the system as a whole.[115] In one of the last extended conversations of which we have record, Mao spoke to "liberated cadres" in the fall of 1974 of his position *vis-à-vis* the political system as being one of "disordering it, and then ruling it." "How could we distinguish bad from good without disorder," he went on. "Socialism is a society of change, it cannot be one of fair winds and quiet waters."[116]

Mao's contribution to the Chinese revolution was an enormous one, but the theoretical legacy he left behind poses substantial problems for his successors, if they were to attempt to implement it. The problems are suggested in the most recent of his comments cited above: "first we disorder it, then rule it." In the absence of a towering revolutionary figure such as Mao became over the course of his career, who will be able with equal confidence to disorder and then rule the vast and diverse political system that unites a quarter of the world's population? In the last decade of his life Mao pitted himself against many of his senior colleagues with whom he had made the revolution, taking them to be power holders corrupted by their exercise of power, and thus members of a new bourgeoisie and enemies of the people. The theory of continuing the revolution under the dictatorship of the proletariat, and the equation of political development with a deinstitutionalization of the political order—with the encouragement of creative disorder, if you will—are fundamentally dependent on the existence of those with sufficient power and authority to main-

[113] 1958l:112.
[114] 1966g:94.
[115] 1966n:35.
[116] 1974.

tain that minimal framework of stability within which is to take place the periodic chaos that aims at rectifying the inevitable errors of those in positions of authority, a framework of stability that will render it possible to "rule" the situation between such periods.

Hua Guofeng, Mao's immediate successor, was at the time of his succession by no means the powerful figure that Mao had been. Although he took pains to establish his legitimacy by constant reference to his predecessor,[117] Hua's policies were more akin to the optimistically pragmatic ideas of the Mao of the 1950s than they were to the theory of continuing the revolution, which a more sober and pessimistic Mao devised in the 1960s. The return to power of Deng Xiaoping in 1977 served to reinforce this tendency on Hua's part.[118] That Hua or his colleagues will grow to the point of being sufficiently authoritative to be able to carry out Mao's challenging theoretical legacy, and that, having so grown, they will choose to do so, seems highly unlikely at this writing. Mao himself, on the contrary, was cautiously optimistic with regard to the implementation of his theory: "The future is bright," he wrote, "but the road ahead is tortuous."[119]

[117] "With you in office I can be at ease," Mao is said to have written to Hua at a meeting between the two men five months before Mao's death.

[118] I have discussed Deng's restoration and the policies he has set forward in a pair of articles: "The Phoenix Restored: Reflections on the Career of Deng Xiao-ping from the Fourth to the Fifth National People's Congress," *Asian Thought and Society* 3:7 (April 1978), pp. 118-125; and "China's New Course," *Current History* 75:439 (September 1978).

[119] 1966g:96.

GLOSSARY OF CHINESE NAMES
AND TERMS

Pinyin Romanization	Wade-Giles Romanization	Characters
Ai Hengwu	Ai Heng-wu	艾恒武
Anshan	An-shan	鞍山
Anhui	An-hui (Anhwei)	安徽
"Bali gongshe de weida jiaoxun"	"Pa-li kung-she ti wei-ta chiao-hsun"	巴黎公社的伟大教训
Beidaihe	Pei-tai-ho	北戴河
Beijing	Pei-ching (Peking)	北京
buduan geming	pu-tuan ko-ming	不断革命
Cai Hosen	Tsai Ho-sen	芽和森
"Chedi pipan 'jieji douzheng xiaomie lun' de fandong miulun"	"Ch'e-di p'i-p'an 'chie-chi tou-cheng hsiao-mieh lun' ti fan-tung miu-lun"	彻底批判阶级斗争熄灭论的谬论
chezhi	ch'e-chih	拘戒
Chen Duxiu	Ch'en Tu-hsiu	陈独秀
Chen Zhengren	Ch'en Cheng-jen	陈正人
Chengdu	Ch'eng-tu	成都
chuli	ch'u-li	处理
Dazhai	Ta-chai	大寨
dazibao	ta-tzu-pao	大字报
dangquanpai	tang-ch'uan-p'ai	当权派
dao	tao	迈
Dao De Jing	*Tao Te Ching*	迈德经
Deng Xiaoping	Teng Hsiao-p'ing	邓小平

PINYIN ROMANIZATION	WADE-GILES ROMANIZATION	CHARACTERS
diulian	tiu-lien	去脸
Donfanghong bao	*Tung-fang-hung pao*	东方红报
Dong Zhongshu	Tung Chung-shu	荃仲舒
duli zizhu	tu-li tzu-chu	独立自主
duomianshou	tuo-mien-shou	多面手
Er Di Zhang	*Erh Ti Chang*	二谛章
Feiqing nianbao	*Fei-ch'ing nien-pao*	匪情年报
feiyue	fei-yueh	飞跃
feng	feng	风
fuhe	fu-ho	符合
Fushun	Fu-shun	抚顺
Fuxi	Fu-hsi	伏羲
Gao Gang	Kao Kang	高岗
Gansu	Kan-su	甘肃
gongzuo fangfa	kung-tso fang-fa	工作方法
guan	kuan	官
guanliao	kuan-liao	官仃
guanliao zhuyi	kuan-liao chu-yi	官仃主义
guannian xingtai	kuan-nian hsing-t'ai	观念形态
Guangming ribao	*Kuang-ming jih-pao*	光明日报
Guomindang	Kuo-min-tang	国民党
Guo Moruo	Kuo Mo-jo	郭沫若
Guo Peiheng	Kuo P'ei-heng	郭佩衡
Hanyu cidian	*Han-yü tz'u-tien*	汉语词典
Hanyu da cidian	*Han-yü ta tz'u-tien*	汉语大辞典
Hangzhou	Hang-chou	杭州
Hebei	Ho-pei	河北
"Heigeer de bianhua	"Hei-erh-ko ti pien-hua	"黑格尔的变化

Glossary

PINYIN ROMANIZATION	WADE-GILES ROMANIZATION	CHARACTERS
xingershangxue yu Zhuang Zi de bianhua xingershangxue bijiao"	hsing-erh-shang-hsueh yü Chuang Tzu ti pien-hua hsing-erh shang-hsueh pi-chiao"	形而上学与庄子的变化形而上学比较"
Heilongjiang ribao	*Hei-long-chiang jih-pao*	黑龙江日报
Hong Lou Meng	*Hung Lou Meng*	红楼梦
Hongqi	*Hung-ch'i*	红旗
hongweibing	Hung-hsing	红卫兵
Hongxing	hung-wei-ping	红星
Hubci	Hu-pei (Hupeh)	湖北
Hu Feng	Hu Feng	胡风
Hunan	Hu-nan	湖南
Hua Guofeng	Hua Kuo-feng	华国锋
Ji Ping	Chi P'ing	纪平
jixu geming	chi-hsu ko-ming	继续革命
Ji-zang	Chi-tsang	吉芷
jizhong	chi-chung	集中
Jiang Jieshi	Chiang Chieh-shih (Chiang Kai-shek)	蒋介石
Jiang Qing	Chiang Ch'ing	江专
Jiangsu	Chiang-su (Kiangsu)	江苏
Jiangxi	Chiang-hsi (Kiangsi)	江西
"Jiang Xia"	"Chiang Hsia"	江峡
Jiaoxue pipan	*Chiao-hsueh p'i-p'an*	教学批判
Jiaoyu geming	*Chiao-yü ko-ming*	教育革命
jiejue	chieh-chüeh	解决
Jinggangshan	*Ching-kang-shan*	井冈山

311

PINYIN ROMANIZATION	WADE-GILES ROMANIZATION	CHARACTERS
jing shang	ching shang	经上
jing xia	ching hsia	经下
Kangda	K'ang-ta	抗大
Kang Youwei	K'ang Yu-wei	康有为
Kangzhan Daxue	K'ang-chan Ta-hsuen	抗战大学
li	li	力
li	li	里
Li Lisan	Li Li-san	李立三
lilun	li-lun	理论
Li Yunzhong	Li Yun-chung	李云仲
Liangshan	Liang-shan	凉山
Lin Biao	Lin Piao	林彪
Lin Qingshan	Lin Ch'ing-shan	林青山
Liu Shaoqi	Liu Shao-ch'i	刘少奇
Luo	Lo	洛
Luo Zhanglong	Lo Chang-lung	罗章龙
Lushan	Lu-shan	庐山
Lu Xun	Lu Hsun	鲁迅
Lunyu	*Lun-yü*	论语
Mao Yuanxin	Mao Yuan-hsin	毛远新
Mao Zedong	Mao Tse-tung	毛泽东
Mao Zedong de geming wenyi luxian shengli wansui	*Mao Tse-tung ti ko-ming wen-yi lu-hsien sheng-li wan-sui*	毛泽东的革命 文艺路线 胜利万岁
Mao Zedong dui Peng-Huang-Zhang Zhou fandang jituan de pipan	*Mao Tse-tung tui P'eng-Huang-Chang-Chou fan-tang chi-t'uan ti p'i-p'an*	毛泽东对彭黄 张周反党集 团的批判

Glossary

PINYIN ROMANIZATION	WADE-GILES ROMANIZATION	CHARACTERS
Mao Zedong ji	*Mao Tse-tung chi*	毛泽东集
Mao Zedong sixiang wansui	*Mao Tse-tung szu-hsiang wan-sui*	毛泽东思想万岁
Mao Zedong xuanji	*Mao Tse-tung hsuan-chi*	毛泽东选集
Mao Zedong xuanji buyi	*Mao Tse-tung hsuan-chi pu-yi*	毛泽东选集补遗
Mao Zedong zhuzuo xuandu	*Mao Tse-tung chu-tso hsuan-tu*	毛泽东著作选读
Mao zhuxi jiaoyu yulu	*Mao chu-hsi chiao-yü yü-lu*	毛主席教育语录
Mao zhuxi wenxuan	*Mao chu-hsi wen-hsuan*	毛主席文选
Mao zhuxi yulu	*Mao chu-hsi yü-lu*	毛主席语录
Mao zhuxi zui xin zhishi	*Mao chu-hsi tsui hsin chi-shih*	毛主席最新知识
Mei Cheng	Mei Ch'eng	枚乘
minban	min-pan	民办
Ming	Ming	明
Mo Jing Yi Jie	*Mo Ching I Chie*	墨经易解
Mo Zi	Mo Tzu	墨子
naquan	na-ch'üan	拿权
Nankai	Nan-k'ai	南开
Nanning	Nan-ning	南宁
Ningxia	Ning-hsia	宁夏
peiyang	p'ei-yang	培养
Peng Dehuai	P'eng Te-huai	彭德怀
putonghua	p'u-t'ung-hua	普通话

PINYIN ROMANIZATION	WADE-GILES ROMANIZATION	CHARACTERS
"Qi fa"	"Ch'i fa"	七发
Qiliying	Ch'i-Li-ying	七里营
qian	ch'ien	乾
Qian Xinzhong	Ch'ien Hsin-chung	钱仗忠
Qin	Chin	秦
Qin Shi Huang Di	Chin Shih Huang Ti	秦始皇帝
Qing	Ch'ing	清
Qu Qiubai	Ch'ü Ch'iu-pai	瞿秋白
quan	ch'üan	权
quanli	ch'üan-li	权力
quanwei	ch'üan-wei	权威
Qun qiu fanlu	*Ch'ün ch'iu fan-lu*	春秋繁露
qunzhong	ch'ün-chung	群众
Rao Shushi	Jao Shu-shih	饶漱石
Renmin ribao	*Jen-min jih-pao*	人民日报
sanfan	san-fan	三反
Sao dang bao	*Sao tang pao*	扫荡报
Seng-zhao	Seng-chao	僧肇
Shandong	Shan-tung	山东
Shanxi	Shan-hsi (Shensi)	陕西
Shenyang	Shen-yang	沈阳
shifen fengfu (bushi lingsui buquan)	shih-fen feng-fu (pu-shih ling-sⁱ i pu-ch'üan)	十分丰实 (不是零碎不全)
Shui hu zhuan	*Shui hu chuan*	水浒传
Sichuan	Szuch'uan (Szechuan)	四川
sixiang	szu-hsiang	思想

PINYIN ROMANIZATION	WADE-GILES ROMANIZATION	CHARACTERS
Sun Zhongshan	Sun Chung-shan (Sun Yat-sen)	孙中山
tai ji tu	t'ai chi t'u	太极图
Tan Jiefu	T'an Chieh-fu	谭戒甫
Tang Junyi	T'ang Chün-i	唐君毅
ti	t'i	体
Tianjin ribao	*T'ien-chin (Tientsin) jih-pao*	天津日报
tiaojie	t'iao-chieh	调节
Tong Ha (Tangxia)	T'ung Ha (T'ang-hsia)	棠下
tubian	t'u-pien	突变
Tuan zhuan	*T'uan chuan*	彖传
Wang Haiyong	Wang Hai-yung	王海容
Wang Ming	Wang Ming	王明
Wang Zhong	Wang Chung [chung]	王中
wei	wei	为
wei	wei	威
weifeng	wei-feng	威风
Wen	Wen	文
wenhua	wen-hua	文化
Wenhui bao	*Wen-hui pao*	文汇报
wenyen	wen-yen	文言
Wenyi hongqi	*Wen-yi hung-ch'i*	文艺红旗
Wuchang	Wu-ch'ang	武昌
wufan	wu-fan	五反
Wuhan	Wu-han	武汉
wuwei	wu-wei	无为

PINYIN ROMANIZATION	WADE-GILES ROMANIZATION	CHARACTERS
Wuwei xian	Wu-wei hsien	无为县
Wu Xun	Wu Hsun	武训
Xi ci	*Hsi tz'u*	系锌
Xiju bao	*Hsi-chü pao*	戏剧报
xiafang	hsia-fang	下放
xiaxiang	hsia-hsiang	下乡
xian	hsien	县
xiaozu	hsiao-tsu	小组
Xin	Hsin	新
Xin	Hsin	伩
Xinhua banyuekan	*Hsin-hua pan-yueh-k'an*	新华半月刊
Xinhua yuebao	*Hsin-hua yueh-pao*	新华月报
Xinmin bao	*Hsin-min pao*	新民报
Xinmin wei	*Hsin-min wei*	新民卫
Xinren wei	*Hsin-jen wei*	新人卫
xiuyang	hsiu-yang	参养
Xingdao ribao	*Hsing-tao* (Tsingtao) *jih-pao*	星岛日报
xiucai	hsiu-tsai	秀才
Xu	Hsu	许
Xushui	Hsu-shui	徐水
Xu Teli	Hsu T'e-li	徐特立
xuanji	hsuan-chi	选集
Yan'an	Yen-an	延安
yang	yang	阳
Yang Xianzhen	Yang Hsien-chen	杨献珍
Yao Wenyuan	Yao Wen-yuan	姚文元

PINYIN ROMANIZATION	WADE-GILES ROMANIZATION	CHARACTERS
Yi jing	*I ching*	易经
yi yin yi yang zhi wei dao	i yin i yang chih wei tao	一阴一阳之为道
yin	yin	阴
yong	yung	用
you quanwei de	yu ch'üan-wei ti	有权威的
you maodun de	yu mao-tun ti	有矛盾的
you xitong de quanli	yu hsi-t'ung ti ch'üan-li	有系统的权力
Yu Gong	Yü Kung	愚公
yundong	yun-tung	运动
Zhang Dongsun	Chang Tung-sun	张东荪
Zhang-Guotao	Chang Kuo-t'ao	张国焘
Zhang Kai	Chang K'ai	张凯
Zhang Kaifan	Chang K'ai-fan	张凯帆
Zhang Qunqiao	Chang Ch'ün-ch'iao	张春桥
Zhang Side	Chang Szu-te	张思德
Zhang Wentian	Chang Wen-t'ien	张闻天
Zhang Zhidong	Chang Chih-tung	张则栋
Zhao lun	*Chao lun*	肇论
zhengquan	cheng-ch'üan	政权
zhengzhi nengliang	cheng-chih neng-liang	政治能易
zhengzhi shili	cheng-chih shih-li	政治势力
Zheng Zhisi	Cheng Chih-szu	郑之思
Zhengzhou	Cheng-chou	郑州
zhi	chih	智
Zhonggong wenhua da geming zhongyao wenjian huipian	*Chung-kung wen-hua ta ko-ming chung-yao wen-chien hui-p'ien*	中共文化大革命重要文件汇编

Glossary

Pinyin Romanization	Wade-Giles Romanization	Characters
Zhongguo dalu yanjiu	*Chung-kuo ta-lu yen-chiu*	中国大陸研究
Zhongguo nongmin	*Chung-kuo nung-min*	中国农民
Zhongguo nongcun de shehui zhuyi gaochao	*Chung-kuo nung-tsun ti she-hui chu-i kao-ch'ao*	中国农村的社会主义高潮
zhonghe	chung-ho	综合
zhongjian jieji	chung-chien chieh-chi	中间阶级
Zhong lun	*Chung lun*	中论
Zhou	Chou	周
Zhou Enlai	Chou En-lai	周恩来
Zhou Shizhao	Chou Shih-chao	周世钊
zhudongxing	chu-tung-hsing	主动性
Zhu Xi	Chu Hsi	朱熹
Zhuang Zi	Chuang Tzu	庄子
ziwei de jieji	tzu-wei ti chieh-chi	自为的阶级
zizai de jieji	tzu-tsai ti chieh-chi	自在的阶级
zuzhi	tsu-chih	组织

LIST OF ABBREVIATIONS

BY	*Mao Zedong xuanji buyi* (Supplement to the Selected Works of Mao Zedong). Ding Wang, ed. Hong Kong: Ming Bao Monthly Press, 1974.
BYK	*Xinhua banyuekan* (New China Bimonthly). Peking: formerly published fortnightly.
CB	*Current Background.* Hong Kong: United States Consulate General.
CE	*Chinese Education.* White Plains, N.Y.: M.E. Sharpe Co., published quarterly.
CLG	*Chinese Law and Government.* White Plains, N.Y.: M.E. Sharpe Co., published quarterly.
CMTP	*Chairman Mao Talks to the People.* Stuart R. Schram, ed. New York: Pantheon, 1974.
CSA	*Chinese Sociology and Anthropology.* White Plains, N.Y.: M.E. Sharpe Co., published quarterly.
FEP	*Four Essays on Philosophy.* Peking: Foreign Languages Press, 1966.
HQ	*Hongqi* (Red Flag). Peking, published monthly.
IS	*Issues and Studies.* Taipei, published monthly.
JPRS	Joint Publications Research Service, U.S. Department of Commerce, Washington, D.C.
MP	*Mao Papers.* Jerome Ch'en, ed. New York: Oxford University Press, 1970.
MTTLP	*Mao Tse-tung and Lin Piao: Post Revolutionary Writings.* K. H. Fan, ed. New York: Anchor, 1972.
PR	*Peking Review.* Peking, published weekly.
PT	*Political Thought of Mao Tse-tung.* Stuart R. Schram, ed. New York: Praeger, 1969.
Q	*Quotations from Chairman Mao Tse-tung.* Peking: Foreign Languages Press, 1966.
REC	*Revolutionary Education in China.* Peter J. Seybolt, ed. White Plains, N.Y.: International Arts and Sciences Press, 1973.
RMRB	*Renmin Ribao* (People's Daily). Peking, published daily.
SC	*Ssu-ch'ing: The Socialist Education Movement 1962-66.* Richard Baum and Frederick W. Teiwes. Berkeley: Center for Chinese Studies, University of California, 1968.
SCMM	*Survey of China Mainland Magazines.* Hong Kong: United States Consulate General.

SCMP   *Survey of the China Mainland Press*. Hong Kong: United States Consulate General.

SR   *Selected Readings from the Works of Mao Tse-tung*. Peking: Foreign Languages Press.

SW   *Selected Works of Mao Tse-tung*. 5 volumes. Peking: Foreign Languages Press, 1966 (vols. 1-4) and 1977 (vol. 5).

WS (1967a) *Mao Zedong sixiang wansui!* (Long Live the Thought of Mao Zedong!). Red Guard publication, 1967. 46 pp.

WS (1967b) *Mao Zedong sixiang wansui!* (Long Live the Thought of Mao Zedong!). Red Guard publication, 1967 (collection without title appended in some versions to WS 1967a). 38 pp.

WS (1967c) *Mao Zedong sixiang wansui!* (Long Live the Thought of Mao Zedong!). Red Guard publication, 1967. 280 pp.

WS (1969)   *Mao Zedong sixiang wansui!* (Long Live the Thought of Mao Zedong!). Red Guard publication, 1969. 716 pp.

WX   *Mao zhuxi wenxuan* (Selected Texts from Chairman Mao). Red Guard publication, n.d.

XJ   *Mao Zedong xuanji* (Selected Works of Mao Zedong). Peking: Renmin Chubanshe, 1969 (single-volume edition of vols. 1-4) and 1977 (vol. 5).

XMW   *Xinminwei* (New People's Health). Red Guard publication.

WHB   *Wenhui bao*. Shanghai. Published daily.

YB   *Xinhua yuebao* (New China Monthly). Peking, formerly published monthly.

YL   *Mao zhuxi yulu* (Quotations from Chairman Mao). Peking: Renmin Chubanshe, 1966.

BIBLIOGRAPHY

CHRONOLOGICAL LISTING OF MAO'S WORKS
CITED IN THE TEXT

Documents of which Mao's authorship is open to question are indicated with an asterisk in parentheses (*) following the bibliographical entry.

1917   "A Study of Physical Education" (April), *PT* 152-160.

1919a   "The Great Union of the Popular Masses" (July-August). Translated by Stuart R. Schram. *China Quarterly* 49 (1972), 76-87.

1919b   "Miss Chao's Suicide" (November), *PT* 334-337.

1920-21 Letters to Cai Hosen (November 1920 and January 1921), *PT* 296-298.

1926   "Analysis of the Classes in Chinese Society" (March), *XJ* 3-11; *SW* I, 13-22.

1927   "Report on an Investigation of the Peasant Movement in Hunan" (March), *XJ* 12-44; *SW* I, 23-62.

1928a   "Why Is It that Red Political Power Can Exist in China?" (5 October), *XJ* 47-55; *SW* I, 63-72.

1928b   "The Struggle in the Jinggang Mountains" (25 November), *XJ* 56-82; *SW* I, 73-104.

1929   "On Correcting Mistaken Ideas in the Party" (December), *XJ* 83-93; *SW* I, 105-116.

1930a   "A Single Spark Can Start a Prairie Fire" (5 January), *XJ* 94-104; *SW* I, 117-128.

1930b   "Oppose Book Worship" (May), *SR* 40.

1933a   "Pay Attention to Economic Work" (20 August), *XJ* 105-112; *SW* I, 129-136.

1933b   "How to Differentiate the Classes in the Rural Areas" (October), *XJ* 113-115; *SW* I, 137-140.

1934a   "Our Economic Policy" (23 January), *XJ* 116-121; *SW* I, 141-146.

1934b   "Be Concerned with the Well-Being of the Masses, Pay Attention to Methods of Work" (27 January), *XJ* 122-127; *SW* I, 147-152.

1935   "On Tactics against Japanese Imperialism" (27 December), *XJ* 128-153; *SW* I, 153-178.

1936   "Problems of Strategy in China's Revolutionary War" (December), *XJ* 154-225; *SW* I, 179-254.

1937a   "On Dialectical Materialism," *JPRS* 50792 (23 June 1970), 1-29.

1937b   Letter to Xu Teli (February), *MP* 5.

1937c   "The Tasks of the Chinese Communist Party in the Period of Resistance to Japan" (3 May), *XJ* 232-248; *SW* I, 263-284.

1937d   "Win the Masses in Their Millions for the Anti-Japanese National United Front" (7 May), *XJ* 249-258; *SW* I, 285-294.

1937e   "On Practice" (July), *XJ* 259-273; *SW* I, 295-310.

1937f   "Policies, Measures and Perspectives for Resisting the Japanese Invasion" (23 July), *XJ* 315-323; *SW* II, 13-22.

1937g   "On Contradiction" (August), *XJ* 274-312; *SW* I, 311-347.

1937h   "Urgent Tasks Following the Establishment of Guomindang-Communist Cooperation" (29 September), *XJ* 333-343; *SW* II, 35-46.

1937i   "Interview with the British Journalist James Bertram" (25 October), *XJ* 344-356; *SW* II, 47-60.

1937j   Inscriptions for the Founding of the North Shanxi Public School (23 October), *MP* 11.

1937k   "The Situation and Tasks in the Anti-Japanese War after the Fall of Shanghai and Taiyuan" (12 November), *XJ* 357-369; *SW* II, 61-74.

1937l   *On Guerrilla Warfare*. Translated by Samuel Griffith. New York: Praeger, 1961.

1938a   *Basic Tactics*. Translated by Stuart R. Schram. New York: Praeger, 1966.

1938b   Speech at a meeting commemorating the anniversary of the death of Lu Xun (March), *MP* 14ff.

1938c   "Problems of Strategy in Guerrilla War against Japan" (May), *XJ* 373-406; *SW* II, 79-112.

1938d   "On Protracted War" (May), *XJ* 407-484; *SW* II, 113-194.

1938e   "The Role of the Chinese Communist Party in the National War" (October), *XJ* 485-501; *SW* II, 195-212.

1938f   Ibid., *PT* 171ff. (translating an earlier version of the article).

1938g   "The Question of Independence and Initiative within the United Front" (5 November), *XJ* 502-505; *SW* II, 213-218.

1938h   "Problems of War and Strategy" (6 November), *XJ* 506-521; *SW* II, 219-236.

1939a   "The May Fourth Movement" (May), *XJ* 522-524; *SW* II, 237-240.

1939b   Speech at the Yan'an Rally in Celebration of International Labor Day (1 May), *Q* 147.

1939c   "The Orientation of the Youth Movement" (4 May), *XJ* 525-533; *SW* II, 241-250.

1939d   "To Be Attacked by the Enemy Is Not a Bad Thing but a Good Thing" (26 May), *Q* 146.

1939e   "Instruction of the Military Affairs Committee on the Question of Consolidating the Anti-Japanese Military and Political College" (July), *CB* 888 (22 August 1969), 3f.

1939f   "Interview with three correspondents from the Central News Agency, the *Sao Dang Bao* and the *Xin Min Bao*" (1 September), *XJ* 550-555; *SW* II, 269-274.

1939g   "Introducing *The Communist*" (4 October), *XJ* 565-577; *SW* II, 285-296.

1939h   "Youth Needs Experience" (5 October), *PT* 353.

1939i   "Recruit Large Numbers of Intellectuals" (1 December), *XJ* 581-583; *SW* II, 301-304.

1939j   "The Chinese Revolution and the Chinese Communist Party" (December), *XJ* 584-617; *SW* II, 305-334.

1939k   "Stalin Is Our Commander" (21 December), *PT* 426-428.

1939l   "In Memory of Norman Bethune" (21 December), *XJ* 620-622; *SW* II, 337-338.

1940a   "On New Democracy" (January), *XJ* 623-670; *SW* II, 339-384.

1940b   Speech at the inaugural meeting of the Natural Science Research Society of the Border Region (5 February), *Q* 204f.

1940c   Introducing *The Chinese Worker* (7 February), *XJ* 685f.; *SW* II, 403f.

1940d   "New Democratic Constitutional Government" (20 February), *XJ* 689-698; *SW* II, 407-416.

1940e   "On the Question of Political Power in the Anti-Japanese Base Areas" (6 March), *XJ* 699-701; *SW* II, 417-420.

1940f   "On Policy" (25 December), *XJ* 720-728; *SW* II, 441-450.

1941a   Preface and Postscript to *Rural Surveys* (March-April), *XJ* 747-752; *SW* III, 11-16.

1941b   "Reform Our Study" (May), *XJ* 753-761; *SW* III, 17-26.

1941c   Speech at the Assembly of Representatives of the Shanxi-Gansu-Ningxia Border Region (21 November), *XJ* 765-768; *SW* III, 31-34.

1942a   "Rectify the Party's Style of Work" (1 February), *XJ* 769-786; *SW* III, 35-52.

1942b   "Oppose Stereotyped Party Writing" (8 February), *XJ* 787-803; *SW* III, 53-68.

1942c   "Talks at the Yan'an Forum on Literature and Art" (May), *XJ* 804-835; *SW* III, 69-98.

1942d   "A Most Important Policy" (7 September), *XJ* 836-839; *SW* III, 99-102.

1942e   "Economic and Financial Problems in the Anti-Japanese War" (December), *XJ* 846-851; *SW* III, 111-116.

1943a   Speech explaining the dissolution of the Communist International (26 May), *PT* 421-423.

1943b   "Some Questions Concerning Methods of Leadership" (1 June), *XJ* 852-857; *SW* III, 117-122.

1943c   Letter criticizing Peng Dehuai (6 June), *CLG* 1:4 (Winter 1968-69), 7-9.

1943d   "Spread the Campaigns to Reduce Rent, Increase Production and 'Support the Government and Cherish the People' in the Base Areas" (1 October), *XJ* 865-868; *SW* III, 131-136.

1943e   "Get Organized!" (29 November), *XJ* 869-881; *SW* III, 153-162.

1944a   Letter to the Yan'an Beijing Opera Theatre after seeing "Driven to Join the Liangshan Mountain Rebels" (9 January), *MP* 77f.

1944b   "Our Study and the Current Situation" (12 April), *XJ* 891-904; *SW* III, 163-226.

1944c   "Serve the People" (8 September), *XJ* 905-907; *SW* III, 227-228.

1945a   "On Coalition Government" (24 April), *XJ* 930-1000; *SW* III, 255-320.

1945b   "The Foolish Old Man Who Removed the Mountains" (11 June), *XJ* 1001-1004; *SW* III, 321-324.

1948a   "On Setting up a System of Reports" (7 January), *XJ* 1159-1161; *SW* IV, 177-180.

1948b   "On Strengthening the Party Committee System" (20 September), *XJ* 1234f.; *SW* IV, 267f.

1948c   "On the September Meeting," Circular of the Central Committee of the CCP (10 October), *XJ* 1236-1244; *SW* IV, 269-278.

1949a   "Turn the Army into a Working Force" (8 February), *XJ* 1295-1297; *SW* IV, 337-340.

1949b   Report to the Second Plenary Session of the Seventh Central Committee of the CCP (5 March), *XJ* 1314-1329; *SW* IV, 361-376.

1949c   "Methods of Work of Party Committees" (13 March), *XJ* 1330-1334; *SW* IV, 377-382.

1949d   "On the People's Democratic Dictatorship" (30 June), *XJ* 1357-1371; *SW* IV, 411-424.

1949e   Proclamation of the establishment of the People's Republic of China (1 October), in *Mao Zedong Ji* (Collected works of Mao Zedong). Tokyo: Mō Takutō bunken shiryō kenyūkai, 1970. x, 361; *PR* 12:44 (31 October 1969), 19.

1949f   Message on Stalin's seventieth birthday (21 December), *BY* 5; *MP* 19.

1950a   Inscription written during a tour of inspection to Heilongjiang Province (27 February) in *Heilongjiang ribao* (28 February 1950); *CB* 885 (31 July 1969), 14.

1950b   Report to the Third Plenary Session of the Seventh Central Committee: "Fight for a Fundamental Turn for the Better in the Financial and Economic Situation in China" (6 June), *RMRB* (13 June 1950); *MTTLP* 103-110. Compare *XJ* v, 15-20; *SW* v, 26-32.

1950c   Closing speech at the Second Session of the First National Committee of the Chinese People's Political Consultative Conference (23 June), *XJ* v, 25-29; *MTTLP* 93ff. Compare *SW* v, 37-40.

1951a   Comment on the work of suppressing and liquidating

counterrevolutionaries (9 March), *WS* (1969), 8; *JPRS* 61269-1 (20 February 1974), 7.

1951b Comment on the work of suppressing and liquidating counterrevolutionaries (24 March), *WS* (1969), 8; *JPRS* 61269-1 (20 February 1974), 7.

1951c Comment on the work of suppressing and liquidating counterrevolutionaries (2 April), *WS* (1969), 9; *JPRS* 61269-1 (20 February 1974), 8.

1951d Resolution of the Third National Conference on Public Security (15 May), *WS* (1969), 5f.; *JPRS* 61269-1 (20 February 1974), 9f.

1951e "Give Serious Attention to the Discussion of the Film, 'The Life of Wu Xun'" (20 May), *XJ* v, 46f.; *PT* 363-365. Compare *SW* v, 57f.

1951f Opening Address at the Third Session of the First National Committee of the Chinese People's Political Consultative Conference (23 October), *XJ* v, 48-52; *MTTLP* 96-101. Compare *SW* v, 59-63.

1951g Comment on the Sanfan and the Wufan Campaigns (30 November), *XJ* v, 53; *SW* v, 64.

1951h Comment on the Sanfan and Wufan Campaigns (30 November), *XJ* v, 53; *SW* v, 64 [different from 1951g].

1951i Comment on the Sanfan and Wufan Campaigns (8 December), *XJ* v, 54; *SW* v, 65.

1952a New Year's message (1 January), *XJ* v, 60; *SCMP* 247 (3 January 1952), 1f. Compare *SW* v, 72.

1952b Comment on the Sanfan and Wufan Campaigns (23 March), *XJ* v, 57f.; *SW* v, 68f.

1952c Inscription for the *Tianjin Ribao* (28 September) in *Wenyi Hongqi* (Art and Literature Red Flag), Red Guard publication; *SCMP* 4000 (14 August 1967), 12.

1952d Comment on the Sanfan and Wufan Campaigns (26 January), *XJ* v, 54f.; *SW* v, 65f.

1952e Comment on the Sanfan and Wufan Campaigns (5 March), *XJ* v, 55-57; *SW* v, 66-68.

1953a Comment on the general line for the transition period, *RMRB* (1 July 1971); *PR* 14:27 (2 July 1971), 12.

1953b Speech at the Fourth Session of the First National Committee of the Chinese People's Political Consultative Conference (7 February), *RMRB* (8 February 1953); *MTTLP* 101f.

1953c   "The Greatest Friendship," a tribute written on the occasion of Stalin's death (9 March), *YB* 42 (April 1953); *MTTLP* 111-115.

1953d   Directive on education work contained in a speech to the Politburo (17 May) in *Jiaoxue pipan* (Criticism of Teaching), Red Guard publication, 20 April 1967; *CSA* 2:1-2 (Fall-Winter 1969-70), 29.

1953e   Talk at the reception for the Presidium of the Second National Congress of the Youth League (30 June), *XJ* v, 83-87; *MP* 80. Compare *SW* v, 95-100.

1954a   Instructions on work of doctors of traditional Chinese medicine, *XMW* (June 1967); *SCMM* (suppl.) 22 (8 April 1968), 8.

1954b   Speech at a Standing Committee meeting of the Central Committee, *XMW* (June 1967); *SCMM* (suppl.) 22 (8 April 1968), 9.

1954c   Directive on work in traditional Chinese medicine (30 July), *WS* (1969), 10-12; *JPRS* 61269-1 (20 February 1974), 12f.

1954d   Letter to the Politburo of the Central Committee concerning studies of the *Dream of the Red Chamber* (16 October), *XJ* v, 134f.; *PR* 10:23 (2 June 1967), 7f. Compare *SW* v, 150f.

1955a   Talk at the National Representatives Conference of the CCP (21 March), *XJ* v, 138-156; *CB* 891 (8 October 1969), 18. Compare *SW* v, 154-171.

1955b   Introductory note to the "Second installment of material on the Hu Feng counter-revolutionary clique" (24 May), *RMRB* (24 May 1955); *MP* 51-54. Compare *XJ* v, 157-159; *SW* v, 172-175.

1955c   Introductory note to the "Third installment of material on the Hu Feng counter-revolutionary clique" (10 June), *RMRB* (10 June 1955); *SCMP* 4000 (14 August 1967), 15. Compare *XJ* v, 162-167; *SW* v, 176-183.

1955d   Report delivered at a conference of secretaries of provincial, municipal and autonomous region committees of the CCP: "On the Question of Agricultural Cooperation" (31 July), *XJ* v, 168-191; in translation in pamphlet under the same title. Peking: Foreign Languages Press, 1955. Compare *SW* v, 184-207.

1955e   Speech at the Sixth Plenary (Enlarged) Session of the

Seventh Central Committee of the CCP (11 October), *XJ* v, 195-217; *JPRS* 61269-1 (20 February 1974), 14-26. Compare *SW* v, 211-234.

1955f Talk opposing right deviationism and conservatism (6 December), *WS* (1969), 25-27; *JPRS* 61269-1 (20 February 1974), 27-29.

1955g Preface and introductory notes to the articles in *The Socialist Upsurge in China's Countryside* (27 December) in *Zhongguo nongcun de shehui zhuyi gaochao*, 3 vols. Peking: Renmin Chubanshe, 1955. Condensed and translated under the same title, Peking: Foreign Languages Press, 1955. Compare *XJ* v, 218-259; *SW* v, 235-276.

1956a Talk on the question of intellectuals at a meeting convened by the Central Committee (20 January), *WS* (1969), 28-34; *IS* 10:8 (May 1974), 95-99.

1956b Speech at the Supreme State Conference (25 January), *RMRB* (26 January 1956); Stuart R. Schram and Hélène Carrère d'Encausse, eds. *Marxism and Asia*. Baltimore: Penguin, 1969, pp. 291-293.

1956c Speech at an expanded meeting of the Politburo of the CCP (April), *WS* (1969), 35-40; *JPRS* 61269-1 (20 February 1974), 30-35.

1956d Editorial: "On the Historical Experience of the Dictatorship of the Proletariat" (5 April), *RMRB* (5 April 1956). Translated and published as a pamphlet under the same title, Peking: Foreign Languages Press, 1957, 1-20. (*)

1956e Speech at an enlarged conference of the Politburo: "On Ten Major Relationships" (25 April), *XJ* v, 267-288; *CMTP* 61-83. Compare *SW* v, 284-307.

1956f Poem: "Swimming" (May), in Willis Barnstone, ed. *The Poems of Mao Tse-Tung*. New York: Harper and Row, 1972. Translated in Jerome Ch'en. *Mao and the Chinese Revolution*. New York: Oxford University Press, 1965, p. 346.

1956g Speech at a Supreme State Conference (2 May), *SCMP* 4000 (14 August 1967), 16.

1956h A talk with music workers (24 August), in *Mao Zedong de geming wenyi luxian shengli wansui* (Long Live the Victory of Mao Zedong's Revolutionary Line on Art and

Literature), Red Guard publication, July 1967; *CMTP* 84-90.

1956i   Opening address at the Eighth National Congress of the CCP (15 September), *RMRB* (16 September 1956); *Eighth National Congress Documents*. Peking: Foreign Languages Press, 1956, pp. 7-11.

1956j   Talk with security guards concerning cultural studies (15 September 1956), *SCMP* 2271 (3 June 1960), 6.

1956k   "In Commemoration of Dr. Sun Zhongshan" (12 November), *XJ* v, 311f.; *MP* 19f. Compare *SW* v, 330f.

1956l   Speech at the Second Plenary Session of the Eighth Central Committee of the CCP (15 November), *XJ* v, 313-329; *PR* 13:17 (24 April 1970), 6. Compare *SW* v, 332-349.

1956m   Instruction at a discussion meeting attended by some of the delegates to the Second Session of the First Committee of the All-China Federation of Industry and Commerce (8 December), *WS* (1969), 61-73; *JPRS* 61269-1 (20 February 1974), 36-45.

1956n   Editorial: "More on the Historical Experience of the Dictatorship of the Proletariat" (29 December), *RMRB* (29 December 1956). Translated in *On the Historical Experience of the Dictatorship of the Proletariat*. Peking: Foreign Languages Press, 1957, 21-64. (*)

1957a   Comments at a conference of provincial and municipal party committee secretaries (January), *WS* (1969), 73-81; *JPRS* 61269-1 (20 February 1974), 46-53.

1957b   Summary of a conference of provincial and municipal party committee secretaries (January), *XJ* v, 330-362; *JPRS* 61269-1 (20 February 1974), 54-62. Compare *SW* v, 350-383.

1957c   A letter discussing poetry (12 January), *BY* 98; *CB* 891 (8 October 1969), 23.

1957d   Speech at the Eleventh Session (Enlarged) of the Supreme State Conference: "On the Correct Handling of Contradictions among the People" (27 February), *RMRB* (19 June 1957); *FEP* 79-133. Compare *XJ* v, 363-402; *SW* v, 384-421.

1957e   Ibid., as reported in *New York Times* (13 June 1957), 1:8, 8:5.

1957f   Speech at the CCP National Conference on Propaganda Work (12 March), *XJ* v, 403-418. Published in pamphlet form, Peking: Foreign Languages Press, 1957. Compare *SW* v, 422-435.

1957g   Talk with the secretaries of provincial and municipal party committees at Qingdao: "The Situation in the Summer of 1957" (July), *XJ* v, 456-465; *MP* 56. Compare *SW* v, 473-482.

1957h   Ibid., as translated in *SCMP* 4000 (14 August 1967), 18.

1957i   Comment on class education in a talk with leaders from the Shanghai Motive Power Institute (July), in *Jiaoyu Geming* (Revolution in Education). Red Guard publication, 6 May 1967; *REC* 26.

1957j   Talk at the Third Plenum of the Eighth Central Committee (7 October), *XJ* v, 466-479; *JPRS* 61269-1 (20 February 1974), 72-76. Compare *SW* v, 498-513.

1958a   A talk concerning *Renmin Ribao* (January), *RMRB* (1 September 1968); *PR* 11:37 (13 September 1968), 26.

1958b   Talk at the Nanning Conference (11 January), *WS* (1969), 145-148; *JPRS* 61269-1 (20 February 1974), 77-80.

1958c   Talk at the Nanning Conference (12 January), *WS* (1969), 148-154; *JPRS* 61269-1 (20 February 1974), 80-84.

1958d   Speech at a Supreme State Conference (28 January), *WS* (1969), 154-159; *CMTP* 91-95. Compare *CLG* 1:4 (Winter 1968-69), 10-14.

1958e   "Sixty Work Methods" (31 January), *WS* (1967b), 29-38; *CB* 892 (21 October 1969), 1-14.

1958f   Comments during a visit to Fushun (February), *BYK* 10 (25 May 1958), 35f.; *SCMP* 1766 (7 May 1958), 2.

1958g   Comments during a visit to the Shenyang suburbs (13 February), *RMRB* (13 February 1958); *SCMP* 1761 (30 April 1958), 4f.

1958h   Comments during a visit to Sichuan Province (March), *BYK* 9 (May 1958), 4f.; *SCMP* 1752 (16 April 1958), 1-4.

1958i   Instructions on national minorities (March), *WS* (1967a), 18; *MP* 83f.

1958j   Talk at the Chengdu Conference (10 March), *WS* (1969), 159-165; *CMTP* 96-103.

1958k   Inspection of agricultural cooperative in Sichuan Province (16 March), *BYK* 9 (May 1958), 6f.; *SCMP* 1753 (17 April 1958), 2f.

1958l   Talk at the Chengdu Conference (20 March), *WS* (1969), 165-172; *CMTP* 103-113.

1958m   Speech at the Chengdu Conference (22 March), *WS* (1969), 172-180; *CMTP* 113-124.

1958n   Comments during a visit aboard the "Jiang Xia" (29 March), *RMRB* (15 April 1958); *SCMP* 1761 (30 April 1958), 1-3.

1958o   Remarks during a visit to farms and factories in Hubei and Sichuan Provinces (April), *RMRB* (4 April 1958); *PR* 1:8 (22 April 1958), 4.

1958p   Speech at the Hankou Conference (6 April), *WS* (1969), 180-186; *JPRS* 61269-1 (20 February 1974), 85-90.

1958q   Article for the inaugural issue of *Hongqi*: "Introducing a Cooperative" (15 April), *HQ* 1 (1958); *PR* 1:15 (10 June 1958), 6.

1958r   Comments during a visit to the Tong Ha Agricultural Producers Cooperative (30 April), ·*RMRB* 1 (May 1958); *SCMP* 1779 (27 May 1958), 6-10.

1958s   First speech at the second session of the Eighth National Party Congress (8 May), *WS* (1969), 186-196; *JPRS* 61269-1 (20 February 1974), 91-99.

1958t   Second speech at the Second Session of the Eighth National Party Congress (17 May), *WS* (1969), 196-209; *JPRS* 61269-1 (20 February 1974), 99-109.

1958u   Speech at the conference of heads of delegations to the Second Session of the Eighth National Party Congress (18 May), *WS* (1969), 220-225; *JPRS* 61269-1 (20 February 1974), 119-124.

1958v   Third speech at the Second Session of the Eighth National Party Congress (20 May), *WS* (1969), 209-216; *JPRS* 61269-1 (20 February 1974), 109-115.

1958w   Fourth speech at the Second Session of the Eighth National Party Congress (23 May), *WS* (1969), 216-220; *JPRS* 61269-1 (20 February 1974), 115-118.

1958x   Speech at a group leaders' forum of the Enlarged Conference of the Military Affairs Commission (28 June), in *Mao Zedong dui Peng-Huang-Zhang-Zhou fandang jituan de pipan* (Mao Zedong's Criticism of the Peng-Huang-Zhang-Zhou Anti-Party Clique). Red Guard publication, n.d., pp. 3-5; *CLG* 1:4 (Winter 1968-69), 15-21.

1958y   Talk with the party secretary and cooperative members in Xushui County, Hebei Province (4 August), *RMRB* (11 August, 1958); *SCMP* 1839 (25 August 1958), 1-6.

1958z   Comments during an inspection tour of Qiliying People's Commune (6 August), *RMRB* (12 August 1958); *SCMP* 1847 (5 September 1958), 2-5.

1958aa   Account of remarks on an inspection tour in Shandong (9 August), *RMRB* (13 August 1958); *SCMP* 1833 (15 August 1958), 3ff.

1958bb   Ibid., as translated in *PT* 349f.

1958cc   Comments during an inspection of Xinlicun Agricultural Producers' Cooperative (10 August), *RMRB* (11 August 1958); *SCMP* 1849 (9 September 1958), 2-4.

1958dd   Comments during a visit to exhibitions of new commercial products and industrial techniques (11-12 August), *RMRB* (16 August 1958); *SCMP* 1837 (21 August 1958), 2f.

1958ee   Directive issued during an inspection of Nankai and Tianjin Universities (13 August), *WS* (1967a), 18; *CSA* 2:1-2 (Fall-Winter 1969-70), 44.

1958ff   Ibid., as translated in *CE* 2:3 (Fall 1969), 45f.

1958gg   Ibid., as translated in *SCMP* 1847 (5 September 1958), 6f.

1958hh   Comments during a visit to agricultural cooperatives in the southwestern outskirts of Beijing (14 August), *BYK* 17 (10 September 1958), 18f; *SCMP* 1837 (21 August 1958), 3f.

1958ii   Remarks during an inspection tour of Anhui, Hubei, and Jiangsu Provinces (September), *WS* (1967a), 18; *PR* 1:32 (7 October 1958), 4.

1958jj   Ibid., as translated in *PR* 1:33 (14 October 1958), 4f.

1958kk   Ibid., as translated in *SCMP* 1886 (31 October 1958), 2ff.

1958ll   Second Speech at the Fifteenth Supreme State Conference (8 September), *WS* (1969), 237-241; *PR* 1:29 (16 September 1958), 4.

1958mm Ibid., as translated in *REC* 33.

1958nn Comments while inspecting Wuhan University (12 September), *RMRB* (29 September 1958); *SCMP* 1906 (3 December 1958), 2-6.

1958oo Comments to women in Wuhan during an inspection tour (14 September), *WHB* (8 October 1958); *SCMP* 1886 (31 October 1958), 5f.

1958pp Comments during an inspection tour of Anhui Province (16-20 September), in *RMRB* (4 October 1958); *SCMP* 1874 (14 October 1958), 1-5.

1958qq Ibid., as translated in *SCMP* 1906 (3 December 1958), 7-9.

1958rr Statement following provincial inspection tour (29 September), *HQ* 10 (1958); *SCMP* 1871 (9 October 1958), 1f.

1958ss Comment on the "Summing up report on the organization of Western doctors who leave their posts to study Chinese medicine" (October), *Xinren Wei* (New People's Health). Red Guard publication, n.d.; *SCMM* (suppl.) 22 (8 April 1968), 10f.

1958tt Speech at the first Zhengzhou Conference (November), *WS* (1969), 247-251; *JPRS* 61269-1 (20 February 1974), 128.

1958uu Ibid., as translated in *JPRS* 61269-1 (20 February 1974), 129-132.

1958vv Letter to Zhou Shizhao (25 November), *WS* (1969), 245-247; *JPRS* 61269-1 (20 February 1974), 126f.

1958ww Talk with directors of various cooperative areas (30 November), *WS* (1969), 251-255; *JPRS* 61269-1 (20 February 1974), 133-136.

1958xx Speech at the Wuchang meeting of the Politburo of the Central Committee of the CCP (Sixth Plenum of the Eighth Central Committee), *YL* 68; *Q* 72ff.

1958yy Speech at the Sixth Plenum of the Eighth Central Committee (19 December), *WS* (1969), 259-269; *JPRS* 61269-1 (20 February 1974), 140-148.

1958zz Talk with directors of various cooperative areas (12 December), *WS* (1969), 256-258; *JPRS* 61269-1 (20 February 1974), 136-139.

1959a Critique of Stalin's "Economic Problems of Socialism in the Soviet Union," *WS* (1967c), 156-166; *JPRS* 61269-1 (20 February 1974), 191-199.

1959b   Comments on a reply to Comrades A. V. Sanina and V. G. Venzher, *WS* (1967c), 121f.; *JPRS* 61269-1 (20 February 1974), 189f.

1959c   "On Dialectics," *WS* (1967c), 123-151; *JPRS* 61269-1 (20 February 1974), 201-225.

1959d   Speech at the conference of the Politburo of the Central Committee (Enlarged) at Zhengzhou (February), *WS* (1967c), 2; *CLG* 1:4 (Winter 1968-69), 22.

1959e   Speech at a conference of provincial and municipal party committee secretaries (2 February), *WS* (1969), 271-279; *JPRS* 61269-1 (20 February 1974), 151-158.

1959f   Talk at a symposium of Xin, Luo, Xu, and Xin local committees (21 February), *WS* (1967c), 3-7; *JPRS* 61269-1 (20 February 1974), 159-162.

1959g   Interview with leaders of Latin American Communist and Workers' parties (3 March), *RMRB* (5 March 1959); *Current Digest of the Soviet Press* 16:25 (15 July 1964), 5f.

1959h   Letter to first secretaries of provincial, municipal, and special district party committees (15 March), *WS* (1967c), 106f.; *JPRS* 61269-1 (20 February 1974), 166f.

1959i   Correspondence to first secretaries of provincial, municipal, and special district committees (17 March), *WS* (1967c), 108-110; *JPRS* 61269-1 (20 February 1974), 167ff.

1959j   Correspondence to members of various party Central Committee departments *et al.* (29 March), *WS* (1967c), 110f.; *JPRS* 61269-1 (20 February 1974), 172f.

1959k   Speech at the Seventh Plenary Session of the Eighth Central Committee of the CCP (April), *WS* (1967c), 51-53; *JPRS* 61269-1 (20 February 1974), 175-177.

1959l   Comments during an inspection of the Tongqiao People's Commune (13 April), *SCMP* 2039 (22 June 1959), 19.

1959m   Letter to production team leaders (29 April), *WS* (1969), 292-294; *MP* 7-9.

1959n   Sixteen articles concerning work methods (May), *WS* (1967c), 58-62; *JPRS* 61269-1 (20 February 1974), 178-181.

1959o   Instructions, context unspecified (29 June-July), *WS* (1967c), 63-65; *JPRS* 61269-1 (20 February 1974), 182ff.

1959p   Criticism of Peng Dehuai's "Letter of Opinion" (July), *BY* 208; *CLG* 1:4 (Winter 1968-69), 25f.

1959q   Speech prior to the Lushan Conference concerning the general line (10 July), *WS* (1967c), 66; *CLG* 1:4 (Winter 1968-69), 44f.

1959r   Speech at the Lushan Conference (23 July), *WS* (1969), 294-305; *CLG* 1:4 (Winter 1968-69), 27-43.

1959s   Comment on Li Yunzhong "Letter of Opinion" (26 July), *WS* (1967c), 72-75; *CLG* 1:4 (Winter 1968-69), 47-51.

1959t   Remarks concerning the printing and distributing of three articles (29 July), *WS* (1967c), 76; *CLG* 1:4 (Winter 1968-69), 52.

1959u   Letter to Zhang Wentian (2 August), *WS* (1969), 305f.; *CLG* 1:4 (Winter 1968-69), 54f.

1959v   Speech at the Eighth Plenary Session of the Eighth Central Committee (2 August), *WS* (1967c), 80-83; *CLG* 1:4 (Winter 1968-69), 60-63.

1959w   Comments on the report concerning the dissolution of Wuwei *xian* mess halls by order of Zhang Kaifan, Secretary of the Secretariat of Anhui Party Committee (6 August), *WS* (1969), 306f.; *CLG* 1:4 (Winter 1968-69), 67f.

1959x   Foreword to "Empiricism or Marxism-Leninism?" (15 August), *WS* (1967c), 87; *CLG* 1:4 (Winter 1968-69), 72.

1959y   Concerning Mei Cheng's "Qi Fa" (16 August), *WS* (1969), 310-312; *CLG* 1:4 (Winter 1968-69), 56-59.

1959z   "The Origin of Machine Guns and Mortars, etc." (16 August), *WS* (1969), 307-310; *CLG* 1:4 (Winter 1968-69), 73-76.

1959aa   Letter concerning two poems (1 September), *WS* (1967c), 94; *CLG* 1:4 (Winter 1968-69), 77f.

1959bb   Speech at an enlarged meeting of the Military Affairs Committee of the CCP and the Foreign Affairs Conference (11 September), *WS* (1969), 312-316; *CLG* 1:4 (Winter 1968-69), 79-84.

1959cc   Letter concerning the development of pig breeding (11 October), *WS* (1967a), 21f.; *JPRS* 61269-1 (20 February 1974), 173f.

1960a   Opinion on the free supply system, *WS* (1967c), 248; *JPRS* 61269-1 (20 February 1974), 233.

1960b   List of classical works recommended to high-ranking cadres, *WS* (1967c), 256; *JPRS* 61269-1 (20 February 1974), 234f.

1960c   Principles of educating youth, *WS* (1967c), 257; *JPRS* 61269-1 (20 February 1974), 236.

1960d   Constitution of the Anshan Iron and Steel Company (22 January), *PR* 13:16 (17 April 1970), 3.

1960e   Editorial: "Long Live Leninism: In Commemoration of the 90th Anniversary of the Birth of Lenin" (16 April), *RMRB* (20 April 1960). Published as a pamphlet under the same title, Peking: Foreign Languages Press, 1960, pp. 1-56. (*)

1960f   Conversation with Edgar Snow (22 October), *JPRS* 50792 (23 June 1970), 49.

1961a   Reading notes on the Soviet Union's "Political Economics," *WS* (1969), 319-399; *JPRS* 61269-2 (20 February 1974), 247-313.

1961b   Speech at the Ninth Plenum of the Eighth Central Committee of the CCP (18 January), *WS* (1967c), 258-266; *JPRS* 61269-2 (20 February 1974), 237-245.

1961c   Speech before a Central Committee conference in Beijing (12 June), *JPRS* 50792 (23 June 1970), 44f.

1961d   Letter to Jiangxi Communist Labor University (31 July), *WS* (1967c), 267f.; *MP* 9f.

1962a   Speech at an enlarged session of the Central Work Conference (also known as the "7000-Strong Meeting"): "A Talk on the Question of Democratic Centralism" (30 January), *WS* (1969), 399-423; *CMTP* 158-187.

1962b   Comment at the working conference of the Central Committee at Beidaihe (6 August), *WS* (1967b), 62-65; *JPRS* 52029 (21 December 1970), 19ff.

1962c   Ibid., translated in *PR* 10:26 (23 June 1967), 28.

1962d   Talk at a meeting of the core group at Beidaihe (9 August), *WS* (1969), 423-429; *JPRS* 52029 (21 December 1970), 22-27.

1962e   Speech at the Tenth Plenary Session of the Eighth Central Committee of the CCP (24 September), *WS* (1969), 430-436; *CLG* 1:4 (Winter 1968-69), 85-93.

1963a   Instruction on the commune education movement (May), *WS* (1969), 436-440; *JPRS* 61269-2 (20 February 1974), 314-317.

1963b   Speech at the Hangzhou Conference (May-June), *WS* (1969), 440-446; *JPRS* 61269-2 (20 February 1974), 318-324.

1963c   Note on "The Seven Well-written Documents of Zhejiang Province Concerning Cadres' Participation in Physical Labor" (9 May), *YL* 36f.; *SC* 67, 70f.

1963d   Draft Resolution of the Central Committee of the CCP on some problems in the current rural work ("The First Ten Points") (20 May), in *Mao Zedong zhuzo xuandu* (Selected Readings from the Writings of Mao Zedong). Peking: Renmin Chubanshe, 1966, pp. 249-51; *SC* 58-71.

1963e   "A Proposal Concerning the General Line of the International Communist Movement," letter of the Central Committee of the CCP (14 June), *RMRB* (17 June 1963). Translated in pamphlet form under the same title, Peking: Foreign Languages Press, 1963. (*)

1963f   Statement supporting the American Negroes in their just struggle against racial discrimination by U.S. imperialism (8 August), *RMRB* (9 August 1963); *PT* 409-412.

1963g   "On the Question of Stalin" (Comment II on the Open Letter of the Central Committee of the CPSU of 14 July 1963) (13 September), *RMRB* (13 September 1963); *PR* 6:38 (20 September 1963), 8-15. (*)

1963h   "Is Yugoslavia a Socialist Country?" (Comment III on the Open Letter of the Central Committee of the CPSU of 14 July 1963) (26 September), *RMRB* (26 September 1963); *PR* 6:39 (27 September 1963), 14-27. (*)

1963i   First comment on the Ministry of Culture and the *Xiju bao* (November), in *Wenyi hongqi*, Red Guard publication, 5 (30 May 1967); *SCMP* 4000 (14 August 1967), 23.

1963j   "Two Different Lines on the Question of War and Peace" (Comment V on the Open Letter of the Central Committee of the CPSU of 14 July 1963) (19 November), in *RMRB* (19 November 1963); *PR* 6:47 (22 November 1963), 6-16. (*)

1963k   Instruction of the Central Committee on strengthening of learning from each other and overcoming conservatism, arrogance and complacency (13 December), *WS* (1969), 446-454; *MP* 86-92.

1964a   Comment on women, context unspecified, in *PR* 15:10 (6 October 1972), 11.

1964b   Talk on health services at a reception with Vietnamese guests (24 January), *WS* (1969), 454; *JPRS* 61269-2 (20 February 1974), 325.

1964c   Instructions given at the spring festival concerning education work (13 February), *WS* (1969), 455-465; *CMTP* 197-211.

1964d   Letter of the Central Committee of the CCP to the Central Committee of the CPSU (29 February), *PR* 7:19 (8 May 1964), 12-18.

1964e   Remarks at a briefing (March), *WS* (1969), 471-479; *JPRS* 61269-2 (21 February 1974), 339-346.

1964f   "The Proletarian Revolution and Khrushchev's Revisionism" (Comment VIII on the Open Letter of the Central Committee of the CPSU of 14 July 1963) (31 March), *RMRB* (31 March 1964); *PR* 7:14 (3 April 1964), 5-22. (*)

1964g   Comment on swimming, context unspecified (June), *RMRB* (25 July 1966); *PR* 9:31 (29 July 1966), 5.

1964h   Talk on putting military affairs work into full effect and cultivating successors to the revolution (16 June), *WS* (1969), 500-504; *JPRS* 61269-2 (20 February 1974), 356-360.

1964i   Ibid., as translated in *Q* 276-279.

1964j   Talk with Wang Haiyong (24 June), *WS* (1969), 526-532; *IS* 9:8 (May 1973), 93-97.

1964k   Instructions regarding the All-China Federation of Literary and Art Circles and the various associations under it (27 June), *RMRB* (28 May 1967); *MP* 97.

1964l   Talk with Mao Yuanxin (5 July), *WS* (1969), 465-471; *CB* 888 (22 August 1969), 14.

1964m   Ibid., as translated in *IS* 9:10 (July 1973), 91-95.

1964n   "On Khrushchev's Phoney Communism and Its Historical Lessons for the World" (Comment IX on the Open Letter of the Central Committee of the CPSU of 14 July 1963) (14 July), *RMRB* (14 July 1964); *PR* 7:29 (17 July 1964), 7-28. (*)

1964o   Talk on methods of solidarity (August), *WS* (1969), 545-548; *JPRS* 61269-2 (20 February 1974), 403-405.

1964p   Instruction concerning a report on health insurance (August), in *Xinren Wei* (New People's Health), Red Guard publication; *SCMM* (suppl.) 22 (8 April 1968), 13.

1964q   Talk on the problems of philosophy (18 August), *WS* (1969), 548-561; *JPRS* 61269-2 (20 February 1974), 384-396.

1964r   Talk on Sakata's article (24 August), *WS* (1969), 561-567; *JPRS* 61269-2 (20 February 1974), 397-402.

1964s   Talk with the Nepalese education delegation (29 August), *WS* (1969), 567-577; *MP* 21-23.

1964t   Conversation with a delegation of French officials (September), in Stanley Karnow. *Mao and China*. New York: Viking Press, 1972, p. 56.

1964u   "China's Great Leap Forward" (December), in *Mao Zedong dui Peng-Huang-Zhang-Zhou fandang jituan de pipan* (Mao Zedong's Criticisms of the Peng-Huang-Zhang-Zhou Anti-Party Clique). Red Guard publication, n.d., p. 27; *CLG* 1:4 (Winter 1968-69), 94f.

1964v   Comment on learning from Dazhai Production Brigade, context unspecified (December), *PR* 14:40 (6 October 1972), 24.

1964w   Highlights of a forum on Central Committee work (20 December), *WS* (1969), 578-597; *JPRS* 61269-2 (20 February 1974), 408-426.

1964x   Comment on social development, context unspecified (21 December), *YL* 174f.; *Q* 203f.

1964y   Comments at a central work conference (27 December), *WS* (1969), 597f.; *JPRS* 61269-2 (20 February 1974), 427f.

1965a   Talk on the four clean-ups movement (3 January), *WS* (1969), 606-614; *JPRS* 61269-2 (20 February 1974), 437-444.

1965b   Interview with Edgar Snow (9 January), in Snow. *Long Revolution*. New York: Random House, 1972, pp. 195-222.

1965c   "Some problems currently arising in the course of the rural Socialist Education Movement" ("The Twenty-three Articles"), *SC* 118-126.

1965d   Instruction to the Central Committee and the Chairman on the question of organizing senior medical personnel in the cities to go to the countryside to train rural doctors (21 January), in *Xinren Wei* (New People's Health). Red Guard publication, n.d.; *SCMM* (suppl.) 22 (8 April 1968), 13.

1965e   Comment on Comrade Chen Zhengren's stay in a primary unity (29 January), *WS* (1967a), 31; *MP* 99f.

1965f   Talk with the Palestine Liberation Organization representatives (16 March), *WS* (1969), 614f.; *Journal of Palestine Studies* 1:2 (Winter 1972), 21, 25.

1965g   Comment on Beijing Normal College's investigation material report (3 July), *WS* (1967a), 30; *MP* 101f.

1965h   Interview with André Malraux (3 August), *WS* (1969), 616-624; Malraux. *Anti-mémoires*. Translated by Terence Kilmartin. New York: Holt, Rinehart and Winston, 1968, pp. 356-377.

1965i   Speech at a working conference (enlarged) of the Standing Committee of the Politburo of the Central Committee of the CCP (September), *HQ* 13 (1967); *MP* 102.

1965j   Talk at the Hangzhou Conference (21 December) in *WS* (1969), 624-629; *CB* 891 (8 October 1969), 51-55.

1965k   Ibid., as translated in *CMTP* 234-241.

1966a   Summary of the forum on the work in literature and art in the armed forces with which Comrade Lin Biao entrusted Comrade Jiang Qing (2 February), *PR* 10:23 (2 June 1967), 10-16. (*)

1966b   Second and third conversations with Mao Yuanxin (18 February), *WS* (1969), 631f.; *JPRS* 49826 (12 February 1970), 29f.

1966c   Talk at an enlarged meeting of the Standing Committee of the Politburo (17 March), *WS* (1969), 640; *JPRS* 61269-2 (20 February 1974), 381.

1966d   Talk at an enlarged meeting of the Politburo (20 March), *WS* (1969), 634-640; *JPRS* 61269-2 (20 February 1974), 375-380.

1966e   Talk with Kang Sheng (28 March), *WS* (1969), 640f.; *JPRS* 42349 (25 August 1967), 9.

1966f   Letter to Comrade Lin Biao commenting on the "Report for making greater success of farming by armed forces units" from the Military Commission's General Logistics Department (7 May), *WS* (1969), 642f.; *MP* 103-105.

1966g Letter to Jiang Qing (8 July), in *Zhongguo dalu yanjiu* (Research on Mainland China). Taipei, 10 November 1972; *IS* 9:4 (January 1973), 94-96.

1966h Comments during a swim in the Yangtze (16 July), *RMRB* (25 July 1966); *PR* 9:31 (29 July 1966), 4f.

1966i Speech at "a certain conference" (16 July), *WS* (1969), 643-646; *MP* 24-26.

1966j Address to regional secretaries and members of the Cultural Revolution Group under the Central Committee (22 July), *WS* (1969), 646-648; *MP* 30-34.

1966k Talk at a reception for Qian Xinzhong and Zhang Kai (2 August), *WX* 47; *JPRS* 49826 (12 February 1970), 6f.

1966l Comments at an enlarged meeting of the Standing Committee of the CCP (4 August), *WS* (1969), 650f.; *JPRS* 61269-2 (20 February 1974), 449f.

1966m Decision of the Central Committee of the CCP concerning the Great Proletarian Cultural Revolution ("The Sixteen Point Decision") (8 August), *RMRB* (9 August 1966); *MP* 117-127.

1966n Talk before the Central Committee work conference (23 August), *WS* (1969), 653; *MP* 35f.

1966o Speech at a report meeting (24 October), *WS* (1969), 653-657; *CB* 891 (8 October 1969), 70-73.

1966p Message of greetings to the Fifth Congress of the Albanian Party of Labor (25 October), *RMRB* (4 November 1966); *PT* 437ff.

1966q Talk at a central work conference (25 October), *WS* (1969), 657-660; *CB* 891 (8 October 1969), 75ff.

1967a "Twenty Manifestations of Bureaucracy" (January), *WX* 59-61; *JPRS* 49826 (12 February 1970), 40-43.

1967b Conversation with Albanian delegation (3 February), *WS* (1969), 663-667; *IS* 10:1 (October 1973), 97-100.

1967c Conversations with Zhang Qunqiao and Yao Wenyuan (12 February), *WS* (1969), 667-672; *SCMP* 4147 (27 March 1968), 1-10.

1967d Comment on a report from the Guangzhou Military District (14 May), in *Mao zhuxi zui xin zhishi* (Chairman

Mao's Latest Instructions). Red Guard publication, November 1968, p. 58; *CB* 885 (31 July 1969), 27.

1967e   Comment on the need for a succession of Cultural Revolutions (18 May), *RMRB* (13 August 1967); *PT* 370.

1967f   Directive on external propaganda work (June), *WS* (1969), 679; *JPRS* 61269-2 (20 February 1974), 462.

1967g   Instructions during an inspection tour in the central and southern parts of China (September), *WS* (1969), 681-686; *SCMP* 4070 (30 November 1967), 1-12.

1967h   Ibid., as translated in *PR* 10:48 (24 November 1967), 1.

1967i   Instructions concerning the Great Proletarian Cultural Revolution, context unspecified (September), *SCMP* 4060 (15 November 1967), 1f.

1967j   Statement following inspection tour: "Our Strategy" (September), in *Feiqing nianbao* (Yearbook of Mainland Affairs). Taipei, 1968, pp. 773-775; *CLG* 2:1 (Spring 1969), 3-12.

1967k   Comment on the situation in the Cultural Revolution (9 November), *RMRB* (9 November 1967); *PT* 370.

1967l   Letter to Lin Biao, Zhou Enlai, and the Central Committee Cultural Revolution Group (17 December), *WS* (1969), 686f.; *JPRS* 61629-2 (20 February 1974), 468.

1967m   Comment on criticism and self-criticism (22 December), *RMRB* (22 December 1967); *MP* 150.

1967n   Speech to the Albanian Military Delegation (1 May), *WS* (1969), 673-679; *JPRS* 61269-2 (20 February 1974), 456-461.

1968a   Comment on the composition of the CCP (1 January), *RMRB* (19 January 1968); *MP* 152.

1968b   Directive concerning the Cultural Revolution (10 April), *RMRB* (9 July 1968); *PR* 11:16 (19 April 1968), 7.

1968c   Statement in support of the Afro-American struggle against violent repression (16 April), *RMRB* (16 April 1968); *PR* 11:16 (19 April 1968), 5f.

1968d   Editorial: "An Epoch-making Document" (16 May), *RMRB* (17 May 1968); *PR* 11:21 (24 May 1968), 8-12.(*)

1968e   Comment on continuing need for universities, context unspecified (21 July), *RMRB* (22 July 1968); *PT* 371.

1968f   Conversation with responsible persons of the Beijing Red Guard Congress (28 July), *WS* (1969), 687-716; *JPRS* 61269-2 (20 February 1974), 469-497.

1968g   Directive regarding leadership of the working class in the education revolution (26 August), *RMRB* (27 August 1968); *MP* 155.

1968h   Directive on the need for the re-education of cadres (10 September), *HQ* 9 (1968); *PR* 11:38 (20 September 1968), 15.

1968i   Talk on victory in the Cultural Revolution, context unspecified (October), *RMRB* (28 April 1969); *MP* 159.

1968j   Comment on cadres' participation in physical labor, context unspecified (5 October), *RMRB* (8 October 1968); *MP* 156.

1968k   Comment on the need for the party to "get rid of the stale and take in the fresh" (14 October), in *HQ* 4 (1968), 7; *PT* 326.

1968l   Draft of the Constitution of the CCP (23 November), in *Xingdao ribao*. Hong Kong, 9 January 1969; *China Quarterly* 37 (1969), 169-173.

1968m   Directive on the use of historical experience (25 November), *RMRB* (25 November 1968); *MP* 157.

1968n   Directive on sending youth to the countryside (12 December), *RMRB* (12 December 1968); *MP* 157.

1969   Speech to the First Plenary Session of the Ninth Central Committee (28 April), in *Zhonggong wenhua da geming zhongyao wenjian huipian* (Collection of important documents on the Chinese Communist cultural revolution). Taipei, 1973, pp. 220-223; *IS* 7:6 (March 1970), 94-98.

1970a   Editorial: "Leninism or Social-Imperialism?" (22 April), *RMRB* (22 April 1970); *PR* 13:17 (24 April 1970), 5-15. (*)

1970b   Conversations with Edgar Snow (10 December), in Snow. *Long Revolution*. New York: Random House, 1972, pp. 167-176.

1971   Talks with responsible local comrades during a tour of inspection (August-September), *CLG* 5:3-4 (Fall-Winter 1972-73), 31-42.

1974   Talk to "liberated cadres" and "Wuhan cadres" in *IS* 11:2 (1975), 91-93.

1975a   Directives on strengthening the dictatorship over the bourgeoisie (9 February), *PR* 18:7 (14 February 1975), 4.

1975b   Directives on the dictatorship of the proletariat (22 February), *PR* 18:9 (28 February 1975), 5.

1975c   Comments on the *Shui Hu Zhuan* (4 September), *RMRB* (4 September 1975); *PR* 18:37 (12 September 1975), 7f.

1976   Comment on class struggle (1 January), *RMRB* (1 January 1976); *PR* 19:1 (2 January 1976), 8-10.

n.d.   Directive on the question of class distinction, *WS* (1969); *JPRS* 61269-2 (20 February 1974), 433f.

BOOKS, MONOGRAPHS, AND THESES

Andors, Stephen. *China's Industrial Revolution: Policy Planning and Management, 1949 to the Present.* New York: Pantheon, 1977.

Arendt, Hannah. *The Human Condition.* New York: Harcourt, Brace and World, 1963.

Avineri, Shlomo. *The Social and Political Thought of Karl Marx.* Cambridge: Cambridge University Press, 1968.

Barnett, A. Doak. *Cadres, Bureaucracy and Political Power in Communist China.* New York: Columbia University Press, 1967.

Baum, Richard. *Prelude to Revolution: Mao, the Party and the Peasant Question.* New York: Columbia University Press, 1975.

———, and Frederick C. Tiewes. *Ssu-ch'ing: The Socialist Education Movement of 1962-66.* Berkeley: University of California, Center for Chinese Studies, 1968.

Bender, Frederic L. *The Betrayal of Marx.* New York: Harper and Row, 1975.

Bennett, Gordon. *Yundong: Mass Campaigns in Chinese Communist Leadership.* Berkeley: University of California, Center for Chinese Studies, 1976.

Bennis, Warren G. *Changing Organizations.* New York: McGraw-Hill, 1966.

Bernstein, Richard. *Praxis and Action.* Philadelphia: University of Pennsylvania Press, 1971.

Blau, Peter M. *Bureaucracy in Modern Society*. New York: Random House, 1956.

Buckley, Michael J. *Motion and Motion's God*. Princeton: Princeton University Press, 1971.

Cell, Charles. *Revolution at Work: Mobilizational Campaigns in China*. New York: Academic Press, 1977.

Chan Wing-tsit. *A Source Book in Chinese Philosophy*. Princeton: Princeton University Press, 1963.

Chang, Parris. *Power and Policy in China*. College Park: Pennsylvania State University Press, 1976.

Ch'en, Jerome, ed. *Mao*. Englewood Cliffs, N.J.: Prentice-Hall, 1969.

——. *Mao and the Chinese Revolution*. New York: Oxford University Press, 1965.

——. *Mao Papers: Anthology and Bibliography*. New York: Oxford University Press, 1970.

Chow Tse-tsung. *The May Fourth Movement*. Cambridge: Harvard University Press, 1965.

Ch'ü Tung-tsu. *Local Government in China under the Ch'ing*. Cambridge: Harvard University Press, 1962.

Cohen, Arthur. *The Communism of Mao Tse-tung*. Chicago: University of Chicago Press, 1964.

Connor, James E., ed. *Lenin on Politics and Revolution: Selected Writings*. New York: Pegasus, 1968.

Creel, Herrlee Glessner. *Chinese Thought from Confucius to Mao Tse-tung*. New York: New American Library, 1960.

Crozier, Michel. *The Bureaucratic Phenomenon*. Chicago: University of Chicago Press, 1963.

Cumming, Robert Denoon, ed. *The Philosophy of Jean-Paul Sartre*. New York: Modern Library, 1965.

Dahrendorf, Ralf. *Class and Class Conflict in Industrial Society*. Stanford: Stanford University Press, 1959.

Desan, Wilfrid. *The Marxism of Jean-Paul Sartre*. New York: Doubleday, 1965.

——. *The Tragic Finale*. New York: Harper and Row, 1960.

Devillers, Philippe. *Ce que Mao a vraiment dit*. Paris: Stock, 1968.

Dittmer, Lowell. *Liu Shao-ch'i and the Chinese Cultural Revolution: The Politics of Mass Criticism*. Berkeley and Los Angeles: University of California Press, 1974.

Djilas, Milovan. *The New Class: An Analysis of the Communist System*. New York: Praeger, 1957.

Downs, Anthony. *Inside Bureaucracy*. Boston: Little, Brown, 1967.

Ellul, Jacques. *The Technological Society*. Translated by John Wilkinson. New York: Alfred A. Knopf, 1967.

Engels, Frederich. *Dialectics of Nature*. Translated by Emile Burns. New York: International Publishers, 1940.

———. *Herr Eugen Dühring's Revolution in Science*. Translated by Emile Burns. New York: International Publishers, 1939.

Etzioni, Amitai. *A Comparative Analysis of Complex Organizations*. New York: Free Press, 1964.

Feuer, Lewis S., ed. *Marx and Engels: Basic Writings on Politics and Philosophy*. New York: Doubleday, 1959.

Foulquié, Paul. *La dialectique*. Paris: Presses Universitaires, 1949.

Franklin, Bruce, ed. *The Essential Stalin*. New York: Doubleday, 1972.

Gerth, H. H. and C. Wright Mills, eds. *From Max Weber: Essays in Sociology*. New York: Oxford University Press, 1958.

Haeckel, Ernst. *The Riddle of the Universe at the Close of the Nineteenth Century*. Translated by Joseph McCabe. New York: Harper and Brothers, 1900.

Harding, Harry Jr. "Mobilization, Bureaucracy and Professionalism: The Organizational Issue in Chinese Politics." Ph.D. dissertation, Stanford University, 1974.

Ho Ping-ti. *The Ladder of Success in Imperial China*. New York: Columbia University Press, 1962.

Hofstadter, Richard. *Social Darwinism in American Thought*. Boston: Beacon, 1944.

Hsiung, James Chieh. *Ideology and Practice*. New York: Praeger, 1970.

Huntington, Samuel. *Political Order in Changing Societies*. New Haven: Yale University Press, 1968.

Illich, Ivan. *Deschooling Society*. New York: Harper and Row, 1970.

Johnson, Chalmers, ed. *Ideology and Politics in Contemporary China*. Seattle: University of Washington Press, 1973.

Karnow, Stanley. *Mao and China*. New York: Viking, 1972.

Kau, Michael Y. M., ed. *The Lin Piao Affair: Power Politics and Military Coup*. White Plains, N.Y.: International Arts and Sciences Press, 1975.

Kirk, G. S. *Heraclitus: The Cosmic Fragments*. Cambridge: Cambridge University Press, 1954.

Kraus, Richard. "The Evolving Concept of Class in Post-Liberation China," Ph.D. dissertation, Columbia University, 1974.

Kuhn, Thomas. *The Structure of Scientific Revolutions*. Chicago: University of Chicago Press, 1962.

Levenson, Joseph R. *Confucian China and Its Modern Fate*. Berkeley and Los Angeles: University of California Press, 1966.

Lewin, Moshe. *Lenin's Last Struggle*. Translated by Alan S. Smith. New York: Pantheon, 1968.

Lewis, John W. *Leadership in Communist China*. Ithaca: Cornell University Press, 1963.

MacFarquhar, Roderick. *The Hundred Flowers Campaign and the Chinese Intellectuals*. New York: Praeger, 1960.

————. *The Origins of the Cultural Revolution*. Vol. I: *Contradictions among the People, 1956-57*. New York: Columbia University Press, 1975.

Metzger, Thomas A. *The Internal Organization of Ch'ing Bureaucracy: Legal, Normative and Communications Aspects*. Cambridge: Harvard University Press, 1975.

Munro, Donald J. *The Concept of Man in Contemporary China*. Ann Arbor: University of Michigan Press, 1977.

Needham, Joseph. *Science and Civilization in China*. Cambridge: Cambridge University Press, 1962.

Peyrefitte, Alain, *Quand la Chine s'éveillera, le monde tremblera*. Paris: Fayard, 1973.

Rice, Edward E. *Mao's Way*. Berkeley and Los Angeles: University of California Press, 1972.

Russett, Barbara. *The Concept of Equilibrium in American Thought*. New York: Harcourt, Brace and World, 1966.

Sartre, Jean-Paul. *The Condemned of Altona*. New York: Vintage, 1961.

————. *Critique de la raison dialectique*. Paris: Gallimard, 1967.

————. *L'Etre et le néant*. Paris: Gallimard, 1953.

Schram, Stuart R. *Mao Tse-tung*. Baltimore: Penguin, 1967.

————. *The Political Thought of Mao Tse-tung*. Second, revised edition. New York: Praeger, 1969.

————. *La "Révolution permanente" en Chine*. Paris: Mouton, 1963.

347

Schram, Stuart R., and Hélène Carrère d'Encausse. *Marxism and Asia.* Baltimore: Penguin, 1969.

Schurmann, H. Franz. *Ideology and Organization in Communist China.* Second, revised edition. Berkeley and Los Angeles: University of California Press, 1968.

Schwartz, Benjamin I. *Chinese Communism and the Rise of Mao.* Cambridge: Harvard University Press, 1951.

——. *Communism and China: Ideology in Flux.* Cambridge: Harvard University Press, 1968.

Selden, Mark. *The Yenan Way in Revolutionary China.* Cambridge: Harvard University Press, 1971.

Selznick, Philip. *Leadership in Administration.* Evanston, Ill.: Row, Peterson, 1957.

Shu, Austin C. W. *On Mao Tse-tung: A Bibliographic Guide.* East Lansing: Michigan State University, Asian Studies Center, 1972.

Singer, Kurt. *The Idea of Conflict.* Melbourne: Melbourne University Press, 1949.

Snow, Edgar. *Red Star over China.* New York: Grove Press, 1968.

Solomon, Richard. *Mao's Revolution and the Chinese Political Culture.* Berkeley and Los Angeles: University of California Press, 1971.

Starr, John Bryan. *Ideology and Culture: An Introduction to the Dialectic of Contemporary Chinese Politics.* New York: Harper and Row, 1973.

——. "Mao Tse-tung's Theory of Continuing the Revolution under the Dictatorship of the Proletariat: Its Origins, Development and Practical Implications." Ph.D. dissertation, University of California, Berkeley, 1971.

——, and Nancy Anne Dyer, compilers. *Post-Liberation Works of Mao Zedong: A Bibliography and Index.* Berkeley: University of California, Center for Chinese Studies, 1976.

Teng Ssu-yü, and John K. Fairbank, eds. *China's Response to the West.* New York: Atheneum, 1963.

Thurston, Anne Fretter. "Authority and Legitimacy in Post-Revolutionary Rural Kwangtung: The Case of the People's Communes." Ph.D. dissertation, University of California, Berkeley, 1975

Townsend, James. *Political Participation in Communist China.* Berkeley and Los Angeles: University of California Press, 1967.

Trotsky, Leon. *The Permanent Revolution.* New York: Pioneer Publishers, 1965.

———. *Problems of the Chinese Revolution.* New York: Doubleday, Doran and Co., 1937.

Tucker, Robert C., ed. *The Marx-Engels Reader.* New York: W. W. Norton, 1972.

Wakeman, Frederic Jr. *History and Will: Philosophical Perspectives of Mao Tse-tung's Thought.* Berkeley and Los Angeles: University of California Press, 1973.

Weber, Max. *Economy and Society: An Outline of Interpretive Sociology.* Edited by Guenther Roth and Claus Wittich. New York: Bedminster, 1968.

———. *The Theory of Social and Economic Organization.* Translated and edited by Talcott Parsons. New York: Free Press, 1964.

Wilhelm, Helmut. *The I Ching or Book of Changes.* Translated by Cary F. Baynes. Bollingen Series XIX. Princeton: Princeton University Press, 1967.

Wilson, Dick, ed. *Mao Tse-tung in the Scales of History.* Cambridge: Cambridge University Press, 1977.

Wittfogel, Karl. *Oriental Despotism.* New Haven: Yale University Press, 1957.

Wolin, Sheldon. *Politics and Vision.* Boston: Little, Brown, 1960.

Womack, Brantly. "The Development of Mao Tse-tung's Political Thought," Ph.D. dissertation, University of Chicago, 1977.

Articles and Papers

Andors, Stephen. "Hobbes and Weber vs. Marx and Mao: The Political Economy of Decentralization in China," *Bulletin of Concerned Asian Scholars* 6:3 (1974), 19-34.

Arendt, Hannah. "Reflections on Violence," *New York Review of Books* 12:4 (1969), 19-31.

Bernstein, Thomas P. "Leadership and Mass Movement in the Soviet and Chinese Collectivization Campaigns of 1929-30 and 1955-56: A Comparison," *China Quarterly* 31 (1967), 1-47.

Blecher, Marc. "The Mass Line in Rural Chinese Communities: Toward a Theory of Consensual Politics," paper presented at the Workshop on the Pursuit of Political Interest in the People's Republic of China, Ann Arbor, Michigan, August 1977.

Bodde, Derk. "Harmony and Conflict in Chinese Philosophy," in *Studies in Chinese Thought*. Edited by Arthur F. Wright. Chicago: University of Chicago Press, 1953.

Boorman, Howard. "Mao Tse-tung as Historian," in *History in Communist China*. Edited by Albert Feuerwerker. Cambridge: MIT Press, 1968.

Burns, John P. "The Election of Production Team Cadres in Rural China, 1958-74," paper presented at the Workshop on the Pursuit of Political Interests in the People's Republic of China, Ann Arbor, Michigan, August 1977.

Chang, Parris. "The Anti-Lin Piao and Confucius Campaign: Its Meaning and Purpose," *Asian Survey* 14:10 (1974), 871-886.

Chang Tung-sun. "A Chinese Philosopher's Theory of Knowledge," *Yenching Journal of the Social Sciences* 1:2 (1939), reprinted in *Etc.: A Review of General Semantics* 9 (1952), 203-226.

Creel, Herrlee G. "The Beginnings of Bureaucracy in China: The Origin of the *Hsien*," *Journal of Asian Studies* 23:2 (1964), 155-184.

Dirlik, Arif. "The Problem of Class Viewpoint versus Historicism in Chinese Historiography," *Modern China* 3:4 (1977), 465-488.

Doolin, Dennis, and Peter Golas. " 'On Contradiction' in the Light of Mao Tse-tung's Essay, 'On Dialectical Materialism,' " *China Quarterly* 19 (1964), 38-46.

Esherick, Joseph W. "The 'Restoration of Capitalism' in Mao's and Marxist Theory," *Modern China*, forthcoming.

Feuerwerker, Albert. "China's History in Marxian Dress," *History in Communist China*. Cambridge: MIT Press, 1968.

————, and Harold Kahn. "The Ideology of Scholarship: China's New Historiography," in *History in Communist China*. Edited by Albert Feuerwerker. Cambridge: MIT Press, 1968.

Frolic, Bernard M. "A Preliminary Discussion of the Pursuit of the Political Interests of Chinese Workers," paper presented at the Workshop on the Pursuit of Political Interests in the People's Republic of China, Ann Arbor, Michigan, August 1977.

Glaberman, Martin. "Mao as a Dialectician," *International Philosophical Quarterly* 8 (1968), 94-112.

Goldman, Merle. "China's Anti-Confucian Campaign, 1973-74," *China Quarterly* 63 (1975), 435-462.

————. "Party Policies toward the Intellectuals: The Unique Blooming and Contending of 1961-62," in *Party, Leadership and Power in China*. Edited by John W. Lewis. Cambridge: Cambridge University Press, 1970.

————. "The Role of History in Party Struggle, 1962-1964," *China Quarterly* 51 (1972), 500-519.

Gouldner, Alvin. "Cosmopolitans and Locals: Toward an Analysis of Latent Social Roles," *Administrative Science Quarterly* 9:2 (1967), 23-45.

————. "Organizational Analysis," in *Sociology Today: Problems and Prospects*. Edited by Robert K. Merton *et al*. New York: Basic Books, 1959.

Hammond, Edward. "Marxism and the Mass Line," *Modern China* 4:1 (January 1978), 3-27.

Holubnychy, Vsevolod. "Mao Tse-tung's Materialist Dialectics," *China Quarterly* 19 (1964), 3-37.

Johnson, Chalmers. "Chinese Communist Leadership and Mass Response: The Yenan Period and the Socialist Education Campaign Period," in *China in Crisis*. Edited by Ho Ping-ti and Tang Tsou. Chicago: University of Chicago Press, 1968.

Kahn, Charles H. "A New Look at Heraclitus," *American Philosophical Quarterly* 1:3 (1964), 189-203.

King, Ambrose Y. C. "The Behavior Patterns of Traditional Confucian Bureaucrats," *Chinese Journal of Administration* 8 (1967), 49-55.

————. "Chinese Bureaucracy in the Transitional Society," *Chinese Journal of Administration* 9 (1967), 28-39.

Kraus, Richard C. "Class Conflict and the Vocabulary of Social Analysis in China," *China Quarterly* 69 (1977), 54-74.

Lichtheim, George. "Oriental Despotism," in *The Concept of Ideology and Other Essays*. New York: Vintage, 1967.

Lubman, Stanley B. "Mao and Mediation: Politics and Dispute Resolution in Communist China," *California Law Review* 55:5 (1967), 1284-1359.

Meisner, Maurice. "Images of the Paris Commune in Contemporary Chinese Marxist Thought," *Massachusetts Review* 12:3 (1971), 479-497.

————. "Leninism and Maoism: Some Populist Perspectives on Marxism-Leninism," *China Quarterly* 45 (1971), 2-36.

Meisner, Maurice. "Utopian Goals and Ascetic Values in Chinese Communist Ideology," *Journal of Asian Studies* 28:1 (1968), 101-110.

———. "Utopian Socialist Themes in Maoism," in *Peasant Rebellion and Communist Revolution in Asia*. Edited by John W. Lewis. Stanford: Stanford University Press, 1974.

Michael, Franz. "State and Society in Nineteenth Century China," *World Politics* 7 (1955), 419-433.

Moody, Peter. "The New Anti-Confucius Campaign in China: The First Round," *Asian Survey* 14:4 (1974), 307-324.

Mueller, Gustav. "The Hegel Legend of 'Thesis-Antithesis-Synthesis,'" *Journal of the History of Ideas* 19 (1958), 411-414.

Munro, Donald J. "The Chinese View of Alienation," *China Quarterly* 59 (1974), 580-583.

———. "The Concept of 'Interest' in Chinese Thought," paper presented at the Workshop on the Pursuit of Political Interests in the People's Republic of China, Ann Arbor, Michigan, August 1977.

———. "Egalitarian Ideal and Educational Fact in Communist China," in *China: Management of a Revolutionary Society*. Edited by John M. H. Lindbeck. Seattle: University of Washington Press, 1971.

———. "The Malleability of Man in Chinese Marxism," *China Quarterly* 48 (1971), 609-640.

Nathan, Andrew J. "The Structural Analysis of Political Conflict Groups," paper presented at the Workshop on the Pursuit of Political Interests in the People's Republic of China, Ann Arbor, Michigan, August 1977.

Nivison, David S. "Communist Ethics and Chinese Tradition," *Journal of Asian Studies* 16:1 (1956), 51-74.

Noumoff, S. J. "The Dialectic and China," paper prepared for the XX Congress of Chinese Studies, Prague, August 1968.

Oksenberg, Michel. "Occupational Groups in Chinese Society and the Cultural Revolution," in *The Cultural Revolution: 1967 in Review*. Ann Arbor: University of Michigan, Center for Chinese Studies, 1968.

Peck, James. "Revolution vs. Modernization and Revisionism," in *China's Uninterrupted Revolution*. Edited by Victor Nee and James Peck. New York: Pantheon, 1976.

Rue, John. "Is Mao Tse-tung's 'Dialectical Materialism' a Forgery?" *Journal of Asian Studies* 26:3 (1967), 464-468.

Schram, Stuart R. "The Cultural Revolution in Historical Per-
spective," in *Authority, Participation and Cultural Change in
China*. Edited by Stuart R. Schram. Cambridge: Cambridge
University Press, 1973.

————. "Mao Tse-tung and the Theory of the Permanent Revolution, 1958-1969," *China Quarterly* 46 (1971), 221-244.

————. "Mao's Thoughts: The Revised Version," *Far Eastern
Economic Review* (7 October 1977), 57-58.

————. "Mao Ze-dong and the Role of the Various Classes in the
Chinese Revolution, 1923-27," in *The Polity and Economy
of China: The Late Professor Yuji Muramatsu Commemoration Volume*. Tokyo: Toyo Keizai Sinposha, 1975.

————. "The Party in Chinese Communist Ideology," in *Party,
Leadership and Political Power in China*. Edited by John W.
Lewis. Cambridge: Cambridge University Press, 1970.

Schwartz, Benjamin I. "China and the West in the 'Thought of
Mao Tse-tung,'" in *China in Crisis*. Edited by Ho Ping-ti
and Tang Tsou. Chicago: University of Chicago Press, 1968.

————. "The Legend of the 'Legend of Maoism.'" *China Quarterly* 1 (1960), 35-42.

————. "Modernization and the Maoist Vision: Some Reflections
on Chinese Communist Goals," *China Quarterly* 21 (1965),
3-19.

————. "A Personal View of Some Thoughts of Mao Tse-tung,"
in *Ideology and Politics in Contemporary China*. Edited by
Chalmers Johnson. Seattle: University of Washington Press,
1973.

————. "The Reign of Virtue: Some Broad Perspectives on Leader and Party in the Cultural Revolution," in *Party, Leadership and Political Power in China*. Edited by John W. Lewis.
Cambridge: Cambridge University Press, 1970.

Sigurdson, Jon. "Rural Industry and the Internal Transfer of
Technology," in *Authority, Participation and Cultural
Change in China*. Edited by Stuart R. Schram. Cambridge:
Cambridge University Press, 1973.

Skilling, H. Gordon. "Group Conflict and Political Change," in
Change in Communist Systems. Edited by Chalmers Johnson.
Stanford: Stanford University Press, 1970.

Skinner, G. William, and Edwin A. Winckler. "Compliance Succession in Rural Communist China: A Cyclical Theory," in

A Sociological Reader on Complex Organizations. Edited by Amitai Etzioni. New York: Holt, Rinehart and Winston, 1969.

Thomas, Paul. "Marx and Science," *Political Studies* 24:1 (1976), 1-23.

Wakeman, Frederic, Jr. "High Ch'ing: 1683-1839," in *Modern East Asia: Essays in Interpretation.* Edited by James B. Crowley. New York: Harcourt, Brace and World, 1970.

————. "The Use and Abuse of Ideology in the Study of Contemporary China," *China Quarterly* 61 (1975), 127-151.

Walder, Andrew G. "Marxism, Maoism and Social Change," *Modern China* 3:1 and 2 (1977), 101-118 and 125-160.

Wang Gungwu. "Juxtaposing the Past and Present in China Today," *China Quarterly* 51 (1975), 1-24.

Whyte, Martin King. "Bureaucracy and Mobilization in China: The Maoist Critique," *American Sociological Review* 38:2 (1973), 149-163.

Wittfogel, Karl. "The Legend of Maoism," *China Quarterly* 1 and 2 (1960), 72-86 and 16-34.

————, and C. R. Chao. "Some Remarks on Mao's Handling of Concepts and Problems of Dialectics," *Studies in Soviet Thought* 3:4 (1963), 251-277.

Womack, Brantly. "Theory and Practice in the Thought of Mao Tse-tung," in *The Logic of "Maoism": Critique and Explication.* Edited by James Chieh Hsiung. New York: Praeger, 1974.

————. "The Practical Roots of Mao Tse-tung's Political Thought, 1919-1935," paper presented to the Annual Meeting of the Association for Asian Studies, Toronto, March 1976.

Wright, Arthur F. "Struggle vs. Harmony: Symbols of Competing Values in Modern China," in *Thirteenth Symposium of Science, Philosophy and Religion.* Edited by L. Bryson. New York: Harper, 1954.

Yang, C. K. "Some Characteristics of Chinese Bureaucratic Behavior," in *Confucianism in Action.* Edited by David S. Nivison and Arthur F. Wright. Stanford: Stanford University Press, 1959.

INDEX

Library of Congress Cataloging in Publication Data

Starr, John Bryan.
    Continuing the revolution.

    Bibliography: p.
    Includes index.
    1. Mao, Tse-tung, 1893-1976—Political and social views.
2. Dictatorship of the proletariat.   I. Title.
DS778.M3S76   320.5'323'0924   78-63597
    ISBN 0-691-07596-4